STUDIES IN HONOR OF
HERMANN COLLITZ

Hermann Collitz

STUDIES IN HONOR OF
HERMANN COLLITZ

PROFESSOR OF GERMANIC PHILOLOGY, EMERITUS, IN THE
JOHNS HOPKINS UNIVERSITY, BALTIMORE, MARYLAND

PRESENTED BY A GROUP OF HIS PUPILS
AND FRIENDS ON THE OCCASION OF HIS
SEVENTY-FIFTH BIRTHDAY,
FEBRUARY 4, 1930

Essay Index Reprint Series

BOOKS FOR LIBRARIES PRESS
FREEPORT, NEW YORK

First Published 1930
Reprinted 1969

P2{c}
C67

STANDARD BOOK NUMBER:
8369-1196-2

LIBRARY OF CONGRESS CATALOG CARD NUMBER:
76-84339

PRINTED IN THE UNITED STATES OF AMERICA

TABULA GRATULATORIA.

W. F. Albright, Baltimore, Maryland.
Ruth Norton Albright, Baltimore, Maryland.
William H. Allen, Philadelphia, Pennsylvania.
Hermann Almstedt, Columbia, Missouri.
A. Asher & Co., Berlin, Germany.
Earle B. Babcock, Paris, France.
Joseph Baer & Co., Frankfurt a. M., Germany.
A. J. Barnouw, New York City.
L. C. Barret, Hartford, Connecticut.
H. M. Belden, Columbia, Missouri.
Harold H. Bender, Princeton, New Jersey.
Adolph B. Benson, New Haven, Connecticut.
Gottlieb Betz, New York City.
Frank R. Blake, Baltimore, Maryland.
George H. Blake, Marietta, Ohio.
John C. Blankenagel, Delaware, Ohio.
D. S. Blondheim, Baltimore, Maryland.
Leonard Bloomfield, Chicago, Illinois.
George Melville Bolling, Columbus, Ohio.
Conrad Borchling, Hamburg, Germany.
Konrad Burdach, Berlin-Grunewald, Germany.
A. Busse, New York City.
F. S. Cawley, Cambridge, Massachusetts.
Klara H. Collitz, Baltimore, Maryland.
William A. Cooper, Stanford University, California.
Roberta D. Cornelius, New York City.
Ephraim Cross, New York City.
George O. Curme, Evanston, Illinois.
Edward P. Davis, Washington, D. C.
Mrs. A. Sanders Dewitt, Detroit, Michigan.
Robert R. Drummond, Orono, Maine.

Franklin Edgerton, New Haven, Connecticut.
Ewald Eiserhardt, Rochester, New York.
E. E. Ericson, Pittsburgh, Pennsylvania.
Hollon A. Farr, New Haven, Connecticut
A. B. Faust, Ithaca, New York.
H. G. Fiedler, Oxford, England.
Robert Herndon Fife, New York City.
George T. Flom, Urbana, Illinois.
Laurence Fossler, Lincoln, Nebraska.
Tenney Frank, Baltimore, Maryland.
Hans Froelicher, Baltimore, Maryland.
Eunice R. Goddard, Baltimore, Maryland.
Julius Goebel, Urbana, Illinois.
Jane F. Goodloe, Baltimore, Maryland.
Chester Nathan Gould, Chicago, Illinois.
Willem L. Graff, Montreal, Canada.
Alexander Green, Boston, Massachusetts.
Edwin Greenlaw, Baltimore, Maryland.
Karl J. Grimm, Gettysburg, Pennsylvania.
Hans Harrassowitz, Leipzig, Germany,
Jacob Wittmer Hartmann, Brooklyn, New York.
J. T. Hatfield, Evanston, Illinois.
Joel Hatheway, Boston, Massachusetts.
Frank Hawley, Durham, England.
Francis J. Hemelt, Washington, D. C.
Edward Hoffmeister, Baltimore, Maryland.
A. R. Hohlfeld, Madison, Wisconsin.
Jacob H. Hollander, Baltimore, Maryland.
Lee M. Hollander, Austin, Texas.
Urban T. Holmes, Jr., Chapel Hill, North Carolina,
J. Preston Hoskins, Princeton, New Jersey,
William Guild Howard, Cambridge, Massachusetts.
Sanki Ichikawa, Tokyo, Japan,
T. R. Jehne, Washington, D. C.
Elizabeth F. Johnson, Rock Hill, South Carolina,
Friedrich O. Kegel, Bethlehem, Pennsylvania.
Robert J. Kellogg, Ottawa, Kansas.
Roland G. Kent, Philadelphia, Pennsylvania.
J. Alexander Kerns, New York City.
Herbert Z. Kip, New London, Connecticut.

Armin H. Koller, Urbana, Illinois.
C. F. Kramer, Jr., College Park, Maryland.
Samuel Kroesch, Minneapolis, Minnesota.
W. Kurrelmeyer, Baltimore, Maryland.
Hans Kurath, Columbus, Ohio.
Berthold Laufer, Chicago, Illinois.
C. H. Leineweber, Bethesda, Maryland.
Fang Kuei Li, Peiping, China.
Enno Littmann, Tübingen, Germany.
C. M. Lotspeich, Cincinnati, Ohio.
Arthur O. Lovejoy, Baltimore, Maryland.
Kemp Malone, Baltimore, Maryland.
A. P. Mattli, New Haven, Connecticut.
Ernst H. Mensel, Northampton, Massachusetts.
Ernst C. P. Metzenthin, Chapel Hill, North Carolina.
Leopold L. Meyer, Houston, Texas.
Fritz Mezger, Bryn Mawr, Pennsylvania.
Truman Michelson, Washington, D. C.
C. W. E. Miller, Baltimore, Maryland.
B. S. Monroe, Ithaca, New York.
Otto Müller, Gettysburg, Pennsylvania.
W. P. Mustard, Baltimore, Maryland.
William Allan Neilson, Northampton, Massachusetts.
N. V. Martinus Nijhoff, 's-Gravenhage, Holland.
John Rathbone Oliver, Baltimore, Maryland.
Carroll H. Owen, Oberlin, Ohio.
John Phelps, Baltimore, Maryland.
Hugo Pipping, Helsingfors, Finland.
Allen W. Porterfield, Morgantown, West Virginia.
Louise Pound, Lincoln, Nebraska.
George M. Priest, Princeton, New Jersey.
Eduard Prokosch, New Haven, Connecticut.
Wm. H. Reed, Tufts College, Massachusetts.
O. P. Rhyne, Clemson College, South Carolina.
Allan Lake Rice, Philadelphia, Pennsylvania.
Leo L. Rockwell, Lewisburg, Pennsylvania.
Ernst Rose, New York City.
R. B. Roulston, Baltimore, Maryland.
Else Saleski, Canton, New York.
H. K. Schilling, Berkeley, California.

Mariele Schirmer, Milwaukee, Wisconsin.
J. H. Scholte, Amsterdam.
Karl A. M. Scholtz, Baltimore, Maryland.
Claire Strube Schradieck, Cleveland, Ohio.
F. N. Scott, Tucson, Arizona.
Edward H. Sehrt, Washington, D. C.
D. B. Shumway, Philadelphia, Pennsylvania.
Eduard Sievers, Leipzig, Germany.
Walter Silz, Cambridge, Massachusetts.
Taylor Starck, Cambridge, Massachusetts.
E. H. Sturtevant, New Haven, Connecticut.
Archer Taylor, Chicago, Illinois.
M. Carey Thomas, Bryn Mawr, Pennsylvania.
R. W. Tinsley, University, Mississippi.
John Tjarks, Baltimore, Maryland.
Axel Johan Uppvall, Philadelphia, Pennsylvania.
B. J. Vos, Bloomington, Indiana.
Ernst Voss, Madison, Wisconsin.
Emma E. Walters, Baltimore, Maryland.
John A. Walz, Cambridge, Massachusetts.
James Skillman Ward, Montevallo, Alaamba.
H. G. Wendt, Jamaica, L. I., New York.
C. E. Werling, Denver, Colorado.
Hans Weyhe, Halle a. d. S., Germany.
Marian P. Whitney, New Haven, Connecticut.
Frederick H. Wilkens, New York City.
Edward J. Williamson, Geneva, New York.
W. D. Zinnecker, West Orange, New Jersey.

Die Oeffentliche Bibliothek der Universität in Basel, Switzerland.
Benedictine High School, Cleveland, Ohio.
Börsenverein der Deutschen Buchhändler, Leipzig, Germany.
Bryn Mawr College Library, Bryn Mawr, Pennsylvania.
Butler University Library, Indianapolis, Indiana.
University of California Library, Berkeley, California.
University of Cincinnati Library, Cincinnati, Ohio.
Columbia University Library, New York City.
Dartmouth College Library, Hanover, New Hampshire.
Universitätsbibliothek, Freiburg i. Br., Germany.
George Washington University Library, Washington, D. C.
Goteborgs Stadsbibliotek, Goteborg, Sweden.
Universitätsbibliothek, Göttingen, Germany.
The Grosvenor Library, Buffalo, New York.
Universitätsbibliothek, Halle a. d. S., Germany.
Staats- und Universitätsbibliothek, Hamburg, Germany.
Harvard College Library, Cambridge, Massachusetts.
Haverford College Library, Haverford, Pennsylvania.
J. C. Hinrichs'sche Buchhandlung, Leipzig, Germany.
Holy Cross College Library, Worcester, Massachusetts.
University of Illinois Library, Urbana, Illinois.
Indiana University Library, Bloomington, Indiana.
James Book Store, Cincinnati, Ohio.
The Johns Hopkins University Library, Baltimore, Maryland.
Universitäts- und Stadtbibliothek, Köln, Germany.
Lehigh University Library, Bethlehem, Pennsylvania.
Universitets-Biblioteket, Lund, Sweden.
University of Maryland Library, College Park, Maryland.
Miami University, Oxford, Ohio.
Bookstore, Mount Holyoke College, South Hadley, Massachusetts
Bayerische Staatsbibliothek, München, Germany.
University of Nebraska Library, Lincoln, Nebraska.

VIII

The Newberry Library, Chicago, Illinois.
New Orleans Public Library, New Orleans, Louisiana.
New York Public Library, New York City.
Library, University of North Carolina, Chapel Hill, North Carolina.
Northwestern University Library, Evanston, Illinois.
Library, University of Oregon, Eugene, Oregon.
Library, University of Pennsylvania, Philadelphia, Pennsylvania.
University of Pittsburgh Library, Pittsburgh, Pennsylvania.
Princeton University Library, Princeton, New Jersey.
Librairie Rivnac, Prague, Czechoslovakia.
Rutgers University Library, New Brunswick, New Jersey
Stanford University Library, Stanford University, California.
Taylor Institution, Library, Oxford, England.
University Library, Uppsala, Sweden.
Vassar College Library, Poughkeepsie, New York.
State College of Washington Library, Pullman, Washington.
Washington University Library, St. Louis, Missouri.
West Virginia University Library, Morgantown, West Virginia.
University of Washington Library, Seattle, Washington.
Library of the University of Wisconsin, Madison, Wisconsin.
Yale University Library, New Haven, Connecticut.

TO PROFESSOR COLLITZ.

The scholar gentleman as a knight of old
Valiant and loyal, chivalrous and bold.

Recks not of self or fame, but takes the field
In the name of truth to make blind error yield.

As olden heroes by the play of swords
He wins in reason's war by force of words.

Such a scholar knight has charmed my mind,
Not less urbane than learned, keen and kind;

The utmost light upon the facts he brings,
And truth once clear, his voice with ardor rings;

Simple, lucid, and trenchant, with careful ease,
He wins at once by logic and the art to please.

In the new world and homeland accounted great,
He wears his knightly plume immaculate.

Georgia L. Field
Elmira College

TO PROFESSOR COLLITZ.

The glory of gray hair and youthful heart
Is yours and yours the glory that you wear
Your crown of scholarship and learning's love
So gracefully — lord master of your art.

Then there are traits that place a man apart
From lesser men, — of these you have full store —
For personality is something more,
A thing inborn, not purchased at life's mart.

Some feet leave earth the richer where they tread,
Some minds that move along life's loftier ways,
Are of themselves a university.

Of such you are and where your path has led,
There still shall flourisch in the coming days,
Blossoms of wisdom and humanity.

Carol Wight
The Johns Hopkins University

TABLE OF CONTENTS.

XII

BIOGRAPHICAL SKETCH

BY KLARA H. COLLITZ

Hermann Collitz was born on Sunday, February 4th, 1855, at Bleckede, a Hanoverian hamlet, a little over a thousand years old, situated on the Elbe, about midway between Hamburg and Magdeburg. His ancestors on the paternal side had been for several generations burghers engaged in various lines of business. His mother whose maiden name was Friederike Schäfer, came from the nearby ancient village of Barskamp. Her father is identical with the 'Hauswirt Schäfer' mentioned in J. K. Wächters *Statistik der im Königreiche Hannover vorhandenen heidnischen Denkmäler*, Hannover 1841, for the reason that his estate included a piece of ground on which at that time was situated one of the largest "Hünengräber" (cairns) then in existence [1].

At the age of seven, Hermann was sent to a private school which had just been opened in his native town. Was it because he had always heard High and Low German spoken alongside of each other at his home or for any other reason that from the outset he manifested a special interest in the study of languages? In this private school two classes were combined in one schoolroom. While young Hermann had been assigned to the beginners' class who were expected to attend to caligraphy, he was found to be listening all the time to the instruction given to the older pupils in Latin and French. Upon examination it was found that he had duly profited from the instruction in languages and hence was allowed to join the upper class. A few years later, English was added to his curriculum and when thirteen years old, he was permitted to join a select class in Greek. Thus he was well prepared

---

[1] This "giant's grave" we are sorry to say is no longer in existence, the stone blocks having been meanwhile used for erecting a church in the village of Stiepelse on the Elbe.

to enter, at the age of fourteen, the Lyceum of the *Johanneum* at Lüneburg. The latter was a municipal Academy which could trace its origin to a school of Benedictines; at the time of the Reformation it became a municipal institution for training in the humanities and as such took its place among the leading schools of this kind in Northern Germany. In the humanistic division of the Johanneum stress was laid chiefly, in accordance with a long tradition, on the study of Greek, Latin and Mathematics. In the spring of 1875, the young scholar passed the final examisations (Maturitätsexamen) and thereupon entered the University of Göttingen in the autumn. The interval between the 'Abiturientenexamen' and the Immatriculation at the University he employed in acquainting himself with the elements of Sanskrit.

At Göttingen, he took up the study of Classical Philology under E. von Leutsch, Herm. Sauppe and Curt Wachsmuth. It must suffice here to mention particularly Sauppe's lectures on Latin Grammar and on Greek and Latin Epigraphy, and Wachsmuth's Introduction to the study of Ancient History. Besides, he pursued courses in Philosophy and the Germanic Languages. In Philosophy, his teachers were H. Lotze and J. Baumann, in Germanic Philology, Adalbert Bezzenberger and W. Müller. The appointment, in 1876, of August Fick, to a professorship of Comparative Philology at the University of Göttingen was an event which had a decided influence on his studies. He not only derived much benefit from Fick's courses on Greek and Latin grammar, but also joined Fick's 'Grammatische Gesellschaft'. In the lectures of the newly appointed professor on Greek and Latin grammar, these languages were given a background in comparative Indo-European Philology. The 'Grammatische Gesellschaft' which met at Fick's house served to supplement these lectures and to give his students practice in independent research. In this connection should be mentioned also Bezzenberger's courses on the Zend-Avesta and in Lithuanian, and a course given by Benfey on the Hymns of the Rigveda.

After three years at the Georgia Augusta, he spent the summer semester of 1878 at the University of Berlin in order to study Comparative Philology and Sanskrit with Joh. Schmidt and Albr. Weber, German Philology with Müllenhoff and Scherer, Celtic with H. Zimmer, and Slavic languages with V. Jagić.

Among his fellow-students were F. Bechtel, Maurice Bloomfield, Paul Deußen, Felix Hartmann, Georg Mahlow and other well-known scholars. In the next semester he returned to Göttingen, chiefly in order to take his Doctor's degree. The subject of his dissertation was the origin of the Indo-Iranian palatal series, embodying a discovery he had made before going to Berlin. This dissertation is to be found in Bezzenberger's Beiträge, vol. III. On the recommendation of his Göttingen teachers he received a stipendium intended for future Privatdozenten which enabled him to give his time for several years entirely to a continuation of his studies and to research work. This was the time when Comparative Philology was undergoing a thorough change as compared with the views held formerly by leading scholars. So the time seemed favorable for replacing Schleicher's *Compendium* by a work more in accordance with current views. This situation accounts for the plan conceived at this time by Fick, Bezzenberger, Bechtel and Collitz to unite in supplying the need for such a work. It was to consist of four volumes, one volume to be contributed by each of the four scholars, namely: 1. Phonology 2. Word-Formation 3. Inflection 4. Syntax. The whole was meant as a set of companion volumes to Fick's *Vergleichendes Wörterbuch* and to be published by the same publisher. This plan, unfortunately, was abandoned after a few years, partly because the project of collaborating in bringing out the Greek dialect inscriptions seemed even more urgent, and partly because soon afterwards Brugmann's *Grundriß* made the need of such a work less imperative. That the work of the Göttingen scholars would have received a form somewhat different from Brugmann's *Grundriß* may be inferred, e. g., from Bechtel's important book *Hauptprobleme der indogermanischen Lautlehre seit Schleicher* (Göttingen 1892).

In 1879 Dr. Collitz returned to Berlin, where he resumed his studies in Indo-European linguistics with some of his former teachers. The plan of collecting the Greek dialect inscriptions had meanwhile made substantial progress and Dr. Collitz was entrusted with the editorship. The first number appeared in 1883 and the first volume was finished in the next year.

Another task undertaken in Berlin was the editing of a dictionary of the Waldeck Low German dialect left in manuscript by the late Karl Bauer. In 1883 he left Berlin in order to accept an appointment at the University Library of Halle where a vacancy had been created owing to the resignation of Karl Verner who had been called to the University of Copenhagen. Collitz had every reason to enjoy the work since it included the writing of the new catalogues (begun by Verner) for General and Comparative Linguistics and for Philosophy. In 1885 he was granted the *venia docendi* at the University of Halle for Sanskrit and Comparative Philology. In the same year, he received a call as Associate Professor of German, to the newly founded Bryn Mawr College, near Philadelphia. Among his early colleagues were Miss Carey Thomas (Professor of English and Dean), Woodrow Wilson (Professor of History), Paul Shorey (Professor of Latin), and Washburn Hopkins (Professor of Sanskrit and Greek). After the latter had been called to Yale University, Collitz's title was changed to that of Professor of German and Comparative Philology.

In connection with the graduate courses he gave at Bryn Mawr College, his studies centered more and more around comparative Germanic Philology. This probably was the reason why he was invited, along with Professor Sievers, to represent Germanic Philology at the Congress of Arts and Sciences held in connection with the Universal Exposition at St. Louis in 1904. For several years he served as von Jagemann's successor in editing the Germanic division of *Modern Language Notes*.

Much as he felt attached to Bryn Mawr College he did not hesitate to accept a call, extended to him in 1907, to fill the newly established chair in Germanic Philology at the Johns Hopkins University. This university, as is well known, had adopted at its foundation the German methods of university study with regard to seminaries, the requirements for a Doctor's degree, and in laying stress, in a general way, on research work. It could claim, moreover, to be foremost in this country especially in the various branches of linguistic studies. This tendency apparently was responsible for the endeavor to foster the study of Germanic Philology. As a matter of fact, the relations between the Germanic department and other philological departments of the University soon became quite intimate.

Germanic Philology, as Professor Collitz conceived it, means on the one hand the comparative study of the Germanic languages in connection with the cognate Indo-European languages, above all Sanskrit, Greek and Latin, on the other hand, a comparison of the Early Germanic languages with each other with a view to the reconstruction of the common ancestor, i. e. the Primitive Germanic. Naturally, however, the instruction of graduate students had to take the form chiefly of grammatical courses combined with the interpretation of texts in the various old Germanic languages, such as Gothic, Old High German, Old Norse, Old Frisian and Old Saxon. The study of Gothic generally was combined with that of the elements of Comparative Philology. Considering that Low German resembles English much more closely than High German, the study of Low German in its various periods seemed to deserve special attention. Professor Collitz therefore made it a point to interpret, in each semester, to his students either portions of the Heliand or one of the Middle Low German dramas or extracts from Klaus Groth and Fritz Reuter. The Johns Hopkins University probably was the only university in the United States where such courses in Low German and Frisian were offered with some regularity. Other courses given by Professor Collitz were General Phonetics, seminary courses on OHG. glosses, on Hartmann's Iwein and other MHG. authors, and on MHG. 'Urkunden'. After the retirement (in 1920) of Professor Henry Wood, provision had to be made for the courses formerly given by him. Professor Collitz took over the graduate course in Faust (Part ii) which had been on his repertory for advanced students at Bryn Mawr College.

In 1911, he attended, as a delegate of the Johns Hopkins University, the centennial celebration of the University of Christiania (Oslo). This occasion furnished an opportunity of visiting Denmark, Sweden and Norway, and to make or renew the personal acquaintance with many Scandinavian scholars, such as Hj. Falk, A. Torp; O. Jespersen, H. Möller, Holger Pedersen, W. Thomsen; E. Wadstein; O. A. Danielsson, P. Persson, E. Hj. Psilander and others. Needless to add that the museums and libraries of the various Scandinavian capitals and Universities were a source to him of both enjoyment and instruction, and that the Codex Argenteus in Upsala was not overlooked.

In the following year there appeared his monograph on the origin of the Germanic weak preterite *(Das schwache Präteritum und seine Vorgeschichte)* as the first volume of the series *Hesperia*. In 1916, the University of Chicago conferred on him the honorary degree of L.H.D.

He was one of the scholars to endorse the call extended by

Professors Leonard Bloomfield, G. M. Bolling and Edgar H. Sturtevant for the organization of the American Linguistic Society. After having attended the organization meeting held in New York in December 1924, he was elected the first President of this Society for 1925. That year the Society met in Chicago together with the Modern Language Association of which Professor Collitz also had been elected President.

Among the festivities which marked the celebration, in 1926, of the semicentennial anniversary of the Johns Hopkins University was a special meeting of the Germanic department to which the former students were invited. Mr. Collitz was privileged to welcome the guests in the name of the department and to read the principal paper on the various meanings of the word 'Dialect'. At the commencement exercises of the next year an oil portrait of him, to which friends, colleagues, and former students had contributed, was presented to the University.

At the age of seventy two, after having served for forty one years as a college and university Professor, he felt entitled to ask to be relieved from active duties and retired with the title of Professor Emeritus of Germanic Philology.

The 24th of November 1928 marked the fiftieth anniversary of the day when the degree of Ph. D. was conferred upon him by the University of Göttingen. On this occasion the Philosophical Faculty of the Georgia Augusta sent Professor Collitz its congratulations together with a beautifully executed new diploma.

BIBLIOGRAPHY
OF PROFESSOR COLLITZ' WRITINGS*).

1878. Ueber die Annahme mehrerer grundsprachlicher *a*-Laute;
BB. 2, 291—305.

Register zu Bezzenbergers Beiträgen zur Kunde der idg.
Sprachen, Bd. 1—8 (1877—1884).

Register zu W. Scherer, Zur Geschichte der Deutschen
Sprache, 2. Ausgabe. Berlin 1878.

1879. Die Entstehung der Indo-Iranischen Palatalreihe; BB. 3,
177—234. (Pp. 177—201 also issued separately as a
Göttingen dissertation.)

Polnische Glossen aus dem 15./16. Jahrhundert; *AfslavPh.*
4, 86—97.

---

*) In quoting current periodicals the following abbreviations have been used:

AnzfdA.	= Anzeiger für Deutsches Altertum und Deutsche Literatur.
AfslavPh.	= Archiv für Slavische Philologie.
AJPh.	= American Journal of Philology.
APA.	= Transactions and Proceedings of the American Philological Association.
BB.	= Beiträge zur Kunde der indogermanischen Sprachen, herausgegeben von A. Bezzenberger.
CP.	= Classical Philology.
DLZ.	= Deutsche Literatur-Zeitung.
IF.	= Indogermanische Forschungen.
JAOS.	= Journal of the American Oriental Society.
JEGP.	= Journal of English and Germanic Philology.
JHU. Circ.	= Johns Hopkins University Circular.
KZ.	= Zeitschrift für Vergleichende Sprachforschung (Kuhns Zeitschrift).
Lang.	= Language, Journal of the Linguistic Society of America.
MLN.	= Modern Language Notes.
Ndd. Korr.bl.	= Korrespondenzblatt des Vereins für niederdeutsche Sprachforschung.
PBB.	= Beiträge zur Geschichte der deutschen Sprache und Literatur (Paul u. Braunes Beiträge, z. Z. hrsg. von Ed. Sievers).
PMLA.	= Publications of the Modern Language Association.
Scand. Studies	= Scandinavian Studies and Notes.
ZfdPh.	= Zeitschrift für deutsche Philologie (Zachers Zeitschrift).

Etymologien. 1. Gr. *Τέφρα*, Lat. *favilla, febris*. 2. Gr. *ῥῖγος*,
Lat. *frigus* = *srîgos; BB*. 3, 321—323.

Skr. car-, cirá-m, Gr. *τελέθω, πάλαι; BB*. 5, 101—102.

Rev. of Brugmann-Osthoff, Morphologische Untersuchungen, vol. I; *AnzfdA*. 5, 318—348.

1880. Rev. of W. Thomsen, Der Ursprung des Russischen Staates;
AfslavPh. 4, 656—663.

Rev. of G. Curtius: Das Verbum der Griechischen Sprache,
vol. II; *DLZ*. 1880, no. 13.

1881. Rev. of Braune, Gotische Grammatik; *ZfdPh*. 12, 480—482.

Rev. of Brugmann-Osthoff, Morphologische Untersuchungen, vol. III; *DLZ*. 1881, no. 29.

Rev. of von Bahder, Verbalabstracta; *DLZ*. 1881, col.
1264 seq.

1882. Rev. of Sievers, Phonetik, 2. Auflage; *DLZ*. 1882, nr. 6.

Rev. of Gust. Meyer, Griechische Grammatik; *BB*. 7,
173—176.

Rev. of Lanman, Noun-Inflection in the Veda; *BB*. 7,
176—184.

Ueber eine besondere Art Vedischer Composita; Abhandlungen des 5. Internationalen Orientalistenkongresses zu
Berlin, Vol. II, 2, 287—298.

Homerisch *ἠύ*-s, *ἐύ*-s und Vedisch *āyú-s; KZ*. 27, 183—189.

Rev. of Ziemer, Junggrammatische Studien; *DLZ*. 1882,
col. 1567.

Der Germanische Ablaut in seinem Verhältnis zum Indogermanischen Vocalismus (I. Teil); *ZfdPh*. 15, 1—10.

Zur Einteilung der Niederdeutschen Mundarten; *Ndd.
Korr.bl*. 7, 81—82.

1883. Sammlung der Griechischen Dialektinschriften von J. Bau-
nack, F. Bechtel, A. Bezzenberger, F. Blaß, H. Collitz,
W. Deecke, A. Fick, H. van Gelder, O. Hoffmann, R. Meister, P. Müllensiefen, W. Prellwitz. Herausgegeben von
H. Collitz. 1. Heft, Göttingen, Vandenhoeck & Ruprecht.

(I. Band, Heft 1—4, 1883—84. — II. Bd., Heft 1—6,
1885—99. — III. Bd., hrsg. von C. F. und F. Bechtel.
1. Hälfte, Heft 1—5, 1888—99, 2. Hälfte, Heft 1—5,
1898—1905. — IV. Bd., Wortregister und Nachträge.
Heft 1, bearbeitet von R. Meister, 1886; Heft 2, hrsg.

von H: C. und F. Bechtel, 1901; Heft 3 und 4, hrsg. von
H. C. und O. Hoffmann, 1910—15.)

Rev. of Henry, Étude sur l'Analogie; *DLZ*. 1883, no. 39.

1884. Sammlung der Griechischen Dialekt-Inschriften. Erster
Band; Göttingen, Vandenhoeck & Ruprecht.

Kretisch ἀλλατᾶν = ἀλλάσσειν; *BB*. 7, 328—329.

Rev. of Berghaus, Sprachschatz der Sassen. Vol. I, II;
DLZ. 1884, col. 272 seq.

Rev. of Hoffory, Professor Sievers und die Sprachphysio-
logie; *ibid.*, col. 1613 seq.

1885. Die Flexion der Nomina mit dreifacher Stammabstufung
im Altindischen und im Griechischen. Teil I, Die Ca-
sus des Singulars; *BB*. 10, 1—71.

(Accepted as "Habilitationsschrift" by the Philosophical Faculty of the
University of Halle, March 1885.)

Die Verwandtschaftsverhältnisse der Griechischen Dialekte.
Göttingen, Vandenhoeck & Ruprecht.

1886. Die Neueste Sprachforschung und die Erklärung des Indogermanischen Ablautes; *BB*. 11, 203—242 (also publ.
separately, Göttingen, Vandenhoeck & Ruprecht) and
(Nachtrag) 304—307.

Ueber das Vergleichende Studium der Niederdeutschen
Mundarten; *Ndd. Korr.bl.* 11, 23—32.

Das *B* im Theraeischen Alphabet; *Hermes* 21, 136.

1887. Wahrung meines Rechtes; *BB*. 12, 243—248.

Ἴφθιμος und ved. kṣi; *AJP*. 8 (1887), 214—217. Reprinted in *BB*. 18, 226—230).

1888. Die Herkunft des schwachen Präteritums der German.
Sprachen; *AJP*. 9, 42—57. (Reprinted in *BB*. 17,
227—244. Translated under the title "The Origin of
the Weak Preterit"; *PMLA*. 3, 196—209.)

1890. On the existence of Primitive Aryan *sh; JAOS*. 15, *Proceedings*, pp. LXV—LXVI.

Review of Benfey's Kleinere Schriften, vol. I; *AJP*.
11, 488—495.

1891. Die Behandlung des ursprünglich auslautenden *ai* im Gotischen, Althochdeutschen und Altsächsischen; *BB*. 17,
1—53.

Rev. of G. A. Hench, The Monsee Fragments; *MLN*. 6,
col. 475—482.

Rev. of Jellinek's Beiträge zur Erklärung der Germanischen Flexion; *AnzfdA.* 17, 275—282.

Ueber Ficks Vergleichendes Wörterbuch der Indogerm. Sprachen; *AJP.* 12, 293—309.

Rev. of Jackson "The Avestan Alphabet and its Transcription"; *ibid.* 12, 489—492.

1892. Rev. of Indogermanische Forschungen (vol. I, no. 1); *AnzfDA.* 18, 169—174.

Die drei indischen Wurzeln *kṣi* und ihre Verwanten im Griechischen; *BB.* 18 (1892), 201—226.

For additional comment on these roots and on the existence in the I.-Eur. parent speech of a palatal *š*- sound in addition to the dental sibilant *s* see the author's articles on Lat. *saeculum* (1921, Festschrift for Bezzenberger) and on *Saturnus* (1930, Oriental Studies ed. by Jal Dastur C. Pavry).

Zur Bildung des Instrumentals der *man*-Stämme im Altindischen; *ibid.* 18, 231—241.

Rev. of Benfey's Kleinere Schriften, vol. II; *AJP.* 13, 484—492.

1893. Articles "Dutch Language", "Flemish Language", and "Frisian Language and Literature"; Johnson's Cyclopædia, Vol. III & IV (1894).

Rev. of Paul's Grundriß der germanischen Philologie (vol. I, no. 1); *MLN.* 8, col. 99—106 & 160—169.

1894. The Aryan Name of the Tongue; Oriental Studies (Papers read before the Oriental Club of Philadelphia, 1888/94. — Boston, Ginn & Co.), 177—201.

Articles "Low German" and "Plattdeutsch"; Johnson's Cyclopædia, Vol. V (1894) & VI (1895).

The Etymology of ἄρα and μάψ; *APhA. Proceedings,* Special Session, 1894, XXXIX—XL.

1895. Two Modern German Etymologies (1. *Schnörkel,* 2. *schmarotzen*); *PMLA.* 295—305.

1897. Der Name der Goten bei Griechen und Römern; *JEGP.* 1, 220—238.

Traces of Indo-European Accentuation in Latin; *APA.* 28 (1897), 92—110.

1898. Zu Goethes Faust. I. Eine mißverstandene Stelle im Vorspiel auf dem Theater; Americana Germanica, vol. II, No. 1 (1898), 87—91.

1899. Sammlung der Griechischen Dialekt-Inschriften, 2. Bd. u.
3. Bd., 1. Hälfte (hrsg. v. H. Collitz und F. Bechtel).
Göttingen, Vandenhoeck & Ruprecht.

Die Niederdeutsche Mundart im Fürstentum Waldeck
(Sonderabdruck aus Bauers Waldeckischem Wörterbuche). Norden, D. Soltau, 1899.

The Vedic word *návedas*. *JAOS.* Vol. XX, Pt. 2, 225—228.

1901. The Home of the Heliand; *PMLA.* 16, 123—140.

1903. Waldeckisches Wörterbuch nebst Dialektproben, gesammelt
von K. Bauer. Im Auftrage des Vereins für niederdeutsche Sprachforschung bearbeitet und herausgegeben von
H. Collitz; pp. XVI + 106 + 320; Norden u. Leipzig
1902; D. Soltau's Verlag.

"German Language"; New International Encyclopædia
(New York: Dodd, Mead & Co.) in vol. 7.

1904. Zum Awesta-Alphabet; Verhandlungen des XIII. Internationalen Orientalisten-Kongresses, Leiden 1904, 107
—108.

1905. Die Herkunft der *ā*-Deklination; *BB.* 29, 81—114.

Inhaltsübersicht: 1. Die *ī*-Deklination im Rigveda 81;
II. Die *ī*-Deklination im Lateinischen 82; Exkurs: Zu den *iē*-Stämmen der
latein. V. Deklination 83; III. Die *ī*-Deklination in den übrigen europäischen Sprachen 85; IV. Parallelismus der *ā*- und der *ī*-Deklination
im Altindischen 89; V. Die *ā*- und *ī*-Deklination im Altiranischen 96;
VI. Zur Vorgeschichte der *ī*-Deklination 98; VII. Ergebnisse für die
ā-Deklination 104; VIII. Abgeleitete Stämme auf *-e-ya-* im Altindischen
109; IX. Die *ā*-Deklination in den europäischen Sprachen 110.

Note. When this article was printed in *BB.*, it should have been
stated that it had been written for the volume Γέρας. Abhandlungen
zur idg. Sprachgeschichte, published in honor of Prof. August Fick
in 1903, but owing to adverse circumstances had been received too late
for publication in that volume.

Sammlung der Griechischen Dialekt-Inschriften, hrsg. von
H. Collitz und F. Bechtel, III. Band, 2. Hälfte. Göttingen,
Vandenhoeck & Ruprecht.

Das Analogiegesetz der Westgermanischen Ablautsreihen;
MLN. 20, 65—68.

Note to Francis Wood's article on German *dürfen; ibid.*
20, 105.

Zum vokalischen Auslautsgesetz der Germanischen Sprachen; *ibid.* 20, 129—131.

1906 Problems in Comparative Germanic Philology; Congress
of Arts and Science, Universal Exposition, St. Louis

(Boston; Houghton, Mifflin & Co.), vol. 3 (Language, Literature, Art), 286—302.

1907 Segimer oder: Germanische Namen in Keltischem Gewande; *JEGP.* 6, 253—306.

Rev. of Gallée, Vorstudien zu einem Altniederdeutschen Wörterbuche; *ibid.* 6, 472—477.

1909 Rev. of Fick, Vorgriechische Ortsnamen; *CP.* 4, 206—209.

Rev. of Streitberg, Die Gotische Bibel I.; *MLN.* 24, 181—183.

1910 Two Supplementary Notes: I. O. Norse *bedenn.* II. Gemination in Anglo-Saxon; *JEGP.* 11, 25—26

Zum Hildebrandsliede; *PBB.* 36, 366—373.

Rev. of Fick, Hattiden und Danubier in Griechenland; *CP.* 5, 508—511.

1911. Rev. of Streitberg, Die Gotische Bibel II.; *MLN.* 26, 182—184.

»Missingsch«; Festschrift, Chr. Walther gewidmet von dem Verein für niederdeutsche Sprachforschung (= Jahrbuch des Vereins f. ndd. Spr. XXXVII, Heft 1, 110—113).

1912 Das Schwache Präteritum und seine Vorgeschichte (Hesperia, Schriften zur Germanischen Philologie 1.) pp. XVI + 256; Göttingen, Vandenhoeck & Ruprecht (Baltimore, The Johns Hopkins Press).

In the preface a review is given of recent contributions to Germanic Philology in the United States. An appendix contains a discussion of the Latin perfect tense and the Greek passive aorist in their relation to the weak preterit. A theory advanced here concerning the origin of the Greek passive aorist has recently found an able advocate in Adolf Walter in the Festschrift for W. Streitberg (Stand u. Aufgaben der Sprachwissenschaft, Heidelberg 1924) p. 351 f.

Rev. of Petzet & Glauning, Deutsche Schrifttafeln des IX. bis XVI. Jahrhunderts, 1. Abteilung; *MLN.* 27, 115—117.

1914. Rev. of Hesperia no. 1; *MLN.* 29, 178—181.

Bemerkungen zum Schwachen Präteritum; *IF.* 34, 209 bis 222.

1915. Sammlung der Griechischen Dialektinschriften, hrsg. von H. Collitz und O. Hoffmann, Vierter Band, IV. Heft, 1.—3. Abteilung (Schluß der Sammlung), Göttingen, Vandenhoeck & Ruprecht.

Rev. of Sipma, Phonology and Grammar of Modern West Frisian; *MLN.* 30, 215—217.

1916. Goethe's use of *vergakelt; MLN.* 31, 75—78.

1917. Rev. of Axel Kock, Brechung und Umlaut im Altschwedischen; *MLN.* 32, 40—44.

Zu den Mittelhochdeutschen kurzen Präterita *gie, fie, lie; MLN.* 32, 207—215, 449—458.

The Etymology of the word *Degen; JHUCirc.* no. 296, 887.

The Greek noun πρόμος; *ibid,* 889.

Ags. *sedel,* Mod. German *siedeln,* Lat. *saeculum; ibid.* 900—902,

1918. Early Germanic Vocalism; *MLN.* 33, 321—333.

Note. An abstract only of a more comprehensive and more detailed treatise which remains to be published. In endeavoring to reconstruct the Primitive Germanic vocalism on the basis of the various Old Germanic languages the author arrived at the result that the common foundation is seen almost unaltered in Gothic. The innovations generally ascribed to Gothic were inherited from Primitive Germanic, whereas numerous and fundamental changes took place afterwards in the West Germanic-Scandinavian period.

The Etymology of Modern German *Ketzer; JHUCirc.* no. 306, 540—541.

Giselher; ibid. 558.

Low German *Ziegenfuß; ibid.* 563.

The Last Days of Ulfila; *ibid.* 566—569.

1919. Middle High German *alrune; MLN.* 34, 52—53.

Rev. of Meillet's Caractères Généraux des Langues Germaniques; *AJP.* 39, 408—418.

Rev. of Gaidoz's Deux Érudits Gallois, John Rhys et L. Reynolds; *ibid.* 205—209.

The Systematization of Vowel-Sounds, or: Bell's Vowel-System modified and simplified; *JHU.Circ.* no. 316, 588—589.

Rev. of Joh. Enschedé's Die Hochdeutschen Schriften aus dem 15. bis zum 19. Jahrhundert; *MLN.* 34, 492—496.

1920. The Causes of Phonetic Change; *JHUCirc.* no. 325, 30—32.

Anglo-Saxon *refnan; ibid.* 52—54.

Three Philological Anniversaries [of Bopp, Rask and J. Grimm]; *ibid.* 61.

1921. Old Icelandic *raun* and *reyna; Scand. Studies* 6, 58—67.

Saeculum; Festschrift für Ad. Bezzenberger, Göttingen, 1921, 8—13.

1922. Germanische Wortdeutungen 1. Gotisch *inn, inna* MLN. 37, 215—217. — 2. Gotisch *duginnan* »beginnen«; *ibid*. 274—297.

Sunufatarungo *JEGP*. 21, 557—571.

1924. Old Norse *elska* and the Notion of Love; *Scand. Studies* 8, 1—13.

Wodan, Hermes und Pūshan; Festskrift tillägnad Hugo Pipping, 547—587. Helsingfors: *Skrifter utg. av Svenska Litteratursällskapet i Finland*, CLXXV.

1925. The Scope and Aims of Linguistic Science (abstract); *Lang*. I, 14—16.

Gothic *siponeis*, a Loan Word from Greek; *AJP*. 46, 213—221.

Gothic *barusnjan ibid*. 358—362.

Das Wort *Ketzer*; Germania, Sievers-Festschrift zum 75. Geburtstage, 115—128.

1926. *Weg*, »Die Wand«. Ein Beitrag zur Deutschen Wortkunde; *The Germanic Review* I, 40—46.

World Languages (Presidential address, Joint meeting of Modern Language Association and Linguistic Society of America); *PMLA*. 41, 43—55; *Lang*. II, 1—13.

A Century of Grimm's Law; *Lang*. II, 174—183.

An address delivered in 1923 on the occasion of the centenary of the 2nd edition of the first vol. of J. Grimm's Grammar. It includes a mnemonic help for remembering the working of the Law.

1927. In Memoriam [James W. Bright]; *Hesperia, Ergänzungsreihe*, no. 10 (Preface).

Rev. of K. Lokotsch, Etymologisches Wörterbuch der Europäischen Wörter orientalischen Ursprungs; *MLN*. 42, 412—414.

1928. Das Schwache Präteritum als Mischbildung; *PMLA*. 43, no. 3, 593—601.

A supplement to the author's monograph on the weak preterit published in 1912. In his present opinion this preterit must be regarded as a complex formation, due to the combination of certain forms of the I.-Eur. perfect middle with a peculiar type of the I.-Eur. simple aorist.

Antediluvian Kings and Patriarchs in the Light of Comparative Mythology; *JAOS*. 48 (1928) p. 341.

(Syllabus of a Paper read at the Washington Meeting of the Amer. Oriental Society. Not yet published.)

1930. König Yima und Saturn; Oriental Studies, edited by Jal Dastur C. Pavry, London [To be published shortly].

Contents: I. Einleitung; II. Yima in den Gāthās; III. Yima im Jüngeren Avesta; IV. Yimō xšaētō (Djemšīd) und ved. kṣaitah; V. Yimō xšaētō und Saturnus.

PERIODICALS AND SERIAL PUBLICATIONS.

(Editor:) Sammlung der Griechischen Dialekt-Inschriften; 4 vols., Göttingen, Vandenhoeck & Ruprecht, 1884—1915 (vol. 3 jointly with F. Bechtel, and vol. 4 with O. Hoffmann).

(Editor:) Hesperia. Schriften zur Germanischen Philologie; nos. 1—18, Göttingen, Vandenhoeck & Ruprecht, and Baltimore, The Johns Hopkins Press, 1912—1929.

(Associate Editor:) Modern Language Notes; vols. 17—28, Baltimore, 1902—1913.

(Co-operating Editor:) Journal of English and Germanic Philology; vols. 8—28, The University of Illinois, 1909—1929.

Vol. 28 was dedicated to Prof. Collitz.

(Co-operating Editor:) American Journal of Philology; vols. 41—50, Baltimore, 1920—1929.

NEUTER PRONOUNS REFERRING TO WORDS OF DIFFERENT GENDER OR NUMBER[1]

BY EDGAR H. STURTEVANT

YALE UNIVERSITY

Nine times in the Iguvinian Tables a relative pronominal form, *porse (porsi, porsei)* refers to an antecedent that is masculine singular or neuter plural, and opinions differ as to the nature of *porse* itself. Bücheler, *Umbrica* 46, 192, 215, saw in *rse* an enclitic particle *de*, with which he compared the final element of Latin *quamde*[2]. Brugmann, *Berichte der Sächsischen Akademie* 1893, 135 f., considered *pö* an indeclinable relative adverb strengthened by an enclitic *di*. But *porse* appears to be related to the conjunction *pure* (from *quod-i*) in the same way as *pirsi* to *pire* (from *quid-i*). Other forms also of the relative show a final particle *i* in Umbrian; but there is no clear trace of a particle *di*. As far as form goes, there is every reason to consider *porse*, like *pure*, the neuter singular of the pronoun with an enclitic *i*. Consequently Bugge, Kuhn's *Zeitschrift für Vergleichende Sprachforschung* 3. 35, suggested that it was a stereotyped neuter used for all genders and both numbers. He has been followed by several scholars[3]. I agree with them in the main, except that I consider the idiom, not a peculiar development of Umbrian[4], but a remnant of a very ancient usage.

In four of the eight passages *porse* is equivalent to Latin *is qui*, and the clause describes a person whose identity is unknown.

---

[1] I am under obligations to my colleagues, Professors Edgerton, Prokosch, and Willard, and to my daughter, Mrs. F. W. Hopkins, for assistance in securing material on languages with which I have little familiarity.

[2] Similarly Von Planta, *Grammatik der Oskisch-Umbrischen Dialekte* 3. 228.

[3] See Buck, *A Grammar of Oscan and Umbrian* 145 (§ 199 f.).

[4] See Bréal, *Les Tables Eugubines* 42: "C'est un commencement d'appauvrissement de la déclinaison qui annonce ce qui s'est passé en italien pour le pronom *che* et en français pour *que*." Cf. *ib.* 355.

The sentences are so similar to one another that it will be enough to cite 6 b 63:

> eno deitu, "etato Iiouinur", *porse* perca arsmatia habiest,
> 'tum dicito, "itatote Iguvini", qui virgam ritualem habebit'.

In 6 a 9 *porsei* refers once to *angluto* 'ab angulo' and once to *anglome* 'ad angulum', which word is probably masculine. In 6 a 19 and 6 b 40 the antecedent is *uaso(r)* 'vasa', which is neuter plural; and *tudero* 'finis', the antecedent in 6 a 15, is also a neuter plural.

The clauses of the first type, in which the antecedent of the relative is an unidentified person, find a close parallel in certain phrases in Latin; for example:

Plautus, *Casina* 451: erit hodie tecum *quod* amas, 'today your sweetheart will be with you'.

Curculio 136: id *quod* amo careo, 'I haven't my sweetheart'.

Cu. 170: qui homo *quod* amat videt, 'whoever sees his sweetheart'.

Epidicus 653: tibi quidem *quod* ames domi praestost, 'there's somebody at home for you to love'.

Poenulus 327: *ecquid* amare videor? : : damnum, 'do I seem to be in love with anybody? : : with loss'.

Cu. 38: ama *quid*lubet, 'make love to anybody you please'[5].

Terence, *Andria* 464: nam *quod* peperisset iussit tolli, 'for he told us to rear the baby'.

Vergil, *Aeneid* 5. 715 f.:

> longaevosque senes ac fessas aequore matres
> et quicquid tecum invalidum metuensque pericli est,

'aged men and sea-weary women and whoever in your company is a weakling and afraid of danger'.

Such sentences as these do not stand alone in Latin; there is a marked tendency to use neuter pronouns and pronominal adjectives to refer to persons who are not fully identified.

Catullus, 9. 11: *quid* me laetius est beatiusve? 'who is happier than I?'

Cicero, *Ad Atticum* 9. 16. 3: Dolabella tuo *nihil* scito mihi esse iucundius, 'be assured that nobody is dearer to me than your Dolabella'.

Pliny, *Epistulae* 1. 221: *nihil* est enim illo gravius, sanctius, doctius, 'nobody is more dignified, more reliable, or better educated than he'.

---

[5] For other examples with *amo*, see Lodge, *Lexicon Plautinum* 1. 112.

Cicero, *Tusculanae Disputationes* I. 7. 13: quid enim tam pugnat
  quam non modo miserum sed omnino *quicquam* esse qui
  non sit? 'for what is so inconsistent as for one who does not
  exist to be unhappy or even to be anything?'

Ad Familiares 6. 184: ego quoque *aliquid* sum, 'I too am somebody'[6].

Livy I. 53. 11: in se ipsum postremo saeviturum, si *alia* desint,
  'that he would finally turn his fury upon himself, if there
  were no others'.

We may fairly conclude from a comparison of Umbrian and
Latin that Primitive Italic employed neuter pronouns and
pronominal adjectives to refer to persons in an indefinite way.
That the usage may be carried back to Italo-Celtic times seems
to follow from a notice in Pedersen's *Vergleichende Grammatik der
Keltischen Sprachen* 2. 64 f., to the effect that Old Irish sometimes
employs the neuter of similar words to refer to persons. Among
his examples are *nechtar n-ái* 'one of the two' and *cechtar n-athar*
'both of us'.

In the Germanic languages of all periods neuter pronouns very
frequently refer to persons, although examples are relatively
few in the Gothic Bible on account of the imitation of Greek
syntax which prevails there. I shall illustrate principally with
Old English.

Gothic. Mark 6. 3: niu *þata* ist sa timrja? 'isn't this the carpenter?'

Old High German. Tatian 81. 2: ih bim *iz*, 'ich bin es'.

Modern High German. *Es* sind Männer. Sind das die Männer?
  Jetzt ist er glücklich; wird er *es* aber immer sein?

Old English. Beowulf 237: *hwæt* syndon ge . . .? who are ye . . .?'

Alfred, *Boethius* 36. 22 (Sedgefield): and he hine het secgan
  hwæt his geferan wæron, 'and he ordered him to say who
  his companions were'.

Aelfric, *Homilies* I. 14. 4 (Thorpe): hu mihte Adam tocnawan
  hwæt he wære? 'how could Adam know who he was?'

Aelfric, *Genesis* 27. 32: *hwæt* eart þu? 'who art thou?'

Bede 4. 156. 1139 (Schipper): ac ic cuðlice wat ge *hwæt* þu eart
  ge for hwon þu gnornast, 'scio enim certissime qui es et quare
  maeres'.

Alfred, *Boeth.* 82. 9: *þæt* eart þu, 'that art thou'.

---

[6] For further examples, see Greene, *Classical Review* 18. 448—450.

Orosius 17. 26 (Sweet): and *þæt* wæron eall Finnas, 'and they were all Finns'.

In one usage the employment of the neuter is extended to all adjectives in the Germanic languages; the neuter is used to combine masculine and feminine nouns, as is well illustrated in the early versions of Luke 1. 6. As we are at present interested merely in the pronouns, I shall quote only the Gothic version in full.

Gothic: wesunuh þan garaihta *ba* in andwairþja gudis, gaggandona in allaim anabusnim jah garaihteim fraujins unwaha, 'and they were both righteous before God, walking in all the commandments and ordinances of the Lord blameless'.

Norse. þau voro retlot bæþe.

Old High German. Tatian: *siu* warun rehtiu *beidu* fora gote.

Otfrid: uuarun *siu bethiu* gote filu drudiu.

Old English: soðlice hig wæron *butu* rihtwise.

In Slavic the neuter singular of the pronoun is used to refer to a masculine or feminine noun of either number which has not been previously mentioned (although this limitation is not consistently observed, and has no importance for our investigation). A few examples will suffice.

Russian. kto *eto* takoy? 'who is that?' *eto* moi deti, 'these are my children'.

The interrogative pronoun, *kto* (Church Slavonic *kŭto*) almost certainly represents a phrase of this type; for *kŭ*- is Sanskrit *kas*, and -*to* is Sanskrit *tad*. The relative pronoun also is used in the neuter singular to refer to a masculine singular or plural. The construction is rare in Old Church Slavonic, but more common later, especially in Old Czech. Two examples from Church Slavonic follow.

Codex Suprasliensis 17. 5: bogu suojemy, *ježe* u nebesexŭ, 'to our God who is in the heavens'.

244. 6: *ježe* jeste 'οἵτινες' (= 'you who are').

In the other Indo-European languages neuter pronouns and pronominal words do not often refer to persons; but there are a few scattering examples such as the following.

Greek. Iliad 3. 178 f.:

> οὗτός γ' 'Ατρείδης εὐρὺ κρείων 'Αγαμέμνων,
> ἀμφότερον, βασιλεύς τ' ἀγαθὸς κρατερός τ' αἰχμητής,

'this is Atreus's son, Agamemnon, ruler of many lands, both a good king and a mighty spearsman'.

Aristophanes, *Equites* 854: μελιτοπῶλαι καὶ τυροπῶλαι· τοῦτο δ' εἰς ἕν ἐστι συγκεκυφός, 'dealers in honey and in cheese; for these have conspired together'.

Plato *Apology* 41: ἐὰν δοκῶσί τι εἶναι, μηδὲν ὄντες, 'if they seem to be somebody, although they are nobody'.

Sophocles, *Trachiniae* 1107: κἂν τὸ μηδὲν ὦ, 'even if I am nobody'.

Sanskrit. Chāndogya Upaniṣad 6. 16. 2: tat satyam, sa ātmā *tat* tvam asi, 'that is truth, that is the self, that thou art'.

Vājasaneyi Saṁhitā 32. 1:

tad evāgnis, *tad* ādityas, *tad* vāyus, *tad* u candramāh,
tad eva śukram, tad brahma, *tad* āpaḥ, sa prajāpatiḥ,

'that is Agni, that is the sun, that is the wind, that is the moon, that is the bright one, that is Brahman, that is the waters, that is Prajāpati'.

Sāma Veda 1. 203:

na *ki* indra tvad uttaram,
na jyāyo asti vṛtrahan,
na *ky* evam yathā tvam [7],

'there is nothing higher than thou, Indra, nothing greater, slayer of Vṛtra, nothing even like thee'.

Except for three Umbrian examples, we have so far confined our attention to the use of a neuter pronoun referring to persons. It is evident, however, that Umbrian *porse* referring to a masculine singular or a neuter plural antecedent cannot be separated from *porse* 'is qui'. In Germanic and Slavic there is no distinction in this matter between personal nouns and others, and elsewhere also neuter singular pronouns sometimes refer to impersonal masculine and feminine nouns or to neuters plural. Particularly important is the use of a neuter singular pronoun to govern a partitive genitive.

Latin. Plautus, *Mostellaria* 627 f.: quasi quadraginta minas; ne sane *id* multum censeas, 'about forty minae; don't think that much'.

Cicero, *Pro Sulla* 17. 49: cum honos agebatur familiae vestrae amplissimus, *hoc* est, consulatus parentis tui, 'when high

---

[7] The stanza occurs also in *Rig Veda* 4. 30. 1, where the usual masculine is employed: *na kir . . . uttaraḥ*, etc.

office for your household, that is, your father's consulship, was at stake'.

Plautus, *Amphitruo* 154: *hoc* noctis, 'this time of night'.

Terence, *Eunuchus* 546: *quid hoc* hominis? 'what sort of a man is this?'

Heauton Timorumenos 77: humani *nil*, 'nothing that concerns man'.

Cicero, *Ad Familiares* 2. 8. 3: *hoc litterarum*, ,this letter'.

De Oratore 1. 47. 207: hominibus *id* aetatis, 'men of such age'.

Caesar, *De Bello Gallico* 3. 16: navium *quod* ubique fuerat, 'what ships they had had anywhere'.

Livy 3. 17. 5: *quicquid* patrum plebisque est, 'all the patricians and plebeians'.

9. 45. 2: ad *id* locorum, 'on all occasions up to the present'.

Gothic. Ephesians 1. 18: *hwa* ist wens? 'what is the hope?' (*wens* is feminine).

Skeireins 7. 14 f.: bigitan was þizei hlaibe *ib* tainjons fullos, *þatei* aflifnoda, 'there was found of these loaves twelve baskets full, that was left'.

Old English. Crist 694: *hwæt* sindon þa gimmas buton god sylfa? 'what then are gems but God himself?' (*gimmas* is feminine plural).

89: *hwæt* is þeos wundrung? 'what is this excitement?' (*wundrung* is feminine).

Alfred, *Cura Pastoralis* 21, p. 154 (Sweet): *hwæt* ryhtlices, 'aliquid iusti'.

Orosius 226. 12 (Sweet): siþþan mæst eall forweard þæt on þæm lande wæs, ge monna, ge nietena, ge wildeora for þæm stence, 'afterwards most all that was in that land perished, both of men and of cattle and of wild things, on account of the smell'.

Russian. eto stol (stoly), 'this (is) a table'; 'these(are) tables'.

Greek. Odyssey 1. 159: τούτοισιν μὲν ταῦτα μέλει, κίθαρις καὶ ἀοιδή, 'their interest is this, the lyre and song'.

Herodotos 4. 23: καρπὸν φορεῖ κυάμῳ ἴσον . . . ., τοῦτο ἐπεὰν γένηται πέπον . . . ., 'it bears fruit like a bean; when this grows ripe' (καρπός is masculine).

Sammlung Griechischer Dialektinschriften 5653. a. 5: ἐς τὴν τρίοδον ἕξς· ἀπὸ τούτō . . ., 'to the fork of the road, six (boundary stones); from there' (τρίοδος is feminine).

Euripides, *Helena* 1687: εὐγενεστάτης γνώμης, ὃ πολλαῖς ἐν γυναιξὶν οὐκ ἔνι, 'of a noble disposition, which in many women does not exist'.

Plato, *Symposium* 196 A: ἡ εὐσχημοσύνη, ὃ . . .

Iliad 21. 360: τί μοι ἔριδος καὶ ἀρωγῆς; 'what is warfare and defense to me?' (cf. Aristophanes, *Lysistrata* 514, etc.: τί δὲ σοὶ ταῦτα).

Herodotus 7. 38: ἐς τόδε ἡλικίης, 'to this age'.

Thucydides 3. 44: ἔχοντές τι ξυγγνώμης.

2. 17: ἐν τούτῳ παρασκευῆς ἦσαν.

Avestan. Yasht 5. 77: avavaṭ daēvayasnanąm, 'so many of the devil-worshipers'.

Yasna 34. 12: kaṭ vašī, *kaṭ* vā stūtō *kaṭ* vā yasnahyā? 'what do you want; what of praise or what of sacrifice?'

Vendidad 5. 33: *cvaṭ* dāmanąm, 'quantum creaturarum'.

Sanskrit. Atharva Veda 7. 97. 2: sam indra no manasā neṣa gobhiḥ . . . sam bhrahmaṇām devahitaṁ *yad* asti, 'bring us together, Indra, with mind, with cattle, . . . with whatever of incantations is god-established'.

Kāṭhaka Saṁhitā 8. 14 = *Taittirīya Saṁhitā* 1. 5. 3. 2 = *Maitrāyaṇī Saṁhitā* 1. 7. 1: yat te, 'whatever of thee (Agni)'.

Śatapatha Brāhmaṇa 10. 4. 1. 10: *etāvat* karmaṇaḥ, 'tantum operis'.

Aitareya Brāhmaṇa 2. 15. 8: *mahati* rātryāḥ, 'in the dead of night'.

In Hittite neuter singular pronouns are frequently used to refer to plural antecedents of either gender [9]. The following examples are typical.

Keilschrifturkunden aus Boghazköi 14. 1. 1. 48 (= Götze, *Madduwattaš* p. 12): [KA]RAŠ-za-kán ku-i-e-eš te-pa-u-eš i[š-par]-te-ir *a-pa-a-at*-ma-kán hu-u-ma-an a[r-ha ha]-áš-pí-ir-pít, 'and what few escaped from (his) army, all those they likewise de[stroyed]'.

Keilschrifttexte aus Boghazköi 4. 10. 1. 50 f.: nu ka-a-šá a-pí-e-da-ni me-mi-ni *LI. IM* DINGIR. MEŠ tu-li-ya hal-zi-ya-an-te-eš nu uš-kán-du iš-ta-ma-áš-kán-du-ya na-*at* ku-ut-ru-

---

[8] See Speijer, *Sanskrit Syntax* 87.

[9] See Hrozný, *Die Sprache der Hethiter* 134₂, 142₃, 143₁; Friedrich, *Zeitschrift der Deutschen Morgenländischen Gesellschaft* 76. 164, *Zeitschrift für Assyriologie*, N. F. 2. 290—296.

e-eš a-šá-an-du, 'and, behold! on this occasion the one thousand gods are called to council; let them see and hear, let them be witnesses'.

KUB I. I. 2. 66—68 (= Götze, *Hattušiliš* p. 20): [n]u-za ki-e KÚR. KÚR. MEŠ dan-na-at-ta ... EGIR-pa a-še-šá-nu-[n]u-un na-*at* EGIR-pa ᵁᴿᵁ Ha-at-tu-šá-an i-ya-nu-un, 'and these devastated lands I caused to be inhabited again; and I made them subject to Hattusas again'.

KBo. 5. I. 2. 38 f. (= Sommer and Ehelolf, *Boghazköi-Studien* 10, p. 8*): VII ANŠU. KÚR. RA KÏR VII GUD KÏR VII MUŠEN KÏR VII ᴰᵁᴳ pu-ul-lu-ri-ya na-*at* IŠ.*TU* LAL šú-u-wa-an, 'seven horses of asphalt, seven cattle of asphalt, seven birds of asphalt, seven *pulluriya* vessels; these filled with honey'.

KBo. 3. 6. 2. 52—53 (= Götze. *Hatt.* p. 22): nu-mu-kán *PA. AN.* ŠEŠ.*YA ku-it* KI.KAL.BA[D] ANŠU.KU[R.R]A. [MEŠ] *ŠÁ* KÚR ᵁᴿᵁ Ha-at-ti ŠÚ-i e-eš-ta, na-an am-mu-ug da-par-ha, 'what infantry and cavalry was, subject to my brother, under my control, that I commanded'.

Neuter plural pronominal forms are used in precisely the same way as the neuter singular, and Friedrich (*ZA NF* 2. 295 f.) thought that the confusion of the two numbers was a secondary development, due to the fact that certain neuter nouns are alike, or nearly so, in singular and plural. The similarity of the Hittite usage illustrated above to what we have found in the Indo-European languages makes it much more likely that the use of the neuter singular to refer to plural antecedents, personal or not, was an inherited construction.

This collective use of the neuter pronoun is obviously akin to Umbrian *porse* with a neuter plural antecedent, to Greek τοῦτο with two masculine plural antecedents (Ar., *Eq.* 854), to Latin *id* referring to *quadraginta minas* (Pl., *Most.* 627 f.) to Gothic *þatei* with a plural antecedent, to Old English *hwæt* and *þæt* with plural nouns, to Russian *eto* with the plural, and particularly to the neuter singular pronoun governing the partitive genitive (e. g. *hoc litterarum*) which we have observed in Latin, Greek, Germanic, Avestan, and Sanskrit. The collective use of neuter pronouns may, then, confidently be ascribed to Pre-Indo-European as well as to Indo-European. The precise history of the other idioms which we have noticed (the use of a neuter pronoun to refer to a person in an indefinite way, or to refer to a masculine or feminine singular antecedent, and the use of a neuter plural to refer to persons of different sex) cannot so easily be determined, although there is a fair probability that they all date from Indo-European times. I do not maintain, however, that every usage here illustrated was inherited by the language which exhibits it. A secondary spread of the neuter construction is possible at any period.

DIALECTIC PHONETICS IN THE VEDA: EVIDENCE FROM THE VEDIC VARIANTS

BY FRANKLIN EDGERTON
YALE UNIVERSITY

1. It is sufficiently familiar to all Indologists that the horizontal classification of the Indo-Aryan languages based on the relative dates of their literatures — Vedic, Sanskrit, Pāli-Prakrit, the modern vernaculars — is anything but rigorously scientific; or, at any rate, that the terms "early" and "late" cannot be universally and lightly applied to the structural features of those dialects on the basis of such relative dating of their respective literatures. On the one hand, we know that dialects recorded at late periods, and showing in general unquestionably late phonology and morphology, nevertheless reveal not a few features which are undeniably "early" — earlier than the corresponding features of some older dialects. This is most familiarly illustrated by the well-known features of Pāli and Prakrit which are clearly pre-Sanskritic, or even pre-Vedic, in character. A by no means exhaustive list is found in Wackernagel, *Altindische Grammatik*, I. 1, p. XIX f.; and see in general Pischel, *Grammatik der Prakrit-Sprachen*, § 6; Geiger, *Pāli* (in *Grundriß der indo-arischen Philologie*), p. 1. Paul Tedesco, in a brilliant study on verbs meaning "give" and "take" in Indo-Aryan, which has not attracted the attention it deserves, has shown convincingly that even modern Indo-Aryan vernaculars contain linguistic features directly inherited from Indo-European, which nevertheless do not appear anywhere in the older recorded literature, Vedic, Sanskrit, or Prakrit [1].

---

[1] *JAOS.* 43. 362 f.; the prehistoric perfect passive participle of IE. root *$d\bar{o}$, "give", namely *$dat\acute{o}$, Vedic and Sanskrit *$dit\acute{a}$ (not found), appears in phonetically regular development in the modern vernaculars (Hindustani $diy\bar{a}$, Naipali

2. The converse of this is the equally familiar fact that the oldest literature we have in India, that of the Veda, reveals not a few traces of the existence of dialects (whether geographical or social in basis is a question which need not concern us now) that were, as regards their phonology, essentially in the stage of Pāli-Prakrit. For examples I may refer again to Wackernagel. *op. cit.*, p. XVIII f., and the literature there quoted in footnote 2.

3. I think, however, that the extent to which such dialectic phonology appears in the Veda has never been fully appreciated. A flood of new light will be thrown on this subject, as on almost every other aspect of Vedic grammar, by the corpus of Vedic Variants (as revealed primarily by the *Vedic Concordance*), which was begun by the late Maurice Bloomfield, and several volumes of which (prepared by him and the present writer) are now practically ready for print [2]. The volume on Phonetics shows, among other things, a large mass of phonetic variations in the repeated mantras of Vedic literature which are of the same character as the phonetic changes characteristic of the Prakrit languages. Obviously these have an important bearing on the question of dialects in ancient India. They seem, indeed, to show the prevalence of dialectic tendencies in Vedic phonology to an extent hitherto unsuspected.

4. The phonetic variants are not all uniform in character. Only to a limited extent do they concern what may be called *purely* phonetic variations, as in the following:

pikaḥ (KSA. *pigaḥ*) *kṣviṅkā nīlaśīrṣṇī te 'ryamṇe* (KSA. °*mṇaḥ*) TS. KSA. The name of this bird is otherwise always written *pika;* the KSA. form *piga* is isolated, and it is hardly possible to doubt that it represents a dialectic pronunciation of the word *pika*, in which we recognize the familiar Prakritic change of surd mute between vowels to sonant. No real lexical change can conceivably be involved. On the other hand, in

pumān enaṁ tanuta ut kṛṇatti RV.: *pumān enad vayaty ud gṛṇatti* AV.,

---

diyō, etc., cf. Bengali, Assamese *diyā*, Marathi *dilā*, etc.), whereas Vedic, Sanskrit, and all Prakrit dialects have secondary and analogical substitutes, generally based on the present stem (Skt. *dattá*, Pkt. *dinna*). If Tedesco is right, and I am fully convinced that he is, this old IE. form must have existed underground, so to speak, during fully two thousand years of recorded speech in India.

[2] For a brief account of the plan of this work and its present status, see *Language*, 5, pp. 129 ff.

the AV. form is, indeed, primarily a phonetic corruption for *kṛṇatti*, but simulates a form of the root *grath, granth*, "tie", which clearly floated before the mind of the redactor. And in other, much more numerous cases, both forms are lexically defensible; we have what are really two different words, standing in a certain phonetic relation to each other. Thus:

mitrāvaruṇā śaradāhnāṁ (MS. *°hnā*) *cikitnū* (MS. *cikittam*, KS. *jigatnū*, AŚ. *cikitvam*) TS. MS. KS. AŚ.

Here *jigatnū*, "swift", is as possible as *cikitnū*, presumably "intelligent" (tho not quoted in the lexica). Nevertheless, the phonetic bearings of even the most intelligible of lexical variants of this sort are obvious, and obviously important for our problem. They occur in such large numbers that they furnish strong support for the purely phonetic variants of the type *pika: piga*, helping to demonstrate the strong tendency for surds to shift to sonants.

5. It must further be emphasized that in no case, perhaps, do the variants point to change exclusively in one direction. That is, the changes from surd to sonant, for instance, are flanked by a perhaps equal number of cases in which an older sonant is replaced by a surd. These are not to be regarded as cancelling each other. Both groups are really evidence for the same tendency, namely, the change of surds to sonants — not the reverse. Broadly speaking, and in so far as it is purely phonetic in nature, the shift of sonant to surd is to be classed as what we call hyper-Sanskritism; that is, a leaning backward to avoid dialectic pronunciation. [2a] It is clear that the high speech avoided these Prakritisms. A quite natural result of this shyness was that it was sometimes overdone; just as, in our own time and land, a half-educated person may refer to the well-known capitalist as "Mr. John D. Rockefellow", because he has painfully learned that the American dialectic word *feller* is vulgar and that in correct English one should say *fellow* instead. So, for instance, a word which contained an original sonant may be anomalously written with a surd, as:

diśāṁ devy (MS. *tevy*!) *avatu no ghṛtācī* TS. MS. AŚ.

The MS. form can only intend the word *devī*, "goddess", unless we suppose an otherwise unknown laletic (nursery) word for

---

[2a] For Prakritic change of sonant to surd in certain obscure dialects see Pischel, *of. cit.* §§ 190—191. It is not impossible that some such dialect may have had some influence on Vedic speech; but it seems to me that the above explanation of these Vedic forms is more plausible.

"mother," which is implausible. Cf. TA. 1. 5. 1 *mātṛk kaścana vidyate;* the comm. simply says that *mātṛk* means *mādṛk*, "like me", and no other interpretation is at all conceivable. Yet both editions of TA., apparently with all known mss., read *mātṛk.*

6. In the rest of this brief report I shall limit myself, in general, to a few examples of the various types of what may reasonably be called purely phonetic variants. The list is, of course, far from exhaustive, even for them; and let it be remembered that they are supported in most cases by a very considerable number of variants which can be more or less defended lexically. The total mass of the materials is highly impressive; I must postpone their full presentation for another occasion. Exact references are not given since they can easily be got in every case from the *Vedic Concordance.*

7. The change from surd to sonant has already been illustrated. Dialectic in a broad sense, whether accurately to be called Prakritic or not, is the shift of voiced aspirates to *h,* as in the adjective *kakuhá,* "tall", exclusively found in the RV., tho its original *kakubhá* occurs in Yajurvedic texts (cf. Grassmann, s. v. *kakuhá;* Wackernagel, p. 251). This very word occurs in both its forms in one variant formula, see the Concordance under *kakubhaṁ rūpaṁ* etc.; and as an instance of a similar case, not noted previously I believe, in which *h* stands for *dh,* I may quote:

gṛdhraḥ śitikakṣī vārdhrāṇasas te divyāḥ (KSA. *vārhiṇasas te 'dityāḥ*) TS. KSA.

Von Schroeder emends the KSA. (7. 10) reading to *vārdhrī⁰,* but I consider this emendation unjustified; there is no reason to doubt that KSA. presents a genuine phonetic variant.

8. It is well known that the Prakrit languages frequently replace dentals by linguals; and, contrariwise, some of them show the reverse tendency. See Pischel, §§ 218—225. We find in the Veda such variants as:

avatasya (SV. *avatasya*) *visarjane* RV. SV.

This very word occurs in two other variants, the RV. showing each time the form *avatá,* for which later texts substitute *avaṭá* (not known in RV.). The theory of Bartholomae (IF. 3. 179), approved by Wackernagel, p. 167, that *avaṭá* is derived from the adverb *avár,* ignores the RV. *avatá* and is, in my opinion, most unlikely. Tho relatively not numerous (perhaps two dozen, including all sorts), the Vedic variants under this head are specially interesting because genuine lexical influences are scanty; they are for the most part purely phonetic in character.

9. There are a number of cases of the familiar Prakritic change of *d* to *j* before *y* (Wackernagel, p. 163), as:

sahasriyo dyotatām (TS. TB. *dīpyatām;* MS. *°riyo jyotatām*) VS. TS. MS. KS. ŚB. TB.

And in this group we find a very interesting case of hyper-Sanskritism:

ava jyām iva dhanvanaḥ AV. Vait. ApMB.: *ava dyām iva dhanvinaḥ* HG.

"Off, the bow-string as it were from the bow!" The HG. variant, in the same passage, would mean literally: "Off, heaven as it were of (or, from) a bowman!" But of course *dyām* is simply a would-be learned or mincing pronunciation of *jyām*, perpetrated by a half-educated person.

10. Similarly the change of *y* to *j*, and that of *j* to *y*, are both Prakritic in character (Wackernagel, pp. 208 f., 163; Pischel, §§ 252, 236).

saujāmin (ŚG. *sauyāmim;* with both understand *tarpayāmi*) AG. ŚG.

The "correct" form of this proper name is *saujāmi*. Cf. AV. 19. 34. 2 a *jāgṛtsyas tripañcāśīḥ* (so mss.), for which read *yāḥ* (or *yāś ca*) *kṛtyās* etc., see note in Whitney *ad loc.*

11. The change of *kṣ* to *kh* (Pischel, §§ 317, 319) is not common, but the following appears to be a certain instance:

idhmasyeva prakṣāyataḥ (ŚŚ. *prakhyāyataḥ*) TB. TA. ŚŚ. ApŚ. The form *prakṣāyataḥ* is none too clear; the TB. comm. and Caland on ApŚ. 4. 11. 5 take it as an unparalleled formation from root *kṣi*, "wasting away, being consumed". It is more probably derived from root *kṣā*, "burn", and means then "burning up, burning away". In any case it seems clear that *prakhyāyataḥ* is merely a phonetic corruption of the other form; see Hillebrandt's critical note on ŚŚ. 4. 12. 10, p. 249.

12. There are a number of instances of the familiar change of *kṣ*, *ts*, and *ps* to *ch* (Wackernagel, p. 158; Pischel, §§ 317 ff., 327, 328). It happens that lexical considerations play a part in most of them, but the following is a sample of a purely phonetic example, unusually complicated in character:

achalābhiḥ (KSA. *acharābhiḥ,* MS. *atsarābhiḥ* [so pada-pāṭha; saṁ-hitā, *matsarābhiḥ*], VS. *ṛkṣalābhiḥ*) *kapiñjalān* VS. TS. MS. KSA.

The form *r̥chárā* occurs in AV. 10. 9. 23. The word means "fet-locks" (of an animal); its original form is unknown. Either MS. or VS. (or both) must be hyper-Sanskritistic back-formations from the "Prakritic" form with *ch*. Note also the Prakritic variation of *r̥: a* in the first syllable (§ 20, below).

13. On *m* for *v* (and the reverse), which may be Prakritic, cf. Bloomfield, *JAOS*. 13, p. XCVII ff.; Wackernagel, p. 197; Pischel, § 251. The cases are few but interesting:

uc chvañcasva (TA. *chmañcasva*) *pr̥thivi mā ni bādhathāḥ* (TA. *vi bādhithāḥ*) RV. AV. TA.

14. The familiar cases of shift between *b* and *v* are certainly dialectic, whether properly to be called Prakritic or not; see Wackernagel, p. 183 f., Pischel, §§ 201, 300. Much uncertainty exists as to the writing of *b* and *v* thruout Sanskrit literary tradition, for reasons pointed out by Wackernagel. The variants are numerous, and fall into three groups of nearly equal size, in two of which *b* and *v* seem respectively to be original, while in the third there is no way of deciding with confidence. They are almost all purely phonetic; few genuine lexical changes are included. School custom may have played a rôle here, alongside of true dialect; thus the Vājasaneyin or White Yajurveda school shows a tendency to prefer *v* (of course not rigorously carried thru). I will content myself with quoting three variants containing the word *paḍbīśa* or *ºviśa* (also *ºviṅśa*), "fetter". It is always spelled with *b* in the RV., which is not encouraging to the view which would connect it with Lat. *vincio* (Wackernagel, p. 183), a view for which the form *ºviṅśa* may seem to lend support (but see § 18 below):

saṁdānam arvantaṁ paḍbīśam (VS. MS. *ºviśam*) RV. VS. TS. MS. KSA.

yac ca paḍbīśam (VS. MS. *ºviśam*) *arvatah* RV. VS. TS. MS. KSA.

atho (ApŚ. LŚ. *nir mā*) *yamasya paḍbīśāt* (VS. *ºviśāt;* LŚ. *ºviṅśāt*) RV. AV. VS. LŚ. ApŚ.

15. Like the *b: v* variants, those between *r* and *l* are perhaps hardly to be called Prakritic in a strict or exclusive sense, since they appear familiarly thruout the history of Sanskrit; *l* constantly encroaches on *r*. Yet at bottom they are of the same nature. There are Prakrit dialects which change every *r* to *l* (Pischel, § 256), and the reverse change is not unknown tho only sporadic

in the dialects recorded (id. § 259); cf. Wackernagel, p. 215 f. The variants are numerous and almost wholly phonetic in character, with scant lexical bearings. A single example must suffice:

aśrīrā (AV. ApMB. *aślīlā*) *tanūr bhavati* RV. AV. ApMB.

The *r*-form of this word is not recorded outside of RV., which is the more remarkable because of its obvious connexion with the common noun *śrī*. For this the suffix *-ra* is no doubt responsible, first by dissimilation of one of the liquids to *l*, and then again by assimilation of the remaining *r* to *l*.

16. The thoro confusion of the sibilants in the middle Indic dialects (Wackernagel, p. 226, § 197 e; Pischel, §§ 227—229) must certainly be connected with the extensive occurrence of the like confusion in the Vedic texts. One or two out of many examples:

śaṁ yor abhi sravantu (MŚ. *śra⁰*) *naḥ* RV. AV. SV. VS. KS. TB. TA. ApŚ. MŚ. HG.

And other cases of *śru = sru*, "flow", so that BR. even postulate a root *śru*, "flow"! Here *s* is original and *ś* secondary; the contrary is the case in:

śukeṣu me (AV. *sukeṣu te*) *harimāṇam* RV. AV. TB. ApŚ.

Since different Prakrit dialects change all sibilants to both *s* and *ś*, both these changes may be directly dialectic and not hyper-Sanskritic. Less numerous, but still not rare, are interchanges between *ṣ* and the other sibilants:

nainad devā āpnuvan pūrvam arṣat (VS. *arśat*) VS. VSK. ĪśāU. The proper form is *arṣat;* VS. comm., *ṛśa gatau*.

17. Especially in Jaina Māhārāṣṭrī (Jacobi, *Ausgewählte Erzählungen in Māhārāṣṭrī*, p. XXII, § 7), but also to some extent in other Prakrit dialects (Pischel, § 353), and in Pāli (Geiger, § 73), *y* serves as a separator or "Hiatustilger" between otherwise juxtaposed vowels, where it has no etymological justification. Traces of such a tendency seem to be found to a rather surprising extent in the Veda, altho to be sure they are always complicated by other considerations; that is, the variant forms are grammatically or lexically explicable. Thus in the following example the evidently secondary reading of TS. is, of course, a correct dative case-form; but it is certainly not very intelligent, and seems to involve a tendency to avoid hiatus between vowels by use of the glide-sound *y*:

vaiśvānaram ṛta ā (TS. *ṛtāya*) *jātam agnim* RV. SV. VS. TS.
MS. KS. PB. ŚB.

There are similar cases in which alternative presence and absence
of *v* and of the nasals may be similarly interpreted (cf. Pischel,
§ 353; Geiger, § 73).

18. In the Pāli-Prakrit languages no syllable can be "over-
long", that is, none can consist of more than two morae. No long
vowel can be followed by more than one consonant, and the
nasalization *(anusvāra, anunāsika)* counts as a consonant; or,
to put it otherwise, a nasalized vowel counts as a long vowel.
Where such combinations originally occurred, either the two
consonants are simplified to one, or the long vowel is shortened.
In the final outcome, after numerous analogical developments,
it boils down to this, that Pāli and Prakrit feel as phonetically
equivalent the following three cases: (1) long vowel plus single
consonant, (2) short vowel plus double consonant, (3) nasalized
vowel plus single consonant [3]. These three come to interchange
at random, with no fixed relation to etymological differences
of origin: Pāli-Prakrit *sīha*, Pāli *sārambha* = Sanskrit *siṅha*,
saṁrambha; Pāli-Prakrit *daṁsana, suṁka = darśana, śulka* (intermediate forms **dassana* or **dāsana*, **sukka* or **sūka*); Pāli-
Prakrit *niḍḍa, nĕḍḍa = nīḍa;* Prakrit *vāsa = varṣa;* Pāli *sāsapa =
sarṣapa*, etc.

The beginnings of this phonetic confusion seem to be present
in certain Vedic variants. For long vowel vs. nasalized vowel,
cf. the variant quoted above, § 14:

atho (LŚ. ApŚ. *nir mā*) *yamasya paḍbīśāt* (VS. *°viśāt*, LŚ.
°viṅśāt) RV. AV. VS. LŚ. ApŚ.

Here there is no lexical variation; we have forms of one and the
same word. Whichever may be the older form (cf. § 14), it is
clear that they are phonetic equivalents.

As for variations between long (double) consonant and long
vowel with single consonant, I know of no variants which can
be called "purely" phonetic. That is, in every case known to
me, both forms of the variant are capable of independent lexical
or morphological explanation. And yet, if we confront such

---

[3] Or, we may phrase it thus: Long vowel, nasalized vowel, and long consonant
are interchangeable. A concise and excellent statement of the conditions is
found in Geiger, *Pāli*, §§ 5, 6. In Pischel the facts are more scattered, and stated
less clearly and less happily; see his §§ 90, 62—65, 74, 76. I do not believe that
word-accent has anything to do with it (cf. Pischel, § 90).

variants as the following with each other, it seems to me hard to doubt that they are bound together by a common phonetic character, which makes its influence distinctly felt in spite of the individually distinct explanations which suggest themselves easily enough under each one:

agne samrāḍ iṣe rāye (ApŚ. rayyai) . . . AŚ. ApŚ.: iṣe rāye (ApŚ. rayyai) . . .VS. MS. ŚB. TB. AŚ. ApŚ. Of course, rayyai (and also rayyā, once in the RV. itself) is connected with the stem rayi, parallel to rai whence comes rāye. I do not question the propriety of this connexion, even tho the stem rayi is usually masculine and these are distinctively feminine forms; other case-forms of rayi, such as rayiḥ, are also occasionally feminine. If these variants were isolated, they would perhaps prove nothing for the phonetic tendency under consideration. But taken with the rest of this group, they do seem to me to suggest an urge in the direction of treating short vowel plus double consonant as the phonetic equivalent of long vowel plus single consonant.

śocasva (VS. also, rocasva) devavītamaḥ (KS. ⁰vittamaḥ) RV. RVKh. VS. TS. MS. KS. ŚB. TA. Roots vī and vid; "god-rejoicing" and "god-finding". Cf. next.

iṣṭam ca vītaṁ (ŚB. AŚ. vittaṁ) ca (ŚŚ. cābhūt) MS. ŚB. TB. AŚ. ŚŚ. Cf. preceding.

indrāya (MS. MŚ. add tvā) suṣuttamam (VS. ŚB. suṣūtamam) VS. MS. KS. ŚB. MŚ. Equivalent bases su-t (with euphonic t after final short vowel of monosyllabic base) and sū.

apsarassu (HG. apsarāsu ca) yo gandhaḥ ApMB. HG. And others with the same interchange. Here noun-declension is concerned; apsarāsu is from an ā-stem apsarā, parallel and secondary to apsaras. This, of course, does not exclude the likelihood of phonetic considerations, any more than in the other cases of this group.

19. There are distinct traces among the variants of the very familiar Prakritic tendency to assimilate adjoining consonants; this is most marked with semi-vowels and liquids, which are easily assimilated to other consonants (cf. Jacobi's table of consonants in the order of their resistance to assimilation, Ausgew. Erz. in Māh., § 27, p. XXXI):

abhinne khilye (TB. khille) nidadhāti devayum RV. AV. TB. The TB. reading is well attested, and can certainly mean nothing but khilye. (Comm. khilībhūte.)

20. A very numerous group of variants concerns interchanges between vocalic *ṛ* and other vowels, *a*, *i*, and *u*; also *ṛ* and consonantal *r* plus vowel; cf. Wackernagel, §§ 9, 16, 19. It is well-known that Pāli and most Prakrit dialects have no *ṛ*; they most commonly substitute *a*, *i*, or *u* for older *ṛ*. And the modern Hindus pronounce *ṛ* (in Sanskrit words) as *ri* in most parts of India (in some regions, notably Mahārāṣṭra, the vowel following the consonantal *r* has rather an *u*-coloring). I select a few instances which show this dialectal phonetics in the Veda most clearly (cf. also § 12 above):

ava sma durhaṇāyataḥ (SV. *durhṛṇ⁰*) RV. SV. Here the RV. has Prakritic vocalism, for which SV. (secondarily, of course) has substituted the more "correct" or "hifalutin" form with *ṛ*.

tejo yaśasvi sthaviraṁ samiddham (ŚG. *samṛddham*) ŚG. PG. ApMB. HG. It is highly likely that *samiddham* is a Prakritism for *samṛddham*, "plenteous", as suggested by Kirste on HG. 1.4.6, and approved by Winternitz, ApMB. Introduction, p. XXIII; "inflamed" (root *idh*) is incongruous in this context (despite the etymological meaning of *tejas*). Yet three texts have the dialectic form, and only one the "correct" *samṛddham* (and even ŚG has a v. l. *samiddham*, in two mss., probably owing to a scribe's recollection of the variant form as found in the other texts).

puraṁdaro gotrabhid (MS. *⁰bhṛd;* TB. *maghavān*) *vajrabāhuḥ* VS. MS. KS. TB. Here we have a curious and most interesting hyper-Sanskritism in MS. All the terms refer to Indra, one of whose regular epithets is *gotra-bhid*, "splitter of the cow-pens (clouds or mountains?)". All the mss. of MS. agree here on the form *gotrabhṛd*, which is otherwise unrecorded. It can only be a pedantic substitution for *gotrabhid*, apparently under the sciolistic assumption that *i* stood for *ṛ*; at any rate, the alteration can scarcely be understood except in the light of this dialectal phonetics. For *gotra-bhṛd* is hardly capable of intelligent interpretation. Perhaps it was felt as meaning "supporting *(bhṛ)* the clan *(gotra)*"; but if so, its incongruity, wedged in between *puraṁdara*, "cleaver of fortresses", and *vajrabāhu*, "armed with the club", is obvious.

tvaṣṭṛmantas (MS. MŚ. *tvaṣṭri⁰;* ApŚ. *tvaṣṭu⁰*) *tvā sapema* VS. MS. KS. ŚB. KŚ. ApŚ. MŚ.

The same Prakritic *u* is substituted for vocalic *ḷ* in one variant: *saṁvatsara ṛtubhiḥ saṁvidānaḥ* (KS. *⁰bhiś cāḳḷpānaḥ*, ApŚ. *⁰bhiś cākupānaḥ*) MS. KS. ApŚ.

tṛṣucyavaso (MS. *triṣu⁰*) *juhvo nāgneḥ* RV. MS. The adverb *tṛṣu* is the only word which can be involved here.

bhṛmiṁ (TB. *bhrumiṁ*) *dhamanto apa gā avṛṇata* RV. TB. The mss. of TB. appear to be unanimous (if we may trust the two editions) in reading *bhrumiṁ*, a form not otherwise recorded, for *bhṛmiṁ*. — The reverse of this, *r* by hyper-Sanskritism for *ru*, is found in the form *pṛṣvā*, occurring several times in texts of the Taittirīya school for regular *pruṣvā;* the somewhat similar phenomena included under the name of *saṁprasāraṇa* may, to be sure, have a bearing on this:

pruṣvābhyaḥ (TS. *pṛṣ⁰*) *svāhā* VS. TS. KSA.

21. There are very many variants in which long diphthongs *(ai, au)* interchange with the corresponding short diphthongs *(e, o)*. In most of these morphological matters are concerned. But in a few, at least, it appears that the shift is purely phonetic, and therefore belongs with the well-known universal law of Pāli-Prakrit by which *ai* and *au* are everywhere reduced:

avārāya kevartam VS.: *pāryāya kaivartam* TB. The word is otherwise *kaivarta*.

sukurīrā svaupaśā VS. TS. KS. ŚB.: *sukarīrā svopaśā* MS. But several mss. of MS., and its pada-pāṭha, read *svaup⁰*, which may then be the correct reading.

22. Allied to these are a number of interesting cases in which we seem clearly to have Prakritic reduction of *aya* to *e*, and *ava* to *o* (Bloomfield, *AJP.* 5. 27 ff.; Wackernagel, p. 53 f.):

namaḥ kiṁśilāya ca kṣayaṇāya (MS. *kṣeṇāya*) *ca* VS. TS. MS. KS. *kṣeṇa* is not otherwise recorded.

to-to (MS. KS. MŚ. *tava-tava*, TS. ApŚ. *to-te*) *rāyaḥ* VS. TS. MS. KS. ŚB. KŚ. ApŚ. MŚ. *to* for *tava*, gen. sg. of the 2d personal pronoun.

23. The insertion of an epenthetic vowel, generally *i*, between two consonants, usually a liquid and a sibilant or *h*, is likewise to be regarded as a Prakritism, tho fairly wide-spread in Sanskrit (cf. Wackernagel, pp. 56 ff., especially p. 57, § 51 end; Pischel, §§ 131—140). It is found in not a few Vedic variants, as in this sigmatic aorist from the root *pṛ*, "cross":

tan naḥ parṣad (MS. *pariṣad*) *ati dviṣaḥ* TS. MS. KS. TB. Note that the meter is against the inserted vowel. (Read *pariṣad* in both occurrences in MS.)

24. These are only a small selection from a very large mass

of variants showing the kind of shifts which are found in Middle
Indic phonology. Granted that many, and under some rubrics
even most, of them may be explained lexically or morphologic-
ally: it would nevertheless be rash to deny that phonetic influences
are concerned even in the latter, especially since they are supported by a very considerable number of purely phonetic cases.
The principle is, indeed, far from being a new discovery, as has
been indicated. But it has never been illustrated so extensively
as it will be in the Vedic Variants; and some of the rubrics here
included are presented for the first time in Vedic phonology.
The special character of the illustrations, namely the occurrence
óf double forms of each variant, with and without Prakritic
phonology, makes them especially valuable and interesting. The
cases of hyper-Sanskritism are perhaps the most interesting of
all, as pointing to a rather definite consciousness, on the part of
the handlers of the texts, of the antithesis between the phonology
of the high speech and that of the popular dialects.

LINGUISTIC MISCELLANY[1].

BY TRUMAN MICHELSON
SMITHSONIAN INSTITUTION; GEORGE WASHINGTON UNIVERSITY.

1. Pāli and Ardhamāgadhī.

As is known Geiger considers Pāli as a kind of Ardhamāgadhī, a 'Verkehrssprache' whose basis was Māgadhī and which Buddha himself spoke. I have protested against this in *Language*, IV, pp. 104—105, without, however, presenting linguistic proof that the differences between Pāli and Ardhamāgadhī are too far-reaching to permit us to label Pāli as a kind of Ardhamāgadhī. Some apparent similarities I have accounted for as being relics of a Māgadhan original of which the Pāli canon is a transformation. It should be noted that Ardhamāgadhī is so much later than Pāli that a good deal of material can not be relied upon, for the changes may be secondary, and some semi-*tatsamas* may have crept in; also influence of Māhārāṣṭrī as the Prākrit literary language par excellence is also to be reckoned with. I therefore only list a few differences such as are quite convincing:- Amg. nom. sing. masc. a-stems, -*e* (in verse -*o* owing to Māhārāṣṭrī influence), P. -*o*; Amg. gen. pl. *rā·i·ṇaṃ*, P. *raññaṃ, rājūnaṃ*; Amg. loc. sing. *taṃsi*, etc., P. *taṃhi* (cf. Sanskrit *tasmin*); Amg. *bemi* (Skt. *bravīmi*), P. *brūmi* (Epic Skt. *brūmi*); Amg. *dhūyā*, P. *dhītā*; Amg. *iha*, P. *idha*; Amg. *ciyatta*, P. *catta* (Skt. *tyakta*); Amg. *giha*, P. *gaha* (Skt. *gṛha*; *ghara* usually replaces *gaha* in P.); Amg. *peccha·i·*, P. *pekkhati*.

2. Asokan Peteṇika.

In my paper "Walleser on the home of Pāli" (*Language*, IV: 101—105) I argued against the derivation of *Peteṇika* from **Prā-*

---

[1] Printed with permission of the Secretary of the Smithsonian Institution.

tiṣṭhānika (a vṛddhi derivative of ·*Pratiṣṭhāna*), laying emphasis on the early ablative *Patithānā*, the later locative *Patithāṇe*, and *Pa·i·thāṇa* (in a compound) which correspond to Sanskrit *Pratiṣṭhāna*. I overlooked some evidence from the middle of the third century B.C. favoring my view, namely, *prātithānasa bhichuno*, no. 12 of the Sanchi *stûpa*, Tope I, p. 98 of E. I. II, ed. Bühler (see also pp. 104 and 387), which means "of the *prātithāna* monk", that is, "of the monk from *Pratithāna* (Sanskrit *Pratiṣṭhāna*)". The βαίθαυα of Ptolemy, also corroborates my view. For the derivation of *Peteṇika*, my old explanation that it stands for **Pāitrayaṇika* (I. F. 24: 52 f.) still holds valid.

3. Girnar traidasa.

Charpentier, *JRAS.* 1926, p. 139 derives *traidasa* from **traidaśa* without referring to the explanation given by Johansson, *Shb.* I, p. 136 (22 of the reprint) or my note *JAOS.* xxxi, p. 234; and incidentally criticises Gray most sharply. Such archetypes as **traidaśa* and **trayadaśa* (in spite of Hultzsch's return to this, *CII*, vol. I [new ed.], p. lvii) will not satisfy the phonetic requirements of the dialects of the Asokan inscriptions. There still is nothing for nor against Johansson's theory that the archetype is **trayēdaśa* from an earlier **trayazdaśa*, as far as the phonetics are concerned. I now hasten to observe that Turner, *Bull S.O.S.* 4, pp. 363, 364 goes back to Johansson's explanation without giving him any credit whatsoever.

4. Additions to Whitney's Root-Book.

Whitney's Root-Book of Sanskrit will ever impress any one who uses it as being truly marvellous. Minor additions have been made from time to time, and probably will continue to be made. In my 'Linguistic Archaisms of the Rāmāyaṇa' (*JAOS.* 25) I added a few items; and in the present paper hope to add a few more, but it should be borne in mind that these are not the result of systematic reading: on the contrary they are the result of reading by snatches in leisure moments.

The following forms (not roots) are listed as occuring only in Classical Sanskrit; they occur in the Bombay edition of the Rāmāyaṇa of 1902: *kuc* (*saṁcukoca*, v. I. 33), *kūj* (*cukūjatus*, vi. 90. 49), *budh* (*buddhvā*, v. I. 102, v. I. 180, v. 48. 39, v. 58. 12, v. 67. 44, vi. 60. 55, vi. 64. 14), *bhāṣ* (*samabhi-bhāṣiṣye*, vii. 15.

25), *vṛdh* (*vardhitum*, v. I. 92), *vraj* (*vraje*, v. 41. 9), *sphuṭ* (*pus-phoṭa*, vi. 77. 7, vi. 77. 16). I may add the infinitive *gaditum* (*gad*) listed by Whitney as occuring in Classical Sanskrit only, occurs in a manuscript of the Rāmāyaṇa in the British Museum, but I have unfortunately mislaid the exact reference.

The form *līyati* is given as occuring in the Upanishads and Classical Sanskrit only: observe, however, *avalīyantī* in the above mentioned ed. of the Rāmāyaṇa at vi. 114. 33.

Listed as occuring but once in the Sūtras is *jigāhire :* but *vija-gāhire* occurs in the Rāmāyaṇa at vii. 31. 35; no middle voice is given for Classical Sanskrit, but the active *jagāha* is given as occuring in Classical Sanskrit and that only.

The gerundive *patitvā*, listed as AV. B., occurs in the Bombay 1898 ed. of the Bhāgavata Purāṇa at v. 17. 6.

Under *kup cukopa* is listed as U.E. It is found in the Bhāgavata Purāṇa at iv. 4. 9, the Kathāsaritsāgara (ed. Nirṇayasāgara), xv. 1. 148, the Raghuvaṅśa (ed. Nirṇayasāgara), 3. 56.

The active perfect of *kruś* is listed as being peculiar to Epic Sanskrit: *cukruśus* occurs in the Raghuvaṅśa at 8. 39, and *cukrośa* in the Bhāgavata Purāṇa at ix. 16. 13.

Under *smṛ sasmāra* is given as E.: it is found in the Bhāgavata Purāṇa at ix. 16. 3 (see also *JAOS.* 25) and Raghuvaṅśa at 15. 45.

Under *sah* the middle perfect *sehe* is given as authorized by native grammarians but non-quotable; the third person pl. *sehire* is found in the Raghuvaṅśa at 12. 94; see also the Kumārasamb-hava (Nirṇayasāgara ed. 1893) at xii. 48.

The infinitive *spardhitum* is listed as AV. B., but it is found in the Nāiṣadhīyacarita (ed. Bombay 1902) at 8. 30.

Under I *pat* the aorist *apāti* is listed as B.: it is found in the Kumārasambhava at xv. 29.

The perfect *mamāda* under *mad* is given as V. B.: see the Kumārasambhava at ix. 51.

The infinitive *śaṅsitum* is listed as E.; it occurs in the Kumāra-sambhava at v. 51.

The aorist *aseviṣṭa* (under *sev*) is listed as non-quotable though authorized by the native grammarians; the 3 pers. dual of the middle of the aorist *aseviṣātām* occurs in the Kumārasambhava at vii. 42. The commentator Mallinātha correctly explains the form as *sevater luṅ.*

The infinitive *hotum*, listed as B.S., occurs in the Kumārasambhava at x. 8.

The gerund *grastvā* is not in the Root-Book; it is found in the Vāyu Purāna (Ānandāśrama ed.) at 7. 72.

The gerund *charditvā* is given as authorized by the native grammarians but non-quotable. It occurs in the Vāyu Purāṇa at 61. 19.

5. The alleged Fox stem *ānemᴀᵈtci-* 'be cold'.

On page 49 of *Bulletin 85, Bureau of American Ethnology*, I have given a stem *ānemᴀᵈtci-* be cold. Professor Leonard Bloomfield calls my attention to the fact that the alleged stem should be divided *ānem* and *ᴀᵈtci*. This is no doubt correct; cf. Fox *ānemi-* 'be in agony'; the stem of the second member is *ᴀ*, which takes post-verbal *-ᵈtci- -t-:* compare Fox *nepᴀᵈtci-* 'be cold, chilled'; *sīgᴀᵈtci-* 'be frozen to death'; *kepᴀtenwi* 'it is frozen over' (*kepi-* 'enclose', *-en-* inanimate copula, *-wi* pronominal ending); Ojibwa *ningī̆katc* 'I am cold' (Jones' *Ojibwa Texts*, 1. 62. 8). *gashkadin* 'it freezes over' (from Baraga); Cree *sŏ̄kᴀtin* 'it is frozen strongly' (restored from Watkins' *sŏkutin*). Professor Bloomfield cited a Menomini correspondent which I have unfortunately misplaced [1].

6. Fox *-tä-*.

Years ago Jones construed *-tä-* as an inanimate copula; and I have followed him in this. Recently Bloomfield has given the form as *-etä-*. Now, no doubt, *-etä-* is the living stem, but presumably historically the stem is *-tä-*, not *-etä-*, as is shown by Fox *kīwā'gwᴀtäwi* "it lies about", *pemipahotäwi* "it goes by" (of a train), *wī̆cᴀtäwi* "it is hot", *nemᴀtäwi* "it is erect", *ä˘ᴀʳkᴀtägɩ* "it is burned". Decisive proof can only be given when the conditions in other Central Algonquian languages are known, excluding Sauk and Kickapoo which are so close to Fox. If *-etä-* is historically correct then we must assume contraction of *ᴀe* to *ᴀ*, and contraction of *oe* to *o*.

7. A non-Algonquian trait of Arapaho.

As I stated years ago Arapaho is a very divergent Algonquian language; and I still adhere to this view. The grammar is funda-

---

[1] Correspondents occur in a number of other Algonquian languages, but unfortunately I have not been able to control the exact phonetics of the words in other sources to make it worth while citing them, save Kickapoo *kepᴀtenwi.*

mentally Algonquian; from time to time I have been able to note some such traits as were previously unknown; the amount of vocabulary that can be shown to be Algonquian apparently is but a small percentage of the total vocabulary: yet as the demonstrable phonetic shifts are very complicated and of an unexpected character, it is always possible that more lexical material will eventually fall in line [1]. So far it has been the lack of certain Algonquian grammatical features that has impressed any one, not the presence of features which are un-Algonquian. I now proceed to list a feature which can not be duplicated so far as I know (and I have had several years of experience with Algonquian languages) in any other Algonquian language, and that is infixation within the primary stem. [For an infixation of this type note Teton Sioux *pahta* "bind" *pawahta* "I bind".] The syllable *-en-* is infixed after the initial consonant to express customary or habitual action (*ne-* is prefixed to stems beginning with *n-*). So we have *be'ninǫ$^{\varepsilon}$*

---

[1] A few notes on the symbols used in this paper: *ʌ* is nearly like *u* in *sun* but with a distinct *a*-tinge; *e* is open; *ē* is long and close; *i* is open; *ī* is long and close; *o* is very open; *ω* is open but long (like *aw* in law); *ă* is as in hat; *ā̈* is as in bad; *ŭ̈* is long unrounded *ŭ̈*; *t* and *k* are unaspirated; *θ* is a surd interdental spirant; *tc* is *ch* in church but unaspirated; *ǫ* is nasal *o*, occuring when not rhetorical only after *n*; *ǫ̃* is nasal *ω*, occuring only after *n* when not rhetorical; *t'* is aspirated *t*, occuring only when terminal; *k'* is aspirated, but occurs only in the combination *-k'ᵘ* (in which *ᵘ* is voiceless); *'* medially before consonants denotes an aspiration, hardly the surd velar spirant; *$^{\varepsilon}$* is a strong glottal stop. The complicated phonetic shifts to which I have alluded are almost all conditioned by the quality of adjacent vowels, palatization being extremely common. Thus normal Algonquian *p* appears as *k*, but as *tc* before palatal vowels (whether these have been subsequently lost or not); *m* as *w* but *b* before *ē̃* and *ī̃*, and after *e*; *x* (surd velar spirant) is the normal correspondent to Fox *'ck*, Ojibwa *ck*, Menomini and Cree *sk* (Central Algonquian *ck* according to Bloomfield) but appears as *s* before *i*; some other shifts are: normal Algonquian *tc* becomes *θ*; Cree *'t*, normal Algonquian *s*, appears as *s*; Cree *t*, normal Algonquian *n*, appears as *θ* (which as a matter of fact Bloomfield without knowing the Arapaho correspondent, set up as the Central Algonquian prototype); *w* appears as *n* as does *y*, though *ny-* appears as *y-*; corresponding to Fox *'c* we have *s*; *ā* becomes *ω*; *u* becomes *i*; *ō* becomes *ī*; which are only a few of the shifts which I have worked out. Thus it happens words which are really Algonquian may be enormously disguised, e. g., Fox *nī'pi^{d}tci'* "my tooth", *nī'pitʌn$^{ni'}$* "my teeth" correspond to Arapaho *nē'tciθ, nē'tcitoᵋ*; Cree *ispimi'k*, Ojibwa *icpimiñg*, Menomini *ispămiah*, Kickapoo *i'pemegi*, Fox *ʌ'pemegi* "above" correspond regularly to Arapaho *ixtcebeᵋ*. — With the words in the text compare Fox *mī-n-* "give", *pī^{d}tci-* "into", *mī'ci-* "fuzzy", *-negwă-* "arm", *-īgwă-* "face", *-'cin-* "fall" (animate), *mī'sī-* "cacare", *nōtaw-* "hear" (animate obj.). Further explanations would involve too much space.

"I give him, her" but *hω't' bĭ'nọ͜ᵋ* "I shall give him, her"; *tcenĭ'θikūθoᵋ* "I put him, her in", *tcenĭ'θikū'tīnω* "I put it in" as contrasted with *hω't' tcīθikū'tīnω* "I shall put it in"; *benĭ'sinesāt'* "he, she has a fuzzy arm", but *hω't' bĭ'sinesāt'* "he, she will have a fuzzy arm" (*tăbinesā'siᵋ* "he broke his arm by falling"); *benĭ'sīēt'* "he has a fuzzy face", but *hă˘bĭ'sīēt'* "he had a fuzzy face"; *tenē'tωnĭᶜt'* "he, she is quiet" but *tē'tωnʌkᶜᵘ* "be quiet!", *hω't' tē'tωnĭᶜt'* "he, she will be quiet"; *henĭtωω'tĭt'* „he gradually pours it out", but *hĭ'tωnω* "pour (sing.) it out!"; *be'nĭhĭt'* "he, she defecates", but *hω't' bĭhĭnω* "I shall defecate". [For the prefixing of the element *ne-* observe *nenē'θetcωt'* "he, she is afraid" but *hω't' nē'θetcωt'* "he, she will be afraid"; *nenĭ'-tʌnọ͜ᵋ* "I hear him, her" but *hω't' nĭ'tʌnọ͜ᵋ* "I shall hear him, her".]

As intimated above, this trait is unique among Algonquian languages; whether it is self-evolved within Arapaho or borrowed from some non-Algonquian stock is a question which I can not answer at present. To an Indo-Europeanist such a question may seem superfluous; it is not to an Americanist: such borrowings are well-recognized (e. g. the post-positions of Upper Chinook are due to Shahaptian influence); it is only debatable as to whether such borrowings can occur on a large scale: this, if I am not mistaken, is the chief point at issue between Boas and Sapir.

A MATTER OF SEMANTICS

BY GEORGE MELVILLE BOLLING

OHIO STATE UNIVERSITY

I wish to treat of a group of words, the formal connections of which have been suggested by others[1]. The semantic relations do not seem to me to have been described satisfactorily, and perhaps this is the reason that there is still difference of opinion about the exact delimitation of the grouþ. The matter may also have a more general interest; for I shall assume a connection not considered under the sense of smell by Bechtel in his work *Ueber die Bezeichnungen der sinnlichen Wahrnehmungen in den idg. Sprachen*, Weimar, 1879.

To begin with the word whose connection is least recognized[2]. In his discussion of the suffix -αλέος Debrunner[3] notes that it is associated above all with *n*-stems, and yet misses the prettiest example, σμερδαλέος : σμερδνός. In classifying the meanings Liddell and Scott place "terrible to see" ahead of "terrible to hear;" but the Homeric usage (and, bar a few imitations, the words are confined to Homer) indicates that historically the reverse is true. So also does the connection to be suggested with σμαραγέω.

First the Homeric usage. The words are used of loud (and frightful) sounds emitted by human organs of speech: σμερδνὸν βοόων O 687 = 732; σμερδαλέα ἰάχων E 302 Θ 321 Π 785 T 41 Y 285 382 443 χ 81; σμερδαλέον δ᾽ ἐβόησεν Θ 92 ϑ 305 ω 537; σμερδαλέον δ᾽ (δὲ μέγ᾽) ᾤμωξεν Σ 35 ι 395; σμερδαλέον δ᾽ ἵπποισιν ἐκέκλετο T 399; νῆες | σμερδαλέον κονάβησαν ἀυσάντων ὑπ᾽ Ἀχαιῶν

---

[1] In the following etymological dictionaries: Walde-Pokorny 2. 691; Walde[2] 478—9; Müller 432; Trautmann 271; cf. also the references given in note 8.

[2] Proposed first by Fay, *Am. Journ. Phil.* 26. 173 (1905) and now approved by Muller.

[3] *Griechische Wortbildungslehre* 165—168.

44

B 334 $= \Pi$ 277. Of other noises: ἀμφὶ δὲ δῶμα | σμερδαλέον κονάβιζε (v. l. κανάχιζε) κ 399 of the wailing of Odysseus' comrades, ϱ 542 of Telemachus' sneeze; αὐτὰϱ ὑπὸ χϑὼν | σμερδαλέον κονάβιζε ποδῶν αὐτῶν τε καὶ ἵππων B 466; and of the crash (κοναβεῖν, κοναβίζειν) of arms, χαλκός N 498 Φ 255, πήληξ O 648, κνημίς Φ 593. Separately may be noted the use of thunder Ζεὺς | σμερδαλέα κτυπέων H 479.

In words that are reactions to such stimuli a shift of meaning can come about in one of two ways. (1) The emotional element may become so far predominant that the sense element becomes indifferent, and the word is then associated with any stimulus that produces such an emotion. (2) A speaker applies an epithet because an object affects him through one of his senses, while a hearer, who is affected more powerfully through another sense, takes the word in an unintended meaning and afterwards uses it accordingly.

As a result of such processes most of the other Homeric examples are in a transitional stage, and their precise meaning cannot be determined. Thus χαλκὸς σμερδαλέος may just as well be "dire clashing" as "dire gleaming," cf. N 192 πᾶς δ' ἄρα χαλκῷ | σμερδαλέῳ κεκάλυπτο. Nor is it pinned down in either direction by the context in:

M 464 λάμπε δὲ χαλκῷ | σμερδαλέῳ, Υ 260 ἦ ϱα καὶ ἐν δεινῷ σάκεϊ ἔλασ' ὄβριμον ἔγχος, | σμερδαλέῳ· μέγα δ' ἀμφὶ σάκος μύκε δουρὸς ἀκωκῇ. Either meaning will suit in either passage; a preference will depend in reality on whether one likes reiteration or contrast. So also in: Σ 579 σμερδαλέω δὲ λέοντε δύ' ἐν πρώτῃσι βόεσσι | ταῦρον ἐρύγμηλον ἐχέτην. Both slayers and slain may have their epithets either from the same or from different sense spheres—contrast or parallelism again. Perhaps it is worth noting also that the only part of the body to which these adjectives are applied is that from which the voice comes. There are no ὄσσε σμερδαλέω nor χεῖρες σμερδαλέαι; but the Gorgon's head is δεινή τε σμερδνή τε E 742, and there is a σμερδαλέη κεφαλή μ 91 on each of Scylla's necks[4], while her voice was commented upon uncomplimentarily (μ 86) a few lines before.

Uncertain similarly is the meaning in B 309 δράκων ἐπὶ νῶτα δαφοινός, | σμερδαλέος and in Υ 65, where σμερδαλέ' εὐρώεντα[5] is

[4] Cf. also Aeschylus, Prom. 355 σμερδναῖσι γαμφηλαῖσι συρίζων φόνον.

[5] On εὐρώεντα cf. Bechtel, Lexilogus 145—146.

said of the dwelling of Aïdoneus. These may be cases in which the change has advanced considerably; and with them may be put: Φ 401 κατ' αἰγίδα θυσανόεσσαν | σμερδαλέην and λ 609 σμερδαλέος δέ οἱ ἀμφὶ περὶ στήθεσσιν ἀορτήρ. Both have, to be sure, to do with arms, but arms of such a nature that an epithet derived from the noise they make is hardly to be expected.

Clear evidence for the completed change is found in but three passages; one connecting with the use of armor, another like B 309 used of a serpent, and the third textually uncertain. They are: Ο 609 πήληξ | σμερδαλέον κροτάφοισι, τινάσσετο μαρναμένοιο, X 95 (δράκων) σμερδαλέον δὲ δέδορκεν [6], ζ 137 σμερδαλέος δ' αὐτῆσι φάνη κεκακωμένος ἅλμῃ [7]. In the scholia on the last passage λευγαλέος and ἀργαλέος (Zenodotus) are cited as variant readings.

I see no possibility for doubting that the words were used originally of sounds. To put it otherwise, σμερδνός must be regarded as a verbal adjective to * σμερδω a verb used of loud noises. On account of the etymological connection with Skt. mṛdnāti, Lat. mordeō, etc.[8], we may say more definitely used of crushing and crashing noises. We should expect it to have been used of the sea and of thunder, which would account for the connotation of terror that it acquired. Such is the range also of σμαραγέω that I should regard as coming from the same base but with different "root determinatives": *smer-, *smer-d-, *smer-āg-. Compare B 210 σμαραγεῖ δέ τε νόντος, Φ 199 δεινήν τε βροντήν, ὅτ' ἀπ' οὐρανόθεν σμαραγήσῃ, and note also its use of the battle crash Hesiod, Theog. 679 (σμαραγίζω ib. 693). The underlying word σμάραγος occurs in Hom. Epigr. 14. 9, while (σ)μαράσσω is said to be cited by Erotianus and by the Etymologicum Magnum 720. 58. We may now note the rhyme with πάταγος "clatter, clash" and its kindred [9]

σμάραγος : σμαραγέω : σμαράσσω
πάταγος : παταγέω : πατάσσω.

Words used of thunder are frequently applied to sounds coming from the bowels. The association is evidenced as early as the

---

[6] Cf. Hom. Hymn 31. 9.

[7] Cf. Aristophanes, Birds 553; Nicander, Th. 815.

[8] Cf. Walde-Pokorny 2. 278—279; Boisacq 884; Walde 495; Muller 275—276; Falk-Torp 2. 1080—81.

[9] If the vocalism of πάταγος has been influenced by that of σμάραγος, the former may derive from the base *petā-, meaning originally "noise made by a fall."

Homeric *h. Merc.* 295 f. by the way (cf. Allen-Sikes, ad loc.) that the infant Hermes parodies the omen of Ζεὺς ὑψιβρεμέτης. Strepsiades too had evidently been struck by the parallelism of βροντή and πορδή and is delighted (Arist., *Clouds* 394) with the explanation of the similarity in which παταγέω (389) and βροντάω (391) had been used. For σμαραγέω Hippocrates 658. 29 is cited, while βρέμω and its cognates will be considered below. The same may be presumed for *σμερδω and we will then note that *smerd- and *perd- were rhyme words[10]. That may help explain why in the differentiation [11] of *perd- and *pezd- the former came to mean the loud sound; and why *σμερδω dropped out of the literary tradition so early and completely that even Aristophanes knew nothing of it.

It gives also the semantic link between σμερδαλέος and a group of Balto-Slavic words, that may be represented by Lith. *smìrdžiu*, *smirdéti* "stink", for which Trautmann reconstructs *smirdyō as a startform. That is, in preference to the suggestions of a "beißender Geruch" or a "reibender, kratzender Geruch" which do not seem adequate, I should derive the specialized meaning of *smerdō "stink" (recognized by Walde-Pokorny) from an earlier meaning "make a crashing noise", the change being aided by the existence of the rhyme word *perdō. Another line, of development from this earlier meaning ends in σμερδνός, σμερδαλέος "frightful to hear", "frightful".

Latin *merda* < *smērdā may be exactly parallel to *pērdā continued by Albanian *pordε*[12], and differ from πορδή only in its vocalism, a restriction that is not surprising, cf. Hirt, *Hdb. d. gr. Laut- u. Formenlehre* 343. To separate Gothic *smarnōs* "σκύβαλα" seems difficult. Falk-Torp 2. 1086—87 connect it with OHG *smero*, etc. thus bringing it into a group with which it contrasts semantically. I should prefer to consider the possibility that within Indo-European itself, under certain conditions at least, -*rdn*- became -*rn*-; for σμερδνός could easily be a new formation in Greek.

---

[10] In the present both verbs seem to have varied between *-ō and *-yō. Greek πέρδομαι may represent either, if the treatment of *-dy- parallels that of *-gy- after consonants as elsewhere; a yō-present would be the normal thing beside the future ἀποπαρδήσομαι

[11] Pedersen, *KZ* 38. 418.

[12] Jokl, *IF* 37. 96. For the change of meaning, contrast dialectic (Carinthian) *Schass* 'πορδή'.

The change of meaning here assumed for Indo-European may be parallelled perhaps in Greek. No instances of βρέμω and the kindred nouns to indicate intestinal noises seem quotable; but from the third century B. C. on βρόμος or βρῶμος (the MSS are said to vary frequently in the spelling) and the compound βρομώ-δης (βρωμώδης) are well attested in the sense "stink," "stinking." Phrynichus (133, Rutherford) seems to have been unable to find warrant for this use in Attic. It seems likely that it started as a euphemism for πορδή and then gained a wider meaning.

ZUR DUENOSINSCHRIFT

VON EDUARD SIEVERS
UNIVERSITÄT LEIPZIG

1. Ueber die Geschichte der 'Duenosforschung' hat neuerdings E m i l G o l d m a n n in einem besonderen Buche [1] so eingehend berichtet, daß ich mich wohl jedes Rückgreifens auf Vergangenes enthalten darf, wenn ich versuche, im folgenden noch einiges zur Erklärung der merkwürdigen Inschrift nachzutragen, um die es sich handelt. Denn so vieles auch im einzelnen darüber bereits richtig gesagt sein mag, eine einleuchtende Gesamtlösung der Aufgabe steht meiner Ueberzeugung nach doch noch aus. Zeugnis dafür ist mir, neben den Unerträglichkeiten in Stil und Gedankenform, mit denen man uns auch hier öfter nicht verschont hat, vor allem die U n s p r e c h b a r k e i t sämtlicher bisher vorgeschlagener Textformen, d. h. die Unmöglichkeit, eben diese Textformen in dem ihnen beigelegten Sinne o h n e S t i m m - h e m m u n g frei so vorzutragen, daß dabei herauskommt, was sonst für jeden Satz verständlicher menschlicher Rede notwendiges Ingrediens ist. Ich meine damit: eine faßbare P e r s o n a l - k u r v e, eine faßbare S t i m m q u a l i t ä t, eine faßbare S a t z m e l o d i e, und dazu bei Verstexten auch noch eine faßbare Art der T a k t f ü l l u n g [2]. Daß das so ist, erklärt sich leicht aus der Art, wie man beim Entziffern und Deuten von Inschriften überhaupt vorzugehen pflegt. Denn ganz natürlich hält man bei solcher Arbeit zunächst nach Buchstabengruppen Umschau, die einem einen Anhalt für die weitere Deutung zu geben scheinen. Von da aus baut man dann weiter, Steinchen an

---

[1] E. Goldmann, Die Duenos-Inschrift, Heidelberg, Carl Winter, 1926; dazu kommen dann noch die weiteren Ausführungen von R. G. Kent, *Language* 2 (1926), 207 ff.

[2] Ueber alle diese Dinge habe ich kurz gehandelt in meinen 'Zielen und Wegen der Schallanalyse' (= ZuW.), Heidelberg, Carl Winter, 1924 (Sonderdruck aus der Festschrift für W. Streitberg: *Stand und Aufgaben der Sprachwissenschaft*).

Steinchen reihend, und oft auch ohne viel zu fragen, ob der so
entstehende, und manchmal sehr locker geschichtete, Haufe von
Kleinstücken in seiner G e s a m t h e i t auch etwas ergibt, was
man für ein mögliches Sprach-, Sinnes- und Stilgebilde halten
kann. Da liegt eben eine Lücke in dem herkömmlichen Verfahren,
die einmal ausgefüllt werden muß, damit eine neue, ergänzende
Kontrolle einsetzen kann. Ich halte es demnach auch nur für
angemessen, beispielsweise auch bei der Behandlung der Duenosinschrift das Arbeitsverfahren einmal direkt umzukehren, d. h.
an erster Stelle nach der G e s a m t f o r m des Textes zu fragen,
und erst nachher zu untersuchen, wie sich diese Gesamtform
zwanglos in einzelne Glieder auflösen läßt. Die dabei zu be-
wältigende Arbeit ist, nach einiger Vorübung, gar nicht so schwer,
wie manche zu denken scheinen: man muß nur d u r c h P r o -
b i e r e n lernen, seinen Text in lebendigem Ton so vorzutragen,
daß er ebenso 'k l i n g t' wie andere menschliche Rede, die man
kennt und versteht. Wende ich dies Probeverfahren (zunächst
also noch ohne bewußte Rücksicht auf den ja erst noch im einzelnen festzulegenden Sinn) auf die Duenosinschrift an, so ergibt
sich mir das Folgende als ein für mich klanglich anstoßfreier
Sprechtext:

A) °J ŏ^- veisat de'ivos / °qo'i mēd mi°tā't!

B) Nei tē'd endo co'smis / vi'rco si°ē'd,
as tē'd nois io'pēt / o'ite·si°a'i
pā˘kā·ri °vo'is!

C) D u°e'n o s mēd fē'ced, / e'n manom °e'inom
d u e'n o i: nē mē'd / ma'los tatō'd!

Darin markieren die Zeichen ', `, ^, ˘ einerseits die T o n -
s t e l l e n (bzw. H e b u n g e n , Nr. 3), andrerseits geben sie die
verschiedenen I n t o n a t i o n s f o r m e n an, die für den hem-
mungslosen Vortrag erforderlich sind, und zwar bezeichnen '
und ` e i n f a c h e (d. h. durch die g a n z e Silbe hindurch-
laufende) S t e i g - bzw. F a l l t ö n e, ^ und ˘ aber 'g e b r o -
c h e n e' S t e i g f a l l - und F a l l s t e i g t ö n e, bei denen
i n n e r h a l b der Silbe ein Wechsel der Tonrichtung statt-
findet [3]. Ferner wolle man beachten, daß die Herübernahme der

---

[3] Weiteres dazu siehe z. B. *Indogerm. Forschungen* 43, 158 ff. (Nr. 99). 45, 124 ff.
(Nr. 10). Auch mag es nicht unangezeigt sein, einmal auf die vor Jahren an einem
freilich etwas versteckten Orte (Kongreß für Aesthetik und allgemeine Kunst-
wissenschaft . . . 1913, Bericht herausgegeben vom Ortsausschuß, Stuttgart,

Schreibungen *virco, iopēt* und *tatōd* aus dem Original nur ortho-
graphisch gemeint ist, daß man aber beim Vortrag *virgo, iobēt* (dreisilbig!) und *datōd* sprechen muß. Die gesperrt gesetzten Wörter
jō^, qo'i und *due'nos, due'noi* verlangen ferner einen gewissen (im
Grunde antithetischen) Nachdruck, auch müssen sie so gesprochen
werden, daß man eine gegenseitige Beziehung zwischen ihnen
herausfühlt. Bei dem Zeichen ° endlich tritt stets der sog. S t i m m-
s p r u n g ein, über den ich anderwärts ausführlich gehandelt
habe [4]. Nach dem Schlusse des mit ° ausgezeichneten Wortes
(oder des durch - abgetrennten Wortstückes, das mit ° eingeleitet
ist) kehrt dann die Stimme jedesmal zu der laufenden Grund-
artikulationsweise zurück.

F. Enke. 1914, S. 461 f.) vorgetragene Beobachtung hinzuweisen, nach der das,
was das gemeine (d. h. nicht besonders akustisch-analytisch eingestellte) menschliche Ohr als 'tiefer' oder 'höher' bzw. als 's t e i g e n d' und 'f a l l e n d' ein-
schätzt, n i c h t l e d i g l i c h auf einer Verschiedenheit der Schwingungszahlen beruht, sondern auf einer K o m p l e x w i r k u n g von Verschiebung der
S c h w i n g u n g s z a h l, S p a n n u n g und K l a n g f a r b e, bei der die
Schwingungszahl durchaus nicht immer der ausschlaggebende Faktor ist. Gra-
phische Aufnahmen, die einseitig nur die Schwingungszahlen aus dem Komplex
herauszuziehen vermögen, können daher auch nichts gegen die vom Menschen
e m p f u n d e n e melodische Abstufung der Rede beweisen. Wohl aber haben
wir für diese ein sehr bequemes Kontrollmittel in den durch lockeres Auflegen
einer Fingerspitze auf die Vorderzunge zu verfolgenden Z u n g e n b e w e -
g u n g e n beim Sprechen. Bei jedem S t e i g t o n speziell schnellt die Zungen-
spitze innerhalb der betreffenden Silbe energisch nach dem Vordergaumen
hinauf, beim F a l l t o n schiebt sie sich (da sie sich nicht wesentlich senken
kann) unter dem kontrollierenden Finger in etwas absteigendem Bogen nach
vorn zu hinweg, so den hinteren Resonanzraum der Mundhöhle vergrößernd
und dadurch die Klangfarbe verdunkelnd. Dieser einfache Versuch wird bei
genügender Sorgfalt der Ausführung niemand im Zweifel lassen: 'S t e i g t ö n e'
in dem von mir gemeinten Sinne sind eben zugleich 'T ö n e m i t S t e i g -
z u n g e', 'Falltöne' aber 'T ö n e m i t Z u n g e n v o r s c h i e b u n g'
(das letztere war a. a. O. noch nicht richtig erkannt: ich glaubte damals noch
Zurückziehung der Zunge mit Herabdrückung der Hinterzunge beobachtet zu
haben).
   [4] S. meine Schrift 'Zur englischen Lautgeschichte' (= *Abhandlungen der
Sächs. Akademie der Wissenschaften, phil.-hist. Kl.* Bd. 40, Nr. I) S. 11 ff. 23 ff.
Weiteres dazu wird eine Abhandlung 'Neue Beiträge zur Lehre von der Kasus-
intonation' bringen, die demnächst am gleichen Ort erscheinen wird, desgleichen
ein weiterer Aufsatz *Elnonensia*, dessen Erscheinungsort noch nicht angegeben
werden kann. — Der Stimmsprung bedeutet einen plötzlichen Wechsel zwischen
den beiden Artikulationsarten der menschlichen Stimme, die ich (s. ZuW. S. 75 ff.)
als N und U (d. h. 'Normalstimme' und 'Umlegstimme') bezeichnet habe. Eine
von diesen Stimmarten ist jeweilen die 'Grundstimme' des einzelnen Textes,
an deren Stelle dann durch den 'Sprung' die andere Art als 'Gegenstimme' tritt.
Ist die Grundstimme N, so geht der 'Sprung' zu U, ist die Grundstimme U,
so 'springt' man zu N (Schemata N/U und U/N). Den ersteren Fall haben wir
bei der Duenosinschrift in dem Stück B, den zweiten in den Stücken A und C.

3. Wenn man sich den Text der Inschrift nach diesen Vorschriften frischweg vorspricht und dazu bei jedem der gesetzten Tonzeichen versuchsweise einmal T a k t schlägt, so wird man wohl alsbald bemerken, daß das Ganze in V e r s e n abgefaßt ist. Bei näherer Prüfung mit Hilfe der von mir eingeführten sog. Taktfüllkurven (ZuW. 77 ff.) entpuppen sich diese Verse als regelrechte S a t u r n i e r , die wieder nach Bau und Abkunft mit dem identisch sind, was ich auf germanischem Boden als 'S a g v e r.s e' bezeichnet habe. Das Wesentliche der ganzen Versart ist die Anwendung des g e r a d e n (sei es steigenden, sei es fallenden) $\dfrac{2 \cdot 2}{4}$ -T a k t e s mit Taktschlag vom Schulterblatt aus (s. dazu vorläufig Sievers, *Zeitschr. f. Assyriologie* Bd. 38 [NF. 4], S. 7).

4. Die drei Absätze A, B, C stammen nicht von einem und demselben Verfasser. Das folgt schon aus der Verschiedenheit ihrer P e r s o n a l k u r v e n (ZuW. 74). Die Personalkurven von A und B gehören zwar beide dem Großtypus I an, sind aber doch unter sich verschieden. Die von A hat annähernd die Gestalt der Figur 4 auf der Kurventafel S. 174 meiner *Deutschen Sagversdichtungen des IX.—XI. Jahrhunderts* (Heidelberg, Carl Winter, 1924), in B aber ist die Figur um 180° gedreht, so daß der keulenförmige Kopf nach oben, die Spitze aber nach unten steht; die Kurve von C aber ist eine Unterform des Typus III, aus der Figur 16 der Kurventafel S. 73 der ZuW. dadurch herzustellen, daß man die beiden Spitzen des Bogens sich noch kreuzend überschneiden läßt. — Dazu treten parallelgehende Verschiedenheiten der S t i m m q u a l i t ä t (ZuW. 90 ff., ausführlicher in meinen 'Metrischen Studien' 4 [= *Abhandlungen der Sächs. Akademie der Wiss., phil.-hist. Klasse* Bd. 35, Leipzig 1918] S. 31 ff.

261. A hat nämlich die Stimmformel U $\dfrac{5w\gamma}{2}$ (weit, steil nach rechts aufschwingend) [5], B die Formel N 2wγ (mitteleng, flach nach innen aufschwingend), C endlich die Formel U $\dfrac{4kq}{2}$ (mitteleng, steil nach rechts aufschwingend) [5]. Trotzdem bilden A B C

---

[5] Diese beiden 'Bruchformeln' zeigen an, daß den Einstellungen auf die Hauptstimmarten 5 w und 4 kq Elemente der Einstellung für die Stimmart 2 eingemischt sind. Hierüber werde ich erst später im Zusammenhang handeln können.

sichtlich eine gewollte Einheit, denn die Kleinheit der Wider-
stände beim Uebergang von A zu B und von B zu C zeigt (nach
Metr. Studien 4, § 184. 193 usw.), daß B als Fortsetzung an A,
und C als Fortsetzung an B 'angearbeitet' ist, d. h. also, daß die
in der Inschrift vereinigten drei Sprüche einem gemeinsamen
Zweck dienen sollten und für diesen von den drei Leuten ge-
schaffen wurden, die an der zweckdienlichen Herstellung des
kleinen Kunstwerks (Abbildungen bei Goldmann Tafel I und II)
ein gleiches Interesse hatten. Diese drei Männer werden wir uns
doch aber wohl in der W e r k s t a t t vereinigt zu denken haben,
in der das aus drei Einzeltöpfchen zusammengesetzte 'Drillingsgefäß' gearbeitet und mit den drei Sprüchen versehen wurde,
die es uns so wichtig machen.

5. Was mögen denn aber die hier gemutmaßten drei Leute mit
ihrem Produkt und ihrer Zusammenarbeit an ihm gewollt haben?
Ich glaube, das ist leicht zu sehen: denn das ist doch wohl bereits
als sicher anzusehen, daß das Drillingsgefäß der A u s f ü h r u n g
e i n e r   s ü h n e n d e n   L i e b e s w i r k u n g   dienen sollte,
bei der im Hintergrunde ein G o t t mitzuarbeiten hat: der Gott
eben, der ja allein imstande war, dem durch Menschenhand
gestalteten Gefäß die gewünschte Einwirkung auf den Empfänger
zu sichern. Daß es ohne einen solchen lenkenden Gott nicht
immer glatt gehen würde, dessen sind die braven Töpfer sicher:
darum soll er eben auch dazu m i t h e l f e n , daß die ganze
Sache in g u t e r   B a h n verlaufe. Und sie sind auch darin
ehrliche und wohlgesinnte Leute, daß sie wünschen, nur ein
b r a v e r Liebhaber möge sich der gewünschten Wirkung des
Gefäßes zu erfreuen haben: 'ein B r a v e r [6] hat', so sagt ja
direkt C, 'dies Gefäß dazu gemacht, daß es einem B r a v e n
zu Händen komme: kein B ö s e r soll es (sc. zum Zweck der
Einwirkung auf die Umworbene) verschenken dürfen.' Und
dafür, daß das Gefäß nicht in unrechte Hände falle, soll auch der
Gott mit sorgen helfen, wenn das Gefäß einmal die Werkstatt
verläßt, in der es entstanden ist: 'd a r a u f möge der Gott sehen,
w e m er mich zuführt' (d. h. 'in wessen Hände er mich geraten
läßt'), wie es in A heißt. Das ist ein ganz einfacher, und auch
ein wohl verständlicher Gedankengang.

---

[6] Die Intonation zeigt, daß in *duenos* und *duenoi* unmöglich Eigennamen
gesucht werden dürfen; denn diese beiden Wortformen entbehren des melo-
dischen Auszeichnungstones, der auch im Lat. die Eigennamen von den gewöhnlichen Appellativen scheidet.

6. Ich glaube demnach den Text nun etwa folgendermaßen umschreiben zu können:

A) D a r a u f schaue der Gott, w e m er mich zuführe!

B) Wenn dir ein Mägdlein nicht hold ist, so heißt er [nämlich der Gott] dich, von uns [nämlich den drei Töpfchen des Gesamtgefäßes] Gebrauch machen, um Frieden für euch zu gewinnen.

C) Ein B r a v e r hat mich gemacht, daß ich einem B r a v e n zu Handen komme: kein Böser soll mich verschenken [dürfen]!

Oder lateinisch:

A) Eo visat deus, c u i me mittat. — B) Ni in te comis virgo siet, ast tē [sc. deus ille] nobis jubet uti pacari [= ad pacandum] vobis. — C) B o n u s me fecit in manum ire [= ut in manum eat] b o n o: ne me malus dato!

7. Das klingt ja nun wohl im ganzen ziemlich glatt und einleuchtend, aber man wird sich doch fragen müssen, ob es auch möglich ist, diesen Sinn sprachlich aus dem heraus zu gewinnen, was dasteht. Ich muß also darüber noch einiges anfügen.

8. Die beiden E i n g a n g s w o r t e können, wie in Nr. 2 bereits angegeben wurde, stimmfrei nur als °jō^-veisat gesprochen werden, d. h. mit Stimmsprung und starkem Nachdruck auf dem steigend-fallenden jō^. Auch muß eine psychisch-syntaktische Bindung zwischen jō und veisat bestehen (bzw. zum Ausdruck gebracht werden, vgl. schon Nr. 2), die das jō^ stimmlich so stark hervorzuheben gestattet, daß das Wort veisat ohne Anstoß dahinter in die Senkung treten kann. Beides gewinnt man sofort, wenn man nur das jō als eine durch sog. 'Akzentumsprung' entstandene satzphonetische Dublette zu dem gewöhnlichen eo 'dorthin' auffaßt, also der Stelle den schon oben gegebenen Sinn 'do'rthin (= da'rauf) schaue der Gott' beilegt, an den sich dann auch das folgende nach Sinn und Klang gut anschließt (auch der so oft beanstandete Konjunktiv mittat kommt damit zu seinem Recht). Auf germanischem Boden ist der hier gemeinte Akzentumsprung ja z. B. aus dem Altnordischen allbekannt, und auch im Altenglischen ist er weit verbreitet, wenn er auch noch nicht in den Grammatiken gebucht ist (vgl. aber z. B. Sievers, Metr. Studien 4, § 102). Aus dem L a t e i n i s c h e n selbst sowie aus dem U m b r i s c h e n (s. v. Planta 2, 732 f.) kenne ich zwar derlei Formen nicht, wohl aber hat das O s k i s c h e gerade bei dem Pronomen, das dem lat. is entspricht, ganz analoge Formen entwickelt, wie joc nsf. apn., jonc asm., jusc npm. zu lat. ea, eum, eōs (statt ii); desgleichen heißt es marruzinisch jafc apf. = lat. eās. Man vergleiche z. B. aus der ebenfalls

in Saturniern laufenden Inschrift der T a b u l a   B a n t i n a
(v. Planta 2, 494 ff.) die Verse

> pon j o'c egmo °co'mparascu'ster 17, 4
> si'om j o c °co'mono 5
> in sua'epis j o n c fo'rtis / meddis mo'ltāum °he'rēst 12
> j o'n c suaepis he'rēst meddis / mo'ltāum °li'citūd 17 (vgl. 26)
> po'izād lī'gud j u s c °ce'nstur 20

oder das marruzinische (v. Planta 2, 549)

> j a'f c ēsuc ā'gine a's⟨s⟩um 274, 8

Man wird also doch wohl auch für das älteste Latein die Existenz
solcher Dubletten für möglich halten dürfen: sie werden nur
später in üblicher Weise durch Ausgleichung wieder beseitigt
worden sein. —

9. Die annoch bestehenden Schwierigkeiten im Absatz B lösen
sich, wie mir scheint, in befriedigender Weise, wenn man aus der
Buchstabenfolge *astednoisiopetoitesiai* zunächst das Stück *iopet*
als (dreisilbig zu sprechendes) altlat. *io'bēt*[7] = lat. *jubet* heraus-
löst, als dessen Subjekt dann natürlich der *deivos* der ersten Zeile
fungieren muß. Das *jubet* fordert dann weiter einen abhängigen
Infinitiv hinter sich, und der steht da, wenn man das folgende
oitesiai unzertrennt läßt. Denn dies *oitesiai* enthält (daran wird
man wohl nicht zu zweifeln brauchen) gewiß nur eine Parallele
zu dem späteren Typus von *amārier, vidērier, opperīrier, īrier,
ferrier* (Sommer, Handbuch[2] 594 f.; Stolz-Schmalz, Lat. Gramm.[5]
328), nur noch ohne das nachträgliche passivisch-deponentiale
Anhängsel -*r*, und insofern allerdings etwas auffällig, als es
meines Wissens der bisher erste Beleg für den ganz vollen Typus
*ūterier (statt des nachher gebräuchlich gewordenen *ūtier*) bei
einem Verbum der 3. Konjugation ist (vgl. indessen doch das
zitierte *ferrier*). Von dem Infinitiv *oitesiai* hängt sodann weiter
das vorhergehende (auch an richtiger Satzstelle stehende) *nois*
'nobis' ab, dessen Pluralität sich, wie man weiß, aus der Dreizahl
der vereinigten Töpfchen erklärt. Etwas schwieriger bleibt syntaktisch das folgende *pākāri vois*, mag man nun *pākāri* aktivisch
oder passivisch fassen. Es muß aber doch wohl auf alle Fälle
ein Z i e l infinitiv sein, im Sinne von etwa 'ad pacandum', wie
schon oben angedeutet wurde (s. auch unten Nr. 22 über *einom*).
Der Dativ *vois* 'für euch' dürfte syntaktisch wieder leichter zu
verstehen sein. Auch die kürzere Form *pākāri* gegenüber dem

---

[7] Das *o* statt *u* ist durch den Fallton hervorgerufen.

emphatischen, zweihebigen o'ite·sia'i mit Volldiphthong am
Schluß (vgl. dazu auch unten Nr. 16 über umbr. *heriei: heri*)
begreift sich wohl aus den besonderen Betonungsverhältnissen
der Stelle. Zur Endung -*esiai* vergleiche man überdies noch das
altindische -*ádhyāi* (wie in *iyádhyāi* usw., Delbrück, *Altindisches
Verbum* § 211) und ähnliches.

10. Nun aber 'der' viel beanstandete 'R h o t a z i s m u s' in
pākāri gegen *oitesiai* mit unverändertem *s*? Ich glaube, um den
braucht man sich nur so lange Sorge zu machen, als man es für
gestattet halten wird, sich auch beim Latein nicht um die Einwirkung der verschiedenen Intonationsarten auf die Ausgestaltung
der Wortkörper zu kümmern. Denn alles hier bisher Zweifelhafte
wird alsbald deutlich, wenn man nur das Verhältnis der in Frage
kommenden *s* und *r* zu den Steig- und Falltönen der einzelnen
Belegstellen ins Auge faßt. So können wir gleich als Ausgangspunkt für weitere Betrachtung feststellen, daß unser *oite'siai*
auf der Silbe *e's* einen Steigton trägt, die Form *pākā'ri* aber auf
dem *ā'r* einen Fallton. Ebenso unbestreitbar ist, daß die sekun-
dären *r* aus *s* früherer wie späterer Zeit (wenigstens soweit ich
das habe verfolgen können) stets auf einen Fallton folgen, und um-
gekehrt die unveränderten *s* der 'vorrhotazistischen Zeit' ebenso
wie die Dauer-*s* der stehenden 'Ausnahmswörter' (wie *cāsa, miser,
caesariēs, nāsus* u. dgl., Sommer 191; Stolz-Schmalz[5] 141) auf
einen Steigton[8].

11. Daß dem Wechsel von *s: r* ein älterer Wechsel von *s: z*
zugrunde liegt, ist allgemein anerkannt, und dieser Wechsel tritt
ja auch, u n d z w a r i n g l e i c h e r V e r t e i l u n g n a c h
S t e i g - u n d F a l l t o n, i m O s k i s c h e n direkt zutage,
sobald man nur dessen metrische Texte richtig als Verse spricht.
So stehen z. B. in der Inschrift der T a b u l a B a n t i n a (v.
Planta 2, 494 ff., Nr. 17), die ja *s* und *z* auch graphisch scheidet,
nebeneinander 'steigtonige *s*' in

> pā'n p̣ieisum brä'teis / auti cā̱'deïs °a'mnūd 17, 6
> e'isū̱c-en °zi'culūd 16
> censā̱'mur ē's u f in °e'ituam 19
> i'n eizeic vi'ncter / ē̱suf co'menei la°mā̱'tir 21 (s. u.)

---

[8] Zur bequemen Veranschaulichung des Verhältnisses kann auch der bekannte
Ausspruch des Pomponius dienen: '*R* litteram invenit, ut pro *Vale'siis Vale'rii*
essent, et pro *Fū̱'siis Fū̱'rii*, der (wie ähnliche andere Angaben) natürlich nichts
anderes zu besagen braucht, als daß man damals angefangen habe, der falltonigen
Dublettform den Eingang in die offizielle S c h r e i b u n g zu gestatten.

neben 'falltonigen z' in

> i'z ī c e i z e i c si'celei / co'mono °ni-°hī'pid 7
> si'om dat e·i z ā's c / idīc ta'ngineis °de'icum 9
> ta'dait e'z u m , nep °fe'facid 10
> po'd pis dat e'i z ā c °e'gmād 10
> i'z ī c co'mono °ni-°hī'pid 14
> po'n censtur Ba'nsaë / ta'utam cen°s ā'z e t 19
> p o'i z ā d lī'gud jusc °ce'nstur 19
> ce'nsāu'm °ange t u'z e t 20
> i'n e i z e i c vi'ncter / ēsuf co'menei la°mā'tir 21 (s. o.)
> in e'i(tuo) sī'vom / pa'ei e i z e i s fu'st 22
> sua'e pis op e' i z o i s com °a'trūd 23
> maᴨim ā'serum e'i z ā z u n c °e'g m ā z u m 24.

12. Die Inschrift des C i p p u s A b e l l a n u s (v. Planta 2, 513 ff., Nr. 177), die überhaupt viel mehr mit Steigtönen arbeitet als die der Tabula Bantina, hat allerdings, dank der abweichenden persönlichen Sprechweise ihres Verfassers [9] nur unverändertes s:

> d e'k e t ā s i u i Nu'vlanui 127, 5
> inim te'erum pud up e'i s ū d / sa'karāklūd °i'st 13
> pru'f t u s e t re'htūd °a'mnūd 16
> mu'inikum mu'inikei / tē'reï °f ū's i d 19
> inim e'i s e i s sakarā'kleis inim °tē'reis 19 f.
> trī'barak°ka't t u s e t 39
> e'kkum svai pid A'bellānūs / trī'barak°ka't t u s e d 41
> e'i s e i tē'rei / ne'p Abel°lā'nūs 46
> a'ut thēsa'urum / pud ē's e i tērei °i'st 48
> e'i s a i viai mefiai / tereme'nniũ °sta'iet 57

Ich betone ausdrücklich, daß man hier an keiner Stelle ohne Stimmstörung ein stimmhaftes z statt des geschriebenen s sprechen kann: wir haben also sicher auch nur wieder den Niederschlag eines rein lautgesetzlichen Zustandes vor uns: der etwaige Einwand, man habe gesprochenes z im oskischen Originalalphabet graphisch nicht ausdrücken können, hat also hier keine beweisende Kraft, da überhaupt keine Belege für klanglich notwendiges z vorliegen.

13. Ganz analog stehen die Dinge auch im A l t u m b r i - s c h e n für den I n l a u t. Das kann man speziell wieder an den ebenfalls metrischen Texten des altumbrischen Teiles der I g u - v i n i s c h e n T a f e l n (v. Planta 2, 557 ff.) ersehen. Die einzige Abweichung vom oskischen Brauch besteht darin, daß das er-

---

[9] Ueber solche persönliche, nicht dialektische Differenzen s. Sievers, *Zur englischen Lautgeschichte* S. 18. 86 Fußnote. — Ich scheide hier und im folgenden, um das Druckbild nicht zu überladen, bei den Texten in altoskischer Schrift nicht zwischen *i*, *u* und *í*, *ú*.

weichte *z* auch schon im A l t umbrischen zu *r* weiterentwickelt ist. Man vergleiche etwa

a) für erhaltenes stimmloses *s* nach s t e i g tonigem Vokal Stellen wie

pī'r ā's ē °ante'ntu 2ᵃ, 19; ähnl. 2 a, 38. 39. 43. 3, 22. 23. 4, 6. 16
svē'pu ē's u m - e k¹⁰ °ē's u n u 1ᵇ, 8; ähnl. 2ᵃ, 3. 4, 29. 5ᵃ, 1. 14 und 1ᵇ, 9. 14. 38. 2ᵃ. 20. 21. 3, 1. 14. 20. 5ᵃ, 4. 5. 6. 11
strū'hçla pe'tenāta / i's e k °aȓve'itū 4, 4
    s v i's e v ē fe'rtū °pū'ne,
e'trē s v i's e v ē / vī'nu °fe'rtū,
te'rtiē s v i's e v ē / ū'tur °fe'rtū 2ᵇ, 14 ff.
i's u n t kre'matru °pru'sektu 2ᵃ, 28; ähnl. 2ᵃ, 36. 3, 16. 17
se'sten t ā's i ārū / u'rn ā s i°ā'rū 3, 2
plē'n ā s i ē'r ur°n ā's i ēr 5ᵃ, 2

b) für *r* aus erweichtem stimmhaftem *z* nach F a l l ton z. B.

a'ȓfertū·re e'r u pe°pu'r k u r e n t 5ᵇ, 5; ähnl. 5ᵃ, 26. 29
    e r e k ē'sunēs-ku °ve'purus 5ᵃ, 11; ähnl. ere 5ᵃ, 4
ē'r a-hunt °ve'ā 1ᵇ, 23; ähnl. 2ᵇ, 22. 3, 12. 14. 31. 32. 4, 1. 5
e're rī ē'sune k ū °r ā'ja¹¹ 5ᵃ, 4; ähnl. 5ᵃ, 24. 26. 29
ē'nuk hapin ā'r u / e·ru's titū, °ze'ȓēf 1ᵃ, 33
se'stentasi ā'r u / u'rnāsi°ā 'r u 3, 2 (vgl. oben a; ähnl. 2ᵃ, 16)
e't ape frā'ter / çe'rsnā·tūr °f ū'r e n t 5ᵃ, 22
pūne pu'rtinçus ka'ȓētu, / pū'fe aprūf °fa'k u r e n t 1ᵇ, 33
pū're ulu be'n u r e n t / °pru'si k u r e n t re'hte / ... 5ᵃ, 25; (ähnl.
    5ᵃ, 28. 5ᵇ, 5
a'ȓfertūre e'ru pe°pu'r k u r e n t 5ᵇ, 5

14. Im A u s l a u t hat sich bekanntlich, auch schon im A l t - umbrischen, eine d r e i f a c h verschiedene Behandlung des ursprünglichen -*s* herausgebildet. Auch diese richtet sich nach der Klangbesonderheit der einzelnen Belegstellen, und diese Besonderheiten hängen ihrerseits wieder von den deklamatorischen Gewohnheiten oder Neigungen der einzelnen Verfasserpersönlichkeiten ab. Das -*s* bleibt nämlich entweder a) erhalten, oder es ist b) geschwunden, oder c) durch *r* ersetzt. In dem Wechsel der verschiedenen Wortausgänge herrscht aber, nach der Ueberlieferung gemessen, keineswegs das sinnlose Durcheinander, das man allgemein anzunehmen beliebt, sondern: a) das e r h a l t e n e -*s*

---

¹⁰ Das *e* dieses Wortes ist, wie die Klangverhältnisse zeigen, sicher lang: *ēsu* gehört also (gegen v. Planta) doch zu osk. *eis-* usw. Die n e u umbrischen Formen *essu* und *Fissiū* in dem einen Satze

    ti'om e s s u bū'e / pera'crī pi°hā'clū
    e'trū o'criper F i's s i ū 6ᵃ, 43

haben sichtlich sekundäre Gemination im Verband mit Vokalverkürzung, denn auch der Name *Fīs-* nebst seinen Ableitungen verlangt sonst stets die Aussprache mit -*īs*- (Belege bei v. Planta 2, 736).

¹¹ Pälignisch *coisātens* 'curaverunt', v. Planta 2, Nr. 253.

ist an vorhergehenden e i n f a c h e n (d. h. die ganze Silbe durch-
laufenden, oben Nr. 2) S t e i g t o n (') gebunden; — b) der
S c h w u n d ist nur nach e i n f a c h e m (d. h. wieder die ganze
Silbe durchlaufendem) t i e f e m F a l l t o n (') eingetreten; —
c) das *r* nur bei h a k e n f ö r m i g e m , tief herabgehendem
S t e i g f a l l t o n (^) innerhalb derSilbe, die es beschließt [12].

15. Daß es sich bei dieser Regelung in der Tat mindestens zum
guten Teil nur um Stilistisch-Deklamatorisches handelt, kann
man besonders deutlich daraus ersehen, daß auch s t e h e n d e
F o r m e l n je nach dem klanglichen Zusammenhang, in dem
sie erscheinen, intonatorisch wie lautlich verschieden behandelt
werden können. So geht z. B. die oft wiederkehrende Formel
°*ařepēs* °*a'rvēs* (am Versschluß) stets auf steigtoniges *arvēs'* oder
arvĭs' aus (letzteres bei besonderer Hochlage der letzten Silbe),
aber das erste Wort heißt entweder *ařepēs'* (oder *ařipēs'*) mit
schließendem Steigton, oder verkürzt mit tief herabgehendem
Fallton am Schluß *ařepē'*, oder endlich *ařepēr*^ mit -*r* und
steigend-fallendem Hakenton. Jede der drei Formen paßt klanglich an die Stelle, wo sie geschrieben steht: keine aber kann
ohne Stimmstörung an eine Stelle geschoben werden, wo wir eine
der anderen Formen lesen. Man vergleicht z. B. die Verse

a) sē'vum kutēf °pe'snī·mū / a'řepēs' °a'rvēs' 1ᵃ, 6.
   fe'itū kutēf °pe'rsnī·mū / a'řipēs' °a'rvīs' 1ᵇ, 7.
        kutēf °pe'snī·mū a'řepēs' °a'rvēs' 1ᵃ, 19. 23
b) ⎰ a'rviu °uste'ntu. / pū'ni °fe'i(t)ū.
   ⎱ ta'çez °pe'snī·mū / a'řepē' °a'rvēs' 1ᵇ. 26
   ⎰   pū'ni fētu. °pe'řaja °fē'tū;
   ⎱ ta'çez °pe'snī·mū / a'řepē' °a'rvēs' 1ᵇ, 44
c)   pe'snī·mū a'řepēr^ °a'rvēs 1ᵇ, 30
   ⎰   pū'ni °fē'tu.
   ⎱ ta'çez °pe'snī·mū / a'řepēr^ °a'rvēs' 1ᵇ, 32

16. Weitere Beispiele aus dem Gebiet der Deklination anzuführen erübrigt sich wohl, da die Regel ausnahmslos zu verlaufen
scheint und man sich die Belege mühelos aus den ausführlichen
Listen von v. Planta zusammenstellen kann. Aber aus dem an
sich begreiflicherweise viel spärlicher vertretenen V e r b a l -
gebiet sei wenigstens die dem lat. *sive—sive* entsprechende Formel
(eigentlich = lat. *velīs—velīs*, oder allenfalls auch indikativisch [13]
vīs—vīs) hergesetzt, bei der übrigens neben der Intonation im

---

[12] Ueber solche 'Hakentöne' s. *Indogerm. Forschungen* 45, 128 ff.
[13] Daß aber die kürzeren Formen mit bloßem *ī* in der Endung mindestens
konjunktivisch sein können, zeigt die deutliche 3. Sing. Conj. *svē pis heri* ... 4, 26.

engeren Sinne auch noch Stimmlage, Tempo und Dynamik maß-
gebend eingewirkt haben. Sie erscheint in folgenden Gestalten:

a) $\begin{cases} \text{te'nzitim } °\text{arve'itu, } / \text{ her}is' \text{ vī'nu her}is' °\text{pū'ni} \\ \text{fe'itu.} \end{cases}$ kutēf °pe'rsnīmū / a'ŕipēs °a'rvīs 1ᵇ, 7

$\begin{cases} \text{va'tuvā fe'rīne } °\text{fe'itū} \\ \text{her}is' \text{ vī'nu her}i' \text{ pū'ni, } / \text{ u'kri-per } °\text{Fī'siū} \end{cases}$ ... 1ᵃ, 4

$\begin{cases} \text{va'tuvā fe'rīne } °\text{fē'tū,} \\ \text{her}i' \text{ vī'nu her}i' \text{ pū'ni. } / \text{ a'rviu } °\text{uste'ntū.} \end{cases}$ 1ᵃ, 22

$\begin{cases} \text{her}i' \text{ vī'nu her}i' \text{ pō'ni } °\text{fētū.} \\ \text{va'tuō fe'rīne } °\text{fē'tū.} \end{cases}$ 6ᵃ, 57

$\begin{cases} \text{a'rvio } °\text{fē'tū.} \\ \text{her}i' \text{ vī'nu her}i' \text{ pō'ni } °\text{fē'tū} \end{cases}$ 6ᵇ, 46

b) $\begin{cases} \text{fo'ndlir-ē a'brof } / \text{ trī'f } °\text{fē'tū.} \\ \text{he'r}iei' \text{ rō'fū, } / \text{ he'r}iei' °\text{pē'jū} \end{cases}$ ... 7ᵃ, 3

   va'tuō fer'īne °fē'tū,

   herie' vī'nu herie' pō'ni °fē'tū ... 6ᵇ, 19

Vgl. ferner die 2. Sing. *sīr*ᴧ neben *sī'* (und *sei'*) = lat. *sīs* (v. Planta
2, 755) und *kūpifiāfā'* 1ᵇ, 35.

17. Ebenso richtet sich im U m b r i s c h e n nach Steig- und
Fallton das Stehen oder Fehlen des auslautenden *m* (*n*), sowie des
-*f* aus -*ns*, wie z. B. in dem Vers

Fu'ntlēr-*ē'* trī*f* a'prūf' / rū'frū' ūte °pē'ju' ... 1ᵇ, 24.

Im letzteren Falle kann es nur fraglich sein, ob direkt ein *f* geschwunden ist, oder ein *s* nach vorherigem Schwund des Nasals
(unter Nasalierung des vorhergehenden Vokals). Die Entschei-
dung ist natürlich auch für die chronologische Frage wichtig,
ich kann aber an dieser Stelle nicht näher darauf eingehen. Ich
begnüge mich also damit, zu sagen, daß mir nach den begleitenden
Umständen die zweite Alternative wahrscheinlicher vorkommt
als die erste.

18. Auch das L a t e i n i s c h e zeigt nun wieder ganz ähnliche
Erscheinungen. Daß auch dort das -*m* nur nach Fallton abfällt,
kann ein Blick z. B. auf die Scipioneninschriften lehren, für den
Abfall des -*s* lassen sich auch genug inschriftliche Zeugnisse bei-
bringen, ganz abgesehen von dem alten Paradebeispiel *facile
omnibu' princeps* u. dgl. Ja selbst aus der späteren Literatur läßt
sich die einstige Gültigkeit der Regel noch demonstrieren an der
Hand der V e r s c h m e l z u n g s f o r m e n m i t *es, est*.

Ich habe daraufhin z. B. den ersten Akt des Plautinischen Amphitruo durch-
gesehen. Dort heißt es aber bei erhaltenem *m* ebenso konsequent im N e u t r u m
mit s t e i g tonigem Ausgang *oppidum'st* 191, *exitum'st* 219, *actum'st* 227, *pugnā-
tum'st* 249, *certum'st* 265. 339. 372, *pessumum'st* 314, *conlubitum'st* 343, *futūrum'st*
374, *datum'st* 418. 538, *quaerundum'st* 423, *factum'st* 431, *redeundum'st* 527 (vgl.

auch *verbōrum'st* 247) wie beim M a s k u l i n u m f a l l tonig -*u'st*: *nātu'st* 179, *additu'st* 250, *itūru'st* 263, *nūllu'st* 293, *superstitiōsu'st* 323, *tūtātu'st* 352, *praefectu'st* 363, *eru'st* 381, *ingressu'st* 429, *sēminātu'st* 482, *scitu'st* 506; desgleichen *exercitūru's* 324, *ēmentītu's* 411, *vaniloquo's* 379. Dagegen ist die Endung -*us* ebenso konstant s t e i g tonig, wenn keine kürzende Verschmelzung eintritt: *conspicātus est* 242, *acceptūrus est* 296, *validus est* 299, *onerandus est* 328, *erus est* 362, *solitus est* 419, *ēlocūtus est* 420, *saevos est* 541. Auch die -*a* der F e m i n i n- formen bleiben trotz der Verschmelzung (wie das -*um* der Neutra) steigtonig: vgl. *dūra'st* 166, *aurea'st* 260, *exorta'st* 274, *scita'st* 288, *nupta'st* 364, *solūta'st* 412, *nūlla'st* 509, *data'st* 534. Dazu halte man das männliche *Sōsia's* 427 und beliebige andere Verschmelzungsformen mit Steigton, wie *quid-*, *quisquam'st* 271. 400, *Sosiae'st* 332; *superque'st* 168, *(con)simile'st* 443. 447, *quale'st* 537 f., *necesse'st* 501; *tibī'st* 350. 364. 402, *mī'st* 406, *similī'st* 446; *adeō'st* 169, *imāgō'st* 265, *eō'st* 345, *signō'st* 421, *factō'st* 505 (2), *curātiō'st* 519; *diu'st* 302. 530. Steigtonig bleiben bei der Verschmelzung auch die *us*, die nicht dem Nom. Sing. von *o*-Stämmen angehören: *onus't* 175, *opus't* 445; *satius't* 176, *domus't* 362.

Da also tatsächlich nur bei den eben genannten Nom. M. Sing. bei der Verschmelzung ein Fallton eintritt, während bei Nicht-verschmelzung auch deren -*us* Steigton behält, so bleibt wirklich nichts anderes übrig, als von einer alten, d. h. vor der Verschmelzung liegenden Doppelheit steigend -*us'*: fallend -*u'* auszugehen, die diesmal zugunsten des falltonigen -*u'* ausgeglichen wurde, während sonst überall die steigtonige Variante den Sieg davon-trug. Wie das steigtonige *onus't* nebst Genossen zeigt, hat also Sommer, *Krit. Erläuterungen* S. 92 ff. darin gegen Leo recht, daß auch eine Kürzung von -*us est* zu -*us't* über -*us'st* an sich m ö g - l i c h ist: aber der männliche Typus -*u'st* ist doch eben t a t - s ä c h l i c h offenbar aus -*u' est* entstanden. — Uebrigens gelten die hier vorgeführten Intonationsregeln auch noch für die klas-sische Latinität.

19. Es stimmt ferner wieder zur Hauptregel, daß in Fällen mit mehrsilbiger Senkung wie *quibus me deceat* Amph. 201, *facinus nequiter* 315, *lassus sum, vectus hūc sum* 329, *servos ne an līber* 343, *servus sum* 356, *inmutātus sum* 456; oder *vīribus superbī* 212, *finibus exercitūs* 215, *vīcimus vī* 237, *complexus cum* 290, wo Satz- und Versmelodie steigtonigen Ausgang des ersten Wortes verlangen, aus klanglichen Gründen auch dessen -*s* mitzusprechen ist, während das *s* aus gleichem Grunde unterdrückt werden muß, wo an entsprechender Stelle ein Fallton auftritt: *opinātu' fui* 186, *instrūximu' legiōnēs* 221, *familiārī' sīs* 354, *sānu' nōn est* 402. Es ist also wirklich nicht abzusehen, warum nicht auch z. B. *mentīris' nunc* 344 und *vocāre'* 382 u. dgl. einfach lautgesetzliche Intonationsdubletten sein sollen. Auch das falltonige *pote's(t)* würde zur Regel stimmen: selbst das ständige *qui's*: *quī'* könnte

schließlich hierher gehören, wie denn auch Formen wie *aĭ-n*
Amph. 284. 344, *pergĭ'-n* 349. 539, *scĭ'-n* 356, *satĭ'-n* 509, *abĭ'-n* 518
tatsächlich den zu erwartenden Fallton zeigen. Auf Zweifelhafteres
möchte ich hier nicht eingehen. —

20. In der intonationsbedingten E r w e i c h u n g eines inneren
und dem intonationsbedingten A b f a l l eines schließenden *s*
gehen also die altitalischen Hauptsprachen (auch die Klein-
sprachen liefern noch einiges einschlagende Material) in solcher
Ausdehnung zusammen, daß man schwer glauben kann, es handle
sich hier n i c h t um bereits uritalische Prozesse, deren Wirkungen
nur hernach durch Ausgleichungen mannigfacher Art wieder
unübersichtlicher gemacht wurden. Einigermaßen abseits steht
nur das Umbrische mit seinem bereits in altumbrischer Zeit
beginnenden auslautenden hakentonigen *-r* (oben Nr. 15), und
das muß denn doch wohl als eine auf s e k u n d ä r e m I n t o -
n a t i o n s w a n d e l beruhende nachträgliche Abbiegung aus
dem älteren steigtonigen *s'* angesehen werden: der lange fallende
Ast des Hakentons hätte dann im Umbrischen ähnlich gewirkt,
wie der einfache Fallton im Vorumbrischen. Für das Umbrische
hätten wir demgemäß neben dem 'älteren' auch noch einen
'jüngeren' Rhotazismus anzusetzen.

21. Damit kann ich denn endlich wieder zum Ausgangspunkt
dieser langen Digression zurückkehren. Wenn nämlich im Oskischen je nach der Intonation inneres *s* und inneres *z*, im Umbrischen inneres *s* und inneres *r* nebeneinander stehen konnten, so
weiß ich nicht, warum ein solches Nebeneinander (das ja akzentisch geschützt war) im Lateinischen unmöglich gewesen sein
soll. Für meine Auffassung der Geschichte des 'Rhotazismus'
vertragen sich also auch das *oite'siai* und das *pākā'ri* unserer
Duenosinschrift auf das beste miteinander. —

22. Zu dem Abschnitt C der Inschrift sind nur noch ein paar
Worte zu sagen. Das *o* von *manom* gegenüber gemeinlat. *manum*
mit altem *u* ist vom Intonationsstandpunkt aus gut verständlich,
wieder als Produkt des Falltons. Das zwischen *en* und *einom*
formelgemäß akzentisch eingeklemmte Wort sinkt nämlich bis
zum Schlusse des *o*, um dann in dem *m* wieder anzusteigen (das
nun als steigtonig erhalten bleibt). In *einom* sehe ich dann syntaktisch wieder einen (an den Supinumgebrauch erinnernden)
Infinitiv des Zieles (wie oben in *pākāri*, Nr. 9), formell einen
akkusativisch gebildeten Infinitiv der Wurzel *ei* 'gehen', der

genau dem germanischen Bildungstypus zumal von Verbis wie
dō-n, *gā-n*, *stā-n* usw. entsprechen würde, der ja seinerseits auch
von einem Suffix *-no-* ausgeht. Neben den oskisch-umbrischen
ebenfalls akkusativischen Infinitiven auf *-um* scheint mir die
Annahme besonders unbedenklich, unser *ei-no-m* könne ein Rest
einer einst weiter verbreiteten Gattung von Infinitiven sein, der
aus der Zeit vor der großen Neuregelung des lateinischen Infinitiv-
wesens stammt.

Ich möchte also glauben und hoffen, daß die im Vorstehenden
verfochtene Deutung der Duenosinschrift auch der sprachlichen
Formkritik gegenüber werde standhalten können.

ON THE NAME *LUCRETIUS CARUS*

BY TENNEY FRANK
THE JOHNS HOPKINS UNIVERSITY

We know so little about the poet Lucretius that we are justi-fied in resenting misinformation which is handed down without hesitation from volume to volume. Many years ago Marx[1] made the statement that the poet's cognomen *Carus* was not found among Romans of the Republican period, and that while rather frequent in the imperial period it belonged regularly to men of low station, that is, to slaves, freedmen and immigrants. He also noticed that *Carus* was frequently found in the Celtic provinces, and therefore concluded that Lucretius was probably a Celt of freedman standing.

Now that several indices of the Corpus have appeared so that any one might have discovered that Marx' statements were erroneous it is a pity that the standard reference books continue to repeat and even to exaggerate these guesses. Mewaldt, who has recently written the article on Lucretius for the great Pauly-Wissowa Realencyclopädie (XIII, 1659 ff., dated 1927) says: "So wird es bei der These von Marx verbleiben müssen." Hosius, in his revision of Schanz (I p. 273, dated 1927) also accepts the statements of Marx, as did Kroll in his revision of Teuffel-Schwabe (I, 473). Finally, the article on *Carus* in the great Thesaurus Linguae Latinae says *ante aetatem imp. non nisi serv. vel lib., cf. Marx.*

Now let us examine the facts in detail. The first edition of vol. I of the Corpus (containing the republican Latin inscriptions) gave one instance of Carus (no. 769) and that belonged to a slave. However the inscription had no right to a place in that volume because its date is 32 A. D. So much for the slave name of *Carus* in republican times. We have no instance of it. The

---

[1] *Neue Jahrb.* 1899, p. 535.

cognomen is, to be sure, rare in republican times in any class, but that has little significance since cognomina came into use late except in the highest nobility and republican inscriptions are relatively few. The fact is that nine-tenths of the well-known cognomina are not vouched for at all in republican records. Marx's statement regarding the rarity of this cognomen among citizens of the republic was, therefore, hardly worth repeating. The fact is that, leaving aside the case of Lucretius, we have found it in republican times only in Livy 39, 55, T. Aebutius Carus, a senator (where it is doubtful because the name seems to reappear as Aebutius Parus in 42, 4, according to the Vienna ms.), in an old inscription (vetustis litteris) of Aquila, in central Italy (C. I. L. I² 1796, Sex. Vibius Sex. ⟨f⟩ Carus), and in the case of a Spanish chieftain (Appian, Hisp. 45). From this evidence we can only say that there was a Celtic name which Appian transliterated into Karos, that the Latin name Carus was in good standing in central Italy before there is any question of Celtic nomenclature there, and that perhaps a senator of the Catonian epoch bore the cognomen.

During the empire, whence most of our inscriptions come, the cognomen is found in all strata of society. The Emperor Carus is late, but before his day there were L. Aemilius Carus (consul about 50 A. D.), D. Junius Carus (a senator), C. Popilius Carus (consul about 148), Salvius Carus (a senator) and Seius Carus (of senatorial rank). The index of nomina of C. I. L. VI, where the cognomen is found about fifty times, will add to the above several centurians and praetorians of respectable standing (2676; 3639; 32 520, VI, 14; 32 536, II, 5; 32 995; 37 184, I, 22). Among the forty that cannot be classified *only two* are distinctly proved to be freedmen (20 304, 16 823), though several of the others appear to be related to freedmen, but are clearly one or two removes from the class. And as it is a well known fact that while freedmen were required to keep their servile cognomina, the children of freedmen were very apt to be given respectable cognomina so that they might have a fair chance at civic and social opportunity. The occurrence of the name Carus in this latter group does not support the Marxian hypothesis.

Those who are not intimate with the inscriptions might readily draw the incorrect inference from the fact that only 25% of the *Cari* of the index are demonstrably of a respectable social class

But the fact is that that proportion is exceedingly high. One has only to compare the use of such servile names as Amandus, Ampliatus, Auctus (cf. the Thes. L. L.), Hilarus, Donatus, Optatus, Successus, or the numberless Greek servile names to realize how estimable the name *Carus* is. A good place to test the tone and quality of names is the second part of the sixth volume of C. I. L. which contains the thousands of inscriptions of the columbaria where the ashes of slaves and freedmen were interred in the early empire. In examining the first two thousand inscriptions in that volume we find the favorite slave names recurring by scores while *Carus* occurs only once (VI 5263) and then in the instance of a *son* of an imperial freedman. In short no one who is familiar with Latin inscriptions could possibly have accepted the Marxian statement. So far is Carus from being a cognomen of servile association that it is one of the most respectable of names outside of the distinctly senatorial group. The fact that the majority of the people who bear it are of humble station is, of course, due to the fact that more than 90% of our epitaphs naturally come from that class.

The reference to Celtic origin has little more value[2]. There is no doubt that there was a Celtic name that resembled *Caros* and that it occurs on Celtic headstones. But the first occurrence of the name in Italy is too early to attribute to Celtic origins. Furthermore, the frequent use of it as a designation of children in Italy shows that it was felt as a *kosename* at Rome in many instances. Carus in fact is found as a name all over the Latin part of the empire and is just about as frequent on the inscriptions of Rome and Italy as in Gaul and Spain. There is not the slightest ground for assuming that Lucretius had any Celtic connections.

It must be because of the Marxian hypothesis that several scholars, especially countrymen of Marx, have assumed that Lucretius was of humble origin and immediately tried to prove that he was unusually deferential in his address to Memmius. Sellar and Munro, to be sure, felt differently, and Merrill [3] well says "Such expressions as *volgus abhorret*, and *impia pectora volgi* show the intellectual aristocrat; but the austere sermon at

---

[2] Brieger has already said so, in *Bursians Jahresbericht*, 1901, 159 ff. The cognomen is surprisingly rare in Cisalpine Gaul whence Marx suggests that Lucretius might have come.

[3] Merrill's edition, p. 14. See also Giri, *Bull. Phil. Class.* 1910—11 and Tolkiehn, in *Woch. Klass. Phil.* 1904, 362.

the opening of the second book on the variety of political ambition is evidence of a freedom of criticism and a liberty of thought and expression which could hardly be found in a person of low social standing at the time". Once we are rid of the prejudices created by the conjectures of Marx I think that no reader of Lucretius will fail to see that the poet speaks like a free citizen conscious of an honorable position in society and that he addresses Memmius as an equal.

AENEID, II, 557

BY JAMES TAFT HATFIELD
NORTHWESTERN UNIVERSITY

That the body of Priam should come to lie on the sea-shore, has doubtless seemed incongruous to others than the writer. During the progress of this study, I was pleased *(Vivant qui ante nos nostra dixerunt!)* to find a short note by J. Mähly in the *Zeitschrift für die österreichischen Gymnasien,* 1887 (38, 415): »Aber wer hat denn das 'ingens corpus' des Königs an das Gestade geschleppt? Verständlicher und natürlicher wäre 'limine'.«

With the city in flames, the gods themselves taking part in its overthrow, Ulysses and Phoenix guarding the spoils and captives, and, at the very close of the book, the Greeks holding all the gates, there was no likelihood that anyone would be inclined to transport the king's body over the wide plain and through the ford of the deep-eddying Xanthus to the Hellespont, some five miles away.

In the cases of Patroclus and Hector, the possession of the hero's corpse became, to be sure, the object of much activity on the part of the warriors: Hector wished to drag away the naked body of Patroclus from the plain, in order to give it to the dogs of Troy (Il. 17, 127), while the Greeks finally brought it to their camp, and rendered it most imposing funeral honors; Achilles was unrelenting in the persistent indignities which he wreaked upon the dead body of Hector (Il. 24, 15), but, in general, the Homeric heroes were content that the bodies of their foes should be devoured by vultures where they fell. This place, in the case of Priam, was a sequestered *limen* of his palace.

This word, from its original meaning, "dividing-line," "sill," has a variety of derived, transferred uses in the Aeneid, but for the purposes of our passage may be held to signify "place of entering in," comparable to the πρώτῃσι θύρῃσιν of Il. 22, 66.

As in the case of *litus*, the word makes a convenient and perfect dactyl in the declined cases, the forms *limine, limina; litore, litora* occurring unnumbered times in the fifth foot; *litore* here is somewhat more frequent than *limine*, as might be expected in a sea-going epic. In this position, *litore* ("place where"), without a preposition, occurs somewhat oftener than the prepositional phrase, *in litore;* whereas *in limine*, in this sense, occurs about eight times as often as the simple *limine*. The clearest cases for *limine*, without preposition, in the fifth foot, and indicating "place where," are:

> tutum patrio te limine sistam (2, 620)

and:

> sedens niveo candentis limine Phoebi (8, 720).

Illustrations could be multiplied as to the indifferent use or omission of the preposition *in* in such constructions, e. g.:

> nudus in ignota, Palinure, iacebis harena (5, 871)

and:

> fulva resplendent fragmina harena (12, 741).

A scribe, accustomed to *litore* in the fifth foot, would very easily substitute it in place of *limine*, though I believe that the current reading *litore* in our line, 2, 557, is found in all standard manuscripts and editions. Precisely this easy substitution is shown in line 8, 555: Palatinus, γ^1, c, and χ read *limina;* Mediceus, Romanus, and γ^2 read *litora*.

The strongest argument for the proposed amendment lies in the fact that the whole action connected with the death of Priam revolves continually about the word *limen*. Aeneas, with his valiant companions, while fighting in burning Troy, is drawn, by the vehemence of the conflict there, to the palace of Priam. The entrance is occupied by attacking Greeks, who have formed a *testudo* (2, 441):

> cernimus obsessumque acta testudine limen.

The more particular description begins with line 453:

> Limen erat caecaeque fores et pervius usus.

The raging Pyrrhus is discovered:

> primo . . . in limine (line 469).

He proceeds in his murderous course (480):

> limina perrumpit postisque a cardine vellit.

Those in the royal apartments are terror-stricken by this invasion (485):

armatosque vident stantis in limine primo.
In describing these events to Dido, Aeneas relates (499 f.):

... vidi ipse furentem
caede Neoptolemum geminosque in limine Atridas.

Priam, driven to fury by the destruction of the city (507 f.):

urbis uti captae casum convolsaque vidit
limina tectorum et medium in penetralibus hostem,

rushes, in spite of his age, against the invader. Pyrrhus butchers
him, after slaying his son Polites.

In view of all these considerations, there seem to be convincing
reasons for reading, at the close of this scene:—

haec finis Priami ... iacet ingens limine truncus.

THE GERMANIC VOWEL SHIFT AND THE ORIGIN OF MUTATION

BY E. PROKOSCH
YALE UNIVERSITY

1. THE INDO-EUROPEAN VOWEL SYSTEM. The foundations of our present understanding of Indo-European phonology have been obtained in two great strides. In 1822 Jacob Grimm correlated the Germanic Consonant System with that of the other Indo-European languages by recognizing the primary factors of the Germanic Consonant Shift. More than half a century later, in 1878, Hermann Collitz, through his discovery of the Palatal Law gave the proof that the Indo-European vowel system was closely akin to that of early Greek and Latin, while the Indo-Iranian vowels, which had been supposed to represent the primitive Indo-European condition, were shown to be a secondary development. Neither Grimm nor Collitz, it is true, stood entirely alone in their discoveries; Rask, Johannes Schmidt and others have furnished meritorious contributions to the new evidence, but in the main the names Grimm and Collitz will always stand out as those of the most important pioneers in our "reconstruction" of the Indo-European consonants and vowels.

In regard to both sound systems, the Germanic languages, especially in their earlier periods, present a network of variations which seem kaleidoscopic at first consideration, but on closer analysis follow more or less clearly distinguishable directions of the type for which Sapir has coined the fortunate term "Drift." The drift in the Germanic Consonant System is especially obvious, and the writer has attempted to formulate it in various articles, especially in *MPh. XV* and *XVI*. The details of the transition of the Indo-European vowels to the various Germanic Vowel Systems have also been investigated at various times, and Collitz's own theories, summed up in *MLN. XXXIII, 321 ff.*, constitute the most important attempt to clarify that involved problem. The writer cannot fully accept certain aspects of Collitz's views on the development of the Germanic vowels, especially his contention that the primitive Germanic and the Gothic vowel system were essentially identical, but he is nevertheless indebted to him for invaluable stimulation and information on this as well as many other linguistic problems.

2. THE GERMANIC VOWEL SHIFT. A mere tabulation of those facts that are accepted by the majority of linguists in the Germanic field reveals for the development of the Germanic vowels a consistent continuity that is no less amazing than that of the Germanic consonants. In fact, the assumption of a vowel shift in the Germanic languages is quite as valid as the assumption of the well established consonant shift, and it might be best to use the term "sound shift" as comprising both groups. To state the external facts of the drift in concrete terms is a relatively easy matter; to explain its meaning or cause is difficult and may at the present stage of linguistic understanding be even impossible.

The term "Germanic Vowel Shift" as I am using it in this paper should be interpreted as comprising the *spontaneous* vowel changes of the pre-historic period before the formation of the several Germanic languages that is, roughly speaking, of pre-Christian times (Collitz's Proto-Germanic and Primitive Germanic). In principle, therefore, it excludes changes that depend on neighbouring sounds, but this is not and should not be, carried through with complete consistency. Also, theoretically the term should not take into account later changes in the individual Germanic languages. But we are justified in including certain indications of a continuation of the trend into historical times.

3. THE VOWEL TRIANGLE. In the following analysis of the Germanic vowel drift it is expedient to make use of that standardized diagram that we are accustomed to term the "Vowel Triangle". This may seem objectionable in view of Russell's recent opposition to that concept (cp. especially *The Vowel*, Columbus, O., 1928), and a brief discussion of his objections is quite unavoidable for the purpose of the present paper. I am, of course, aware of the fact that in spite of such over-conventionalized diagrams as we find, for instance, in Viëtor-Rippmann's *Elements of Phonetics* the term "triangle" is not to be taken in its geometrical sense but merely indicates the acceptance of

intersecting spheres of tongue articulations in which the distances between the "points of articulation" are wider for "high vowels" than for "low vowels." The use of a triangle in representing this theory merely takes into account the practical fact that even within a given language (say, German) the contrasts between the various low-vowels [a, *a*, æ] are generally less marked than those between front and back mid-vowels and between front and back high-vowels, and that for certain practical purposes it is expedient, but hardly more than that, to sum up all low vowels in the convenient although rather vague symbol [a]. In that sense, there is really no contradiction between the triangle and Bell-Sweet's rectangular scheme. The latter merely goes to the other extreme of standardization, assigning to the low vowels the same latitude that is given to the high vowels. The writer has attempted to compromise between these extremes in his *Sounds and History of the German Language* (p. 38) by using a spherical diagram of this shape:

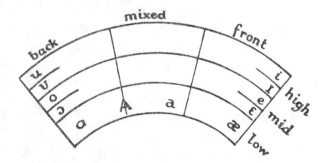

The top curve in this diagram is supposed to run approximately parallel to the roof of the mouth, while the bottom line roughly symbolizes the tongue in its lowest position. Evidently this diagram does not strive for physiological or geometrical accuracy any more than the triangle, or, for that matter, the rectangle of the English school, but it does give recognition to the belief in the existence of "high-vowels," "front-vowels," etc. Nor does it seem to me that Russell's admirable investigations have shaken that assumption in the least.

I wish to go on record with an expression of the highest appreciation of the fundamental scientific value of Russell's experimental work. His x-ray photographs of vowel articulations are beyond comparison the clearest and most reliable that have ever been published; in fact, most similar attempts dwindle into insignificance before Russell's attainments. But I am unable to reconcile his photographs (and his tables, as well) with his conclusions. He characterizes the vowel triangle as a "fallacy" and goes so far as to say (p. 149): "It is only by the biggest stretch of the imagination that we can make out anything which at all resembles points of tongue arching which would remotely correspond to even the three extremities of the triangle, $\begin{smallmatrix} u & i \\ & a \end{smallmatrix}$."

To arrive at tangible results I made minutely accurate tracings of Russell's outlines of tongue and hard palate (p. 257 ff. and p. 110 ff.) and super-imposed and concentrated them into one diagram by means of transparent tracing paper (the transparent diagram which Russell himself attaches as a help in comparing his pictures with the "traditional sweet terminalogy" (*sic*; p. 257) is quite meaningless for the purpose). In that way I obtained a composite outline, in which the "points of articulation" are located in the following way:

Russell   IPA

I was amazed to find that this careful tabulation of Russell's own results did not substantiate his skepticism. More than that: the "points of articulation" in this diagram that is, the points of highest tongue elevation, are in principle identical with those contained in the newest diagram of the International Phonetic Association, in which the four "fundamental" points [i, u, *a*, *a*] were also obtained by X-ray photography (*Lautzeichen und ihre Anwendung*, Berlin, 1928, p. 20 ff.). The relatively greater altitude of the latter diagram possibly indicates an extreme articulation, for the purpose of the experiment, but I am by no means sure on that point; several other interpretations are possible. Russell's outlines show the most surprising resemblance with those contained in Bremer's *Deutsche Lautlehre*, published as early as 1893 (p. 160 f. and table II), gained not by photography but by extremely skillful and conscientious mechanical measurements. Of course, they cannot claim the same reliability as Russell's results, but they are thoroughly confirmed by them. Bremer's diagrams are also substantially in agreement with several other of Russell's statements, notably the assumption that "the point of arching for *u* is not much farther back than is that for the front vowels" (*The Vowel*, p. 160). Indeed, a part of his results almost seems another illustration of a remark of Sievers' in his lectures on Phonetics which I took down in shorthand as a student in 1905: »Die Experimentalphonetik hat bis jetzt nichts gefunden, was die besten Phonetiker nicht ohnehin wußten.« Doubtless, in view of the great progress in experimental phonetics during these twenty-five years, Sievers himself would nowadays not maintain this view in full, but in the present case it seems only slightly exaggerated as far as the "points of articulation" are concerned. Here, indeed, Russell has in the main confirmed the previous statements of the "best phoneticians," notably Bremer, and his quotations from Viëtor, Jespersen, Meyer and others do not prove the opposite for this part of his contentions.

True, the opposition to "points of articulation" is only a part of Russell's results. His discoveries in regard to the movements of the epiglottis, velum, and back of the tongue are to a large extent new contributions of the greatest value, but I cannot admit that these factors eliminate the concept of points of articulation. All of these elements of articulation constitute an interlocking complex, although up to a certain degree each element may vary independently from the others. The point of articulation is, of course, not the *cause* of any given vowel articulation but merely its most characteristic symptom. Taken alone, it means nothing. It is obviously true, as Russell points out, that any vowel can be articulated with a virtually flat tongue. It is also true, I might add, that variations of the angle of the jaws are by no means indispensable; many men are in the habit of speaking while holding a pipe firmly between their teeth, thus insuring an invariable angle of the jaws. All of this does not in the least controvert the fact that in average articulation each vowel family ranges within a given sphere of tongue elevation, which in a diagram such as that of Bremer or of the IPA may quite legitimately be indicated as a point of articulation. That these spheres of articulation are apt to intersect is no proof to the contrary.

(Compare *Sounds and History of the German Language*, p. 38 f.)
I consider it therefore justified and even necessary to retain in
the present analysis the concept and general scheme of the vowel
triangle, all the more since in the investigation of earlier periods
of the language it is obviously impossible in most cases to define
the tongue positions with the accuracy of a contemporary X-ray
picture. The general trend of vowel changes is quite certain
nevertheless.

4. VOWEL QUANTITY AND VOWEL SHIFT. There exists
a striking parallelism between the quantity of Indo-European
and Germanic vowels and the Germanic Vowel Shift, all the more
striking since it presents a sharp contrast to similar groups of
phonetic changes in other Indo-European languages. As will be
shown below, in the Germanic languages long and short vowels
move in opposite directions, thus increasing the divergency
between the two series. Thus IE *ā* became Gc. *ō* (HG. *ū*) while
IE *ŏ* became Gc. *ă*. Nowhere else is such a contrasting treatment
to be found. In Indo-Iranian, both *ē*, *ō* and *ĕ*, *ŏ* are lowered to
ā, *ă*. In the Romance Languages the deciding factor is not quantity
but position in closed or open syllable. Slavic at first glance seems
to offer a partial analogy since here as in Germanic (and Lituanian)
ō and *ā* on the one hand and *ŏ* and *ă* on the other fall together.
This fact is frequently considered a sort of connecting link between
Germanic and Slavic (thus Kretschmer, (*Einführung in*) *die indogermanische Sprachwissenschaft*, p. 54). But, as a matter of fact,
the apparent similarity in this respect between Germanic and
Slavic leads to opposite results. In Slavic *ō* is lowered to *ā* (Lat.
dō-num; Sl. *dā-ti*) while *ă* is raised to *ŏ* (L. *ar-āre*: Sl. *or-ati*). It can
safely be said that this vowel change was merely the first step,
or an accompanying and completing factor, in the obliteration
of the difference between long and short vowels; in Old Bulgarian
a is long while *o* is short, but in the later development this distinction disappears. — Vowel fronting or narrowing, which is such
a common process in Greek dialects, in Celtic, and in Romance
and Germanic Languages that developed on Celtic soil, is either
restricted to long vowels or at least far more general with them;
but no contrary movement toward vowel widening or relaxing,
such as we shall find in Germanic, occurs in those languages on a
significant scale.

5. LONG VOWELS. The historical facts of the development

of the Germanic long vowels are well understood and its general direction is easily established. Its graphic representation by means of the vowel triangle (see below) shows a remarkable uniformity comparable in consistency and simplicity to the Germanic consonant shift. If we arbitrarily arrange the vowels in the diagram in such a way that the direction of the current of breath follows our customary direction of writing, that is, from left to right (this is Sievers' preferred arrangement), we may state symbolically that the Germanic vowel trend follows a "clock-wise" direction:

This uniformity is too constant to be accepted as accidental, but what is its significance? Two definitions of the trend offer themselves, one physiological and one acoustic; they do not exclude but rather support and confirm one another. *Physiologically*, it appears that the articulation of Germanic long vowels moves farther and farther away from the resting position of the tongue *(Ruhelage)*. I am aware of the fact that this position is difficult to define and varies both individually and nationally. Still, we are on fairly safe ground if we say that *in pausa* the mouth is closed or nearly closed and the tongue is well forward, its point being at or near the lower teeth so that the *i*-position is approximated. Every Germanic long-vowel change means a step farther away from this basis. If we examine the series $\bar{e} > \bar{æ} > \bar{a} > \bar{o} > \bar{u}$ we find the following: the tongue is at first lowered as far as possible with corresponding widening of the angle of the jaws (IE $\bar{e}$ > Gc. $\bar{æ}$ NWGc. $\bar{a}$); when the lowest point has been reached, the articulating activity is further increased by withdrawing the tongue, leading to its physically unavoidable elevation towards the soft palate ($\bar{a} > \bar{o}$). The latter aspect of the process becomes still more evident in the historical continuation of this change in a part of the Germanic languages: Lat. *fráter*, Goth. *bróþar*, OHG *bruoder*, NHG *Bruder*. The facts as such are incontestable; the Germanic consonant shift seems to represent an analogous increase of articulatory activity.

However, this plain statement of actual physiological facts does not *explain* the Germanic vowel shift but merely *describes* it. In the case of consonants, the physical contact (tongue-roof or lip-lip) produces a distinct muscular feeling which is capable of increase or decrease according to the degree of expiratory pressure or muscular tension. The articulation of vowels is not accompanied by any muscular feeling of similar distinctness and we are hardly justified in attributing the change, say, from $\bar{a}$ to $\bar{o}$, merely to a tendency towards greater articulating energy, although in point of fact the tongue *is* withdrawn, the angle of the jaws *is* widened and incidentally the lips *are* more or less rounded.

A partial explanation of the phenomenon is offered by Sievers, *Grundzüge der Phonetik*[5], p. 279: »Kurze und lange Vokale schlagen bekanntlich bei derartigen Verschiebungen häufig entgegengesetzte Wege ein. . . . Hiefür liegt der Grund wohl in dem auch sonst vielfach zur Anwendung kommenden Gesetz, daß die Artikulationen eines Lautes um so energischer und sicherer vollzogen werden, je stärker derselbe zum Bewußtsein kommt, d. h. je größer seine Stärke und Dauer ist. Dies erklärt beim langen Vokal sowohl eine Steigerung in der spezifischen Zungenartikulation (nach Stellung und Spannung) als der Rundung, falls solche vorhanden ist. Beim kurzen Vokal dagegen, der nur einen momentanen Zungenschlag erfordert, wird leicht das eigentliche Maß der Entfernung von der Ruhelage wie der Spannung nicht erreicht, d. h. es wird eine Wandlung von Vokalen mit stärkerer spezifischer Artikulation zu Lauten von mehr neutraler Artikulation angebahnt, sowohl was Zungen- und Lippenstellung als was Spannung betrifft.« This is doubtless correct as far as it goes, but it does not explain the fact that Germanic vowels follow this tendency with such unalterable consistency while other languages, as has been pointed out above (and numerous instances could be added) carry it out only casually or even proceed in the opposite direction.

An explanation may be found in the same principle that has actuated so many other changes in the Germanic languages, namely, the striving for contrasts, (cp. author, "*Inflectional Contrasts in Germanic, JEGPh. XX, 468 ff.*) Sievers' definition of the underlying cause is abstractly true, but the effect followed only where the contrast between long and short vowels, as subsequent linguistic history shows, was sharply outlined in speech consciousness, that is, principally in the Germanic languages. Variation in the degree of speech consciousness had been a chief starting point for contrasts in quantity; it led gradually to an increase of muscle tension and secondarily to such progressive changes in the position of the tongue as have been described.

But incidentally an *acoustic* aspect of the problem is suggested by the fact that each step of the long-vowel shift implies a lowering of the vowel pitch. While personally inclined to interpret this consistent lowering of the pitch of long vowels as merely an incidental physical effect of the progressive variation of the resonance chambers, I must admit that it is by no means impossible to consider it the primary cause. It might be argued that the greater carrying power of low-pitch vowels led to changes of articulation in that direction in the case of long and therefore relatively emphatic vowels, while short vowels followed the opposite trend. But I am skeptical as to this interpretation.

6. THE SHORT VOWELS are less clearly understood as far as the historical facts are concerned. So much is certain: ŏ (and ə in syllables with the Germanic accent) became ă; ŭ became ŏ, especially in West-Germanic and Norse, under certain conditions; ĭ became ĕ under more or less analogous conditions, and ĕ became ĭ under the opposite conditions. The exact relation between Gc. ŏ and ŭ must be considered a moot question but there is no clear evidence of any Germanic change from ŏ to ŭ. — A conditional change of ă to ĕ takes place in historical times, too late to appear in (literary) Gothic. For this, see section 7.

Diagram B on page 76 schematizes the trend of these changes, broken lines indicating conditional changes. It is obvious that the direction of this contrary-clock-wise development is just the opposite of the process observed with long vowels, so the explanation should be simple since we would merely have to assume muscular relaxation for the short vowels as against muscular tension for the long vowels. But we are somewhat hampered by the uncertainty of the historical facts. Since the problem has been restated so admirably by Collitz (cp. § 1) I may restrict myself to the briefest remarks. These three points are in doubt:

1. Did Gc. ŏ and ĕ change to ŭ and ĭ in Primitive Germanic everywhere except before *h* and *r* (and in West Germanic before *i* and *u* in the following syllable)?

2. Did IE *ŭ* and *ĭ* change to *ŏ* and *ĕ* under the same conditions in which Gc. *ŏ* and *ĕ* were preserved, namely, before *h* and *r* and in West-Germanic before *a* in the following syllable?

3. Was the Germanic vowel that developed before IE *m̥*, *n̥*, *l̥*, *r̥*, perhaps *ŏ* rather than *ŭ*, as Loewe assumes, and did this *ŏ* change to *ŭ* under the same conditions as those in which IE *ŭ* was preserved?

If these questions are answered in the affirmative, Diagram B is wrong and we must assume this development instead:

At first, IE *ŭ* is lowered to Prim. Gc. *ŏ* just as IE *ŏ* had been lowered to *ă*. Later, the two mid-vowels (*ĕ* and *ŏ*) are raised to high-vowels unless prevented by *h* or *r* (Collitz); still later, these two high-vowels, *ŭ* and *ĭ* (IE as well as Gc.), are lowered under the influence of a following low-vowel, while the mid-vowels are raised before high-vowels. In that case we should have to assume alternating stages of different phonetic tendencies in Germanic. But in view of its great uniformity in other respects, e. g. in the development of the long vowels, such an assumption of contradictory drifts could only be justified by definite historical evidence. But the facts in the questions formulated above are ambiguous and can be used equally well for the affirmative as for the negative.

Therefore clearness must be sought elsewhere than through historically accessible material, and I believe that we have here a striking instance of the methodical value of the concept of phonetic tendency, in the sense of the assertion of Vendryes (*Mél. ling.*, p. 116): "Une loi phonétique ne peut donc être reconnue valable que si est d'accord avec les principes qui régissent le système articulatoire de la langue au moment où elle agit ... La notion de tendance phonétique est plus exacte theorétiquement, et pratiquement plus féconde que celle de loi phonétique. Elle seule permet de déterminer avec précision la cause des changements phonétiques et d'interpreter scientifiquement ceux mêmes qui paraissent le plus rebelles à toute discipline scientifique."

Perhaps the following is in keeping with the facts: Apparently (and for this Russell's experiments have given new evidence) the articulating spheres of *i* and *e* are not only contiguous but even overlap, so that *e* is not infrequently pronounced with a higher tongue elevation than *i*. Germanic *e* and *i* virtually constitute one phonetic concept (one phoneme). Its articulation was determined by various factors. When unaccented it inclined towards the resting position, and *i* resulted. In accented (non-nasal) syllables its development depended on the vowel of the following syllable. If that was low (Gc. *a, æ*) the mid-vowel variety of the phoneme prevailed regardless of its origin from IE *i* or *e*. Thus IE **ni-zdom, *wiros* became Gc. **nesta-, *wera-*, and *e* was preserved in the present stems of the fourth and fifth classes of strong verbs *(neman, etan)*. Under all other circumstances *i* resulted: It remained, for instance, in the preterite plural of the first class, and it resulted in the 2nd and 3rd sing. pres. of the fourth and fifth classes: OHG *zigum, nimit, gibit*. Certain details of this general trend require comment. First of all, the negative effect of a low-vowel in the following syllable did not overcome the underlying trend towards *i* when the latter was supported by association with other grammatical forms, therefore the "*a*-Umlaut" did take place in isolated words like **nesta-, *wera-*, but the high-vowel variety of the phoneme was protected by analogy with the other verb forms in the past participles of the first class of strong verbs: *gizigan, gistigan*.

The effect of *u* in the following syllable is not easy to judge. I am at present inclined to believe that in this respect Old High German presents the original Germanic condition, insofar as there the *e-i* phoneme yields *i* if followed by *u (gibu, nimu)*. Gothic does not help us in that respect, since it gives the preference to *i* regardless of the following vowel, and conditions in Norse and Old English appear to be secondary.

Thus the interchange between *ĕ* and *ĭ* in Germanic, aside from Gothic, is conditional in the sense that it really rests on a spontaneous trend just as much as the change of *ŏ* to *ă*, but it is either supported or counteracted by association with the vowel of the following syllable. I dare not decide whether this association is chiefly psychological or chiefly physiological, nor has this old controversy any bearing on the general problem. The change of *ŭ* to *ŏ* is analogous in character, but it is simpler insofar as there is no corresponding change of *ŏ* to *ŭ*. We can say: *ŭ* follows the general trend of short vowels, that is, the tongue elevation is lowered (the muscles of the tongue are relaxed) so that *ŏ* results, but this change, too, is conditional. It takes place only under conditions that favor it, namely, under the associative influence of a following low-vowel: OHG *gibotan*.

7. THE ORIGIN OF MUTATION. The conditional changes
ŭ > ŏ and ĕ > ĭ followed the general Germanic trend and belong
to the Primitive Germanic period, although in Gothic the inter-
ference of new phonetic laws has largely obscured them. They
implied the establishment of a new linguistic device of great
importance, namely, the influence of inflectional vowels on the
quality of stem vowels. At first it functioned only as a contributing
factor that either favored or hampered a phonetic tendency of
somewhat unstable character, but it affected the inflection,
especially of the verb, so strongly that it could hardly remain in
this tentative condition. It was bound to disappear or to spread.
Gothic, with its strong leveling tendency, discarded it by stand-
ardizing ŭ and ĭ. In West Germanic and Norse, however, the new
device became one of the most important morphological factors.

First of all, probably in Primitive Germanic times, although
not apparent in Gothic, the variation between ŭ (both IE ŭ and
Gc. ŭ from ḷ, ṛ, ṃ, ṇ,) and ŏ, and between ĕ (IE ĕ) and ĭ, spread to
IE ĭ. That was natural, although against the basic phonetic trend,
which, however, exerted a restricting influence, as stated above.

The leveling tendency of Wulfila's Gothic did not accept this
change as a distinguishing element in its inflection; but it spread
widely in the other Germanic Dialects. It was first transferred
to Germanic ă, affecting it in the direction of the basic trend as
diagram B indicates. Due to the great number of nouns with
the stem vowel ă, this change became a frequent plural characteristic and brought about corresponding changes of other stem
vowels that had no longer any connection with the original
direction of the Germanic Vowel Shift. It is not impossible that
in Old English and Norse the mingling with speakers of Celtic
and Finnic languages may have favored the adoption and spread
of the new device since the Celtic "consonant colors" and the
Ugro-Finnic "vowel harmony" in their results resemble vowel
mutation, although their phonetic basis is different. But the
origin of mutation is doubtless to be sought in the Germanic
Vowel Shift.

8. LATER DEVELOPMENTS do not belong to the scope of
this paper, which is limited to general Germanic conditions,
nor was the influence of consonants taken into consideration in
the discussion of the Vowel Shift. I believe that in strictly Germanic vowel development it represents only a negative element.

Nasal combinations prevent the change of $\breve{u}$ to $\breve{o}$ under the influence of a following $\breve{a}$, but require $\breve{\imath}$ instead of e regardless of the following vowel. This means that a nasal vowel is not subject to the influence of the following vowel, the nasal combination forming a more effective syllable division than other consonants or consonant groups. Moreover, nasalization, perhaps on account of the lower pitch of nasal vowels, tends to preserve the low pitch of $\breve{u}$. — Influences exerted by h, r, and other consonants are not Primitive Germanic but independent phenomena in the several Germanic languages which have nothing to do with the vowel drift.

SALIC *LITUS*

BY LEONARD BLOOMFIELD
UNIVERSITY OF CHICAGO.

1. The term *litus, lidus, letus, ledus, laetus* in the Salic Law [1] designates a person of the semi-servile class intermediate between serf and free Frank: *adscriptus glebae, Höriger*. In the ill-preserved Frankish glosses of the Law our word appears as *letu, lexm̄, ledo, lito* (4 MSS), *leciim, l&', l&us* (2 MSS) [2]. From the Salic Law *litus* was taken into the other laws and into documentary use.

Grimm, l. c., recognized *litus* as the latinized form of a Frankish word, which he set up as **lita-*; this he connected, by vowel-variation, with OHG *laz* and cognates, of the same meaning; this, in turn, with the adjective **lata-* "slack, lazy" (Go *lata* "oknēre" etc.), and thus with **lētō* "I let" (Go *lētan*, etc.). Aside from the romantic view of the meaning, — the master is keen, the servant slack, — we know today that an alternant with PGic *i* (PIE *e*) has no place in the alternation of PGic *ē : ō : a*.

Von Kralik, *Neues Archiv der Gesellschaft für ältere deutsche Geschichte* 38 (1913), 430 developed a new etymology: he supposes that the *i, e* of the Merovingian scribes represents a PGic *ē*, early Frankish [e:] or [ɛ:], and connects our word with fourth-century Latin *laetus* "semi-servile Germanic colonist on Gallic soil", and with OHG *lāz* "litus" and cognates (whose vowel is now known to be long); all three represent a PGic **lēta-* in the sense of a past participle of the verb **lētō* "I let": **lēta-* is "con-

---

[1] Ed. Hessels, *Lex Salica* (1880), with index; cf. Schramm, *Sprachliches zur Lex Salica (Marburger Beiträge zur romanischen Philologie*, 3 [1911]), with stemma of MSS on p. 2. On the meaning of our term, see Grimm, *Deutsche Rechtsaltertümer*, I⁴ (1899), 424 (305); Schröder-Künszberg, *Deutsche Rechtsgeschichte*⁶ (1922), 239 with references.

[2] See Grimm in Merkel's ed. (1850), xxx. Hessels' Index (not his text) gives one of the two last-named occurrences as *letur*.

quered person who has been *left* on his land or *allowed* to settle on ours". That a type **lēta-* had the meaning of a past participle is proved by the parallel formation Go *fralēts* "apeleutheros", OHG *frīlāz* "libertus", etc.

This led Meyer-Lübke, *Romanisches etymologisches Wörterbuch* [2] *(Sammlung romanischer Elementar- und Handbücher*, III, 3 [1924]), no. 4994, to derive OFr *liege* "bound by feudal tie" from a type PGic **lētika-* "vassal" [3]. This **lētika-* Gamillschegg, *Etymologisches Wörterbuch der französischen Sprache* (1926 ff.), s. v. *lige*, explicitly connects with our *litus, letus*, which he identifies, ignoring the difference of meaning, with the words for "libertus", citing the Go word as *"lēt"*. The forms *litus* and OFr *lige* he explains, regardless of geography, as due to "**līt*", a late Go variant of *"lēt"*.

We thus obtain a whole series of words in the three related meanings "libertus", "inquilinus", and "adscriptus glebae" — a confusion of forms and meanings which needs ordering.

2. The Gic type **-lēta-* as second member in words for "libertus" occurs in Go *fralēts* (1 Cor 7, 22) and possibly in the variant reading *fralatz* in *Lex Baiwariorum* (ed. Schwind, *MGH Legum* 4⁰ 1, 5, 2 [1926]), 338. Another compound appears in the variants, *friilaz*, etc., l. c., fem. *frilaza*, 358, and in glosses, *libertus: frilaz*, etc., Steinmeyer-Sievers, *Die althochdeutschen Glossen* I, 760, 41; II, 122, 16; 611, 28; III, 426, 41; 645, 26. In OE the word is an *n*-stem: *frioleta, freolæta*, etc., Sweet, *Oldest English Texts (EETS* 83), 75; 105; 115; Wright-Wülcker, *Anglo-Saxon and Old English Vocabularies* I, 111, 22; Wright, *A Second Volume of Vocabularies* (1873), 51. Another compound is OHG *liberti: hantlazza*, Steinmeyer-Sievers II, 139, 37.

This queer formation is paralleled, as von Kralik 431 points out, by OHG *superstitem: aftarlaz*, St-S I, 318, 3. It may be a personalization of the neuter action noun in Go *aflēt, fralēt* "aphesis", in the manner of NHG *Bedienung*, Go *hliftus* "thief", OB *sluga* "servant"; cf. Brugmann, *Grundriß* [2] II, 1 (1906), 599; 610 and Brugmann-Delbrück, *Grundriß* [1] III (1893), 110. As Grimm remarks, it would not do to confuse "libertus" with "litus"; accordingly, von Kralik sees in his **lēta-* "litus" only a parallel formation with Go *fralēts* "libertus". However, queer

---

[3] With the erroneous statement (due to misreading of von Kralik 435; repeated by Gamillschegg) that *terrae laeticae* occurs in the *Lex Baiwariorum*.

as is a second member *-lēta(n)- in passive meaning, an uncompounded *lēta- would be queerer still. Except for a possible confusion in German (cf. below, §3), the above words for "libertus" are in all likelihood entirely distinct from the terms litus and lāz.

3. Latin laetus in the second half of the fourth century designates semi-servile Germanic (Batavian, Frankish, Suebian, Alemannic) colonists in Gaul; laetus in Gaul is what inquilinus, at this time, is in the other provinces [4].

Kluge, Urgermanisch (Paul, Grundriß der germanischen Philologie[3], 2 [1913]), 33 takes laetus to represent a Gic word with PGic ē; the ae would represent, then, a stage intermediate between the ē reflected in Suebi (Caesar), Segimerus (Tacitus) and the historical German ā. Bremer, PBB 11 (1886), 1 has, indeed, shown that PGic ē long remained in Frankish: names in -merus do not appear with a before 500 A. D. A Frankish [ɛ:] is reflected in OFr biere, Meyer-Lübke no. 1038; cf. von Kralik 434. This interpretation leads, of course, to the etymology worked out by von Kralik. However, it is nothing more than a possibility. Latin ae for the early Frankish form of PGic ē occurs nowhere; Ammianus, who has laetus (ed. Clark, 1910) 16, 11, 4; 20, 8, 13; 21, 13, 16, writes Teutomeres 15, 3, 10. Pliny's[5] glaesum "amber" (for which Tacitus has glesum) leaves us at a loss: has it PGic ē (Müllenhoff, ZfdA 23 [1879], 23; Bezzenberger, KZ 44 [1911], 291) or ai (Osthoff, MU 4 [1881], 145) or a (Bremer, PBB 11 [1886], 16)? A fourth-century Roman may have represented the quality of Gic short e by his ae; cf. Zosimus' spelling with Gk short e. The consonant may have been Gic þ; cf. Kluge, l. c., 31. To name extreme possibilities, laetus may represent a Gic *lēta- or a Gic *leþu-.

4. The type *lēta- is in the WGic vernaculars the equivalent of litus. In OE it occurs but once, in the oldest laws, as læt, and is glossed þeowa (Liebermann, Die Gesetze der Angelsachsen, I

---

[4] For occurrences and meaning see Schönfeld in Pauly-Wissowa, Realenzykl.[2], s. v.; of the older discussions Böcking, Notita dignitatum II (1853), 1044 is the fullest. One notes especially Theodosiani libri xvi (edd. Mommsen et Meyer, 1905) 13, 11, 10 terrae laeticae, and Zosimus (ed. Mendelssohn, 1887) 2, 54, 1 eis Letoús, éthnos Galatikón. — Du Cange's mention, s. v. leti, of Vita S. Gildae Sapientis relates only to the name Letavia; cf. the text (ed. Mommsen, MGH Auct. Antiqu. 13 [1898]) 96, 12. — Hardly our word is Jordanes' (ed. Mommsen, MGH Auct. Antiqu. 5, 1 [1882]) 108, 3 liticiani (later MSS litigiani, litiani) among a list of Gic tribal names; cf. below, § 8.

[5] Brüch, Der Einfluß der germanischen Sprachen auf das Vulgärlatein (Sammlung romanischer Elementar- und Handbücher V, 1 [1913]) 16 is in error when he attributes the word to Caesar.

[1903], 4, 26) [6]. In OFris we have the plurals *letar, lethar* (on the
th see van Helten, *Altostfriesische Grammatik* [1890], 90), *letan*
and the compounds *let(h)ma, letslachta, letslachte, letslaga* (Richthofen, s. vv.). Van Helten, *Verhandelingen der K. Akademie van
Wetenschappen Amsterdam, afd. Letterkunde*, n. r. 9 (1907), 104,
points out that West Frisian spellings with *ee* assure a long vowel.
The MLG (Schiller-Lübben, *Mittelniederdeutsches Wörterbuch*, s. v.
lat [7]) and MDu forms (Verwijs en Verdam, *Middelnederlandsch
woordenboek*, s. vv. *laet* and *late*; a wealth of examples) do not
show the vowel quantity. The later forms here, as in HG, show
n-inflection. In OHG we have, as a variant of a gloss cited § 2
above, *libertini*: *laza* (St-S III, 645, 26); this must be due to a
confusion of the two words. But a gloss on the *Lex Ribuaria,
litus*: *laz* (St-S II, 354, 30) is unmistakable. In Latin documents
we have Hucbald (MGH *Scriptores* 2 [1829]) 361, 50 *sunt qui
lassi dicuntur*; Nithard (ibid.) 668, 46 *qui lazzi illorum lingua
dicuntur;* 669, 3 *frilingis lazzibusque;* 377, 45 (spurious but old)
multis lazzis; Constitutiones et acta publica (ed. Weiland, *MGH
Legum* 4° 4, 1 [1893]) 88, 14 (1035 A. D.) *illis qui dicuntur lazi*
(with variants *laz, lass, lasz); Diplomata regum* 4 (ed. Bresslau,
MGH [1909]), 296, 16 (1035 A. D.) *illis qui dicuntur laszi*. Our
word has little life in HG; for the later usage see Lexer, *Mittel-
hochdeutsches Wörterbuch* s. v. *lazze;* Haltaus, *Glossarium Ger-
manicum* (1758) 1195; Grimm, *Deutsches Wörterbuch* 6, 212. The
modern *Lasse* in learned works is artificial. It survives in opprobrious terms; so probably *prostituta: huorra lazza*, St-S I, 344, 41.
In modern dialects it is subject to popular etymology (*Latz*
"latchet, bib") which even the dictionary-makers seem to accept.
Alsatian (Martin-Lienhardt, *Wörterbuch der elsässischen Mundarten* 1 [1899], 633; Stoeber, *Die deutschen Mundarten* 3 [1856],
483 recognized the origin) *ful, dumm wi e Latz; Hanslatz* (1575
A. D.), etc.; Swabian (Fischer, *Schwäbisches Wörterbuch* 4 [1914],
1019) in field names *Latz, Burenlatz, Lätzen*, as an opprobrious
term, and in the name of the Shrovetide and Pentecostal clown
or dummy, *Latzmann* (cf. Sartori, *Sitte und Brauch* [*Handbücher
zur Volkskunde*, 7—8], 3 [1914], 231; Birlinger, *Volkstümliches*

---

[6] The passage in Palgrave, *Rise and Progress* II (1832), ccxxxiv (Liebermann
I, 400) cited by Richthofen, *Altfriesisches Wörterbuch* (1840), s. v. *let*, contains
a different word; cf. Liebermann III (1916), 237 and here, below, § 6.
[7] Von Kralik 432 too readily accepts the popular etymology *(Sachsenspiegel)*
there cited.

aus Schwaben, 2 [1862], 114; references due to Archer Taylor);
in the passages from older literature note especially the far-
fetched popular etymology from the Zimmer Chronicle in explanation of Latzwein "low grade of wine"; Swiss (Staub-Tobler,
Schweizerisches Idiotikon, 3 [1895], 1546) Lāz "Dirne", Latz
"awkward fellow"; Lätsch, Latsch "clumsy, stupid person" (col.
1529) may be a contamination of our word. The [ts] of the modern
dialects probably does not point to old tt, but rather takes rank
among the examples of [ts] from old final t; cf. Swiss šuts "Schuß"
guts "Guß" (Streiff, Die Laute der Glarner Mundarten [Beiträge
zur schweizerdeutschen Grammatik, ed. Bachmann, 8; 1915], 78;
see Behaghel, Geschichte der deutschen Sprache [5] [Paul, Grundriß, 3;
1928], 420, with references).

5. Grimm, we have seen (§ 1), took Salic litus and variants
to represent a Frankish *lita-; von Kralik sets up Frankish
*lēta-. Van Helten, PBB 25 (1900), 425 explains the spelling
lidus (ledus) as due to Romance weakening of intervocalic t,
citing a few graphs of Latin words with d for t. Graff, Althoch-
deutscher Sprachschatz 2 (1836), 191 seems to be alone in suggesting
a prototype with OHG d (i. e., PGic þ). Actually, however, the
MSS of Lex Salica do not often write d for Latin t; the few instances are suspiciously concentrated on a few words. The only
word comparable in this respect with litus, is fritus "king's
peace", from Gic *friþu-. In the list below, the Latin words
with d for t occur once each, unless otherwise stated. The vowel
variations of litus and fritus are here ignored.

MS	litus	lidus	fritus	fridus	Latin words with d for t
1	9	0	9	1	dode, poledrum
2	9	0	6	2	strada
3	6	2	1	8	—
4	3	2	0	6	deladore, emancada, mederit, repedit 2, sudem, uinidore
5	7	0	6	2	tribudarium
6	8	1	6	3	dido ("digito") 4, mederit, legadario
7	6	1	0	5	tribudarium
8	6	0	0	6	poledrum
9	5	0	0	6	tribudario, medere
B	5	0	0	6	toscada ("toxicata")
F	4	0	0	6	—
G	4	0	0	6	medere
H	4	0	0	5	poledrum
Leiden	2	6	2	8	sudem 2, polledrum 2, capridum
Herold	2[8]	7	0	8	sudenn ("sutem"), puledrum 2
Emendati	(1)	7—8	0	7—8	sudem 2, puledrum 2

[8] In appendices.

Of inverse writings I find only: MS 2 *retat* (reddat), MS 7 *petica*. Special factors are involved in MSS 1, 2, 6, 9 *quatru-*, *quatro-;* MS 5 and Herold *spato, spathum, espatauerit;* MSS 1, 2, 3, 4, 6, B, F, G, H, Emm *cinitum*, etc. (cinaedum?). Confusion in final position is another matter: MS 2 *aliquit;* MSS 3 (twice), 4 (twice), 7 *aput;* and MS 4 *torquid;* MSS 8 (twice), Leiden *capud*.

The spelling *letus* appears also in the glosses of the lost MSS d'Este (Hessels, col. xxii) and Thou (Merkel's ed., xcvii).

The divergence between *liius* and *fritus* may be due to the fact that the latter was in living use in German as *fridu*, in Romance (names) as **fredu-*, while the former was known only from law writings; even our MSS 1 and 2 once mistake the word and write *lex*. The Carolingian reform (Herold, Emendati) normalizes to *lidus, fredus;* the semi-reformed Leiden matches its two archaic *litus* with two similar *fretus*.

The later tradition of *litus* (see Du Cange, s. v.) derives from the Salic Law. In the laws *d*-spellings prevail, with *t* in MSS that otherwise also show Merovingian irregularities. Forms with *t* occur in the Saxon laws (ed. Richthofen, *MGH Legum* f⁰ 5 [1889]), beside *frido, fredo; Lex Ribuaria* (ed. Sohm, ibid.), with *d*-variants and misunderstandings *libertum, licitum*, beside *fretus, fredus;* Roman Law of the Burgundians (ed. Bluhme, *MGH Legum* f⁰ 3 [1863]), with one misunderstanding, *et*, beside *Fredegisclus, Fredemundus; Lex Frisionum* (ed. Richthofen, ibid. and Patetta, *Mem. r. Accad. d. Sc. di Torino*, ser. 2, t. 43 [1893]), beside *freda;* Alemannic Laws (ed. Lehmann, *MGH Legum* 4⁰ 5, 1 [1888]) *Pactus*, fragment 2 *litus*, fragment 5 *lita* in one MS, where the rest have *lida* and miswritings (French?) *lisa, lesa*, beside *fridus, fredus*, except once (8th century MS) *freto*. Both *lidus* and *fredus* have *d* in *Lex Francorum Chamavorum* (ed. Sohm, *MHG Legum* f⁰ 5) and *Leges Langobardorum* (edd. Bluhme et Boretius, *MGH Legum* f⁰ 4[1868]). The *Formulae* (ed. Zeumer *MGH Legum* 4⁰ 5 [1886]) have the derivative *letimonium, litimunium*, with *lidemonio* in one MS. The archaic *freta* keeps up: *Lex Baiwariorum* (ed. Schwind, *MGH Legum* 4⁰ 1, 5, 2 [1926]) in the archaic MSS; *Lex Romana Raetica Curiensis* (ed. Zeumer, *MGH Legum* f⁰ 5 [1889]).

In the charters, on the other hand, *litus* is normal; so *Diplomata*

Karolingia (ed. Mühlbacher, MGH [1906][9]) 113; 119; *Diplomata Regum* (*MGH*, 1 and 2 ed. Sickel [1884. 1893]; 3 and 4 ed. Bresslau [1903. 1909]) passim. Spellings with *d* are rare: *Dipl. Kar.* 177 *lidos*; *Dipl. Reg.* 1, 401, 39; 529, 25; 2, 38, 41. A late form is *liddo* with *n*-inflection, in the spurious documents *Dipl. Kar.* 401; *Dipl. Reg.* 1, 294, 1; it is genuine after the year 1000: *Dipl. Reg.* 3, 626, 1; 4, 168, 31 [10]. Intermediate forms are *litones*, *littones*, *Dipl. Reg.* 3, 10, 24; 4, 218, 17. The *n*-inflection and probably the double writing of the consonant are due to vernacular HG *lāzze*. These documents consistently write *freda*.

Litus and its variants represent a purely graphic learned tradition derived from the Salic Law. The spellings of the Salic Law are inconclusive; what they tell is in favor of *þ* as the consonant of the underlying Frankish word; unfortunately they give us no counter-example of a word with Frankish *t*.

We have seen that von Kralik takes the vowel of *litus* to represent Gic *ē*; he blames the Merovingian scribes for the spellings with *i*. Certainly Brüch, *ZsfrP* 38 (1917), 701 errs when he says that *litus* is "so gut wie immer mit *i* geschrieben"; yet the orthography of the Salic Law does not warrant von Kralik's conclusion. In stressed syllables of Latin words fluctuation of *i* and *e* is almost entirely confined to certain forms where special factors come into play: a type *ficit* of perfects with suffix zero (namely, *fecit, fregit, venit, *presit* and compounds), with *i* written for *ē*; and a type *reteneat* of compounds with *e* written for *i* on the model of the simple word (namely, *exteterit, perdederit, vendederint, reteneat*). Outside of this, *i* for Latin *ē* occurs only in the few cases listed below, and *e* for Latin *ī* only once (MS 2 *deuidant*), for Latin *i* twice (MSS 2 and 9 *fedem*)[11]. The table below ignores the fluctuation of *t* and *d*.

Note especially that MS 2, which does fairly often (34 times in all) write *i* for Latin *ē*, has only one *litus* and no *fritus*.

The d'Este and Thou glosses had *letus*.

---

[9] I owe the references in this volume to C. A. Williams of the University of Illinois.

[10] At *Dipl. Reg.* 1, 108, 18 it is an erroneous emendation of Sickel's.

[11] Special cases are (omnes) *cinitum, cinidum*, etc. (cinaedum?); MS 7 *sipem*; the various spellings, *inium*, etc., in all the MSS, for *aeneum* "kettle". I do not count the river-name *Ligerim, Ligere* "Loire" or "Lys, Leye" (see Hessels 633), written variously with *i* and *e*. MS 1 has *praeserit* once, MS 6 thrice, beside once *praesit*.

MS	litus	letus	laetus	fritus	fretus	ficit	reteneat	Latin words with i for ē.
1	2	7	1	4	6	4	1	tricinus, nonaginus, plibium, uicissimus
2	1	6	2	0	8	15	3	accidant, succidant, dibilem, tricinus, quinginus, iudicitur, manire, minsis, pleuium, secricius, suspinsus, uiro, dibeo 7
3	1	7	0	0	9	3	1	—
4	5	0	0	3	3	0	0	plebium
5	7	0	0	0	8	3	1	plebium
6	9	0	0	0	9	0	0	plebium, requiritur
7	7	0	0	3	2	10	1	dibilem, minsis, plebium, ritem
8	6	0	0	0	6	6	1	plebium
9	0	5	0	0	6	3	4	dibilium (pointing to dibilis?)
B	4	1	0	0	6	2	0	—
F	4	0	0	0	6	1	0	—
G	3	0	1	0	6	2	1	dibilem
H	3	0	1	0	5	2	0	dibilem
Leiden	7	1	0	0	10	1	1	—
Herold	9	0	0	2	6	3	2	requiritur
Emendati	8—9 0	0	0	7—8	1	2	—

The difference between the vowel writings of *litus* and *fridus* may, again, be due to the living character of the latter word. The occasional *laetus* is doubtless due to the familiar if irrelevant word-picture of *laetus* "glad".

In the later laws the norm is *lidus* with *i*, *fredus* with *e*. MSS of the older type for *Lex Alamannorum* show variants with the reverse vowels: *letus, frido*. The charters consistently write *litus*; exceptions are *letos Dipl. Reg.* 1, 413, 33; 2, 127, 36; 3, 133, 30; 4, 18, 34; *laetos* 1, 66, 34. For **friþu-* they write *freda*.

In Gic names the Merovingian scribes write **-mēra-* as *-merus*, later as *-marus*, never with *i*; cf. Bremer, l. c.

In so far as the spellings of *litus* tell us anything, they suggest a **liþu-* parallel with **friþu-*. In both words the fluctuation between *i* and *e* may date back to the Gic prototype and there be due to the familiar alternation (OHG *fihu, fehu; sciff, sceff*); in **friþu-* the living usage of Romance names later favored the *e*.

6. A Gic **liþu-*, **leþu-*, though swamped by **lēta-*, has left some traces. ON *liðar* ("ðat eru fylgðrmenn") is set up as an *n*-stem (Cleasby-Vigfusson, Fritzner) and may well represent a type PGic **galidjan-* "one who travels along" [12]; yet a technical

---

[12] The compounds *sumar-liði, vetr-liði* are irrelevant.

term *liþu- may have been merged with it and may also have contributed to the formation of lið n. "retinue" (*galidja-). ME lith is doubtless from the Norse (NED), though the phrase land and lith (reinterpreted in ne lathes ne landes, Liebermann I, 400; cf. above, footnote 6) is reminiscent of OFris umbe lond ne umbe lethar. In German we have the standing expression der tiefal unde sine lide (Notker, ed. Piper [1883], 2, 116, 10; 619,8), des tiefels lide (occurrence, MSD³ [1892] 1, 166; 2, 259; Lexer, Mhd. Wb. 1, 1938); strangely, of Christ's followers, Notker 2, 187, 31 [13]. This is scarcely *liþu- "limb", though it may have been so reinterpreted; in the same way E limb of Satan may be a reformation of an older *lith of Satan. Finally, MHG lidelōn, lidlōn (Benecke-Müller-Zarncke, Mhd. Wb. 1, 1042; Lexer 1, 1940 and Nachträge, 301; Schmeller, Bayer. Wb.² 1 [1872], 1442), taken by Heyne (Grimm, D. Wb., s. v. Liedlohn) as a derivative of OHG līdan "travel", is specifically payment to the humbler sort of servants: Liedlohn soll man vor allen Schulden zahlen; Verdienter Liedlohn schreit zu Gott im Himmel (Bächtold-Stäubli, Handwörterbuch des deutschen Aberglaubens [1929], s. v. Dienstbote).

The adjective type *liþuga-, *leþaga-, MHG lidec, ledec, NHG ledig is not exactly synonymous with frei (cf. especially, the modern use of lediglich); as Heyne, l. c. s. v. points out, it reflects a term of social organization whose import is lost to us. The meaning "free" appears also in the sister tongues, e. g. ON: lauss ok liðugr, G los und ledig. It survived best in HG because it was there taken into elevated language (MHG poetry) as a synonym of vrī.

7. OFr lige, liege, borrowed in Prov litge, It ligio, E liege, latinized to ligius, and hellenized to lizios (Du Cange, s. v. ligius), occurs typically in ome liges "vassal" (Godefroy, s. v.) and derivatives. However, we have some divergent uses: lige seigneur "liege lord"; le roy vertueux, franc et liege; property is given en lige; quitte et lige "free"; esligier, eslegier "to free" [14].

<hr>

[13] Graff's reference, Ahd. Sprachschatz 2, 191, to litten in the Vienna Genesis, though confirmed by Massmann, Deutsche Gedichte (BNL I, 3 [1837]) 2, 305, verse 5673, is to be canceled: the MS has luten, Dollmayr, Die Sprache der Wiener Genesis (QF 94 [1903]), 2, for liuten "people"; cf. p. 72, line 2 and Hoffmann, Fundgruben 2 (1837), 79, 32. — The Vienna Notker has lidir at 3, 102,6.

[14] To the occurrences in Godefroy T. A. Jenkins kindly adds the following: Guernes, Vie St. Thomas 1854. 1856 huem liges; 2517 lige seigneur; Ambroise,

The distribution of *i* and *ie* does not agree with that in any native type (Brüch, *ZsfrP* 38 [1907], 701) [15].

The older etymologies are given by Du Cange, s. v. *ligius*. Diez, *Wörterbuch*[5] (1887) decides that G *ledig* is the source. This has been widely accepted (Nyrop, *Grammaire historique* 1[1889], 9; Mackel, *Französische Studien* 6 [1887], 82; Körting, *Lateinisch-romanisches Wörterbuch*[3] [1907], no. 5506; and others) but questioned on account of the discrepancy of meaning. Similarly G. Paris, *Romania* 12 (1883), 382 derived *esligier* as *ex-* plus G *ledigōn*, against Tobler, *Jahrbuch f. rom. u. engl. Lit.* 8 (1867), 342, who took it to be *ex-lītigāre*. Tobler's explanation fails to account for the *e*-varaint, *eslegier*; one suspects that the *elitigare* of medieval law (Du Cange, s. v.) is a learned re-interpretation: *Capitula* (ed. Boretius, *MGH Legum* 4°, 2, 1 [1883]) 337, 1 *res litigosa nullathenus potest dare neque vendere antequam elitigetur.* Note the spellings *Dipl. Imper.* (ed. Pertz, *MGH* 1872) 107, 20 *evindecatum atque elidicatum*; 108, 11 *evindicatas adque elidiatas*; similarly *Formulae* (ed. Zeumer, MGH), see Index, p. 753.

Baist, *ZsfrP* 28 (1904), 112 derives *lige*, following an old etymology, from Gic *leoda-* "people (collective)", *leudi-* pl. "people", which appears in medieval Latin writings as *leudis*, *leodis*; *eligier* he derives from *leudis* "wergeld". This fails to account for the Fr forms with *i*; nor does it seem that *leodis* in Latin usage ever went farther than "retainer".

Thomas (*Dict. gén.*[6] [1920], s. v.) connects *lige* with *litus (*liticu-)*, as do Meyer-Lübke and Gamillschegg, cited at the beginning of this article. But *litus, letus* is a merely graphic and learned tradition which could not lead to such phonetic development as is implied in *lige*. There is no trace of an adjective in *-icu-* or of a verb derived from *litus*. Moreover, a noble or even a freeman who entered into the feudal relation would not call himself *litus* "adscriptus glebae"; the two relations were entirely different.

In spite of Baist, l. c., *ledig* and *lige-ligius* have some uses in common. Beside *erledigen: esligier-elidigare*, we have *los und*

Guerre sainte, ligece; *Vie de Guillaume le Mareschall* 2019 *homes liges*; Chrestien, *Erec* 3868 *home lige*; *Charette* 1731 *chose lige*.

[15] However, it is perhaps not so clear-cut as Godefroy's examples lead one to suppose; thus *Aiol et Mirabel* (ed. Foerster, 1876 ff.), beside the normal Picard (Foerster, p. 495) *en liege*, verse 10 210, has also *hon liges*, verse 7590. (Reference due to T. A. Jenkins).

ledig: *quitte et lige*. Du Cange, s. v. *ledighman* and Haltaus 1214 give us, from the 13th century, such turns as these: *ligius homo, quod Teutonice dicitur ledighman*; *homines legii dicti ledigman*; *homo suus absolutus, quod vulgo ledighman nuncupatur*; *erit adjutor noster, quod ledichman dicitur in vulgari, contra quemlibet hominem in hoc mundo* (cf. *semper liberi vasalli erimus*). With *ledigez eigen, ledigez guot* (Lexer, Haltaus) cf. OFr *chose lige, sa lige mansion*. The OFr word is a loan from an antecedent of the documented MHG *ledec, lidec*; probably both the native and the Fr word changed their meanings before the time of our records; some semantic common ground is left.

8. Our records are of technical terms; we have not the spoken forms from which these terms were specialized.

There seems to have existed a PGic or early general Gic term (spread by loans at the time of the new settlements?) **leþu-*, **liþu-*, with the derived adjective **liþuga-*, **leþaga-* and verb **uz-liþugōmi*, **uz-leþagōmi*. The meaning of these words seems to have been close to that of **frija-* "free", but in some way more restricted [16].

It is barely possible that Jordanes' *liticiani* (footnote 4, above) is an early trace of the adjective, in a specialized technical use, as a synonym of *laeti*. The *laeti* of the fourth century may similarly reflect our **leþu-*, but it is ambiguous, since it may just as well reflect Gic **lēta-*.

The earliest relatively certain deposit is the *letus, litus* of the Salic Law. If Gic **leþu-*, **liþu-* was close to "free person" (in some way more restricted than **frija-*), then the technical term **liþu-*, *litus* must at the time of its specialization have stressed the advantageous phase of adscriptio glebae, perhaps in contrast with the fate of other conquered persons or groups, who were reduced to thraldom, servitudo. Whether ON *liðar* "retainers" has **liþu-* at least as a component, is uncertain. In WGic speech **liþu-* was soon crowded out by **lēta-*, an entirely different word, of unknown origin, — perhaps at first the name of some conquered tribe. Our *litus* is a "Latin" (that is, of course, an artificial, graphic) word, the prescribed equivalent, in Latin-writing, of the vernacular *lāt, lāz*. Relics of **liþu-* are OHG *lide* "followers (of Satan)" and MHG *lide-lōn* "wages".

---

[16] Ultimate connection with **liþu-* "limb" or with **līþō* "I travel" is a matter beyond our ken.

While *leþu-, *liþu- has come down to us only in a highly specialized use, the adjective *leþaga-, *liþuga- has perhaps been somewhat generalized in meaning by the time of our records. Yet in ON liðugr and even more in the WGic languages it shows traces of specialization in the legal sphere. In the language of MHG poetry, however, it became an elevated synonym of vrî; with this, its career was made. Of the servile connotation in which the underlying noun had once been specialized it shows no trace; its French loan lige, liege has on the contrary been carried into the noble sphere of the feudal relation, again with traces of older meaning.

The verb doubtless lurks behind the elidiare, elitigare "free from legal claims" of medieval law. In German it has remained close to the adjective: erledigen is merely the verb of ledig; but the French loan-word elegier, eligier does not share the specialization of liege, lige.

These words are different from *lēta-, synonym and successful rival of *leþu-, *liþu-, and from derivatives of *lētō "I let", such as Go fralēts "libertus".

DER GENITIV PLURAL AUF -ē IM GOTISCHEN

VON EDWARD H. SEHRT

GEORGE WASHINGTON UNIVERSITY

Das Gotische zeigt im Gegensatz zu allen anderen Sprachen der indogermanischen Sprachgruppe im Genitiv Plural sämtlicher Stämme beim Masculinum und Neutrum (die ō- und *ein*-Stämme natürlich ausgenommen) die eigentümliche Endung -ē: *dagē-waurdē, hairdjē-kunjē, gastē, suniwē, attanē-hairtanē, brōþrē, nasjandē, mannē*. Ja diese Endung kommt auch beim Femininum der *i*-Stämme *(qēnē)* und der weniger zahlreichen Stämme auf -*u (handiwē)*, auf -*r* (sehr wahrscheinlich, obwohl nicht belegt: **swistrē, *dauhtrē)* und der konsonantischen *(baurgē)* vor. Im großen und ganzen ist jedoch ein deutlicher Unterschied zwischen dem Plural der Maskulina-Neutra und dem der Feminina vorhanden; die letzteren haben bis auf die erwähnten Ausnahmen -ō *(gibō-fráistubnjō, laiseinō, qinōnō, manageinō)*, die ersteren -ē. Das -ē beim Femininum findet sich nur bei den Stämmen, wo das Maskulinum stark vertreten ist; also wohl Ausgleich innerhalb der betreffenden Deklinationsklassen. Bei den ō-, jō-, wō- und *ein*-Stämmen, die überhaupt keine Maskulina haben, ist nur -ō vorhanden [1]. Das Femininum der *n*-Stämme hat gleichfalls nur -ō. Wie fest im Bewußtsein sonst bestimmte Endungen für Mask.-Neut. und Fem. der a- und ō-Klassen liegen, zeigt sich auch beim Dat. Plur. *attam, hairtam—qinōm*.

Die Ansetzung einer indogermanischen Endung -ēm, die eine Ablautform [2] zu -ōm (ai. (ved.) *vŕkām, dēvā́m*, gr. *λύκων*, lat. *deum, fabrum*, inschriftl. *Romanom*, osk. *Núvlanúm*) sein soll, entbehrt jedes Haltes. Auch innerhalb des Germanischen ist, trotz der Behauptung R. Kögels, *PBB 14, 114*, daß altsächs. *kinda*,

---

[1] Vgl. auch die fem. Verbalabstrakta auf -*eins (naiteins)*.

[2] Vgl. O. Bremer, *PBB* 11, 37; dazu Streitberg, *Urgerm. Gramm.*, S. 231.

friunda, Hrodbertinga[3] u. ä. Genitive auf -*ēm* seien, keine Spur aufzudecken. Also muß mit einer spezifisch gotischen Neuerung gerechnet werden. Van Helten, *PBB 17*, 570 *ff.* vermutet daher eine qualitative Angleichung an das -*e*- der Endung -*eso* beim Gen. Sg. Diese Auffassung scheint mir unannehmbar, erstens weil das Gotische jedes kurze *ĕ* (außer vor *r, h*, und *hv*) in *ĭ* verwandelt hatte und deshalb eine qualitative Angleichung von vornherein unmöglich ist, und zweitens ist die Annahme einer Beeinflussung eines Endungsvokals durch den Vokal einer Mittelsilbe immerhin bedenklich. Unter diesen Umständen wird es wohl nicht ungerechtfertigt sein, einen neuen Versuch zu einer Erklärung zu machen[3a].

Außer beim Gen. Plur. kommt das lange -*ē* im Gotischen in den folgenden Fällen vor: beim Instr. der Pronomina *þē, hvē*; beim Dat. der Indefinita *hvammēh, hvarjammēh, ainummēhun*; bei den Adverbia *nē, hvadrē, hidrē, jaindrē, swarē, simlē, bisunjanē* (*hvēh* 'jedenfalls') und den Konjunktionen *swē, untē, þandē*. Was den Ursprung der Endung bei den Pronominibus betrifft, gehen die Meinungen auseinander. In *þē* und *hvē* sehen die meisten Forscher einen alten [nominalen?[4]] Instrumental (vgl. ved. *vĭkā*, ai. Adv. *paçcā*; daneben ther. *τῆ-δε* 'hier', lak. *πή-ποκα*)[5], was wohl das Richtige trifft[6], zumal die syntaktische Funktion sich mit der Bildung deckt. Bei *hvammē-h* herrscht noch vorläufig keine Uebereinstimmung. Paul, *PBB 2*, 239 ff., Möller *ebd.* 7, 490, Bremer, *ebd.* 11, 35 f., Kluge, *Urgermanisch* halten es für einen Ablativ; J. Schmidt, *Festgruß an Böhtlingk*, S. 3, Collitz, *BB. 17*, 13 ff. für einen Dativ; Streitberg, *Urgerm. Gramm.* S. 269, Bethge bei Dieter, *Laut- und Formenlehre*, S. 554, u. a. für einen Instrumental. Es ist sogar bei vielen überhaupt noch die Frage, ob got. *hvamma* [*daga* usw.] und *hvammē-h* auf dieselbe Urform zurückgehen. Streitberg, *Got. Elementarbuch*[5]. [6]. S. 171 bemerkt folgendes

---

[3] S. Schlüter, *Untersuchungen zur Gesch. d. altsächs. Sprache*, S. 108; Collitz, *Bezz. Beiträge* 17, 13.

[3a] In der Zeit zwischen der 1. und 2. Korrektur bin ich zufällig auf einen wichtigen Aufsatz von Brugmann (*IF* 33, 272—284) gestoßen. Seine Beweisführung deckt sich z. T. überraschend mit der meinigen, aber das Endergebnis ist verschieden, da er den Gen. Pl. auf *ē* aus einer denominativen Adjektivbildung auf -*ēi̯a*- herleitet.

[4] Streitberg, *Urgerm. Gramm.*, S. 273.

[5] Brugmann, *Kurze vergl. Gramm.*, §§ 471, 503.

[6] Vgl. Collitz, *BB. 17*, 19.

über den Dativ: »Der got. Dativ ist ein Mischkasus. Er entspricht formell dem idg. Instrumental (*a*- und maskul. *i*-Stämme), dem Lokativ (fem. *i*-; *u*- und kons. Stämme aller Genera) und dem Dativ (*ō*-Stämme), niemals jedoch der idg. Ablativbildung«. Das mag wohl zum großen Teil richtig sein, schließt aber nicht aus, daß durch *syntaktische Verschiebung* ein ablativischer Sinn auch im Dativ enthalten sein kann, oder daß sogar Adverbia kasuelle Funktion übernehmen. Es ist ja allgemein bekannt, daß das Baltisch-Slavische den Ablativ als Gen. benutzt. Wackernagel [7] (*Mel. de Saussure*, 125 ff.) hat für den Gen. Sg. der *o*-Stämme (gall. Gen. *Segomari*, ir. Gen. *maicc*) im Italo-keltischen Anschluß an indo-iranische Adverbia auf -*ī* hergestellt, indem er Wendungen wie *multī facio* mit ai. *samī kr̥* verband. Aehnlich läßt Sommer [8] die Form *peregrē* neben *peregrī* (Lokativ) durch Adverbia auf -*ē* beeinflußt sein. Solche formelle und syntaktische Verschiebungen sind also in den indogermanischen Sprachen nichts Außergewöhnliches. Ob nun auch in den gotischen Adverbia auf -*ē* wie *simlē, swarē, bisunjanē, hidrē, jaindrē* und *hvadrē* ein Ablativ auf -*ēd* [9] (vgl. lat. *facilumēd* 'facillimē', ai. *paçcāt* > **poskēd*) oder ein Lokativ auf -*ām* [10] stecke, ist auch immer noch eine Streitfrage. Eng mit den Adverbien auf -*ē* hängen die auf -*ō* zusammen: *galeikō, sinteinō, usdandō, andaugjō, allandjō, þiubjō, sniumundō, unwēniggō, ussindō, sundrō, hvaþrō, jainþrō* usw., worin die meisten Forscher einen idg. Ablativ auf -*od* sehen (vgl. got. [Präp.] *undarō* = ai. *adharād*; lat. *Gnaivōd*). Um die Erhaltung der Länge zu erklären, haben einige, wie z. B. Jellinek, zu der Hypothese gegriffen, daß das -*d* erst spät abgefallen sei und den vorausgehenden Vokal vor Verkürzung geschützt habe. Dagegen Streitberg [11] und Collitz [12]. Wie dem auch sein mag, jedenfalls sehen die Endungen -*ē* und -*ō* bei Formen wie *swarē, simlē*, vielleicht auch *bisunjanē, þiubjō, sniumundō* wie erstarrte Kasus von Substantiven aus. Sie können allerdings auch übertragen sein. Besonders bei Wörtern wie *swarē* und *simlē* ist mit einer Uebertragung des -*ē* aus den Adv. *hvē* und *þē* zu rechnen. Ob man nun die Erhaltung einer ursprünglichen idg. Endung oder eine Neu-

---

[7] Vgl. auch Wackernagel, *Vorlesungen über Syntax*, Basel 1920, S. 299.
[8] *Handbuch der latein. Laut- u. Formenlehre*, § 193, S. 340.
[9] Bethge bei Dieter, *Laut- u. Formenlehre*, S. 540.
[10] Streitberg, *Urgerm. Gramm.*, § 152.
[11] *Ebenda*, S. 182.
[12] *Bezz. Beiträge*, 17, 18 Anm.

bildung annimmt, muß man doch für die o-Stämme, denn bei diesen allein sind die betreffenden Endungen in erster Linie zu suchen, einen vorgermanischen Kasus auf -ē und -ō voraussetzen. Bei dem Kasus (ob Instr. oder Abl.) auf -ē war ein Anhalt an dem Instr. des Pronomens þē, hvē, wie auch im Westgermanischen (ahd. *tagu, wordu — diu*) [13] gegeben. Im Altindischen besteht auch ein Zusammenhang zwischen *vṛkéna-téna*. Solche alte Beeinflussungen lassen sich auch sonst nachweisen: Ai. gen. sg. masc. *dēvásya* nach *tásya*; instr. sg. fem. *sénayā-táyā*; im Griech. gen. sg. ϑεοῖο-τοῖο, nom. pl. ϑεοί-τοί, gen. pl. χωράων-τάων, loc. pl. ϑεοῖσι-τοῖσι; im Latein. nom. pl. *lupī* nach *istī*, gen. pl. *bellōrum-istōrum, mensārum-istārum*, loc. pl. *bellīs-istīs*, abl. sg. *bellō(d)* nach *istōd*.

Ich nehme nun an, daß auch im Gotischen ein Instr.-Abl. **dagē, *waurdē* einst bestand [14]. Adverbia wie *simlē, swarē* können wohl erstarrte Reste davon sein (siehe jedoch oben). Das Althochdeutsche und Altsächsische haben den (Abl.-) Instrumental auf -ō (vgl. got. *galeikō* usw.) bei Substantiven der o- (und i-)- Deklination [15] erhalten. Wie im Gotischen sind auch im Althochdeutschen Instrumentalformen zu Adverbien geworden. Vgl. ahd. [16] *allu werku* 'summopere'; *diu dingu, disu dingu* 'hactenus; *diu mezu* 'quemadmodum' u. a. m. (Vgl. auch *hiutu* 'heute', *hiuru* 'heuer'). Im Altnordischen kommt der alte Instrumental auf -ō nur noch beim Dativ des Adjektivs (z. B. *blindu, -o*; vgl. anorw. *hú*) und vereinzelt bei den Substantiven [17] vor. Die andere Form auf -ē ist wie im Gotischen auch auf den Instr. des Pronomens beschränkt (*hvé, þvé* [hat sein v vom Fragepronomen bezogen]). Im Altenglischen fungiert der alte Lokativ auf -i als Instrumental (adverbial: *thys geri* 'horno', *aengi thinga* 'quoquomodo', *gihuuelci uuaega* 'quocunque', *sume daeli* 'partim'; *hraecli* 'amiculo', *gaebuli* 'aere alieno') [18]. Die Instrumentalform auf -ō ist nur noch beim Pronomen *(hwon [hū], þon)* erhalten. Das Altfriesische hat den Instr. noch beim Pronomen: *thiu, hwiu*.

Zwei von den gotischen Adverbien *(simlē* [19], *bisunjanē)* werden

---

[13] Für das Angelsächs. vgl. Sievers *PBB* 8, 329 ff.

[14] Vgl. Grimm, *Deutsche Gramm.* IV, 707.

[15] Vgl. Wilmanns, *Deutsche Gramm.*, Abteilung III, 663.

[16] *Ibid.*, Abteilung II, 620.

[17] Noreen, *Geschichte der Nordischen Sprache* [3], S. 164.

[18] Sievers, *PBB* 8, 324 ff.: Dieter, *Laut- u. Formenlehre* S. 554, 666.

[19] Vgl. H. Ehrlich, *Zur idg. Sprachgeschichte*, S. 70.

auch als Gen. Pl. aufgefaßt; ob mit Recht, wird sich schwer
entscheiden lassen. Die Frage ist nur, ob das -ē in diesen Wörtern
zum alten (Abl.-) Instrumental gehöre, oder ob es wirklich die
neue Genitivendung sei. Die enge Beziehung zwischen (Abl.-)
Instrumental und Gen. Pl. ist auch sonst im Germanischen
bezeugt. Im Altsächsischen stehen nebeneinander: *ōðaru uuordu
gibiodan* (Hel. 3208) — *gibōd torohtero tēcno* (Hel. 5943); *that he
thene uueroldcuning sprācono gespōni endi spāhun uuordun* (Hel.
2719). Im Althochdeutschen hat dieser Genitiv Plural in den
adverbialen Bestimmungen der Art und Weise stark um sich
gegriffen [20], besonders bei *worto*: *kurzero worto lēren, wīsero worto
warnōn, gāhero worto sprechen, frenkisgoro worto sagēn; petōno
pittiu* 'prece posco' [21] usw.; dann in Wendungen wie *sulīchero
dāto* 'auf solche Weise', *managero dingo* 'in mannigfacher Weise'
giborganero werko 'im verborgenen'. Im Angelsächsischen führt
B e h a g h e l [22] aus dem Beowulf 3209 an: *swā sē secg secgende
wæs lāðra spella*. Dieser instrumentale Genitiv wird wohl nach
Behaghel durch Verschiebung der Gliederung aus dem partitiven
hervorgegangen, muß aber alt sein, da er gleichzeitig im Angelsächsischen, und Althochdeutschen belegt ist. Ob das Gotische
ihn auch gekannt habe, läßt sich nicht nachweisen, wie so manches
andere, dessen einstige Existenz aber über allen Zweifel erhaben
ist. Es dürfte dasselbe auch hier der Fall sein. Ein instr. Genitiv
ist allerdings auch im Gotischen vorhanden, besonders bei Verben
des Füllens [23]: *grēdagans gasōþida þiuþē* πεινῶντας ἐνέπλησεν ἀγα-
θῶν. Daneben der instr. Dativ [24]: *hvaþrō þans mag hvas gasōþjan
hlaibam* πόθεν τούτους δυνήσεταί τις χορτάσαι ἄρτων. Vgl. *gairnida
sad itan haurnē* ἐπεθύμει χορτασθῆναι ἐκ τῶν κερατίων. »Danach
konnte sich bei Verben, die sonst mit dem Instr. verbunden
wurden, auch ein Gen. einstellen« [25]. Zum Beispiel, neben dem
Instrumental got. [26] *ni blandaiþ izwis hōram;* ags. *heolfre geblonden;*

---

[20] Wilmanns, *Deutsche Gramm.* III, § 256.

[21] Vgl. Delbrück, *Synkretismus,* S. 216.

[22] *Deutsche Syntax,* § 430.

[23] Vgl. ai. *sōmasya jatháram pŗnēthām;* daneben meistens der Instr.: *sōména
jathávam ápipratāmandata.* Ebenso bei lat. *implēre.* Für das Germ. vgl. Delbrück,
Synkretismus, S. 34.

[24] Vgl. auch den Gen. u. Instr. bei got. *brūkjan: daupeinim brūkjan* "baptisma-
tis uti" Sk. III, 10 (vgl. ags. *linenum hræglum brūcan*); sonst der Gen.: *ainis
hlaibis brūkjan* ἐκ τοῦ ἑνὸς ἄρτου μετέχομεν.

[25] Delbrück, *Synkretismus,* S. 216.

[26] Da der got. Dativ (wie auch gewöhnlich im Germ.) die Funktion des Instru-

7*

aisl. *blóþe blanda* erscheint der Genitiv: ags. *nīða geblonden,*
altsächs. *baluwes giblandan* [27]. So auch bei *hladan, wasjan* usw.
(das vollständige Verzeichnis sämtlicher hier in Betracht kom-
mender Verba bei Delbrück, *Synkretismus*).

Bei einer Besprechung des Gen. Plur. im Gotischen darf die
Form des Genitivs der ungeschlechtigen Personalpronomina
(meina, þeina, seina, ugkara, igqara, unsara, izwara) nicht außer
acht gelassen werden. Zwar gehen die Meinungen über die Endung
stark auseinander: Brugmann 2, 569, denkt an einen alten
Ablativ; Janko *IF. Anz.* 15, 253 an einen Abl. oder Instr.; Bethge
bei Dieter, *Laut- und Formenlehre* S. 552 an einen Akk. Pl. Neut.
oder Akk. Sing. Fem.; Walde, *Auslautsgesetze* S. 91 an einen
alten Lokativ **mei* »bei mir« $+$ *nē* [vgl. lat. *supernē*]. Alle stimmen
aber soweit überein, daß sie in allen drei Numeri einen Kasus
der Possessivpronomina sehen. Dieser Kasus wird wohl im Singular zu suchen sein, war auch ursprünglich kein Genitiv und wurde
schließlich auf den Plural übertragen.

Man könnte auch zur Erklärung des Gen. Plur. auf -*ē* vom
Pronomen ausgehen, indem man die Form *þizē* durch Beeinflussung des Instrumentals *þē* entstehen und dann durch Ver-
mittelung des Adjektivs [28] auf das Substantivum übertragen läßt,
was wohl die Beschränkung des -*ē* auf den Gen. Plur. der Stämme,
die nur Maskulina und Neutra enthalten, leicht erklärt, aber für
andere oben besprochenen Einzelheiten nicht genügt.

Der angeblich spurlos verschwundene Instrumental auf -*ē* im
Gotischen ist im Gen. Plur. der *o*-Stämme erhalten.

---

mentals mit übernommen hat, ist es nicht immer sicher, ob wir es mit einem
ursprünglichen Dativ oder Instrumental zu tun haben.
[27] Delbrück, a. a. O. S. 14.
[28] Vgl. Sievers, *PBB* 2, 107.

GOTHIC SYNTACTICAL NOTES

BY ALBERT MOREY STURTEVANT
UNIVERSITY OF KANSAS

I. *Du usfilhan ana gastim*, εἰς ταφὴν τοῖς ξένοις, Mat. XXVII, 7.

The question here has reference to the construction of the particle *ana* and of the dative *gastim*.

Streitberg [1] construes *ana* as an adverb in direct connection with the infinitive *usfilhan;* i. e., *du usfilhan ana* = "to bury [strangers] *in*".

To this interpretation G. W. S. Friedrichsen in his scholarly monograph *The Gothic Version of the Gospels* (London, 1926) objects [2] on the ground that the verb *(us)filhan* elsewhere always governs the *accusative, not the dative* case.

But there is no reason for construing the dative *gastim* as the object of the infinitive *usfilhan*. The dative *gastim*, it seems to me, is best construed as having the same function as the Greek dative τοῖς ξένοις which it translates; i. e., ἠγόρασαν τὸν ἀγρὸν τοῦ κεραμέως εἰς ταφὴν τοῖς ξένοις, "They bought the potter's field *for a burial for strangers*" = "to bury strangers in", Gothic *du usfilhan ana gastim*.

Friedrichsen construes the particle *ana [gastim]* "in respect of [strangers]" as a preposition, apparently because he believes the dative *gastim* to be the object of the verb *usfilhan*. But the fact that we may assume the dative *gastim* to be a dative of interest exactly equivalent to the Greek dative τοῖς ξένοις renders his contention highly improbable.

The very fact that Friedrichsen raises the question as to the rection of the verb *usfilhan* tempts one to believe that he has here

---

[1] Cf. *Got. Bibel*[2], Voc , p. 35.

[2] Cf. p. 140: ". . . taking *ana* closely with *gastim*, and not, as Streitberg (see *W. B.*), with *du usfilhan: (us)filhan* governs the accusative case, not the dative . . ."

been led astray by the English translation "for burying strangers in". But the infinitive *usfilhan* [3] is a verbal substantive and has no voice, corresponding exactly to the Greek verbal noun ταφὴν "burial" (active or passive); i. e., εἰς ταφὴν τοῖς ξένοις = *du usfilhan gastim* "[the field to be used] for a burial for strangers" = "for strangers to be buried in".

Streitberg does not anywhere discuss the dative case *gastim* but there is no reason to believe that he considers it as the object (instrumental dative) of the infinitive *usfilhan,* as Friedrichsen implies.

Finally, as to the troublesome particle *ana,* which Friedrichsen falsely construes as a preposition. As an adverbial modifier of the verbal substantive *usfilhan* the particle *ana* is used in its literal sense of *location,* denoting the field *where* strangers are buried; cf. Eng. "for burying strangers *in*". This is a clear case of an addition (inflation) for the sake of explicitness. On the other hand, if we construe *ana* with Friedrichsen as a preposition in connection with *gastim* (i. e., *ana gastim* = "in respect of strangers") the inflation tends rather to confusion than to explicitness, for *ana* in this sense occurs far less frequently than in its primary sense of location.

II. *The Gothic Preterite for the Greek Present.*

Streitberg [4] mentions the fact that the Greek present tense (aside from the historical present) is sometimes represented by the Gothic preterite and quotes one example: John XIV, 9, *swalaud melis miþ izwis was;* τοσοῦτον χρόνον μεθ᾽ ὑμῶν εἰμί "Have I been so long a time with you?"

Streitberg makes under this heading no attempt to explain the discrepancy between the Gothic and the Greek tense. It will be seen from the following that the Gothic present tense sometimes represents the same time function as the Greek present tense and

---

[3] For the reading *du usfilhan* Friedrichsen *(loc. cit.)* suggests *du usfilha.* There is no justification for this emendation; the reading of the text is clearly *du usfilhan.* Apparently Friedrichsen has made this emendation to fit his interpretation of *ana* as a preposition, inasmuch as *usfilh* is a *noun* and as such could not properly have an adverbial modifier (cf. *du usfilha ana* "for a burial *in*"), which is not true of the verbal substantive *usfilhan* (cf. *du usfilhan ana* "to be buried *in*").

[4] Cf. *Got. Elementarb.*[5-6], § 299, 2.

sometimes does not, a fact which Streitberg should have brought out under the category in question.

The example which Streitberg quotes, belongs to the category of the *durative perfect* (i. e., time begun in the past and continuing in the present) and therefore the Gothic preterite *was* does not violate the function of the Greek present εἰμί. Since the verbal action involves two points of time (the past and the present), either one of these points of time may be utilized to express the durative nature of the verbal action; cf., e. g., the Greek present tense εἰμί with the German (Luther) present "So lange *bin* ich bei euch?", and the Gothic preterite tense *was* with the English perfect "*Have* I *been* so long with you?"

Further examples of this nature are: Luke XV, 29, *swa filu jere skalkinoda þus;* τοσαῦτα ἔτη δουλεύω σοι; "These many years *do* I *serve* thee" (Goth. *skalkinoda* = "have served and do now serve"); Mark VIII, 2, *unte ju dagans þrins miþ mis wesun*[5]; ὅτι ἤδη ἡμέραι τρεῖς προσμένουσίν μοι; "Because they *continue* with me now three days" (Goth. *wesun* = "have been and are now").

In certain cases, however, the Gothic preterite, used in the function of a durative perfect, violates the present time function of the Greek verb. In such cases no adverbial element of time is expressed and there can, therefore, be no doubt that the Greek present represents time without reference to action begun in the past. The Gothic preterite, therefore, here represents an expansion of the Greek present into a durative perfect.

Examples of this nature [6] are as follows:

John XIX, 4, *ei witeiþ þatei in imma ni ainohun fairina bigat;* ἵνα γνῶτε ὅτι ἐν αὐτῷ οὐδεμίαν αἰτίαν εὑρίσκω; "That ye may know that I *find* no crime in him" (Goth. *ni bigat* = "have not found and do not now find"). For εὑρίσκω in this phrase the Gothic scribe elsewhere regularly uses the present tense *bigita* (cf. John XVIII, 38; XIX, 6).

---

[5] Cf. Luke XV, 31, *þu seinteino miþ mis [wast jah] is;* σὺ πάντοτε μετ᾽ ἐμοῦ εἶ; "Thou *art* ever with me". The interpolated preterite form *wast* is evidently based upon the Latin *[tu mecum] fuisti [semper et es]*, but the Latin *fuisti* (= Grk. εἶ) represents the principle involved.

[6] Textual corruptions (due to confusion with other passages or to the influence of the Latin) are, of course, excluded from my discussion; cf., e. g., John VIII, 45, *rodida:* λέγω; John VI, 37, *gaf:* δίδωσιν, etc. See Friedrichsen, *op. cit.,* pp. 81, 234.

John XIV, 31, *ei ufkunnai so manaseþs þatei ik frijoda attan meinana*; ἵνα γνῷ ὁ κόσμος ὅτι ἀγαπῶ τὸν πατέρα; "That the world may know that I *love* the Father" (Goth. *frijoda* = "I have loved and do now love").

Cases of this kind must be clearly distinguished from genuine perfect presents (i e., where the Goth. preterite represents present time as a *result* of an action begun in the past); cf. Mat. VI, 2, 16, *andnemun mizdon seina*; ἀπέχουσιν τὸν μισθὸν αὐτῶν; "They *have* their reward" (Goth. *andnemun* = "They have received and therefore now have"); cf. *haband* (Mat. VI, 5) = ἀπέχουσι.

The foregoing analysis shows that the Gothic preterite may represent the Greek present tense under three different conditions: 1) when the Greek present functions as a durative perfect, 2) when the Gothic has expanded the Greek present into a durative perfect, and 3) when the Gothic uses a preterite (= perfect) present for the Greek present [7].

III. *Sei inna uswaurkeiþ*, Col. I, 29.

The whole passage reads: *du þammei arbaidja usdaudjands bi waurstwa sei inna uswaurkeiþ in mis in mahtai*; εἰς ὃ καὶ κοπιῶ ἀγωνιζόμενος κατὰ τὴν ἐνέργειαν αὐτοῦ τὴν ἐνεργουμένην ἐν ἐμοὶ ἐν δυνάμει; "Wherounto I labor also, striving according to his working which worketh in me mightily".

The question under consideration concerns the relative pronoun *sei*, which should, according to the Greek original, refer back to *waurstwa* and therefore be in the neuter *(þatei, is ei* [8]*)* and not in the feminine gender *(sei)*.

Streitberg [9] meets this apparent incongruence in gender by deriving the form *sei* from an adverb IE **sei* > Lat. *sī* (as in *sī-c* "so" < **sei̯-ke*), in which case the relative form *sei* must be considered as genderless (cf. OHG *só*: ON *sem, es: er*, etc.) and may therefore refer back to the neuter antecedent *waurstwa*.

Professor Curme [10], on the other hand, maintains that the relative *sei* represents the regular feminine form, referring not

---

[7] In all other cases of the genuine preterite present the Gothic is in accord with the Greek; cf. Mark I, 11. *galeikaida*: εὐδόκησα; Luke XVI, 4, *andþahta*: ἔγνων; John VIII, 52, *ufkunþedum*: ἐγνώκαμεν; John XVII, 7, *ufkunþa*: ἔγνων, etc.

[8] Wrede's emendation, *Ulfilas*[12].

[9] Cf. *op. cit.*, § 346, 1, Anm.

[10] Cf. "Is the Gothic Bible Gothic", *JEGPh.*, X, 358 ff.

to the preceding neuter *waurstwa* but to the following feminine *mahtai*. This contention he supports by the fact that in Gothic, as well as in Greek, the relative often preceded its antecedent.

Professor Curme further contends that the Gothic scribe has entirely reconstructed the passage so that it reads (according to Curme's translation): "Whereunto I labor, striving with energy by the aid of that power *(mahtai)* which works within me".

I agree with Professor Curme on both these points and that Streitberg's recourse to an adverbial relative *sei* (see above) is unnecessary.

Yet at the same time the difference in sense between the Greek original and the Gothic translation indicates not a deliberate reconstruction of the original Greek on the part of the Gothic scribe, as Curme implies, but simply a case of corrupted text [11].

In reconstructing his relative clause *(sei inna uswaurkeiþ)* in place of the Greek participial construction *(τὴν ἐνεργουμένην)* the Gothic scribe apparently became confused as to the correct antecedent of his relative and falsely construed it with *mahtai* instead of with *waurstwa*. This confusion may be attributed to the fact that in Gothic the relative often precedes its antecedent. The omission of the equivalent for the Greek αὐτοῦ (= Goth. *is*) is further evidence of confusion and of a corrupted text.

With this type of attraction in gender compare II Cor. V, 17 *jabai hwo in Xristau niuja gaskafts;* εἴ τις ἐν Χριστῷ, καινὴ κτίσις; "If any man is in Christ, he is a new creature".

It is here perfectly evident that the feminine pronoun *hwo* (instead of *hwas* = Gr. τις) is due to the influence of the following feminine substantive *gaskafts* [12].

Now, since the Gothic relative often preceded its antecedent it is most reasonable to assume that in our passage in question the Gothic scribe falsely construed his relative with the following substantive *mahtai* instead of with the correct antecedent *waurstwa*, resulting in an attraction of gender similar to that existing in IICor. V, 17 (i. e., *hwo* for *hwas*).

---

[11] This is also Streitberg's view *(Got. Elementarb.*[5-6], § 346, 1, Anm.; *Got. Bibel*[2], p. 488) but he is unable to explain how the corruption came about.

[12] Cf. similarly the Latin *it vg:* "si *qua* in Chr. nova creatura".

Cf. likewise John XVII, 3, *so h þan ist so aiweino libains* "This is the eternal life"; where, however, the Gothic feminine *soh* corresponds to the Greek feminine αὕτη [δέ ἐστιν ἡ αἰώνιος ζωή].

IV. *þo s a m o n frisaht ingaleikonda af wulþau in wulþu; τὴν αὐτὴν εἰκόνα μεταμορφούμεθα ἀπὸ δόξης εἰς δόξαν;* "We are transformed into the same image from glory to glory", II Cor. III, 18.

At first blush one is tempted to view the Gothic accusative *þo samon frisaht*, used with the medio-passive *ingaleikonda*, as an imitation [13] of the Greek accusative *τὴν αὐτὴν εἰκόνα* and not as a native Gothic construction.

However, when we consider the fact that the Gothic passive *in-galeikonda* is compounded with the prefix *in-*, it is quite possible to construe the accusative *þo samon frisaht* as due to the influence of this prefix *in-*, denoting the goal of the verbal action. The prefix *in-* (= Grk. *μετα-*) here denotes a change [14] from one condition *into* another. As there is no essential difference between a verbal prefix and a preposition we might construe the accusative *þo samon frisaht* as object of *in-* in close connection with the verb [15], whereas in our Modern Germanic languages a fully developed prepositional construction must be used; cf. Eng. "We are transformed *into* the same image", Germ. (Luther) "Wir werden verkläret *in* dasselbige Bild", etc.

It seems to me, therefore, that it is a moot question as to whether the Gothic scribe in preserving the Greek construction here did violence to his native Gothic idiom.

V. *Galeik ist barnam sitandam in garunsim jah wopjandam a n þ a r a n þ a r i s (προσφωνοῦσιν τοῖς ἑτέροις);* "It is like unto children sitting in the market places and calling out *one to the other*", Mat. XI, 16.

Since the form *anþar* is nominative and yet stands in apposition with the dative *barnam*, we evidently have here a case of anacoluthon. This lack of strict grammatical agreement is due to a *constructio ad sensum.* The reciprocal relation "one —

---

[13] So Gerhard H. Balg in his translation (1895) of Braune's *Got. Gramm.*[4], "Explanatory Notes" (p. 132), under this passage: "... this acc., with a pass. vb., is an imitation of the corresponding Greek passage".

[14] Cf. also *in-maidjan* "to transform"; Mark IX, 2, *inmaidida sik = μετεμορφώθη.*

[15] Cf. *anakumbjan miþ: miþanakumbjan* with dative rection (Luke V, 29, *wesun miþ im anakumbjandans:* Mark II, 15, *miþanakumbidedun Jesua*); similarly *bisitan: sitan bi* with accusative rection (Luke I, 65, *ana allaim agis þaim bisitandam ina:* Mark III, 32, *jah setun bi ina*). Cf. Germ. "er durchfliegt die Luft": "er fliegt durch die Luft".

the other" usually occurs in connection with a finite verb, *anþar* (nom.) standing in partitive apposition with the plural subject and *anþar-* (oblique case) standing as object of the verb; cf., e. g., *anþar anþarana munands sis auhuman*, "Each accounting the other better than himself" (Ph. II, 3); *timrjaiþ ainhwarjizuh anþar anþarana*, "Build ye each other up" (Th. V, 11); *sijum anþar anþaris liþus*, "We are members one of the other" (Eph. IV, 25).

In our passage in question the participial construction *(si-tandam ... wopjandam)* is in sense equivalent to a relative clause, hence the nominative *anþar* is felt to be in partitive apposition with the subject of a finite verb, just as in the cases quoted above; cf. *galeik ist barnam þoei sitand ... jah wopjand anþar anþaris*, "Like unto children *who* sit ... and cry out *one to the other*".

That the nominative *anþar* in the original passage with participial construction is good Gothic, is shown by the fact that in the original Greek we have nothing corresponding to *anþar*. It is unfortunate for our discussion that in the parallel passage (Luke VII, 32), where the participial construction *(sitandam jah wopjandam)* occurs, the Gothic translator avoids the *anþar — anþar-* construction (cf. *wopjandam seina misso*, προσφονοῦσιν ἀλλήλοις).

VI. *Jah fagino in izwara, ei galaubjaiþ, unte ni was jainar;* καὶ χαίρω δι᾽ ὑμᾶς, ἵνα πιστεύσητε, ὅτι οὐκ ἤμην ἐκεῖ; "And I am glad for your sakes *that* I was not there, to the intent that ye may believe", John XI, 15.

The clause *unte ni was jainar* is the object of the verb *fagino*, hence we should expect in the place of the conjunction *unte* either *þatei* or *ei* which are regularly used [16] after verbs of "rejoicing" and of "wondering"; cf., e. g., Luke X, 20, *ni faginoþ, e i ..*: μὴ χαίρετε ὅτι; John XIV, 28 *faginodedeiþ ei*: ἐχάρητε ἂν ὅτι.

Why then did the Gothic scribe in our passage deviate from the normal usage of *þatei* or *ei* in favor of *unte*?

The reason for this, I think, is obvious. The Greek ὅτι may either serve as a conjunction introducing a substantive clause

---

[16] Cf. Streitberg, *Got. Elementarb.*[5-6], § 354, 3. Besides *þatei* and *ei* the dative form *þammei* is also sometimes found after *faginon*; cf. *faginoþ miþ mis þammei bigat lamb mein*; συγχάρητέ μοι ὅτι εὗρον τὸ πρόβατόν μου, Luke XV, 6.

(= Goth. *þatei: ei* "that") or represent a causal conjunction
(= Goth. *unte* "for which reason, because"). The passage may,
therefore, be interpreted as meaning "I rejoice *because* [17] I was
not there". Had the Gothic scribe here used the regular particle
þatei or *ei* instead of *unte*, the clause introduced by the particle
(þat)ei (i. e., *(þat)ei ni was jainar*) could have been construed
as the object of the verb *galaubjaiþ* instead of the verb *fagino;*
i. e., *ei galaubjaiþ (þat)ei ni was jainar* "That ye may believe
that I was not there".

To avoid such a misinterpretation [18] the Greek ὅτι is rendered
by the particle *unte* which (unlike the particle *þatei : ei*) cannot
properly be construed with the verb *galaubjaiþ* but only with
the verb *fagino;* i. e., *fagino . . . unte* "I rejoice because (= that)"

VII. *Unte for þatei : ei : þei.*

As has been shown above, the Greek ὅτι may correspond either
to Gothic *þatei :ei: þei* "that", introducing a substantive clause,
or to Gothic *unte* "because, for".

I have found one passage in which on account of this double
meaning of the Greek conjunction ὅτι the Gothic scribe evidently
used *unte* for *þatei : ei : þei*, namely Luke I, 58: *jah hausidedun . .
unte gamikilida frauja armahairtein seina;* καὶ ἤκουσα . . . ὅτι
ἐμεγάλυνεν κύριος τὸ ἔλεος αὐτοῦ; "And they heard *that* the Lord
had magnified his mercy".

There is no possibility of construing *unte* = ὅτι here (after a
verb of "hearing" [19]) as having a causal sense, yet Streitberg
makes no mention of this misuse [20] of the particle *unte* either
in his *Got. Elementarb.*[5-6] or in his *Got. Bibel*[2] (Voc. under *unte*).

Since this use of *unte* = ὅτι in the sense of "that" introducing
indirect discourse does not occur elsewhere, we may best explain
its occurrence here as due to the influence of the Latin *quia*,

---

[17] Cf. Lat. Vulgate *"quoniam non eram ibi"*.

[18] In our modern versions of this passage we avoid the ambiguity in question
by changing the order of the clauses so that the last clause immediately follows
the first; cf. Eng. "And I am glad for your sakes that I was not there, to the
intent that ye may believe", Germ. (Luther) "Ich bin froh um euretwillen,
daß ich nicht da gewesen bin, auf daß ihr glaubet".

[19] For the usage of the conjunction *þatei: ei: þei* after verbs of "hearing",
"seeing", etc. compare Streitberg, *op. cit.*, § 355.

[20] Braune, however, in his *Got. Gramm.*[9] (Voc. p. 185) gives besides *denn* and
weil, the meaning *daß*, which would indicate that Braune recognizes the misuse
of *unte* under discussion.

which also had the double sense of "because, inasmuch as" and "that" (cf. OHG *(h)uuanta*, Tatian): cf. Luke I, 58 "et audierunt ... *quia* magnificavit Dominus misericordiam suam".

VIII. *Jah qens meina jramaldrozei in dagam seinaim;* καὶ ἡ γυνή μου προβεβηκυῖα ἐν ταῖς ἡμέραις αὐτῆς; "And my wife well advanced in her days", Luke I, 18.

It will be noted that the Gothic here employs the comparative degree of the adjective *(jramaldrozei)* to render the Greek positive προβεβηκυῖα.

The same phrase is used in Luke II, 36 regarding the prophetess Anna — *jramaldra dage managaize* (προβεβηκυῖα ἐν ἡμέραις πολλαῖς) — but here in the positive degree corresponding to the Greek. Why then did the Gothic scribe in the first passage employ the comparative degree?

In the first passage the age of the wife of Zacharias is connected with the question of childbirth, so that we may construe the comparative *jramaldrozei* as meaning "older [than that she can give birth to a child]" = "too [21] old [to give birth to a child]". Such an idea is not present in connection with the age of the prophetess Anna.

This usage of the comparative *jramaldrozei* is obviously equivalent to the so-called absolute comparative; i. e., *jramaldrozei* = "older [than women who can give birth to a child]", in which a second party is implied. In the Greek this distinction between positive and comparative is not always observed, the idea being viewed (as in our passage) from the standpoint of only one party[22]; cf. *Marja Jacobis þis minnizins* (τοῦ μικροῦ), "Mary the mother of James the less", Mark XV, 40.

IX. *þairh injeinandein armahairtein gudis unsaris, in þammei gaweisoþ unsara urruns us hauhiþai;* διὰ σπλάγχνα ἐλέους ἡμῶν, ἐν οἷς ἐπισκέψεται ἡμᾶς ἀνατολὴ ἐξ ὕψους; "Because of the tender mercy of our God, whereby the dayspring from on high shall visit us", Luke I, 78.

It will be noted that there is a lack of agreement in gender between the relative *þammei* (= οἷς) and its antecedent *arma-*

---

[21] Cf. ON "ertu ok myklu *vitrari* maðr, en þú munir vilja..." "Thou art also a much *wiser* man than that thou shouldst wish..." = "*too* wise a man to wish".

[22] Cf. Streitberg, *op. cit.*, § 274 a.

hairtein; instead of *in þammei* we should expect *in þizaiei* fem. (in agreement with *armahairtein*).

The Greek phrase διὰ σπλάγχνα ἐλέους (= Lat. *viscera miseri-cordiae* "bowels of mercy") has been recast by the Gothic scribe into *þairh infeinandein armahairtein* "durch erbarmendes Mit-leid" [23], "because of *pitying* (= tender) mercy", wherein a verbal action *(infeinandein)* is implied. The relative *þammei* may then be construed as a *neuter singular* referring to the *act* [of mercy] implied in the present participle *infeinandein;* i. e., *in þammei =* "by which *act* [of mercy], whereby".

In view of the Greek plural οἷς [24] (which must refer back to σπλάγχνα) the Gothic scribe could not possibly have used *þammei* with reference to *gudis unsaris.*

Streitberg [25] makes no reference to this type of apparent incongruence of gender (i. e., between relative and antecedent).

X. *Jah gairnida s a d itan haurne;* καὶ ἐπεθύμει χορτασθῆναι ἐκ τῶν κερατίων; "And he would fain have eaten his fill of the husks".
Luke XV, 16.

This same phrase *saþ itan* (= χορτασθῆναι) occurs again in Luke XVI, 21.

Regarding this phrase Friedrichsen [26] says: "In German "er wollte sich satt essen" . . . Nothing could be more obviously idiomatic."

Of course the German "er wollte sich satt essen" translates perfectly the idea expressed in the Gothic, but the German idiom does not correspond to the Gothic idiom. For an exact parallel to the Gothic idiom Friedrichsen might have quoted the English "he would fain have eaten his *fill* (adj.) of". The Gothic adjective *sad (saþ)* is not a predicative adjective (masc. sing., cf. *sadana*), as is the German *satt*, but a substantivized neuter = "a sufficient amount of, enough". We find several such examples of the substantivized neuter singular of the strong adjective in Gothic [27]: cf. *þiuþ* = τὸ ἀγαθόν, *ubil* = τὸ πονηρὸν

---

[23] Cf. Streitberg, *Got. Bibel²*, Voc., p. 34, under *infeinan.*

[24] Cf. Lat. "per viscera misericordiæ Dei nostri, *in quibus* visitavit nos, oriens ex alto".

[25] Cf. Streitberg, *Got. Elementarb.⁵⁻⁶*, § 236, "Inkongruenz der grammatischen Genera".

[26] Cf. *op. cit.*, pp. 67—68.

[27] Cf. O. Erdmann, *Die Grundzüge der deutschen Syntax*, § 48.

(Luke VI, 45); *þata ubil* (John XVIII, 23); *þata leiht* (II Cor. IV, 17), etc.

It will be noted that the adjective *sad* denotes the idea of *quantity* and therefore easily lends itself to the collective idea, — hence the substantive usage. This is of course a Common Germanic idiom; cf. the Gothic substantive usage of *sad* with the substantive usage of the adjective for "enough" in all the Germanic languages (Eng. *"enough* of the husks", Germ. *"der Trebern genug"*), similarly ON *fátt manna* "few men", *mart manna* "many men". The Gothic adjective *sad* in our passage is thus syntactically equivalent to the substantive *filu* with the partitive genitive.

We find no cases of *manag* "much" plus the partitive genitive (parallel to ON *mart manna*), presumably because the substantive *filu* is thus used in place of *manag*. But the substantive *filu* is, of course, not capable of comparison and therefore in the comparative degree "more" we find the neuter singular of the adjective *managizo* substantivized in exactly the same way as is *sad* in our passage; cf. *nibai m a n a g i z o* [28] *wairþiþ izwaraizos garaihteins* [28] *þau þize bokarje; ἐὰν μὴ περισσεύσῃ ὑμῶν ἡ δικαιοσύνη πλεῖον τῶν γραμματέων*, Matt. V, 20.

This latter passage illustrates the point in question, viz. that the reason for the substantivization of the neuter singular adsective *(sad)* is due to the idea of *quantity* — i. e., a collective substantive (cf. German *genug, viel, mehr*).

XI. *Jah Jacobau þamma Zaibaidaiaus jah Johanne broþr Jacobaus*, Mark. III, 17.

The Gothic datives *Jacobau* and *Johanne* correspond to the Greek accusatives *Ἰάκωβον* and *Ἰωάννην*, direct objects of *ἐποίησεν (gawaurhta)* in verse 14; i. e., "He made James and John to be his disciples".

These Gothic datives obviously represent a scribal error for the accusative. Directly following the passage in question we read: *jah gasatida i m namna Bauanairgais:* "And gave *to them* the names Boanerges". Similarly in the preceding verse (16), *jah gasatida S e i m o n a namo Paitrus;* "And gave to Simon the name. Peter".

---

[28] With Goth. *managizo izwaraizos garaihteins* compare Germ. *der Kinder mehr*.

The Gothic datives *Jacobau: Johanne*, therefore, obviously represent a later contamination [29] with the dative construction after *gasatida* (cf. *im: Seimona* hence *Jacobau: Johanne*). This anacoluthon was further favored by the fact that the verb *gawaurhta*, which governs these two names *(Jacobau: Johanne)*, is so far separated from them.

XII. *Ei sahwazuh izei usqimiþ izwis, þuggkeiþ h u n s l a saljan guda;* ἵνα πᾶς ὁ ἀποκτείνας ὑμᾶς δόξη λ α τ ρ ε ί α ν προσφέρειν τῷ θεῷ ; "That whosoever killeth you shall think that he offereth *a service* to God", John XVI, 2.

The Greek singular λατρείαν "religious service" is here rendered by the Gothic plural [30] *h u n s l a* "sacrifices". There is no reason to assume that the form *hunsla* represents a dative (instrumental) singular after the verb *saljan* "to sacrifice", especially since the verb *saljan* elsewhere requires an accusative [31] rection, just as does *atbairan* [32] = προσφέρειν which is the Greek verb for *saljan* in our passage. The form *hunsla* undoubtedly represents an accusative plural.

But why should the Gothic scribe have translated the Greek singular λατρείαν by a plural *hunsla*? There is no reason for considering *hunsla* as a *pluralis tantum* [33], especially since the singular form [34] of this word is regularly used to translate the Greek θυσία "sacrifice".

The plural form is, it seems to me, best explained as due to the plural idea inherent in the subject *sahwazuh (= πᾶς ὁ)* "whosoever" = "all who".

The subject *sahwazuh* "whosoever" *(= πᾶς ὁ)* is a collective pronoun; although singular in form it is plural in sense, denoting

---

[29] There is no reason to believe that Wulfila himself used the dative case for these two names; the contamination was most probably due to a visual error on the part of a later scribe. Streitberg does not mention (*Got. Bibel²*, under this passage, p. 173) this contamination nor is it discussed by Friedrichsen *(op. cit.)*.

[30] Cf. Streitberg, *Got. Bibel²*, Voc. p. 61, under *hunsl*.

[31] Cf. ICor. X, 20, *ak þatei saljand þiudos;* ὅτι ἃ θύει τὰ ἔθνη; "The things which the Gentiles sacrifice".

[32] Cf. Mat. V, 24, *atbair þo giba þeina;* πρόσφερε τὸ δῶρον σοῦ.

[33] Nor does Streitberg include this plural form in his list of *pluralia tantum* (*Got. Elementarb.⁵⁻⁶*, § 238). To this list I should add *haurja* = ἀνθρακιὰν "coal-fire", John XVIII, 18.

[34] Cf. Mat. IX, 13; Luke II, 24; Eph. V, 2; Skeir. I, 5.

a number of individuals who perform the same act. The Gothic scribe, contrary to the Greek, viewed the verbal action from the standpoint of a plural subject *(constructio ad sensum)*; consequently the object *(λατρείαν)* of the verb was pluralized *(hunsla)* corresponding to the several acts on the part of the subject.

The Greek viewpoint is *singular*, i. e., "Every one who killeth you shall think that *he offereth his service* to God"; the Gothic viewpoint is *plural*, i. e., "All who kill you shall think that *they offer their services* to God". For this type of fluctuation between a singular and a plural object compare German "Sie nahmen *den Hut* ab" and English "They took off *their hats*".

SCANDINAVIAN-POLISH RELATIONS IN THE LATE TENTH CENTURY

BY SAMUEL H. CROSS
HARVARD UNIVERSITY

The contacts between Scandinavians and Slavs in Russian territory during the ninth and tenth centuries are treated in respectable detail by both Russian and Norse sources. The Russian *Primary Chronicle*, composed about 1116 and covering the period 850—1110, preserves a coherent tradition of the establishment of Scandinavian domination over the Slavic and Finnish tribes of Northern Russia by three totally legendary brothers, ostensibly of Swedish origin [1]. This tradition, covering the extension of Scandinavian overlordship down the Dnieper valley toward the Black Sea, reflects the foundation of Scandinavian trading posts and colonies at strategic points along the Russian watercourses and the gradual consolidation of the peaceful but disunited Slavic tribes into a state dominated by a ruling class of immigrant Scandinavian warrior-merchants. Their voyages of trade and piracy had carried them as far as the Caspian, Byzantium, and the northern coast of Asia Minor before 900. The activities of these Norse colonists are abundantly attested both by archaeological remains and by the testimony of contemporary oriental observers [2]. Intermarriage with daughters of the numerically

---

[1] Лаврентьевская Летопись ed. E. F. Karski (Leningrad, 1926), 19—21. Cf. W. Thomson: *Relations between Ancient Russia and Scandinavia* (Oxford 1877), *passim*; V. Klyuchevski: Курс Русской Истории I (Moscow, 1904), 150—173; L. Niederle: *Slovanské Starožitnosti* I [4] (Prague 1925), 90—126, and for summary of literature on Varangian question, *ibid.*, 278—281; *Manuel de l'Antiquité Slave* I (Paris 1913), 198—207.

[2] Cf. T. J. Arne: *La Suède et l'Orient* (Uppsala 1914), 18—61, 220—231; J. Marquart: *Osteuropäische und Ostasiatische Streifzüge* (Leipzig 1903), 203—204, 330—353. F. Westberg: 'К Анализу Восточных Источников О Восточной Европе', Ж. М. Н. П., N. S. XIII (Leningrad 1908), 364—404; XIV, 1—52. D. A. Khvolson: Известия Ибн-Даста о Ховарах, Славянах и Руссах, (Leningrad, 1869). A. S. Cook: "Ibn Fadlan's Account of Scandinavian Merchants on the

dominant Slavic masses rapidly deprived these energetic immigrants of their exclusively Scandinavian character. Especially after the conversion of Vladimir I (988), intensive contact with Byzantine civilization oriented the Varangian princes more and more toward the intellectually superior south, and restricted the influence of their original northern habitat. The route from the Baltic to the Black Sea via the Russian watercourses[3], which remained open until blocked by Turco-Tatar nomads toward the end of the twelfth century, insured notwithstanding, as long as it was practicable, a constant influx of Scandinavian adventurers, some of whom enlisted in the service of the Russian princes, while others went on southward to seek gainful employment on the Bosporus[4]. The Russian state thus became a recognized haven of refuge for princes whose sojourn in Scandinavia was, for one reason or another, fraught with momentary peril, while intermarriage between the Russian and the Scandinavian ruling families kept alive the sense of kinship uniting the Norse princes with the house of Rurik.

The closest relations between Scandinavia and the early Russian state prevailed during the reign at Kiev of a friend and contemporary of St Olav: Yaroslav the Wise (978—1054), who was himself son-in-law of Olaf Skotkonungr and father-in-law of Harald Harðráði[5]. For this period the Norse sources (e. g., *Agrip, Morkinskinna, Fagrskinna, Heimskringla, Eymundarþáttr Hringssonar*) supply abundant data as to contacts between Scandinavia and Russia. The various sagas dealing with Olaf Tryggvason also contain a considerable body of information (most of it legendary

---

Volga in 922," *Journ. Eng. and Germ. Philol.* XXII (Trbana 1923), 51—63. V. G. Vasilievski: 'Русско-Византийския Изследования', Летопись Археографической Коммиссии IX—X (Leningrad, 1893), pt. 2 M. Rostovtzeff: *Iranians and Greeks in South Russia* (Oxford 1922), 210—222; "Les Origines de la Russie Kiévienne," *Revue des Etudes Slaves* II (Paris 1922), 5—18).

[3] Лавр. Лет., 7. Cf. A. Bugge: "Die nordeuropäischen Verkehrswege im frühen Mittelalter", *Vierteljahrsschrift für Soz. u. Wirtschaftsgeschichte* IV (Berlin 1905—1906), 245—252. A. Szelagowski: *Najstarsze Drogi z Polski z Wschód* (Cracow 1909), 9 ff.

[4] Cf. V. G. Vasilievski: 'Варяго-Русская и Варяго-Английская Дружина в Константинополе XI в XII Веков', Ж. М. Н. П., CLXXVIII (March, 1875), 76—152.

[5] Cf. F. Braune: »Das historische Rußland im nordischen Schrifttum des X. bis XIV. Jhdts.«, *Festschrift für E. Mogk* (Halle 1924), 150—196. S. H. Cross: "Yaroslav the Wise in Norse Tradition", *Speculum* IV (Cambridge, 1929), 177—197, and the sources there cited.

or distorted in transmission) concerning his sojourn at the court of Yaroslav's father Vladimir I, and his entirely unhistorical connection with the latter's conversion to Christianity. The *Bjarnar Saga Hitdoelakappa* also preserves some remnant of tradition concerning the participation of a Norwegian adventurer in the conflicts of Vladimir with the nomads about 1008. It is thus to be expected that the Norse historical compilations of the twelfth and thirteenth centuries might present corresponding material concerning Scandinavian intercourse with the Western Slavs of the Baltic seaboard during substantially the same epoch, in the course of which the trading centers established by Viking raiders along the Baltic maintained close contact with the Wendish tribes then engaged in their perennial struggle against Saxon expansion.

Among the Norse sources, the earliest (the *Ágrip* and the anonymous *Historia Norwegiae*) contain but scanty references to such contacts. The *Fagrskinna*, the two full redactions of Oddr's *Saga of Olaf Tryggvason*, the *Jómsvíkingasaga*, the *Heimskringla*, and the *Knytlingasaga* expend considerable detail and extensive romantic embellishment upon the relations between the Danes and the Slavic tribes adjacent to the mouth of the Oder during the last half of the tenth century, especially in connection with the foundation and history of the Danish colony at Jómsborg, on the island of Wollin. The Slavic tribes nearest this center were obviously either Pomeranian or Polish. Before their subjection and absorption by German invaders, the Pomeranians never reached a sufficiently high intellectual level to permit the crystallization of any tradition concerning this early period. Western culture penetrated Poland itself only during the thirteenth century after an interval of internal disruption in which the memories of Mieszko I, the prince who first brought Poland into the circle of European states, had fallen into almost complete oblivion. The Poles therefore possess no literary monument of historical nature in any way comparable with the Russian *Primary Chronicle*, and for the second half of the tenth century, the earliest Polish sources offer practically no information against which the data of the Norse sagas may be checked. We are thus limited to the evidence of Widukind, Thietmar of Merseburg, and Adam of Bremen (together with Helmold and occasionally Saxo Grammaticus) for material either contemporary or slightly later and applicable as a corrective to the extant Norse texts, none of which antedates the last quarter of the twelfth century. For the early life of Olaf Tryggvason prior to 986, Snorri Sturluson himself found little scaldic material to supplement oral tradition and the scanty literary efforts of his precursors. By the time the Norse historical sagas took shape as written literature, Scandinavian contacts with Poland proper must also have been severely restricted. After the death of Boleslav Krzywousty (the Wrymouthed) in 1138, Poland was partitioned among his heirs, and the whole Baltic seaboard west of the Vistula was lost to German conquest. From 1229 forward, the penetration of the German military orders into East Prussia and Lithuania definitely cut the Poles off from the sea. The coincidence of a period of civil strife in Norway, together with the gradual collapse of the Polish principate, which did not recover until the coronation of Vladislav Łokietek in 1320, provided an interval in which earlier information, unfixed by consignment to writing and uncontrolled by continuous contact between the nations concerned, could degenerate into a body of inaccurate legend wherein the remote Icelandic compiler or *sagnamaðr* could hardly be expected to distinguish fact and romance. The Norse sources dealing with Scandinavian-Wendish relations in the second half of the tenth century thus merit the closest critical scrutiny before their content is in any wise historically acceptable.

While the Oder and the Vistula as trade routes never attained the importance of the Dnieper and the Volga, they still played no mean part in the early mediaeval communication system. The finds of Arabic coins not only along the upper Oder in Silesia, but also along the courses of the Warta and Notec, indicate that the Oder basin likewise fell within the range of the oriental commercial influence which was so extensively felt in Northeastern Russia and in Sweden in the course of the ninth and tenth centuries [6]. During the Viking Age and early in the ninth century, such Baltic trading points as Hedeby and Slesvig in Denmark, or Birka and Sigtuna in Sweden, were the centers of Viking commerce. The raids of the Vikings along the south shore of the Baltic [7] resulted either in the capture of Wendish coastal towns

---

[6] Cf. Niederle III [2], 369—374; R. Ekblom, in *Arch. Slav. Philol.* XXXIX (Berlin 1925), 210.

[7] Bugge: *Verkehrswege* 232—235, 237—251.

or the foundation of new Viking settlements adapted both for trade with the interior and as intermediate stations for voyages toward destinations further eastward. Among these were Reric in Mecklenburg, Svarinshaugr (Schwerin), and Truso, on the eastern arm of the lower Vistula. For the contact of Scandinavians with Polish and Pomeranian tribes, the most important center of this sort seems to have been a Danish settlement at Jómsborg, situated at the mouth of the Oder on the island of Wollin, apparently upon or near the site of the modern town bearing the latter name [8]. This colony, at least until its destruction by Magnus in 1043, has the reputation of having been the outstanding Danish settlement on the Baltic, and is correspondingly celebrated in the Sagas [9].

The related saga material is, in fact, so contradictory and so complicated with romantic accretions that one Swedish investigator has been led to deny the existence of Jómsborg altogether [10]. As will presently appear, however, regardless of the extensive fiction surrounding this Danish strong-point, the evidence of Danish contact with at least one historical Polish prince through some Scandinavian outpost near the mouth of the Oder is too well-established to justify such ruthless rejection of the whole Jómsborg tradition, though the archaeological remains gathered on the spot are remarkably scanty, as far as any proof of lasting and organized Scandinavian occupancy is concerned.

In the earliest Norse historical compilations, Jómsborg and the *Jómsvíkingar* do not appear, apart from a brief mention of the settlement as Olaf Tryggvason's winter-quarters on his return

[8] Cf. J. C. H. R. Steenstrup: *Venderne og de Danske for Valdemar den Stores Tid* (Copenhagen 1900), 25—59; Bugge, *loc. cit.*, 238—239; A. Stubenrauch: »Untersuchungen im Anschluß an die Vineta-Frage«, *Balt. Studien* n. F. I—II (Stettin 1897), 67—133; Niederle, *op. cit.* III, 150, and literature there cited.

[9] *Heimskringla* ed. F. Jónsson, III, 43, 44: "En er Magnús konungr kom til Vindlandz, þá lagði hann til Jómsborgar ok vann þegar borgina, drap þá mikit fólk ok brendi borgina ok landit víða út í frá ok gerði þar it mesta herverki", corroborated by citation from Arnórr Jarlaskáld, cf. F. Jónsson: *Skjaldedigtning* A 355, B 308. This destruction appears to have been only temporary, however, as a *ciuitas Vulinensis* is again mentioned in 1140 (Niederle III, 149, n. 7). Helmold, however (*Chron. Slav.* ed. G. H. Pertz [Hannover 1868] 15), refers to Jómsborg as long since destroyed: "*quondam fuit* nobilissima ciuitas Iumneta ... omnes enim *usque ad excidium* eiusdem urbis paganicis studiis oberrarunt".

[10] L. Weibull: *Kritiska Undersökningar i Nordens Historia omkring Ár 1000* Lund 1911), 178—195.

from Russia in 986 [11]. The traditions of its foundation are highly conflicting. Sveinn Agason asserts that Harald Gormsson (Blátonn) fled before his son Sveinn Tjuguskegg into *Sclavia*, where he is said to have founded the city called Jómsborg [12]. The *Fagrskinna* (second quarter of thirteenth century) [13] contains the statement that King Harald, while raiding in Vindland, caused the construction of a great fortress at a site called *at Jómi*, later known as Jómsborg, with the supplementary information that the *Jómsvíkingar* seized a good part of the realm of Búrizleifr, who then ruled over Vindland [14]. A similar tradition is preserved in the *Knytlingasaga*, according to which Harald possessed a great domain *(jarlsríki)* in Vindland. He thus caused the construction of Jómsborg, where he established a considerable garrison, who were known as *Jómsvíkingar* [15]. A parallel group of sources attributes the foundation of Jómsborg not to Harald, but to Sveinn Tjuguskegg's foster-father Palnatoki. The *Jómsvíkingasaga* thus dates its establishment by this legendary hero as subsequent to Sveinn's accession, and in the various redactions of this saga, the *Jómsvíkingar* appear not as Búrizleifr's enemies, but as his allies, a role which they likewise play in the Arnamagnaean redaction of Oddr [16]. Snorri Sturluson omits any statement as to the foundation of Jómsborg, but Saxo Grammaticus attributes its establishment to Harald [17]. Obviously, if Harald was its founder, the establishment of Jómsborg would fall somewhere between 950 and 986; if the foundation is attributed to Sveinn Tjuguskegg, it must have occurred after the latter date, which appears intrinsically improbable. Modern authorities in general

---

[11] *Ágrip*, in *Fornmanna Sögur* X (Copenhagen, 1835), 392: "[Ólafr] hafþi iþuliga vetrseto sina i Veinlandi i borg þeirri er heit Jómsborg," and *Historia Norwegiæ* ed. G. Storm, p. 113.

[12] *M. G. SS.* XXIX, 32: "Qui [Haraldus] cursu celeri fugam arripiens ... ad Sclauiam usque profugus commeauit ibique, pace impetrata, primus urbem fundasse dicitur quae Hynnisburgh nuncupatur."

[13] Cf. F. Jónsson: *Oldnor. og Oldisland. Litt. Hist.* II (Copenhagen 1923), 611—620.

[14] *Fagrskinna*, ed. P. A. Munch and C. R. Unger (Oslo 1847), 42: "Haraldr konungr herjaði á Vindland ok lét gera borg mikla, þá er heitir at Jómi, ok er su borg köllud siðan Jómsborg ... Jómsvíkingar unnu mikit af ríki Búrizleifs konungs, er þá réð fyrir Vindlandi."

[15] *Forn. Sög.* XI (Copenhagen 1828), 179: "Hafði hann mikit jarlsríki i Vindlandi; hann lét þar gjöra Jómsborg, ok setti þar herlið mikit ... þeir voru kalladir Jómsvíkingar."

[16] *Forn. Sög.* XI, 73, 74; X, 285.

[17] ed. A. Holder (Straßburg 1886), 325 [9].

thus accept as historical the foundation of Jómsborg by Harald Gormsson [18]. From these variants in the tradition, however, it would appear that the compilers of the historical sagas knew nothing positive of the foundation of Jómsborg, and in this instance gave free rein once more to their habitual practice of legitimating some doubtful feature of their narrative by attaching it to a known personage whose chronology and general character harmonized at least ostensibly with the situation in question. In view of the extensive and self-contradictory increments of the whole Jómsvíking tradition, Weibull is entirely justified in his contention that "the Norse Jómsborg and the Jómsvíkings *as the Danish and Icelandic traditions knew them* never existed" [19].

There is, however, one element of analogy connecting Jómsborg with Scandinavian colonization in Russia which, though not noticed heretofore, is capable of casting some light on the actual status of this stronghold. The Scandinavians who penetrated Russia actually founded no new towns there, but rather, through their superior energy and military ability, became in time the ruling class both in the older cities on the Dnieper and in the newer settlements like Novgorod and Rostov, which were themselves the product of Slavic expansion. In the case of Jómsborg, the commercial interest of the site cannot have been intrinsically as great as that of Novgorod (to cite an outstanding example in Russia), though the sheltered mouth of a major river connecting with a prosperous hinterland was *ipso facto* of obvious importance. There is, moreover, relatively satisfactory archaeological evidence of a Wendish settlement on the site of Wollin during the tenth century [20]. The Danish tradition as expressed by Saxo states: "Haraldus, armis Sclauia potitus, apud Iulinum, nobilissimum illius prouinciae oppidum, competencia militum presidia collocauit." Without regard to other elements of the tradition, this text means nothing more than that Harald, on one of his raids in Vindland, set a garrison in the already existent Slavic town on the site of Wollin, which is precisely what the Swedes in Russia appear to have done repeatedly. Such a garrison, provided with suitable harbor facilities, then served as a base for further raids

---

[18] Cf. J. W. Thompson: *Feudal Germany* (Chicago 1928), 534, 535, and notes; J. C. H. R. Steenstrup, *op. cit.*, 34.

[19] *Op. cit.*, 178—195.

[20] Stubenrauch, *op. cit.*, 94—126.

or trading expeditions into the interior, from which resulted the increased contact between Poles and Danes substantiated by German sources for the period. The absence, however, of archaeological evidence as to any impressive and specifically Scandinavian settlement on the site of Wollin also casts a shadow of doubt on the fulsome description of Jómsborg supplied by Adam of Bremen [21]. Jómsborg is thus by no means to be conceived as a grandiose mediaeval mercantile port, but as a small Slavic town dominated by a Danish garrison, who used it as a starting-point for their characteristic expeditions of combined trade and piracy.

The statement in the *Ágrip* and the *Historia Norwegiæ* that Olaf Tryggvason, upon returning from Russia, made Jómsborg his winter-quarters while raiding Flanders, England, Scotland, and Ireland, has already been cited. Neither in the *Ágrip* nor in the latter is there any reference to a marriage of Olaf in Vindland. A tradition to this effect first appears in the *Fagrskinna*, where this wife is called Geila the Wend, and later identified as daughter of Búrizláfr, King of Vindland, and thus sister to both Gunnhildr, wife of Sveinn Tjuguskegg, and Ástríðr, wife of Jarl Sigvaldi of Jómsborg. (*Fgsk.*, 56, 59). The Arnamagnaean redaction of Oddr contains a long account of the princess Geira, who, upon Olaf's arrival in Vindland, was exercizing the sovereignty in her father Búrizláfr's absence (*Forn. Sög.* X, 233 ff.). In this text, no reference is made to Jómsborg in connection with Olaf's arrival in Vindland, to which he was driven southward from Bornholm by storm. Geira, upon learning of his arrival from her chief councillor Dixin, despatches the latter to invite Olaf to her court. At Dixin's instigation, her marriage with Olaf is soon consummated. The princess lives but three years as Olaf's consort, and after her death he quits Vindland, according to Oddr (Arn.), to undertake his second (apocryphal) voyage to Russia, but according to Snorri (*Hskr.* I, 306), only to extend his raids to the North Sea. This same redaction of Oddr also recurs later to Geira as Olaf's former wife in connection with his voyage to Vindland to recover the dowry of his third wife Þyri, Sveinn Tjuguskegg's

[21] ed. B. Schmeidler (Hannover 1917), 79, 80. Cf. C. Niebuhr: »Die Nachrichten von der Stadt Jumne«, *Hansische Geschichtsblätter* XXIII (Munich, 1917), 367—375, pointing out that Adam's descriptions of both Jómsborg-Iumneta and Kiev show signs of bring derived from some ἔκφρασις on Constantinople.

sister [22]. It is, however, rather more than a coincidence that the Stockholm redaction of Oddr omits all passages associating Olaf with Geira. In any case, Snorri adopts substantially the same account provided by the Arnamagnaean redaction, not only as to Olaf's marriage to Geira (*Hskr.* I, 294—295, 297) and her death (*ibid.*, 306), but also with regard to his recovery of Þyri's dowry from Búrizláfr (*ibid.*, 422—423, 429), with the addition that Þyri herself suggests this errand will prove particularly easy on account of Olaf's long-standing friendship with the Wendish king. Snorri rejects Olaf's second voyage to Russia, but accepts the erroneous association of Olaf Tryggvason with Otto II's campaign against Harald Gormsson in 974 [23]. It is likewise significant that the traditional site of Olaf's adventure with Geira was not unanimously localized near Jómsborg and the mouth of the Oder, as may be gathered from the statement of Oddr (Arn.): "Geira drottning ríkði þar er Germanía heitir til vestrhalfu, oc er þangat beiði betri landzcostr oc svâ lýðrinn" (*Forn. Sög.* X, 235).

Before attempting any conclusion as to the degree of historical verity attributable to the Geira tradition, it is essential to analyze the various phases of the Norse material dealing with her supposed sister Gunnhildr. The first mention of the latter, as of Geira, appears in the *Fagrskinna* (p. 42), and in Oddr [24]. According to the former, when Jarl Sigvaldi learned of the death of Harald Gormsson [25], he immediately made peace with Búrizláfr of Vind-

---

[22] *Forn.*, *Sög.* X, 340: "En til þessa veitti Ástríðr konungi lið, dóttir Búrizleifs konungs, oc hann var oc hinn mesti vin Ólafs konungs, af því er hann hafði verit í Vinðlandi, þá er hann átti dóttur hans.

[23] As Olaf was born in 968, and returned from Russia only in 986—987, such participation is historically impossible. For the activity of Búrizláfr in this connection, v. *infra* p. 136.

[24] Arn., *Forn. Sög.* X, 285 ff.; Stkh., in *Kong Olaf Tryggvesöns Saga af Odd Snorreson*, ed. P. A. Munch (Oslo, 1853), 29, 30.

[25] The accounts of Harald's death are varied and interesting. According to *Fgsk.* (p. 51), he died of an illness. The redactions of Oddr give no particulars. The *Hskr.* represents him as attacked by Sveinn, and receiving in battle a wound from which he died (I, 318, 319). Adam of Bremen, who claims to have derived his information from Sveinn Ulfsson, the grandson of Sveinn Tjuguskegg, recounts that the latter was supported against his father by the anti-Christian party, and that Harald, beaten and severely wounded, "elapsus est ad ciuitatem Sclauorum, quae Iumna dicitur [= Jómsborg]", where "post aliquot dies ex eodem uulnere deficiens in Christi confessione migravit" (*ed. cit.* I, 27, 28). According to the *Jómsvikingasaga* (*Forn. Sög.* XI, 64, *Flatey.* I, 161, 162), he is assassinated by Palnatoki (cf. also Saxo Gram., *ed. cit.*, 332, according to whom Harald, beaten by Sveinn, flees to Jómsborg for assistance, and upon landing after a second battle with his son, is killed by Palnatoki).

land, with whom the Jómsvikings are represented as waging constant war, and after marrying his daughter Ástríðr, proposed to entice Sveinn Tjuguskegg to Vindland. Journeying to Seeland for this purpose, he employed a successful ruse to lure Sveinn on board his ship, and forthwith set sail for Jómsborg. On his arrival there, he informed Búrizláfr of Sveinn's capture, and also proposed to release the Danish king upon the latter's acceptance of such terms as Sigvaldi should dictate. Búrizláfr likewise consented to conclude peace with Sveinn on conditions to be set by the Jarl of Jómsborg. These stipulations included the marriage of Sveinn to Gunnhildr, whose dowry was to include the Wendish territory which the Danes had seized, while Búrizláfr was betrothed to Þyri, Sveinn's sister, who later married Olaf Tryggvason. In the Arn. redaction of Oddr, the account of the marriage of Sveinn and Gunnhildr is yoked up with the story of the union of Sigvaldi with Búrizláfr's third daughter Ástríðr. Sigvaldi, in fact, demands her hand, but the Wendish king stipulates as a preliminary that Sigvaldi shall first kidnap Sveinn. The abduction is then recounted with extensive elaboration. As soon as Sveinn is in his power, Sigvaldi frankly explains the situation to his captive, and suggests the advisability of a match between the Danish king and Gunnhildr. As Sveinn has no choice but to assent, the Jarl then visits Búrizláfr and puts forward his proposition covering Gunnhildr's marriage to Sveinn, which is duly celebrated. In this redaction, the Þyri-Búrizláfr match does not appear at all in this connection, but instead (*Forn. Sög.* X, 309), Búrizláfr makes independent application for Þyri's hand considerably later. In the Stockholm redaction of Oddr, the situation is very briefly described with totally different implications. At the time of Harald Gormsson's death, Sigvaldi is already married to Ástríðr. Búrizláfr conspires with Sigvaldi to deprive Sveinn of his throne. The Jarl thus captures Sveinn, releasing him only on payment of ransom and the celebration of his marriage to Gunnhildr. Here again, there is no relation between the marriage of Gunnhildr and the union of Þyri with Búrizláfr. The *Jómsvikingasaga* (*Forn. Sög.* XI, 99 ff.) adds the detail that, of the Wendish princesses, Ástríðr was the oldest and Geira the youngest. The basis of the narrative corresponds in the main to the Arn. redaction of Oddr, but with the addition that Ástríðr herself suggests as a prior condition to her marriage with Sigvaldi that he either secure the refund of all previous payments made by Búrizláfr to the Danes or else kidnap Sveinn Tjuguskegg. The Jarl succeeds in capturing Sveinn, and then announces to the Danish king that out of personal friendship he has planned the marriage with Gunnhildr. Sigvaldi now claims Astríðr, having fulfilled his part of the contract, and also secures from Sveinn the desired refund prior to the latter's marriage with Gunnhildr. In the *Jómsvíkingasaga*, there is again no mention of any alliance between Þyri and Búrizláfr. The *Hskr.* (I, 319, 320) is closest to the Arn. redaction of Oddr, but represents Sigvaldi's marriage to Ástríðr as having already taken place before the abduction of Sveinn. The Danish king, fearing for his life, consents to a reconciliation with Búrizláfr, sealed by his own marriage to Gunnhildr and the betrothal of the Wendish king to his sister Þyri [26].

The only consistent elements emerging from this welter of contradictory detail are the capture of Sveinn by Sigvaldi and the latter's mediation in the arrangement of a marriage between the Danish king and a Wendish princess. The sources dealing most extensively with the Gunnhildr-episode (both redactions of Oddr, *Jómsvíkingasaga, Hskr.*) are curiously reticent as to the chronological relation between the marriage of Geira and the former, though Olaf's return from Russia and the accession of Sveinn Tjuguskegg (and therefore the latter's marriage with Gunnhildr) are, according to the customary dating, separated by only two years at the most. In fact, if the implications of the Geira episode are strictly followed, Olaf should have been in Vindland when the abduction and marriage of Sveinn occurred. In view, however, of the faulty nexus between the two sets of traditions, the conclusion is indicated that Geira, if she existed, was actually not related to Gunnhildr and Búrizláfr at all. The Arn. redaction of Oddr (*supra*, p. 122) classes her as a Wendish princess in Western Germany. Olaf's early association with the Jómsvikings is mentioned in but two sources (*Ágrip, Forn. Sög.* X, 392, and *Hist. Norw.*, p. 113), and is never picked up again in later works save in a brief note in Oddr (Arn.) mentioning a tradition that Olaf once besieged Jómsborg (*ibid.*, 238), which is obviously in contradiction with the statement of the sources cited that he made that center his winter-quarters. It therefore appears

---

[26] For the subsequent development of the Þyri-Búrizláfr motive, v. *infra.* p. 129.

that a scanty tradition regarding Olaf's temporary union with a Wendish princess has been connected by the saga-compilers with the account of Gunnhildr's marriage, and has then been extensively used to motivate Olaf's later success in recovering Pyri's dowry in Vindland. The rejection of any relationship between Gunnhildr and Geira is further justified by the fact that while there is scaldic confirmation for Olaf's raids in Vindland, there is none whatever for any contact between Olaf and the *Jómsvíkingar*.

According to the *Fagrskinna* (p. 43), Gunnhildr bore Sveinn two sons, Knútr inn Ríki and Harald. This tradition is repeated in both redactions of Oddr (Stkh., *loc. cit.*, 37, 38; Arn., *Forn. Sög.* X, 313) and in the *Knytlingasaga* (*Forn. Sög.* XI, 183), as well as in the *Hskr.* (I, 319). The same sources unanimously add that Sveinn later married Sigríðr Stórráða, the widow of Eiríkr Sigrsaeli of Sweden (died 993), who is stated to have been the mother of Olaf Skotkonungr by her first husband [27]. The *Hskr.* is the only source stating explicitly that Gunnhildr died before Sveinn's marriage to Sigríðr.

It so happens that the marriage of Sveinn to a Wendish princess is attested by German sources considerably closer to the event. Thus Thietmar of Merseburg, referring with some animus to the Scandinavians, writes:

"Sed quia nullus ad comprehendendas aquilonaris regionis uarietates, quas natura pre caeteris mirabiles ibidem operatur, et crudeles populi istius executiones sufficit, omitto et de geniminibus uiperarum, id est filiis Suenni persecutoris [i. e., Sveinn Tjuguskegg] pauca edissero. Hos peperit ei Miseconis filia ducis, soror Bolezlaui successoris eius et nati; quae a viro suimet diu depulsa non minimam cum caeteris perpessa est controuersiam." [28]

The generation of vipers mentioned is speedily identified by Thietmar as "praedicti fratres Harald et Cnut" [29]. The prince appearing as Miseco, the father of Bolezlavus, his own successor, is Mieszko I, Prince of Poland (died 992) [30], the father of Boleslav Chrobry. Thietmar is thus in agreement with the body of Norse tradition as to the parentage of Knut. Adam of Bremen, however, writes:

---

[27] *Fgsk.*, 59, 64; Oddr (Stkh.) 38, (Arn.) *Forn. Sög.* X, 313; *Hskr.* I, 419.

[28] VIII, 39; ed. F. Kurze (Hannover 1889), 216.

[29] VIII, 40; *ibid.*, 218.

[30] For a general account of Mieszko, cf. H. Zeißberg: "Miseco I (Mieczyslaw), der erste christliche Beherrscher der Polen" *Archiv für Kunde österreich. Geschichtsquellen* XXXVIII² (Vienna 1867), 27 ff.

"Post mortem diu optatam Herici [Eiríkr Sigrsaeli], Sueinn ab exilio regressus optinuit regnum patrum suorum anno depulsionis uel peregrinationis XIIII. Et accepit uxorem Herici relictam, matrem Olaph [Olaf Skotkonungr], quae peperit ei Chnud." [31]

As Weibull has remarked, it would hardly seem likely that Adam of Bremen should have erred in a matter of recent genealogy where the grandson of Sveinn Tjuguskegg was his immediate source, though his statement that fourteen years elapsed between the deaths of Harald Gormsson (986) and of Eiríkr Sigrsaeli (993) shows that in dealing with foreign subjects he was by no means exempt from the capacity to err [32]. Saxo Grammaticus likewise mentions Sveinn's marriage to Eiríkr's widow, whom he names Syritha, and characterizes as having borne to Sveinn his son Knut [33]. And finally, the *Cnutonis Res Gestae* relate that Knut, after succeeding to the throne, went with his brother Harald to *Sclavonia*, whence he brought back their mother who was so-journing there. [34]

The evidence of the Norse sources, along with Thietmar and, by implication, the *Cnutonis Res Gestae*, thus indicates Knut's mother to have been of Slavic origin. Adam testifies, however, in contradiction with Norse tradition, that Knut and Olaf were sons of the same mother. If the mother of Knut was a Slavic princess, and if, at the same time, Knut and Olaf Skotkonungr were half-brothers by the same mother, the widow of Eiríkr Sigrsaeli cannot have been a Swedish lady. In fact, not only must Eiríkr's widow in this case have been Slavic, but she and Sveinn's Slavic wife (i. e., Gunnhildr) must have been one and the same person.

It is only by analysis of the traditions surrounding Sigríðr Stórráða that this radical correction of the sources can be justified. Sigríðr first appears in the *Morkinskinna* [35] casually mentioned as the mother of Olaf Skotkonungr and his sister Ástríðr. In the

---

[31] II, 39; ed. Schmeidler, 99. He later (II, 73) refers to Knut and Olaf as "germani fratres".

[32] *Undersökningar*, 109. That Adam was less infallible in matters of recens genealogy than Weibull's remark would signify is also indicated by Adam't statement that Sveinn Tjuguskegg's daughter Ástríðr (her Christian name was Margaret) was married to Richard II of Normandy (II, 54, *ed. cit.*, 114), when she was really the wife of his son Robert I.

[33] *Gesta Danorum* ed. A. Holder (Straßburg 1886), 337, 340.

[34] Ed. G. H. Pertz (Hannover 1865), 12.

[35] Ed. C. R. Unger (Oslo 1867), 17.

same connection, she is characterized in the *Fagrskinna* (p. 59) as daughter of Skǫglar-Tosti and mother of Olaf Skotkonungr, instrumental in influencing her second husband, Sveinn Tjuguskegg, to avenge the slight put upon her by Olaf Tryggvason through his unceremonious breaking of their engagement. She is later referred to (ibid., 110) as the mother of Ástríðr by Sveinn Tjuguskegg and as the previous wife of Eiríkr Sigrsaeli. The statement of Adam of Bremen (II, 39) that Sveinn married Eiríkr's widow (whose name he does not mention) has already been noted, together with the related passage in Saxo Grammaticus, who gives Eiríkr's widow the name Syritha. Saxo is thus the first author to use the name Sigríðr or its approximation. Details of Sigríðr's marriage to Eiríkr first appear in Oddr (Stkh., p. 7), where it is stated that, according to common gossip, Eiríkr divorced her on account of her temper, but that she knew he had made a previous vow to Odin, according to which he had but a *few* years to live, which was dangerous for her in view of the Swedish custom that a queen should not survive her deceased husband. This same redaction (p. 29) later reports that, in accordance with his vow to Odin, Eiríkr committed suicide when *ten* years had elapsed after his successful battle with Styrbjǫrn, in connection with which his vow had been made. The Arn. redaction (*Forn. Sög.*, X, 220) first amplifies the corresponding data to the immolation of a surviving consort over a deceased king by the statement that Eiríkr had only *ten* more years to live, and then, in a later passage (*ibid.*, 283) repeats the terms of the vow, adding that at the time of Eiríkr's divorce of Sigríðr he made her queen in Gautland. Snorri Sturluson apparently undertook some elimination of the prolific romantic elements of the tradition as it existed to this point in his own day, since he confines himself to the following statements: (1) Sigríðr, daughter of Skǫglar-Tosti, was married to Eiríkr Sigrsaeli (I, 245), by whom she had a son Olaf [Skotkonungr]; (2) Eiríkr died of illness at Uppsala *(ibid.)* ten years after Styrbjǫrn's death (993—94); (3) upon the arrival of Harald grenzki in Sweden (994), Sigríðr was a widow, and had considerable estates in that country (I, 338). He thus rejects the whole tale of Eiríkr's vow and of his divorce from Sigríðr.

The next series of traditions associated with Sigríðr concerns her relations with Olaf Tryggvason. She does not appear in this connection at all prior to the *Fagrskinna* which, as indicated above (p. 127), notes her hostility to Olaf on account of their broken engagement, but without detailed motivation (*ed. cit.*, p. 59). The episode of the imitation gold ring offered as a gift from Olaf Tryggvason to Sigríðr appears, however, in both redactions of Oddr, which likewise report Olaf's subsequent meeting with her and the scornful slap dealt her with his glove when she refused to be converted. Both redactions also mention this episode as the basis for her pronounced hostility to Olaf [36]. Snorri adopts substantially the same version. This enmity of Sigríðr toward Olaf Tryggvason is connected with his personal history only at one point, viz., in the events preceding the battle of Svölð, with the story of which has been interwoven a considerable amount of romantic embellishment connected both with Sigríðr and with Þyri, the sister of Sveinn Tjuguskegg.

The motives underlying the collision between Olaf Tryggvason and his enemies at Svölð are variously explained in the earlier texts. According to Adam of Bremen (II, 39, p. 100), Olaf, hearing of an alliance between Sveinn Tjuguskegg and Olaf Skotkonungr, and believing Sveinn easy prey, declared war upon him at the instigation of his wife *Thore* ("cuius instinctu bellum Danis intulit," *ibid.*, 36, p. 98). Olaf Tryggvason is thus the aggressor. In the *Ágrip*, however, the quarrel arises from Sveinn's retention of the items promised and stipulated as Þyri's dowry after her marriage to Olaf Tryggvason, who, with a view to wiping out the insult entailed, projects an expedition against Denmark (*Forn. Sög.* X, 393). While troops are being gathered in Norway, Olaf sails over to Vindland, but his soldiery turn back as soon as he is out of the country, so that he is obliged to depend solely on Wendish support. Sveinn now allies himself with Olaf Skotkonungr and Eiríkr Hákonarson, and the allies attack and defeat Olaf Tryggvason *"furir Siolandi"*. In Theodric's *Historia de Antiquitate Regum Norwagiensium* [37], Sveinn, Olaf Skotkonungr, and Eiríkr Hákonarson are the aggressors, catch Olaf Tryggvason unprepared, and defeat him "iuxta insulam quae dicitur Svold et iacet prope Slauiam". In this text, there is not the slightest

---

[36] Stkh., pp. 29, 31, 32; Arn., *Forn. Sög.* X, 284, 292, 293.

[37] *Mon. Historica Norvegiae* ed. G. Storm (Oslo 1880), 23, 24. For the most recent and a very satisfactory analysis of the sources on the battle of Svölð, cf. J. Schreiner: 'Olaf Tryggvasons Siste Kamp' in *Festskrift til H. Falk*, (Oslo 1927), pp. 54—77.

reference to Þyri. The *Historia Norwegiae* [38] gives an account similar to that of the *Ágrip*, relating that, when Sveinn retains Seeland, the dowry of his sister "nomine Thyri, quam prius dux quidam de Sclauia desponsauerat inuitam", Olaf declares war upon him. The Norwegian king, as in the *Ágrip*, endeavors to collect a force wherewith to attack the Danes, but the Norwegians are unwilling to cross the frontiers, so that Olaf Tryggvason is obliged to seek aid among the *Sclavi*, "quos in piratica fidissimos habuerat socios". Sveinn, upon hearing of Olaf's preparations, concludes an alliance with Olaf of Sweden and Eiríkr Hákonarson. The three take Olaf of Norway by surprise as he is sailing *past Seeland*, where they attack and defeat him.

As far as the earlier Norse sources may be credited, the basic element of these narratives seems to consist in a territorial dispute between Sveinn and Olaf Tryggvason, whether or not connected with Þyri's dowry; it can no longer be determined with certainty who was the aggressor. The romantic increment of this episode in the later texts is attached to the fundamental account as supplied by the fairly congruent narratives of the *Ágrip* and the *Historia Norwegiæ*, both of which include as points of departure: Þyri's betrothal to a Wendish prince prior to her marriage with Olaf Tryggvason, Sveinn's retention of her dowry, Olaf's preparation for hostilities, his journey to Vindland, the alliance of Sveinn, Olaf Skotkonungr, and Eiríkr Hákonarson, and the fatal naval engagement. Subsequent elaborations, which first occur in the redactions of Oddr, thence find their way, for the most part, into the *Hskr.*, and are summarized in the *Fagrskinna*, include: an extended account of Þyri's marriage to Búrizláfr, her flight from Vindland, her marriage to Olaf of Norway, her incitement of Olaf to war against Sveinn, and her request that Olaf recover her property in Vindland; Olaf's successful errand to Búrizláfr in this connection; and finally, the activity of Sigríðr Stórráða in urging Sveinn to avenge on Olaf Tryggvason the disgrace he had visited on the Danish king by marrying Þyri without Sveinn's permission.

The various development of these elements may best be seen from the summaries following:

(a) Oddr (Stkh.): Þyri, though betrothed to Búrizláfr, stays at home in Denmark, unwilling to go to Vindland and consummate the marriage until forced

[38] *Loc. cit.*, 116, 117.

Festschrift Collitz.

9

to do so by Sveinn, who is chiefly influenced by the protests of his wife Gunnhildr. Þyri, even after the marriage, refuses to live with Búrizláfr, who allows her to depart. She flees to Falster, and sends a messenger to Olaf Tryggvason requesting his protection. Olaf goes to Falster, where he marries Þyri without consulting Sveinn Tjuguskegg, who resents this slight (pp. 36, 37). After Sveinn's marriage to Sigríðr Stórráða, she keeps his resentment hot, and finally (p. 46) induces him to concoct a plot with Olaf Skotkonungr whereby the latter shall pretend his readiness to be converted and plan a meeting with Olaf Tryggvason, by which pretext the Norse king shall be enticed out of his kingdom and thus laid open to attack. Olaf Tryggvason falls into the trap, and when Olaf Skotkonungr does not show up at the rendezvous (p. 48), sails on to Vindland, where he recovers Þyri's property. Meanwhile Sveinn, Olaf Skotkonungr, and Eiríkr Hákonarson prepare to attack him.

(b) Oddr (Arn.): Olaf Tryggvason's attention is first called to Þyri by one of his companions (*Forn. Sög.* X, 293). Búrizláfr, however, asks successfully for her hand in Denmark, and returns home to Vindland, whither Þyri is supposed to follow. She refuses to do so, however, until Búrizláfr requests Gunnhildr to intervene with Sveinn so that he may induce her to set out (p. 309). The marriage is consummated, but Þyri refuses food for eleven days, and on the twelfth the king allows her to depart. She flees to Falster, whence she sends messengers to Aki, her foster-father at Olaf's court (the same person who had previously spoken to Olaf concerning her). Olaf goes to meet her at Falster, and they are married (p. 313). Sveinn is displeased at the news, and shortly after, Gunnhildr dies, whereupon he marries Sigríðr. She subsequently (p. 333) incites him to hostility against Olaf Tryggvason, and devises a plot whereby Olaf Tryggvason, Olaf Skotkonungr, and Sveinn shall meet the following summer at the Brenneyar. Eiríkr Hákonarson and his brother Sveinn join with Olaf Skotkonungr in the conspiracy. Olaf Tryggvason consents to the meeting, and meanwhile Þyri urges him to recover her property in Vindland (p. 337). Olaf Tryggvason sets out for Vindland, where he celebrates a reunion with his old friends Dixin, Búrizláfr, and Astríðr, and recovers the dowry of Þyri (pp. 339, 340). In both redactions of Oddr, Sigvaldi of Jómsborg is Sveinn Tjuguskegg's emissary to Olaf Skotkonungr.

(c) *Heimskringla* (I, 419—430): Búrizláfr complains of the non-fulfillment of the contract whereby he is to marry Sveinn's sister Þyri. Sigvaldi goes to Denmark and brings her back to Vindland, where she is married to Búrizláfr. She refuses all sustenance *for a week*, and finally flees to the woods with her foster-father. They escape thence to Denmark, but dare not stay there in fear of Sveinn's anger. They thus move on to Norway, where Þyri addresses herself for protection directly to Olaf Tryggvason. Being a persuasive woman (*"orðsnjǫll"*, says Snorri), she immediately wins his sympathy to the extent that he proposes marriage. Upon its celebration, Þyri begins to regret her lost belongings in Vindland, and suggests that Olaf should have no difficulty in recovering them, as long as Búrizláfr is such an old friend. The king thus plans a voyage for this purpose, disregarding the counteradvice of his friends because Þyri taunts him with being afraid of her brother Sveinn. He thus arrives in Vindland, and accomplishes his mission successfully. Sigríðr is meanwhile inciting Sveinn Tjuguskegg to attack Olaf. Sveinn therefore crosses over to Sweden to conclude an alliance with Olaf Skotkonungr and Eiríkr Hákonarson, so that they may attack Olaf while he is on his voyage to Vindland.

(d) *Fagrskinna* (pp. 58—61): At Gunnhildr's instigation, Sveinn forces Þyri to depart for Vindland and marry Búrizláfr. After seven days, however, she escapes to Denmark, and thence to Norway, where she becomes Olaf's wife without

Sveinn's consent. After leaving Vindland, which he had visited for the recovery of Þyri's dowry, Olaf sails toward Denmark, and in the neighborhood of Svölð- comes into collision with the combined fleets of Sveinn Tjuguskegg, Olaf Skot- konungr, and Eiríkr. Olaf Skotkonungr was there to avenge Olaf Tryggvason's insult to his mother Sigríðr, who had also incited Sveinn to avenge the affront Olaf had put upon him.

This body of tradition which, in view of its extensive variations, must be viewed entirely as fiction, arises logically from an effort to motivate the hostility of Sveinn Tjuguskegg and his con- temporaries toward Olaf Tryggvason. The impulse to the wholesale introduction of feminine influences derives initially from the supposition that the quarrel first rose over Þyri's marriage portion, so that she was the injured party likely to spur Olaf Tryggvason to aggression. In the versions which made Sveinn Tjuguskegg the aggressor, it was then necessary to supply a similar motivation, hence the general appearance of Sigríðr Stórráða in this role. In both redactions of Oddr, Gunnhildr exercizes great influence over Sveinn, especially in connection with the marriage of Þyri. On the other hand, since another parallel tradition existed accord- ing to which Gunnhildr was Olaf Tryggvason's sister-in-law, it would be incongruous if she were to prove hostile to him. The necessity thus arose of postulating as second wife for Sveinn Tjuguskegg the entirely mythical Sigríðr Stórráða, around whom other legends could be centered. The somewhat nebulous character of the whole account is further indicated by the absence of precise information as to Gunnhildr's death; only Snorri (I, 419) remarks specifically that she "took sick and died" [39], but with very indefinite indication of chronology, and the dubious explanation "sem nú var áðr frá sagt." [40]

There remains one further item requiring interpretation in this connection, viz., Scholium 25 to Adam of Bremen, according to which Eiríkr Sigrsaeli of Sweden made an alliance with "Boliz- laus", king of Poland, against the Danes and married "either his daughter or his sister." [41] The Polish prince thus designated is

---

[39] Cf. Oddr (Arn., *Forn. Sög.* X, 313): "En er Sveinn konungr spyrr þetta, lícar honum stórilla, er þetta var gert at úleyfi hans [i. e., marriage of Olaf Tryg- gvason and Þyri]; oc litlu síþarr andaðiz Gunnhilldr drotning, er átti Sveinn konungr."

[40] Substantially the same conclusion is reached by Weibull (*Undersökningar* 124, 125), who suggests an analogy with the Sigurd-legend, urging that Brynhild is the prototype for the evolution of Sigríðr.

[41] Ed. Schmeidler, p. 95: "Hericus rex Sueonum cum potentissimo rege Polanorum Bolizlao fedus iniit. Bolizlaus filiam uel sororem Herico dedit. Cuius

undoubtedly Boleslav Chrobry, Mieszko's son, who actually did control most of Russia for a brief period (1018—1019), and who likewise subjected both the Prussians and certain Slavic tribes west of the Oder. Mieszko, however, had died in 992; Eiríkr Sigrsaeli died in 993—994. The period within which this marriage could have been consummated and the otherwise totally unknown Slavo-Swedish attack on the Danes could have been executed is thus reduced to an impossibly narrow margin. While Schmeidler attributes this scholium to Adam himself (*op. cit.*, XLII), this attribution by no means exempts it from the possibility of error, particularly since Adam was apparently misinformed anyway as to the date of Eiríkr's death (v. *supra* p. 127). Furthermore, Boleslav in 992—994 was in no position to undertake a war against the Danes. In the first place, he had no navy and as yet no direct contact with the sea. In the second, he was supporting the Saxons during 992 against a Slavic revolt [42], and shortly thereafter was involved in a serious Russian offensive into Galicia [43]. The fact that Adam did not know whether it was Boleslav's sister or his daughter whom Eiríkr was supposed to have married shows that his information was dubious. As a matter of fact, Boleslav was born in 967 (cf. Zeissberg, *op. cit.*, 102) and thus could have had no marrigeable female issue in 992—994. The conclusion is therefore justified that we are here confronted with a very scanty trace of the original marriage of Gunnhildr to Eiríkr Sigrsaeli, which must actually have taken place some eight years previous. Adam, already familiar with Sveinn's marriage to a daughter of Mieszko, appears to have received subsequent information of the marriage of Eiríkr to a princess of the same family. Since Adam obviously did not know the name of the princess concerned, and, unlike Thietmar, was unfamiliar with the tradition of Mieszko's daughter's divorce, he naturally concluded that two separate individuals were involved. Since the

---

gratia societatis Dani a Sclauis et Suconibus iuxta impugnati sunt. Bolizlaus rex christianissimus cum Ottone tercio confederatus omnem Sclauoniam subiecit et Ruzziam et Pruzzos, a quibus passus est sanctus Adalbertus, cuius reliquias tunc Bolizlaus transtulit in Poloniam."

[42] *Ann. Sax.*, in *M. G. SS.* VI, *sub anno*.

[43] Лавр. Лет., *ed. cit.*, *122 ad* 992; *Ann. Hildesheim*, *M. G. SS.*, III, 69 ad 992: "Bolizlao vero, Misachonis filius, per se ipsum ad dominum regem uenire nequaquam ualens — imminebat quippe illi grande contra Ruscianos bellum — suos sibi satis fideliter milites in ministerium regis direxerat."

evidence is overwhelmingly in favor of the Slavic origin of the mother of Knut the Great, it may be inferred that Gunnhildr was first married to Eiríkr Sigrsaeli, by whom apparently she was divorced [44]. After Eiríkr's death, she married Sveinn Tjuguskegg. During his campaigns in England, she returned to live in Poland, and was brought home from there by Knut after his accession to the throne.

The various traditions surrounding Ástríðr, referred to in the younger Norse sources generally as Búrizláfr's third daughter, have already been briefly noted (*supra* p. 123). Aside from the daughter whom Thietmar of Merseburg and Adam of Bremen mention as married to Sveinn Tjuguskegg, we have no further data as to Mieszko's female issue. He seems to have been first married in 965—966 to Dobrava, daughter of the Czechish prince Boleslav I, and then, upon her death (977), to the former nun Oda, daughter of the German margrave Thiedrich [45]. Dobrava is attested as the mother of Boleslav Chrobry [46]. It is thus apparent that any daughters of Mieszko who acquired Scandinavian husbands in the eighties of the tenth century must have been children of Dobrava and sisters of Boleslav [47]. In view, however, of the romantic elaborations, particularly in the redactions of Oddr and of the *Jómsvíkingasaga*, which surround the conditions of Ástríðr's marriage to Sigvaldi, and the complete lack of evidence elsewhere as to any very consistent and close relations between Poles and Danes, it is rather more likely that Ástríðr was actually the daughter of some minor Pomeranian prince in the vicinity of Wollin, and was linked up with Búrizláfr-Mieszko in the general

---

[44] The phrase of Thietmar (VIII, 39) "*a uiro suimet diu depulsa*" was rightly taken by J. M. Lappenberg (*M. G. SS.* III *ad loc.*) to refer to Eiríkr, not to Sveinn, as F. Kurze (*ed. cit.*, 216, n. 5) interprets it. Kurze also considers, on the basis of the scholium of Adam, that this princess was previously married to Eiríkr: "quae antea Erici regis Sueciae uxor fuisse apud Adam II c. 33, schol. 25 et c. 36 traditur" (*ibid.*, n. 4). Kurze was, however, unfamiliar with the Norse sources, since he remarks of Mieszko's daughter (*ibid.*): "nomen ei fuisse Sigrid Storråda Lappenberg *argumentis ignotis nisus* dixit."

[45] *Ann. Pol., M. G. SS.* XIX, 615, *Ann. Cracov. Vet.,* ibid., 577, Thietmar IV, 55—56, pp. 94, 95.

[46] *Ann. Pol.* iv, *M. G. SS.* XIX, 615.

[47] The tradition preserved in Gallus (*Mon. Pol. Hist.* I, 399) that Mieszko, while a pagan, had seven wives, is rather to be regarded as analogous to the story presented by the Russian *Primary Chronicle* (Лавр. Лет., 79) regarding Vladimir's maintenance, before his conversion, of *six hundred* concubines, who are simply intended to place him in the same class with Solomon and thus to make the contrast between his pagan and his Christian life the more impressive.

process of combination of initially unrelated elements which seems to have taken place in the evolution of the sagas of the *Jómsvíkingar* and of Olaf Tryggvason [48].

The foregoing analysis of Norse material dealing with the relations between Scandinavians and Wends at the mouth of the Oder in the last decades of the tenth century suggests that the extent of these contacts was considerably more restricted than a literal reading of these sources would indicate. It remains to confirm this conclusion by examining the details of Polish history during this period with a view to determining what relations exist between the well-attested activities of the contemporary Polish princes and the implications of the Norse texts.

Regardless of the statement of Oddr (*Forn. Sög.* X, 285) that Búrizláfr was a vassal of the king of Denmark, there is no evidence elsewhere that the Poles during the reign of Mieszko were particularly concerned with controlling the mouth of the Oder or that their northern boundary lay north of the Warta river. The region known as Pomerania, bounded on the west by the Oder, on the south by the Warta and the Notec, and on the east by the Vistula, was indeed inhabited by Slavic tribes closely related to the Poles, but hardly identical with them. The Russian *Primary Chronicle* characterizes them as a subdivision of the Vistulan Slavs, while Helmold, likewise writing in the twelfth century, clearly differentiates them from the Poles [49]. Though generally not so inclusive, the name *Pomerania* also applied in the twelfth century to the west bank of the lower Oder, while the border with Poland proper ran up the Notec through the frontier towns of Zantok, Uzda, and Naklo [50]. Some indication that the Polish outposts lay somewhat further north on the Oder than generally supposed might conceivably be drawn from Widukind's mention that

---

[48] The Arn. redaction of Oddr (*Forn. Sög.* X, 285) thus mentions an otherwise unknown þyri as a fourth daughter of Búrizláfr in addition to Astríðr, Gunnhildr, and Geira.

[49] Лавр. Лет., 6: "Slověne prišedše sědoša na Visle prozvašasja Ljachove i ot těch Ljachov prozvašasja Poljane, Ljachove, druzii Lutiči, ini Mazovšane, ini Pomorjane." Helmold: *Chron. Slavorum* ed. G. F. Pertz (Hannover 1868) I, 40, p. 88: "Otto . . . adiit peregrinationem ad gentem Sclauorum, qui dicuntur Pomerani et habitant inter Oderam et Poloniam." Cf. Adam of Bremen IV, *13*, p. 241: "Trans Oddaram comperimus degere Pomeranos, deinde latissima Polanorum terra diffunditur." Cf. also Gallus, *Mon. Pol. Hist.* I, 394.

[50] Cf. L. Niederle: *Slovanské Starožitnosti* III (Prague, 1919), 152.

Wichmann incited the *Vuloini* to attack Mieszko in 967 [51]. It is clear, however, that in the official Saxon conception Mieszko's territory extended in 972 only to the Warta, since the Polish prince is expressly characterized as "imperatori fidelem tributumque usque in Uurta solventem". [52] This passage is practically the only extant reliable indication of the geographical extent of Poland in the course of Mieszko's principate. While it has sometimes been assumed [53] that Pomerania was in some degree subject to Poland even in Mieszko's time, the best evidence points to its first conquest by Boleslav Chrobry during the early years of his reign [54]. Mieszko, in fact, during his later years appears to have been too constantly engaged in disputes with his Czechish neighbors or, as an ally of the Saxons, in campaigns against the pagan Slavs along the Elbe, to have been able to undertake any organized expansion up the Oder toward the sea.

The historical evidence of Mieszko's relation of vassalage to the contemporary Saxon emperors obviously precludes attaching any significance to Oddr's statement that he was a vassal of the Danish king. In 966, Mieszko had married Dobrava, sister of Boleslav II of Bohemia, and apparently through her influence was converted to Christianity [55]. At this period, conversion was synonymous with political dependence, and we thus find him

---

[51] Widukind: *Res Gestae Sax.* ed. K. A. Kehr (Hannover 1904) II, 69 (pp. 120, *122*): "[Wichmannus] egit cum Sclauis qui dicuntur Vuloini quomodo Misacam amicum imperatoris bello lacesserent." The identity of this tribe has been variously defined. L. Giesebrecht (*Wendische Geschichten* I [Berlin 1843] 189, 190) wished to locate them further south in Brandenburg, but their name clearly connects them with the island of Wollin, so that they can be placed with relative certainly on the lower Oder. So J. Steenstrup: *Venderne og de Danske* (Copenhagen 1910), *35, 36*; Niederle, *op. cit.*, III, 149, 150.

[52] Thietmar ed. F. Kurze I, 29 (p. 37). As Thietmar's father supported Mieszko when the latter was attacked at the time by the Margrave Odo, his information would appear trustworthy.

[53] W. Barthold: *Geschichte von Rügen u. Pommern* I (Hamburg, 1839) 337; A. Naruszewicz: *Historya Narodu Polskiego* I (Cracow 1859) 156.

[54] Cf. Helmold I, *15* (p. 36): "Eodem quoque tempore Bolizlaus, Polonorum cristianissimus rex, confederatus cum Ottone tertio, omnem Sclauiam, que est ultra Odoram, tributis subiecit." Cf. Adam of Bremen, schol. *25, supra*; W. von Sommerfeld: *Geschichte der Germanisierung des Herzogtums Pommern oder Slavien* (Leipzig 1896) *16*, dates this conquest in 995, presumably on the basis of Giesebrecht, *op. cit.*, I, 231, 232. In any case, there was a bishopric at Colberg under Boleslaw's friend Reinbern about 1000 (Thietmar IV, 45; p. 90).

[55] Thietmar IV, 55; pp. 94—95; *Ann. Pol., M. G. SS.* XIX, 614—615; *Ann. Cracov. Vet., ibid.* 577.

present as a vassal at Otto I's court in Quedlinburg on Easter Day, 973, together with his Czechish brother-in-law [56].

To what extremes Mieszko's subservience to Saxon authority extended may be gathered from Thietmar's subsequent lament, in connection with the presumption of Boleslav Chrobry, that the latter's father (Mieszko), as long as Margrave Odo lived, never even dared appear before him in a fur-trimmed cloak, much less remain seated if the Margrave arose [57]. Mieszko's loyalty to his suzerain, however, was not entirely invariable. Regardless of the fact that in 973 he put his son as a hostage in the hands of Otto I, he became involved the following year, just prior to Otto II's Danish expedition, in a conspiracy against the Emperor with Henry II of Bavaria, Bishop Abraham of Freising, and Boleslav of Bohemia [58]. Upon Otto's return from Denmark, he undertook in 975 a punitive expedition against Bohemia and apparently, with less success, against Mieszko [59]. Hence, if the Norse sources understood Búrizláfr to be prince of Poland, their statements as to his participation as a German ally in any operations against Harald in 974 belong to the realm of fable [60]. From the statement of the *Annales S. Trudperti* that Otto's expedition against Mieszko was unsuccessful, the conclusion may be drawn that during Otto II's reign, Mieszko's relations with the imperial court were in abeyance. In view of the Emperor's difficulties elsewhere, first in Bohemia (977), then in Lorraine (978—980), next in Italy (980—983), and finally, the revolt of the Elbian Slavs in 982, he was in no position to enforce obedience upon the Polish prince.

---

[56] *Ann. Altah. Maior.*, 2nd edit. ed. E. von Oefele (Hannover 1891), p. 11; Thietmar II, 31, p. 38.

[57] Thietmar V, 10; p. 113: "Vivente egregio Hodone pater istius Bolezlaui Miseco domum qua eum esse sciebat crusinatus intrare vel eo assurgente numquam praesumpsit sedere."

[58] *Ann. Altah. Maior.*, p. 11; Lambert of Hersefeld, ed. O. Holder-Egger (Hannover 1894), 42.

[59] *Ann. S. Trudperti*, M. G. SS. XVII, 280: "Otto imperator cum Polanis uincitur, et Miseco dux filius Bolizlai uictor existens Polemiorum gentem ab eius imperio seiunxit."

[60] The idea of introducing Búrizláfr into the narrative of Harald Gormsson's conflict with Otto II rose very naturally from the verses of the *Vellekla* (F. Jónsson: *Skaldedigtning* A 117) which speak of Wends as forming a part of Otto's army. Cf. *Hskr.* I, 300: "þás með fylki Frísa Fór gunnviður sunnan (Kvaddi vígs) ok Venða (Vágs blakriði) Frakka." The use of Wendish allies from the Slavic tribes west of the Oder is by no means unknown, as is shown by Henry II's similar enlistment of the Luticians against Boleslav Chrobry in 1005 (Thietmar: VI, 22; pp. 146, 147).

It has generally been assumed heretofore that Otto's campaign of 979 against certain Slavic tribes outside the boundaries of the realm was directed against the Poles [61], but its results were apparently negative. Mieszko thus took no active part in German affairs until after the death of Otto II, when he was disposed to support Duke Henry of Bavaria, the first guardian of the youthful Otto III, in his efforts to seize the realm. The Polish prince was thus present at Henry's court in Quedlinburg on Easter Day 984 [62]. After the diet of Rara and the conclusion of peace between Henry and the partisans of the five-year old Emperor, both Mieszko and Boleslav of Bohemia returned to their previous feudatory relationship, and were present once more at Quedlinburg at Easter 986 [63]. In the course of the same year, Otto initiated a new campaign against the Elbian Slavs, in which he was joined by Mieszko, who brought him the present of a camel [64]. A further Saxon sally against the Elbian Slavs in 987 [65] resulted in the reconstruction of the border blockhouses along the river ("renouatis iuxta Albim castellis", says Thietmar), showing that at the moment the Saxon frontier followed the course of the Elbe. During 990, Mieszko became involved in a conflict of uncertain origin and issue with Boleslav of Bohemia which seems to have caused considerable momentary commotion without modifying the territorial status of either prince [66]. The next Easter (991), Mieszko again appeared before Otto and Theophano, whose death occurred the following June [67]. In the same year, Mieszko made his final appearance as a German ally in Otto's first successful attack upon Brandenburg [68]. The Luticians, however, shortly retook the city, with the result that Otto resumed operations against it in 992; Mieszko was prevented from appearing in person in consequence of a threatened Russian attack, but sent a detach-

---

[61] Giesebrecht: *Wend. Gesch.* I, 255: Zeißberg, *loc. cit.*, 87 n., based on *Gesta Episcoporum Cameracensium*, M. G. SS. VII, 442, 443.

[62] Thietmar IV, 2; p. 65.

[63] *Ibid.* IV, 9; p. 69.

[64] *Ann. Altah. Maior.*, p. 15. *Ann. Hild.* and *Qued.*, M. G. SS. III, 67. Lambert (p. 46) substitutes *Boemos* for *Sclauos*, which is obviously an error, in view of Boleslav's attendance at court the same spring.

[65] *Ann. Altah. Maior.*, p. 15; Thietmar IV, 18, p. 74; *Ann. Hild.* and *Qued. ibid.*

[66] Thietmar IV, 11, pp. 70—72.

[67] *Ann. Hild.* and *Qued.* M. G. SS. III, 68; Thietmar IV, 15, p. 73.

[68] *Ann. Hild.* M. G. SS. III, 68.

ment commanded by his son Boleslav (v. *supra* p. 132). Mieszko himself died in June of this year [69].

It thus appears that the Pyri episode connected in the Norse sources with Búrizláfr cannot by any means be attached to Mieszko I, since, in the first place, he had been a Christian for some twenty-five years; and for the further reason that, since Pyri's marriage to Olaf Tryggvason took place after the latter's occupation of the Norwegian throne (hence in 995 or later), Mieszko had already been dead for at least three years when Pyri's marriage to Búrizláfr is supposed to have occurred. It has also been shown (v. *supra* p. 131) that the account of this marriage is chiefly fiction, quite apart from the historical fact that Mieszko's second wife Oda, whom he married after Dobrava's death (977), actually survived him [70].

There is similarly no historical basis for assuming any more intimate contact between Poles and Scandinavians during the early reign of Boleslav Chrobry. It has already been shown (v. *supra* p. 132) that the report in Scholium 25 to Adam of Bremen concerning a joint Suedo-Slavic attack on the Danes connected with an alleged marriage of some female relative of Boleslav to Eiríkr Sigrsaeli is, in all likelihood, entirely apocryphal. In 992, immediately after his accession, Boleslav, was threatened by a Russian incursion which occupied his attention for the next two years. In 995, Boleslav once more joined Otto III, this time in an expedition against the Obodriti in Mecklenburg [71], and shortly thereafter initiated his campaigns into Pomerania, which culminated in 997 by his recovery of the relics of St. Wojciech (Adalbert) from the Prussians [72]. We also find him seizing the pretext of a revolt among the Elbian Slavs to advance his western frontier to the Bober. The death of Boleslav II of Bohemia in 999 and the subsequent disorders provided him with an opportunity for the recapture of Cracow and the simultaneous annexation of Silesia and a part of Moravia. By this expansion of Polish sovereignty, however temporary it was likely to prove in consequence of the as yet deficient internal organization of Poland

[69] Thietmar IV, 58, p. 96; cf. Zeißberg, *op. cit.*, 98, 99 n.

[70] Thietmar IV, 57, p. 96: "cum magno honore ibi degens usque ad finem uiri."

[71] *Ann. Hild.*, M. G. SS. III, 91: "Rex Abodritos uastauit, urbes et oppida disiecit; occurrit in auxilium Bolizlau filius Misaco cum magno exercitu."

[72] *Ann. Qued.* M. G. SS. III, 73, 74; cf. Adam of Bremen, Schol. 25.

itself, Boleslav automatically became an outstanding European figure. It was accordingly in 1000 that Otto III undertook his celebrated pilgrimage to Gnesen. The Polish prince cannot well have entertained any interest in petty Scandinavian quarrels in 999—1000, so that, like the other components of the Pyri episode, the tradition of Olaf Tryggvason's gathering of assistance at this juncture among the Wends of the lower Oder must be rejected without reserve.

In summary, then, the only historical elements in the extensive body of Norse tradition surrounding the contact of the Jómsvikings with the Slavs at the mouth of the Oder and the relations of the latter with the Scandinavians in general toward the close of the tenth century consist in the probable presence of a Danish garrison at the Slavic town of Wollin and the marriage of a daughter of Mieszko I of Poland first to Eiríkr Sigrsaeli and later to Sveinn Tjuguskegg. As is shown by the marriage of Yaroslav the Wise to Ingigerðr some twenty years later, close political affiliation was not an essential of dynastic unions at this period. From the evidence of Scandinavian trade with central and eastern Europe via the Oder and the Vistula [73], it appears that these marriages with Scandinavian princes must have originated in a desire on the part of Mieszko and Boleslav to maintain friendly relations with Scandinavian warrior-merchants passing through the entrepots of Gnesen and Kruszwica. The romantic evolution of the *Jómsvíkingasaga* also appears to have favored the concentration about the legendary Búrizláfr of all surviving recollections of contacts with the Wends of the Baltic seacoast, particularly with those tribes residing between Holstein and Rügen, practically all of whom had been reduced to submission by the Germans before the thirteenth century. The apparently enigmatic prevalence of the name Búrizláfr-Búrizleifr as a cognomen of Slavic princes, which, in spite of its Slavic aspect, has no Slavic counterpart whatever [74], is hardly to be explained satisfactorily from any confusion of Mieszko I with his son, but rather by the greater Scandinavian familiarity with Boleslav Krzywousty (the Wrymouthed), who from 1102 to 1129 was

---

[73] R. Ekblom: »Die Waräger im Weichselgebiet«, *Arch. Slav. Philol.* XXXIX (Berlin 1924), 210.

[74] In the tenth century, the Polish form, if derived from *burja*, "storm", and the suffix -*slav*, should have been **Burzislaw*, which never occurs.

uninterruptedly engaged in the subjection of Pomerania, and who, after the reduction of Stettin in 1121, allied himself in 1130 with Nicholas of Denmark (son of Sveinn Ulfsson, and therefore great-grandson of Sveinn Tjuguskegg) for the conquest of Wollin. This alliance was sealed by the marriage of Boleslav Krzywousty's daughter Rikiza to the Danish king's son [75]. From Boleslav Krzywousty, the name appears to have become the characteristic appellation for Wendish princes in the Norse sagas, while the transformation of the first two syllables results from the supposed analogy with *Jarizleifr-Jarisláfr*, the Norse equivalent of *Yaroslav* [76] who, by virtue of his historical relationships with St Olaf and Harald Harðráði, was the Slavic ruler most frequently mentioned in the whole body of Norse literature reflecting the Russian adventures of these two princes.

[75] Saxo Gram. XIII, p. 420. *Knytlingasaga* 89 (*Forn. Sög.* XI, 327): "Magnús Nikulásson fekk Rikizu dottur *Búrizláfs* Vindakonungs, þeirra synir voru þeir Knútr ok Nikulás."

[76] For the variation between -*zláfr* and -*zleifr*, cf. *Óláfr*: *Aleifr*, A. Noreen: *Altisländ. u. altnorweg. Gramm.* 3rd edit. (Halle 1903), 39.

BLOTNAUT

BY CHESTER NATHAN GOULD

THE UNIVERSITY OF CHICAGO

I.

Although many scholars have in recent times referred to the worship of cattle in ancient Scandinavia [1], no one has collected and evaluated the evidence.

Cattle are mentioned in the tales of origins, as in the story (1) of the origin of the world and the gods in the Younger Edda. [2] A dripping frost turned into the cow Auðhumla, from whose teats ran four rivers of milk. These rivers nourished the giant Ymir from whose body earth and sky and sea were made. The cow licked the frost-stones "and the first day a man's hair came out of the stones in the evening, the next day a man's head, and the day after that the whole man was there." This man was Buri, the ancestor of the gods. (2) There are two slightly differing versions of the tale of Gefjon and the origin of the island of Zealand. Gefjon, kin of the Æsir, hitched to a plow her four giant-begotten sons, who, in the first version were oxen, or whom, in the second, [3] she changed to oxen. She was to have as much land as she turned over in a day; she plowed so deep that she dragged a piece of land, now the island of Zealand, out into the sea.

---

[1] E. g., J. de Vries, ZfdPh XXXV (1928), 281. Gudmund Schütte, Hjemligt Hedenskab i allmenfattelig Fremstillning (Køb. og Kris. 1919) 121 ff. E. H. Meyer, Germanische Mythologie (Berlin 1891), Par. 141; see also index under the names of the various animals. Finnur Jónsson, "Gudenavne-Dyrenavne," Afnf XXXV (1918), 309 ff. Kaarle Krohn, Skandinavisk Mytologi (Helsingfors, 1922), 79. Eugen Mogk in Hoop's Reallexikon der germ. Altertumskunde (Straßburg, 1911 to 19), s. v. rind. Karl Helm, Altgerm. Religionsgeschichte (Heidelberg, 1913) I, 202—213. Hjalmar Falk, "Odensheite," Vid.-Selsk. Skr. II. H.-F. Kl. (Kristiania, 1924), No. 10.

[2] Gylfaginning, chap. VI.

[3] Gylfaginning, chap. I; "Ynglinga saga," chap. V in Finnur Jónsson, Heimskringla (Køb. 1893—1900), I. Axel Olrik, »Gefjon«, Danske Studier 1910, 1. ff. Magnus Olsen, Stedsnavne Studier (Kristiania, 1912), 49 ff.

The instances of cattle used in ritual are particularly interesting. [4] (3) The oldest written record of cattle-worship among peoples from present Scandinavian territory concerns the Cimbri. [5] They released captive Romans on parole, requiring them to take oath on a bronze bull. [6] (4) The *Viga-Glums saga* relates as follows: "The man who should take a temple-oath took in his hand a silver ring which had been reddened in the blood of a neat which had been sacrificed." [7] (5) In the North German Nerthus ritual cows drew the sacred image of the goddess about the country in a car. [8] (6) Oxen, or more likely, bulls, were sacrificed in case of famine. "Then the Swedes performed great sacrifices at Upsala. The first autumn they offered oxen, and the crops were not bettered either." [9] The next year they triedh uman sacrifices and in the following year they sacrificed the king. (7) In Sweden an old bull intended for sacrifice had been so pampered that he became violent and broke away into the woods and was a source of danger.[10] (8) Saxo relates that a certain Danish king who was harrying in Sweden made an offering with *furuis hostiis*, "black victims," to secure divine favor, and that the Swedes perpetuated

---

[4] One is tempted to regard the vivid pictures of five bulls carved on the rocks at Tegneby, Aspeberget, in Tanums Socken, Tanums Härad in Bohuslän as an indication of bull-worship in Sweden in the bronze age. The manner in which they are depicted suggests that they are symbols of fertility. We know, however, so little of the purpose of these rock-pictures that one dares only to suggest this interpretation as a possibility. Reproduced in *Bidrag till kännedom om Göteborgs och Bohusläns fornminnen och historia*, VIII (1906), 514. Also Oscar Montelius, *Vår forntid* (Stockholm, 1919), 138.

[5] "Caius Marius," in *Plutarch's Lives*, IX, 525 = *Loeb's Classical Library* (London and New York), Greek Authors, CI (1920). The Cimbri arrived in Italy about 100 B. C., having left Jutland some twenty years before.

[6] The function of the bull here resembles that of the *sonargǫltr*, the boar. "In the evening there was making of vows. The *sonargǫltr* was led forth; men laid thereon their hands and made vows on the vowing-cup". See *Helgakviða Hiǫrvarðssonar*, prose following stanza 30. "King Heiðrekr had a big boar fed (i. e. reared). He was as big as the biggest bulls and so handsome that each hair seemed to be of gold. The king laid one hand on the boar's head and the other on his bristles and took this oath . . ." See Jón Helgason, *Heiðreks saga* (Køb., 1924), text *R*, 54 [5]. Text *H*, 54 [25], adds that the king worshipped Freyr and gave him the biggest boar he could get. The oaths were taken on Yule-eve. Text *U*, 129 [4] tells in addition to this that the boar was to be sacrificed to Freyr for good crops early in February.

[7] Guðmundar þórláksson, *Islenzkar Fornsögur*, gefnar út af hinu islenzka Bókmentafélagi (Kaupmannahöfn, 1880—83) I, 76.

[8] Tacitus, *Germania*, chap. XL. It was published in 98 A.D.

[9] *Ynglinga saga*, chap. XV.

[10] *Ynglinga saga*, chap. XXVI.

this offering in the form of an annual sacrifice. Saxo added concerning it: *Fröblod Sueones uocant.* "The Swedes call it Frey-sacrifice." [11] The "black victims" were in all probability black cattle. (9) Þorvarðr bought the carcass of a slaughtered bull and offered it to an elf. [12] One could give a living animal to a god. (10) Þorgils Þórðarson had once given a calf to Thor. Later Þorgils, who in the meantine had become a Christian, was sailing to Greenland. He dreamed that Thor was trying to win him back to heathenism and that Thor had finally said, "If you are not going to be good to me give me my goods anyway." When Þorgils awoke he remembered the calf, which was now an ox, and threw it overboard. [13] (11) ". . . before Þorkell went away from Þverá he went to Frey's temple and led thither an old ox and spoke thus: 'Frey', said he, 'has long been my confidence and received many good gifts from me and repaid them well. Now I give you this ox in order that Glumr may leave Þverá no less against his will than I go now. And do you let signs be seen, whether you accept or not.' And the ox gave a start and cried out and fell down dead." [14]

Bulls were employed in the ritual of the duel. (12) The participants had taken their positition on the duelling ground. "Then was led up a big old bull. It was called a *blótnaut.* [15] That should he kill who had the victory. It was sometimes one neat; sometimes each one who went on an island (i. e. fought a duel) had his own led up." After the victor, Egill Skallagrimsson, had killed his opponent he "sprang up quickly and to that place where the *blótnaut* was standing, grasped with one hand its muzzle and with the other a horn and turned the bull so that its feet stuck up and its neck broke." [16] (13) Kormákr disabled Þorvarðr in a duel and the

---

[11] Alfred Holder, *Saxonis Grammatici gesta Danorum* (Straßburg, 1886), 30.

[12] Vald. Asmundarson, *Kormáks saga* (Reykjavík 1893), chap. XXIII.

[13] Guðbrandr Vigfússon und Theodor Möbius, *Fornsögur* (Leipzig, 1860), 142.

[14] Guðmundur Þorláksson, *Íslenzkar Fornsögur*, Gefnar út af hinu íslenzka Bókmentafélagi (Kaupmannahöfn, 1880—83) I, 29.

[15] *Blótnaut*, from *blóta*, "to sacrifice, to worship," and *naut*, "neat," signifies (a) "a bovine animal destined for sacrifice," or (b) "one which is the object of worship."

[16] Finnur Jónsson, *Egils saga Skallagrímssonar nebst den gröszeren gedichten Egils* [2] (Halle, 1924), chap. LXV, sect. 20 ff. The editor says this manner of killing a bull is of course fictitious. This deed was similar to but far less difficult than "bulldogging a steer", a fairly common exhibition feat of American cowboys. "In this a steer is set galloping at full speed, the cowboy after him. A quick cow-pony will soon catch up with a steer, and, just at the moment that the pony forges beside the steer, the rider must throw himself

latter had to yield. "Kormákr saw where the neat stood and killed it." (14) The outcome of the duel was not satisfactory and it was tried again, but the same man was victorious as before, and "Kormákr killed the *blótnaut* according to custom." [17] (15) Two brothers were leaving home for the duelling ground where one of them was to fight a *berserkr*. "Þorbjǫrn asks his brother Gísli, 'Which of us, brother, shall fight the *berserkr* today, and which shall kill the calf?' Gísli answers, 'I advise this, that you kill the calf, but Bjǫrn and I shall test each other'." [18]

There are accounts of cattle which were objects of worship. Some of these tales concern cows. (16) King Ólafr Tryggvason once asked a peculiar old man who came to him at Eastertide at Ǫgvaldsness why the ness and farm were so named. The old man answered: "Ǫgvaldr was a king and a great warrior. He worshipped most a cow and had her with him wherever he went by sea or land. It seemed beneficial always to drink her milk. . . . He was buried in a mound a short way from this ness and in another mound near by the cow was laid, and there people set up the *bautastones* w h i c h still stand." [19] (17) The people of King Eysteinn of Upsala "had great faith in a cow, and they called her Sibilia. She was so much worshipped (and as a result, enchanted) that men could not endure her bellowing. And for that reason the king was accustomed, when he was expecting a (hostile) army, to have this same cow in front of the lines, and so much craft of the devil was in her that his enemies, as soon as they heard her, became so wild that they fought each other and did not look out for themeselves." In Eystein's message to his army he said. "We shall have with us the cow Sibilia, our god." Ragnar's

---

from the galloping horse to the horns of the galloping steer, grasping the horns in such a way as to turn the animal's head, then throwing himself to the ground, by main force he must twist its neck and drag the steer over to the ground, taking care not to get the horns pinned in his body while doing so." (Francis Rolt-Wheeler, *The Book of the Cowboy* [Boston, 1921], 390.) The object is to turn the steer over and tie its feet, but sometimes the animal's neck gets broken in the process. There is no reason for doubting that an Icelander could do what was imputed to Egill.

[17] Vald. Ásmaundarson, *Kormáks saga*, chap. XXIII.

[18] Konrad Gíslason, *Tvær sǫgur af Gísla Surssyni* (Køb. 1849), 80.

On the sacrifice of cattle in Scandinavia in recent times see Nils Lid, "Norske Slakteskikkar," fyrste luten, *Vid.-Selsk. Skr.* II. H.-F. Kl. (Oslo, 1923), No. 4, 128; Paul Heuergren, *Husdjuren i nordisk folktro* (Örebro, 1925), 249—52.

[19] *Flateyjarbók* (Christiania 1860—68), I, 375—76.

sons defeated the cow by no mortal means, but by superior magic. [20]

Arngrímr Jónsson's Latin summary of the lost *Skjoldunga saga* describes this same *vaccam diabolicam*. [21]

Bulls were worshipped. (18) A hero wished to find the origin of an *úrarhorn*, [22] the quest of which had been imposed upon him. He learned that King Haraldr had harried Bjarmaland, and that the inhabitants had taken an animal and worshipped it; they called it an *úrr*. It became enchanted and destroyed men and animals and subjected everything under itself. When King Haraldr came to capture the beast a stern woman approached him in his sleep and told him how to kill the *úrr*, but in return demanded the horn in the front of its head. When she got this she took it to the temple, where it still was at the time. [23] (19) There is a Norwegian tale of the suspected worship of a bull that was at the head of a herd. Þorsteinn accused Hárekr in the presence of

[20] Magnus Olsen, *Volsunga saga ok Ragnars saga loðbrókar* (Køb. 1906—08), 132—33, 138, 144, 147, 148—49.

[21] Axel Olrik, "Skjoldunga saga i Arngrim Jonssons Udtog," *Aarbøger f. nord. Oldk. og. Hist.*, 1894, 133.

Felix Liebrecht, *Zur Volkskunde* (Heilbronn, 1879), 72—2, says: "Die . . . Kuh Sibilia hat ihr Analogon (auch im Namen) in der göttlichen Kuh Sabala, die durch ihr Brüllen dem Vasischtha hundert Könige verschafft, welche das Heer Visvamithras vernichten (Julius Braun, *Naturgeschichte der Sage* [München, 1864—5] II, 431 ff. Angelo de Gubernatis, *Die Thiere in der indogermanischen Mythologie* [Leipzig, 1874], 56 f.)." Liebrecht gives further references to what he regards as parallels. The passage which he here has in mind is in Manmatha Nath Dutt, *The Ramayana, translated into English Prose*[2], etc. (Calcutta, 1891—4) II, 124—8. See also Ralph T. H. Griffith, *The Rámáyana of Válmiki translated into English Verse* (London and Benares, 1870—4) I, 226—33.

The word *Sabala* or *Çabala* or *Savala*, as it is variously transliterated, means 'spotted', or 'Dappleskin' as Griffith translates. Its resemblance to Sibilia is a matter of chance. The latter was probably made up from elements contained in the foreign names wich pleased this age, such as *Marsibil*, *Blancia*, *Maria*, *Cecilia*, and has nothing to do with Latin *sibylla*. There is no manuscript authority for making the first vowel of Sibilia long, as is often done.

[22] The horn of an aurochs, OE *úr*, Icel *úrr*, a species of wild cattle, coexistent with the European bison in Northern Germany in the eleventh century and persisting longer in Sweden, Poland and Lithuania. The last of the species, a cow, died in the Polish province of Masovia in 1627. See Otto Keller, *Die antike Tierwelt* (Leipzig 1909—13) I, 34. The events described in (15) are placed "west of the river Vína" (i. e. Dvina), in Bjarmaland, the Perm. Mogk in Paul's *Grundriß d. germ. Philol.*[2] (Straßburg 1900—1909) II, 845—47 inferentially puts this saga in the fourteenth century. There were plenty of aurochsen at this time, but I do not know that they ranged as far north as the Perm.

[23] *FAS* III, 637. Reykjavík edition III, 494.

King Ólafr Tryggvason of worshipping a *blótnaut* in secret. Hárekr
said there was little to this, but the king demanded to see the animal
and they went into the woods until they came to a large herd of
cattle. "There was with them a bull so terribly big and ugly that
the king thought he had never seen the like. The bull bellowed
frightfully and acted most viciously. Hárekr said, 'Here is the
bull, my lord, and I am so fond of this neat that he is very af-
fectionate to me.' 'I certainly see it,' said the king, 'and he
looks ugly to me'." The king directed Þorsteinn to kill the bull
and seized Hárek's possessions and drove him from the country. [24]
(20) A king's sister was held captive by a giantess who intended
to make the princess her s u c c e s s o r as p r i e s t e s s of a heathen
temple. The hero Herrauðr and his man Bósi found that the
giantess ate a two-year-old heifer for a meal. "There is a bull in
the temple, enchanted and worshipped. He is bound with iron
bands; he is to cover the heifer and (thus) the poison is mixed
with her, and all become betrolled who eat (of her flesh). She is
to be prepared for food for Hleiðr, the king's sister, and she
(Hleiðr) will become just as much a troll as the temple-priestess
was before." The heroes kill the heifer, break the bull's neck, slay
the old priestess and rescue the princess. [25]

Pampered bulls kept for cult purposes became dangerous and
gave rise to fantastic tales. (21) "It happened one day that
Hjálmþér was playing at tables with the king's daughter. Hervör
asked what he was to do for his winter's lodging. He said he had
to hunt up a calf. 'Whither do you have to seek it?' says she. 'The
king will not tell me anything about that,' says he. 'That is no
calf,' says she, 'but rather an old bull in the nineties; he eats
live-stock and kills men and horses. He is more cruel than any
other animal; he has killed all the men who have gone after
him and have asked my father for lodging for the winter. It is
the greatest *blótnaut*. . . . He is in a high and strong enclosure in
the center of the land; he must not be turned loose, for then he
breaks down fortifications and castles and does much harm
to men and beasts.'" Hjálmþér's enchanted companion, Höðr,
secretly takes upon himself the task of killing the bull, accomplishes this in a violent struggle and brings home the hide and

---

[24] *Flateyjarbók* I, 261 f., and *Fornmannasögur* (Kaupmannahöfn, 1825—37)
II, 131—33.

[25] Otto Luitpold Jiriczek, *Die Bósa saga in zwei Fassungen nebst Proben aus
den Bósa-rímur* (Straßburg 1923), 26 ff.

horns as required by the king. At Yule the company drinks from the horns. [26]

(22) The Icelander who translated chap. XXXIII of the Book of Exodus in the latter half of the fourteenth century [27] had on his tongue's end a suitable word for the golden calf worshipped by the Children of Israel. He called it a *blótkálfr*. [28]

Dangerous cattle are often supernatural in nature or origin. They may be cows with uncanny powers, as in the *Ragnars saga*. (23) "The people of the town own two neat-cattle, and they are heifers, and men had left because they could not stand their bellowing and sorcery. . . . They now take and turn loose these cattle which they believed in, and when the heifers are let loose they run hard and bellow frightfully." A hero with supernatural powers kills the heifers and contributes to the defeat of the people of the town. [29] The troublesome animals are more often bulls [30] and of supernatural origin. (24) Þórolfr bægifótr made trouble for his neighbors in his lifetime and still worse trouble after his death. When nothing else would stop his spooking people dug up his body and burnt it far from the dwellings of men, and the country-side had rest. But a broken-legged cow that had been turned loose on the range after preliminary recovery from its injury had been seen licking the ashes where Þórolfr had been burned. Some people said they had seen her there with a dapple-gray animal. [31] At any rate she was with calf when she came home in the fall. She bore a heifer calf towards spring, but, strange to say, soon after bore another calf, and this time with great difficulty because it was so big. When it bawled the sound was so evil that an old woman with second sight urged that it be killed. But the calf was so superior that the owner kept it for a bull, and it was soon larger and stronger than other cattle of its age. The summer after it was three years old it became violent and

---

[26] "Hjálmþérs saga ok Ölvis," *FAS* III, 498. Reykjavík edition III, 383. A somewhat semilar story is in Jón Arnason, *Islenzkar þjóðsögur og æfintyri*, (Leipzig 1862—64) II, 363.

[27] Mogk, Paul's *Grund. d. germ. Philol.*² II, 896.

[28] C. R. Unger, *Stjorn, gammelnorsk Bibelhistorie fra Verdens Skabelse til det Babyloniske Fangenskab* (Chr., 1862), 312 f.

[29] Magnus Olsen, *Vǫlsunga saga ok Ragnars saga loðbrókar*, 131.

[30] In a version of the *Hervarar saga (Heiðreks saga)* given by Rafn there is mention of "berserkir roaring like *blótneyti*." See *FAS* I, 425. For Modern Icel. *blótneyti*, "ugly bull," see Vigfusson, *Icel.-Eng. Dict.*, Oxford 1874, *s. v. blótnaut*.

[31] The characteristic color of supernatural cattle in Iceland. See (25) *infra*.

killed its owner. [32] The farm-hands pursued it into a swamp where it mysteriously disappeared. [33] The reader of the saga is supposed to know without being told that the bull is the son of Þórolfr and his reincarnation. (25) Ólafr pái had a remarkably fine bull, dapplegray with four horns, one of which stuck out in front of its forehead. When the bull was eighteen years old the front horn fell off and Ólafr had him killed. The next night Ólafr dreamed that a large angry looking woman came to him. She said, "You have had my son killed and caused him to come to me in a mishandled condition, and for that you shall get to see your son all bloody at my bidding; I shall also pick out the one whom I know you would least of all wish to lose." [34]

(26) Only a few of the ox-names which are transmitted in the þulur [35] and in various passages in the sagas interest us. [36] The following are connected with names for Othin: Jǫrmuni, related to the Othin-name Jǫrmunr and probably understood here as 'big ox,' Jǫrmunrekr, similarly related to Jǫrmunr, and probably understood as 'leader of the oxen,' Ǫlgr, 'snorter,' an Othin-name. Sveiður and Sveiðuður are in ablaut relationship to the Othin-names Sviður and Sviðuður. These two ox-names are related to sviða, 'spear,' and probably mean 'horned.' There is a similar relationship between the ox-name Svigðir, 'with curved horns,' and the Othin-name Sveigðir. The ox-name Vingnir is a name of Thor. The ox-name Freyr is the name of the god Freyr. [37] I say "ox-name," but in the old sources uxi also refers to bulls, and since only an entire male would be a suitable sacrifice in a fertility cult, these names may be meant for bulls rather oxen.

(27) The following words referring to cattle were used as names of men: Kálfr, 'calf,' was frequent in Iceland, sporadic but ancient in Norway, Kvígr, 'bull-calf,' was used occasionally,

[32] The details of the owner's unsuccessful fight are like those of Hörð's successful fight (21) in FAS III, 498—501. Reykjavík edition III (1889), 383—85.

[33] Hugo Gering, Eyrbyggja saga (Halle 1897), 221—29.

[34] Kr. Kalund, Laxdœla saga (Halle 1896), 88—89.

[35] Finnur Jónsson, Den norsk-islandske Skjaldedigtningen (Køb. og Krist. 1912—15), A I, 650, 675. B I, 656, 669.

[36] The kenningar for bull in Meissner, "Die Kenningar der Skalden," Rheinische Beiträge und Hilfsbücher z. germ. Philol. u. Volksk. I (Bonn u. Leipzig, 1921), 111, sec. 30, contain nothing of religious import.

[37] On all names connected with Othin see Falk, Odensheite, s. v. and on the others see his page 44 ff. For references to the occurrences of the same see Finnur Jónsson, Lexicon poeticum antiquae linguae septentrionalis (Køb. 1913—16), s. v.

as also *Uxi*, 'ox,' or 'bull.' All of these are also used as nicknames [38].

The foregoing represents what we find on the subject. [39]
Equally important is what we do not find. (28) The prototheme
blót- is recorded in the lexicons with only three deuterothemes
that are the names of animals: -*kálfr*, -*naut*, -*neyti*, all referring
to cattle. That is; there is no such word listed in any dictionary
as **blóthestr*, **blótgoltr*, **blótsvin*. While such words may have
been used, they played such an unimportant role that they have
not been recorded, nor have they lived down to modern times. [40]

II.

In former times much of the material presented here was
considered of little value by reason of its lateness, but the study
of current tales and customs has changed our point of view in
this respect. In evaluating such sources we do not so much ask
if a given event occurred at a stated time or place, as we ask if
the story has preserved a non-christian tradition or usage.

It is of course difficult to tell how much of the Younger Edda
is due to Snorri's fondness for telling a good story, but since there
is not much of a story connected with Auðhumla it is likely that
the account of her is a bit of old tradition (1). The story of Gefjon
and her sons sounds like a local tradition, some skipper's jesting
account of the origin of the island which his craft is approaching (2).
The agreement of the Cimbrian bull-cult with the Scandinavian
as to object and with the *sonargoltr* cult as to content confirms
our belief in Plutarch's account (3). Similarly the linguistic
equation *Nerthus-Njǫrðr* satisfies us as to Tacitus (5). Nos. (6),
(7), (8), (9), similar in kind but in independent texts, confirm
each other as to contents, as do also Nos. (12), (13), (14), (15).
The story of the deification of a milch-cow (16) differs from the
others, Auðhumla being too far removed in kind to be compared.

---

[38] E. H. Lind, *Norsk-isländska dopnamn och fingerade namn frdn medeltiden*
(Upsala och Leipzig 1905—15), and the same author's *Norsk-isländska personbinam
frdn medeltiden* (Upsala 1920—21), *s. v.* Names used only as nicknames are not
included in (24).

[39] The material in folk-tales and folk-customs is not included here. Many things
in de Gubernatis' section, "Der Stier und die Kuh in der germano-skandinavischen
und fränkisch-keltischen Sage" of his *Die Thiere in der indogermanischen Mythologie*, 172—203, do not belong within the limits of this study.

[40] *Blótvargr* means "a person given to profanity," *vargr* having lost its original
meaning, "wolf" Cp. Swedish *slitvarg*, "a person who tears his clothes."

The passage which follows this in the saga says that people believed that the peculiar old man was the devil who had taken on the form of Othin. There is no adequate motivation for the insertion of the Ǫgvald incident, but contemporaries may have known a reason for its inclusion. This story is hardly a deification of a source of food; it is more likely a sarcastic hit at some act or habit of King Olaf's which it was both unnecessary and unwise to point out. I should not attribute to it any value as a source of information as to ancient beliefs. Nos. (17), (18), (20) contain tales of cattle that became enchanted by the worship offered them and in this point show a mutually confirmatory agreement. The behavior of Sibilia (17) is very like that of the two heifers (23) in the same saga and unlike that of any other cattle in old Scandinavian tradition. Hermann suspects a foreign source, but one wishes a closer investigation, [41] for Hermann gives no reason for the faith that is in him when he attributes them to the Irish. Both (18) and (20) are laid in Bjarmaland, which was inhabited by Finnish tribes. The passage in the *Bósa saga* which just precedes (20) says that the temple is that of Jómali. He was a Finnish deity. Thus (18) and (20) are intended to be descriptions of Finnish usages; but voyages to Bjarmaland were always rare and had stopped entirely, at least from Icelandic ports, when this saga was written, and little was known of the country. These accounts tell less of conditions in Bjarmaland than they do of what an Icelander could imagine. The main feature, the bull-cult, was native to his own country. No. (19) is in the saga of King Ólafr Tryggvason, a work which contains much historical truth. One suspects that the accusation of bull-worship was only a scheme to enable the king to seize Hárek's property. Had there not been a general belief that people did worship bulls, the king would have invented some other charge. No. (21) is of course a wholly imaginary tale, though suggested by facts, and so of interest. The bull of which it tells reminds us of those in (7) and (18). No. (23) has been discussed; (24) sounds like a local tradition that had grown up around a story of a violent bull that had killed its owner. No. (25) may well be fact and Ólafr pái may have had

---

[41] H. F. Feilberg, *Bidrag til en Ordbog over den jyske Almuesmål* (Køb. 1886—1911) III, 908 a, 21. Paul Hermann, 'Isländische Heldenromane', Thule XXI (1923), 155 note 2, 157 note 1. Ewald Liden in *Festskrift til Finnur Jónsson* (Køb., 1928), 361 ff.

such a dream, supernatural origin having.been suggested by the color of his bull and the stern woman by some such tale as that of the woman who cursed Hadingus for slaying a supernatural being after he had killed an *inauditi generis beluam.* [42]

While the Icelander of the early Christian centuries officially rejected the heathen gods, he often lived in a lively fear of them, and we are justified in thinking that cattle-names reminiscent of the old gods may well have been a bid for their protection over the cattle (26). Such names for human beings as *Kálfr, Kvígr, Uxi* may have arisen from the nicknames given to the preceding generation of men, a frequent development; but it is possible that they arose as cult-names, [43] a possibility to which insufficient attention has been given in Germanics.

III.

It is probable that the annual journey of the goddess Nerthus was to insure the multiplication of crops and herds, and there must have been a definite reason for yoking cows to her car, whereas oxen were the normal draught-animals for Northern Germany. At any rate sterile oxen which could signify only barrenness gave way to fertile females (5).

Bull-worship is a far flung fertility cult. We know it especially from the accounts in the Old Testament of bull-worship in Samaria, and from the Mithras worship in the lands held by the Roman armies. The Swedes sacrificed "oxen," more likely bulls, to avert famine and secure fertility. The meaning of No. (8) becomes clear when we notice that the story is an attempt to explain the origin of the *Fröblod,* the famous annual sacrifice in Upsala, here named after Freyr, the god of fertility, the god whose name is given to a bull (26). Cattle then, and primarily bulls, play a leading part in the Scandinavian cult of fertility.

One of the stories included above (19) is of special interest in determining the character of the Scandinavian cattle cult. It is not in a legendary or romantic source such as the *Ynglinga*

---

[42] Holder, *Saxonis Grammatici gesta Danorum,* 29.

[43] Hans Naumann, "Altnordische Namenstudien," *Acta Germanica,* neue Reihe, Heft I (Berlin 1912), 172. Note Christian cult-names, as Spanish names for men; *Jesus, José María, Juan Bautista,* for women; *Asunción, Circoncisión, Concepción, María de Jesus,* for either sex; *Encarnación.*

saga, which provides us with version 2 of (2), with (6) and (7), or the Younger Edda, which contains (1) and version 1 of (2), or the *Fornaldarsögur*, from which we have (17), (18), (20), (23); it is in a king's saga, which carries the air of verisimilitude and the assumption that its contents are historical facts. Here a man was accused of worshipping a certain bull and the accusation apparently seemed plausible to his contemporaries. The bull was the head of this man's herd. The two bulls of supernatural origin (24), (25), also in non-romantic sagas, were likewise regarded as choice breeding animals and also apparently the heads of their respective owners' herds. Does not this point the way?

The bull is important; the modern scientific breeder says, "The bull is half the herd." His qualities affect all the young stock; his virility is of special concern, for if he is infertile there are neither calves nor milk and a year is wasted. Was not the worship of cattle primarily a domestic fertility cult, carried on at each farm, centering on the bull, and intended to insure an annual crop of calves? In heathen times it may well have been a public affair of greater proportions (7), (8), but in Christian times it could survive only on a modest scale. Possibly each sort of domestic animal that was of any economic importance enjoyed such a cult. [44] In many countries the church took over this function and annually blessed the domestic animals.

When a fertility cult was once established it could develop off-shoots, as in the cow Auðhumla (1), a "cow of plenty," another side of fertility, and so important a figure that the systematized mythology of Snorri gave her the prime place in the stories of origins as the first living creature, the nourisher of the infant world, the bringer-to-light of the ancestor of the gods.

The Cimbrians regarded an oath as binding when it was taken on the image of a bull (3), a symbol of fertility and in Sweden associated with the god of fertility, Freyr. Similarly oaths were taken in Sweden on the boar, also a symbol of fertility and associated with Freyr, and in Iceland on a ring reddened in the blood of a sacrificed neat (4).

It is difficult to interpret the slaying of the bull in the duelling ceremony (12), (13), (14), (15). This was part of the *holmganga*,

---

[44] For the horse, see "Vǫlsiþáttr" in *Flateyjarbók* II, 331—36, for the boar, Falk, *Odensheite s. v. þrór*, for various animals, Nils Lid, "Joleband og Vegetasjons-guddom," *Vid. Akad. Skr.* II. H.-F. Kl. (Oslo), 1928, No. 4.

the ritualistic trial by battle, not of the informal *einvígi*. Karl Müllenhoff considered it a thank-offering, [45] which it may well have been, but our information is so slight that we can only surmise. At any rate the persistence of the name *blótnaut* in these cases is a witness to the religious character of the act of slaying the bull.

We do not know what Þorvarðr wished to gain by giving the carcass of the slain bull to an elf (9), but probably he desired the strength to overcome Kormákr in the impending second duel, an idea not far removed from the fundamental concept of the bull-cult.

The pampered and therefore illnatured bulls that were in early times kept for sacrifice and the venerated herd-bulls that grew ugly with age gave rise to tales of dangerous *blótnaut* (7), (21); the Icelandic romancers made such a bull part of the temple equipment of a foreign heathen religion (20) and by way of good measure added a heifer as ritual food for the priestess. For another heathen temple they provided an *úrarhorn* (18) and added the story of an *úrr* whose behavior was like that of the *blótnaut* of (21). It is interesting that the horn of a wild animal, a thing of a culturally more primitive order than the horn of a domestic bull, was considered appropriate ritual furniture. The inclusion of a drinking horn in the ritual equipment was not chance, for drinking was a fundamental part of the rite. [46] Oxen were used in the story of Gefjon and her sons (2) because they are the strongest domestic animals known in the North. [47] I see no religious import in this tale, nor should I care to claim such for Ǫgvald's cow (16). "Our god" Sibilia (17) and the two heifers in which men believed (23) seem to be a romancer's insertion.

Among the ox-names (26) there is much that is interesting but nothing very convincing except the name Freyr. We have already noted the bull sacrifices to this god (8).

The frequent use of *blótkálfr* and *blótnaut* in the thirteenth and fourteenth centuries and the occasional use of *blótneyti* (28), together with the accurate use of *blótkálfr* in the latter half of the fourteenth century for the golden calf used in the Samaritan

[45] *Altnordisches Leben* (Berlin, 1856), 300.

[46] Maurice Cahen, "Ètudes sur le vocabulaire religieux du vieux-scandinave. La libation." *Collection linguistique publiée par la société de linguistique de Paris.* — IX (1921).

[47] Feilberg, *Bidrag*, III, 907 b. l. 51 ff.

bull-cult (22) is evidence that after several centuries of Christianity the Icelanders had some knowledge of cattle-worship. The persistence of *blótneyti* in Modern Icelandic with the meaning 'ugly bull' shows that the mental picture of the vicious pampered sacrificial bull of earlier times and the illnatured cult-herd-bull of later times was so widespread and tenacious that it gave the word a permanent foothold in the language. The complete absence of other compounds of animal-names with the prototheme *blót-* shows that cattle-worship, and in the light of the accounts we have collected here, bull-worship mainly, was the chief animal-cult known in Icelandic tradition and practice (28). It was probably a simple domestic fertility rite intended to insure the productivity of the farmer's herd.

HÁVAMÁL 136

VON HUGO PIPPING
UNIVERSITÄT HELSINGFORS

Der codex regius liefert uns die Strophe in folgender Gestalt:

> Ramt er þat tre   er riþa ſcal
>   avllom at vpp loki
> baúg þv gef   eþa þat biðia mún
>   þer leſ hvers aliðo.

In normalisierter Schreibung lesen wir[1]:

> Ramt er þat tré,   er ríða skal
>   ǫllom at upploki;
> baug þú gef   eða þat biðia mun
>   þér læs huers á liðo.

Diese Strophe ist in der Literatur häufig besprochen worden. Wenn wir uns an die im 20. Jahrhundert geführte Diskussion halten, sind — abgesehen von den Wörterbüchern — vor allem folgende Literaturstellen zu berücksichtigen:

F. D e t t e r und R. H e i n z e l, *Sæmundar Edda* II., Leipzig, 1903, S. 136, Strophe 132.

B j. M. Ó l s e n, *Arkiv för nordisk filologi*, XXXI, S. 85—89.

E r n s t A. K o c k, *Notationes Norrœnæ. Lunds Universitets Årsskrift*, Andra delen 1924, § 207, S. 6 f.

B. S i j m o n s und H. G e r i n g, *Die Lieder der Edda.* Dritter Band: *Kommentar.* Erste Hälfte: *Götterlieder.* Halle (Saale), 1927, S. 141 f., Strophe 135.

Abgesehen von dem Ausdruck *geſa baug* und dem Pronomen *þat*[2], glaube ich, daß unsere Strophe kein Wort enthält, das nicht von mehreren der genannten Autoren richtig aufgefaßt wurde.

Ob das *tré* als ein Türzapfen (D e t t e r - H e i n z e l) oder als

---

[1] Vgl. G u s t a v N e c k e l *Edda* I, Heidelberg, 1914, S. 38.
[2] Von G e r i n g *Die Edda*, Leipzig und Wien, 1892, S. 104 richtig übersetzt.

ein Schlagbaum (F. J ó n s s o n) gedacht werden soll [3], ist eine Frage, von deren Beantwortung unsere Auffassung des Grundgedankens der Strophe keineswegs abhängt. Beide können sich drehen *(riða)* und müssen stark (vgl. *ramt*) sein, um die betreffende Bewegung oft ausführen zu können. Abwegig scheint mir [4] B j. M. Ó l s e n s Gedanke, daß unter dem *tré* ein Knüppel zu verstehen sei. Ebensowenig kann ich E r n s t A. K o c k beistimmen, wenn er glaubt, daß *ramt* hier 'zauberkräftig' bedeutet. Allerdings sagt ein altes dänisches Sprichwort: 'Ofte gielder Dør Stakkarls Vrede' [5], was so zu verstehen ist, daß die mit den Flüchen eines a b g e w i e s e n e n Bettlers beladene Tür großen Gefahren ausgesetzt ist. In unserer Strophe wird aber gesagt, daß ein Türzapfen, welcher sich oft dreht, um Bettler h e r e i n z u l a s s e n , stark sein muß. Es hat keinen Zweck, das Wort *ramt* i n d i e s e m F a l l e als 'zauberkräftig' aufzufassen. Der freundlich empfangene Bettler flucht eben nicht.

E r n s t A. K o c k s Bedenken gegen die übliche Uebersetzung von *(ramt) er*, d. h. 'muß sein' [6] oder 'må være' [7], scheinen mir unbegründet. Ein Vers kann gut sein, ohne den höchsten Anforderungen der Logik zu genügen, und es ist erlaubt, ihn bei der Uebersetzung zu verdeutlichen.

Mit F i n n u r J ó n s s o n [8] und S i j m o n s [9] halte ich es für ausgemacht, daß sich *þat* auf den abgewiesenen Bettler bezieht. Die neutrale Form ist ganz korrekt, weil das Geschlecht des Bettlers unbestimmt ist [10]. Der Singular erklärt sich durch den Wunsch des Dichters, einen konkreten Fall zu schildern, und steht also in keinem Widerspruch mit dem Plural *ǫllom*. F. J ó n s s o n ('folkene') und S i j m o n s ('das Bettelpack') scheinen dem Pronomen *þat* eine kollektive Bedeutung beilegen zu wollen, was ich für unrichtig halte. G e r i n g [11] gibt die strenge richtige Uebersetzung 'er'.

---

[3] Auch andere Uebersetzungen sind vielleicht denkbar. Vgl. F r i t z n e r III, S. 101 a ("Træklinke") und H u g o P i p p i n g *Studier nordisk filologi* XVIII. 4, S. 6. G e r i n g (S i j m o n s - G e r i n g S. 141) schreibt: "riegel".

[4] Vgl. E. A. K o c k S. 6 und S i j m o n s - G e r i n g S. 141 f.

[5] Vgl. D e t t e r - H e i n z e l , wo M o l b e c h als Quelle angegeben wird.

[6] H u g o G e r i n g *Die Edda* (1892), S. 104.

[7] F. J ó n s s o n *Hávamál*, S. 135.

[8] F. J ó n s s o n *Hávámal* S. 135.

[9] S i j m o n s - G e r i n g S. 142.

[10] Vgl. M. N y g a a r d *Norrœn Syntax*. Kristiania 1905, S. 80, § 81.

[11] H u g o G e r i n g *Die Edda* (1892) S. 104.

Die Hauptschwierigkeit hat der Ausdruck *baug þú gef* den Uebersetzern bereitet.

Ich kann unmöglich G e r i n g beistimmen, wenn dieser Forscher meint, daß der *baugr* ein *fiotorláss* sei, mit dem man die Tür zu versehen habe. Wie B j. M. Ó l s e n S. 86 bemerkt, ist *gefa baug* ein, mindestens gesagt, sehr gesuchter Ausdruck für 'einen Ring anbringen'. Und vor allem versteht man nicht, warum die Anbringung einer neuen Schließvorrichtung an die Tür die üblen Folgen der Flüche abwehren könnte. Allerdings ließe es sich denken, daß die Form des neuen Schlosses an einen Gegenstand erinnerte, der eine abwehrende Kraft besaß. Aber wenn der *baugr* als ein Abwehrmittel betrachtet werden soll, läßt sich eine gute Erklärung der Strophe herausfinden, ohne daß man die Hypothese vom *fiotorláss* herbeizieht. B j. M. Ó l - s e n (S. 86) bestreitet übrigens, daß es jemals eine Schließvorrichtung gegeben habe, welche den Namen *baugr* führte.

Beim Studium der zweiten Halbstrophe ist vor allem folgendes zu beachten:

1. Einerseits enthält diese Halbstrophe eine Aufforderung, den Bettler so zu behandeln, daß seine Flüche kein Unheil anstiften können.

2. Anderseits kann die zweite Halbstrophe keine Aufforderung zu Freigebigkeit enthalten, denn in der ersten Halbstrophe wird vor den Gefahren der übertriebenen Gastfreundschaft gewarnt. Auf keinen Fall dürfen wir aus der zweiten Halbstrophe eine Aufforderung herauslesen, jedem Bettler einen Ring aus wertvollem Metall zu geben, denn eine solche Praxis würde noch teurer kommen als die Gastfreundschaft, vor welcher die erste Halbstrophe warnt [12].

Unser Dilemma ist indessen nicht so unbequem, wie man bisher gedacht hat. Es liegt hier ein Spiel mit dem doppelsinnigen Worte *baugr* vor. *Baugar* nannte man die Metallringe, welche die Fürsten ihrem Gefolge verschenkten, aber *baugr* war auch der Name des Afterringes, den man zu zeigen pflegte, wo es darauf ankam, den üblen Wirkungen des bösen Blickes vorzubeugen.

Daß *baugr* in zwei anderen Eddagedichten in der Bedeutung 'Afterring' benützt wurde, glaube ich in einer früheren Schrift dargelegt zu haben [13]. Meine Lesung und Deutung von Alv. 5:6

---

[12] Vgl. S i j m o n s - G e r i n g S. 141.
[13] H u g o P i p p i n g *Studier i nordisk filologi* XVIII, S. 27—29 und 35—38.

huerr hefir þik baug[r] um borit?
'qui te anus peperit?'

hat nachträglich eine gute Bestätigung gefunden. Dr. E. H. L i n d
teilt mir mit, daß man in einer Gegend von Värmland die tiefste
Verachtung in der Weise kundzugeben pflegte, daß man von
einem andern sagte, er sei 'auf die Welt geschissen.'

Der Volksglaube, daß man den bösen Blick abwehren kann,
wenn man der gefährlichen Person den Hintern zeigt, ist von
F e i l b e r g erörtert worden [14].

Der Sinn unserer Strophe ist also folgender: Jeden Bettler
kann man nicht hereinlassen, ohne zu verarmen. Aber wenn man
gezwungen ist, einen Bettler abzuweisen, zeige man ihm den
Hintern, um den üblen Wirkungen des bösen Blickes zu entgehen.

Man wird mir die Frage stellen, warum es *gefa baug* und nicht
sýna baug heißt, wenn von dem eben beschriebenen Gestus die
Rede ist. Diese Frage ist nicht schwierig zu beantworten. Der
Dichter hat das Zeitwort *gefa* gewählt, weil *gefa baug* den Gedanken des Zuhörers auf die Gabenspenden der Fürsten lenkt,
wobei eine Verhöhnung des Bettlers beabsichtigt wird. Der Fürst
gibt seinem Gefolge Ringe — gib du dem Bettler einen Ring,
aber nur den Afterring. Vor seinen Flüchen brauchst du keine
Angst zu haben, denn der Gestus schützt dich.

Ein ähnliches Spiel mit dem Doppelsinn des Wortes *baugr* findet
man in Hrbl. 42, wie ich a. a. O. S. 28 f. gezeigt habe.

Die richtige Uebersetzung der Strophe 136 in Hávamál dürfte
also folgende sein:

*Stark muß der Türzapfen sein, wenn er sich drehen soll, um alle
hereinzulassen. Zeige (dem Fremden) den Hintern, sonst wird er
alles Unheil auf deine Glieder herabwünschen.*

---

[14] H. F. F e i l b e r g „Der böse Blick in der Volksüberlieferung." *Zeitschrift
des Vereins für Volkskunde*, XI.

THE USE OF OLD ENGLISH SWA IN NEGATIVE CLAUSES[1]

BY ESTON EVERETT ERICSON
UNIVERSITY OF PITTSBURGH

In a recent article [2], Professor Kemp Malone raises the question as to whether or not an adverbial (i. e. non-conjunctive) *swa* may be used to introduce a negative clause. The passage under discussion is Beowulf 1138—1145:

> he to gyrnwræce
> swiðor þohte   þonne to sælade,
> gif he torngemot þurhteon mihte,
> þæt he Eotena bearn inne gemunde.
> *Swa* he ne forwyrnde woroldrædenne,
> þonne him Hunlafing hildeleoman
> billa selest on bearm dyde [3];

The *swa* in this passage Professor Klaeber lists under modal adverbs in his vocabulary, and in his notes he further refines it into "under these circumstances", "in this frame of mind". To this rendering Professor Malone objects, on the ground that "the use of an adverbial *swa* to introduce a negative clause is excessively rare". His judgment is that this *swa* is a causal conjunction, to be compared with the *swa* in line 2184 of the same poem.

The purpose of this study is to throw further light on the use of *swa* in negative clauses [4].

---

[1] This article constitutes a section of a longer study, soon to be published, on "The Use of *Swa* in Old English."

[2] "The Finn Episode in Beowulf" — *JEGPh*. XXV: 157—172.

[3] So, Klaeber. Malone emends *woroldrædenne* to *woroldrædende*, and by the use of a comma after *gemunde*, makes the *swa*-clause subordinate. He follows Olrik in considering *Hunlafing* the name of a sword. See Malone's article on "Hunlafing", *MLN*. XLIII, 300 ff. For Klaeber's reaction to Malone's reading see his second edn. of *Beowulf*: Sup. P. 430.

[4] The following clarification of my least familiar abbrevations may be of assistance to the reader: AEx = Ælfric's *Exodus*; AGen = Ælfric's *Genesis*:

I. *Swa þeah* in Negative Clauses.

Swa þeah is used to introduce negative clauses, in three different ways: (1) as a true conjunction: "although", (2) as a pseudo-conjunction: "yet", "nevertheless"; (3) as an adversative adverb: "yet", "however".

A. As a subordinating conjunction.

1. And. 812 ff:

> . . he wundra worn wordum cyðde,
> *swa þeah* ne gelyfdon larum sinum
> modblinde menn.

> (He wrought many a wonder by His word, *though* men, blind of heart, believed not in his teachings. — Kennedy)

See also ASHom. 3, 169.

B. As a pseudo-conjunction [5].

2. DG. 27, 2:

> he wearð þa þurh Godes ælmihtiges fultum mid þam mægene gestrangod to þam swiðe, þæt se þe ær wæs ealdor wæpnedmanna . . . . *swa þeah* ne geswac he to manienne his gingran, etc.

Filling in the blur in the manuscript with the part following *wera ealdorman* in Ms. C, I translate:

> (He was by the help of the Almighty God so strengthened in that power, that he who ere now had been governor of men, after that undertook also the instruction and overlordship of women, *yet* he did not desist from warning his disciples, etc.) [6]

C. As an adversative adverb.

3. Beow. 972:

> no þær ænige *swa þeah*
> fea-sceaft guma frofre gebohte;

ASHom. = *Anglo-Saxon Homilies* (Grein: *Prosa*, Vol. 3); BH = *Blickling Homilies*; BR = *The Benedictine Rule* (Grein: *Prosa*, Vol. 2); Chm. = *Charms* (Grein-Wülker: *Poesie*, Vol. 2); DG = *Dialogues of Gregory* (first 75 pages of Hecht's edition in Grein: *Prosa*, Vol. 4); LAS = *Laws of the Anglo-Saxons* (Liebermann); PB: = The Poems of *Boethius*; PPs. = *Paris Psalter*; PNT = Ælfric's *Preface to the New Testament*; POT = *Preface to the Old Testament*; VPs = *Vespasian Psalter*.

[5] For an extended discussion of this matter see Pp. 161—162.

[6] Another case is DG. 33, 12. There the rebuke administered to Peter (*wite . . weorce*) serves as the antecedent clause, to which the *swa þeah* clause is the subsequent clause.

(*Yet* the wretched creature, etc.)
Other cases: Interior: Beow. *2968*. DG. *23, 17. 60, 33. 66, 23* (H). EH.
3, 1919. Or. *56, 1. 134, 16. 29. 146, 35*. ASHom. *4, 105. 9, 270*. Josh. *9, 18*.
Final: Beow. *1929*. Guth. *464*[7]. ASHom. *4, 229*.

II. *Swa* in Concessive Clauses.

A. As a true conjunction: "although", "though".

1. Gen. 391 ff.:

> *Swa* he us ne mæg ænige synne gestælan,
> þæt we him on þam lande laðᵈ gefremedon, he hæfðᵈ us
> þeah þæs leohtes bescyrede, etc.
> ("*Although* he cannot impute to us any sin, etc.")

2. Ex. 80 ff.:

> hæfde witig god
> sunnan siðᵈfæt segle ofertolden,
> *swa* þa mæstrapas men ne cuðᵈon . . ("*though* earth-dwellers knew not, etc.")

3. Rid. 7, 4:

> unrimu cyn, eorþan getenge,
> næte mid niþe, *swa* ic him no rine, ("*though* I touch them not")

4. Rid. 23, 13:

> þa þa hors oðᵈbær
> eh ond eorlas æscum dealle . . . .
> *swa* hine oxa ne teah . . . ("*though*[8] no ox pulled it")

5. Or. 206, 3:

> and him his sunu ham onsende, se wæs on his gewealde,
> *swa* he nyste hu he him to com. ("*though* he knew not how, etc.")

B. *Swa* as a pseudo-conjunction.

Some difference of opinion exists among grammarians as to the status of the word *yet*. Certain authorities classify it as a coordinating conjunction, but even these would not contend that it is of the same rank as *and, but,* and *or*. My opinion is, that *yet* is a concessive adverb, and that while it is often found in a conjunctive capacity, it is never a real conjunctive adverb like *where* or *when*, both of which may be replaced by prepositional phrases; for example:

1. No crops grow *where* (i. e. "in the place in which") it never rains.
2. He spoke *when* (i. e. "at the time at which") his turn came.

---

[7] Gollancz (*The Exeter Book:* EETS, 104) omits *swa* from the text.
[8] Thorpe (*Codex Exoniensis*) translates this one as "so that", but the meaning is plainly concessive.

Festschrift Collitz.   II

The ordinary concessive conjunction in English is *although (though)*, but "upside-down" subordination often causes *although* to be replaced by the concessive adverb *yet*. In such cases, what originally stood as the concessive clause is strengthened by being stated as an independent clause, the original independent clause remaining, however, as before, and being attached loosely to the new independent clause by the word *yet* with the meaning of "in spite of *that*" (i. e. "in spite of" the idea expressed in the first clause). For a case of such reversed subordination, compare the first Case 4, Page 163, with its Latin original:

> *Cumque* moratus esset cum ea per annos viginti, filios aut filias ex ea non accipit.

or the following pair:

> *Although* he was there, he offered no help.
> He was there; *yet* he offered no help.

The term "pseudo-conjunction" may be fittingly applied to the *yet* in such instances as the above. In Old English, *swa* is sometimes used as such a pseudo-conjunction, in the sense of "yet".

1. And. 493 (Krapp's version):

> Ic wæs on gifeðe iu ond nu (þa)
> syxtyne siðum on sæbate,
> mere hrerendum mundum freorig,
> eagorstreamas; (is ðys ane ma),
> *swa* ic æfre ne geseah ænigne mann,
> þryðbearn hæleða, þe gelicne,
> steoran ofer stæfnan. (".. sixteen times
> .. I've been to sea ... *yet* [9] mine eyes, etc.")

2. Or. 252, 21:

> com micel fyrbyrne on Romeburg, þæt þærbinnan
> forburnon XV tunas, *swa* nan man nyste hwanan
> þæt fyr com. (.. which burned fifteen wards; *yet* [10]
> no man knew, etc.)

3. Or. 260, 18:

> þær wæron xxx M ofslagen, and at þam geate of-
> tredd, *swa* nan men nyste hwonon sio wro(h)t com.
> (".. trodden to death at the gate; *yet* [10] no man, etc.")

---

[9] So Root, Kennedy, and Krapp. Grein has "wie," but in what sense it is hard to tell.

[10] Pauli-Thorpe has "and" for both these cases.

4. ASHom. 10, 73:

Hi ða wæron samod drohtniende ætgædere twentig
wintra, *swa* hi nan bearn ne begeaton. (".. living
together twenty years; *yet* they had begotten, etc.")

III. *Swa* in Result Clauses.

1. Finn. 41:

Hig fuhton fif dagas, *swa* hyra nan ne feol, etc.
("*so that* none of them fell")

2. Beow. 1506:

Bær þa seo brimwylf, þa heo to botme com,
. . . .
swa he ne mihte, no he þam modig wæs,
wæpna gewealdan[11]. ("*so that* he could not . . .")

3. Az. 60:

tosweop and toswengde þurh swiðes meaht
liges leoman, *swa* hyra lice ne scod. ("*so that*
it injured not, etc.")

4. Or. 198, 8:

and þa burg on niht abræc, *swa* þa nyston þe þærinne wæron.
("captured the city . . . *in such a way* that, etc.")

5. AGen. 8, 12 b:

and abad swa ðeah seofan dagas and asende ut culfran;
swa heo ne gecyrde ongean to him. ("sent out a dove
so that[12] *[with the result that]* she did not return ..")

Other cases: Beow. *2006*. Gen. *381. 471. 611. 733.* Dan. *639.* Az. *187.*
El. *340.* And. *986.* Or. *296, 34.* ASHom. *10, 298.* AEx. *34, 38.*

IV. *Swa þæt* in Result Clauses.

1. And. 260:

Him ða ondswarode ælmihti god,
swa þæt ne wiste, se ðe þæs wordes, etc.
("*so that* he knew not, etc.")

2. EH. 3, 156:

swiðe geswenced wæs, *swa þæt* he for þy
sare ne mihte furþon his hand to muþe gedon.
(".. severely weakened .. *so that* he could not, etc.")

---

[11] I use Kock's punctuation. See *Anglia* 46: 83.
[12] The Laud and the Cambridge Mss. do not have this *swa*, and Grein-Wülker
omits it. The Latin is "quae non est reuersa ad eum." The result notion fits as
well as any, although a bromidic transitional *swa* (= "and") may be intended.
The translator apparently means to equate *quae* with *heo*.

3. BH. 173, 18:

> .. to Cristes þeowdome gecyrdon .. *swa þæt* hie
> .. wendan noldan. (".. turned to Christ's ser-
> vice .. *so that* they would not return.")

4. ASHom. 10, 96:

> and ðær wunode fif monþa fæce, *swa þæt* ðær nænig
> ærendraca betweonan ne ferde him and his ge-
> mæccan. ("*so that* no messenger passed, etc.")

5. AGen. 20, 18:

> For þan ðe God gewitnode ealle hys wimmen, *swa þæt*
> heora nan ne mihte habban ænig cild .. ("*so that* none
> of them could have a child, etc.")

Other cases:

> DG. 67, 17. 72, 9. EH. 2, 1157. 4, 1716. 3749. 3931. 5, 396. VPs. 103, 35.
> BR. 70, 14. ASHom. 10, 402. AGen. 9, 23. AEx. 9, 10—11. Deut. 9,9.

V. *Swa* in Causal Clauses.

1. Beow. 1142 (Malone's version):

> þæt he Eotena bearn inne gemunde,
> *swa* he ne forwyrnde woroldrædende
> þonne him Hunlafing, hildeleoman,
> billa selest, on bearm dyde;

Klaeber's translation of the last three lines of this passage
(Beowulf: note, P. 170) is as follows:

> "Under these circumstances (or, in this frame
> of mind) he did not refuse (him, i. e. Hunlaf-
> ing) the condition, when Hunlafing placed the
> battle-flame (or: Battle-Flame), the best of
> swords, on his lap."

Klaeber, then, considers the *swa*-clause an independent one, and
the *swa* a modal non-conjunctive adverb.

Malone uses a comma after *gemunde* and takes the *swa*-clause
to be a dependent causal clause modifying *gemunde*. He also
emends *woroldrædenne* to read *woroldrædende*. His translation is:

> "in which he would be mindful of the Euts,
> *since* he did not prevent his lord when he
> (Hnæf) laid in his (Hengist's) lap Hunlafing,
> the battle-gleamer, the best of bills." — JEGPh. XXV: *158—159*

In this case, it seems to me that Malone is on the right track.
Waiving the matter of *woroldrædende*, we may form a judgment
on the basis of the position of adverbial and conjunctive *swa* in
negative clauses. As I hope to show in the course of this article,
adverbial (non-conjunctive) *swa* occurs almost without exception

in the interior or final position (See Pp. 167—174) [13]. Conjunctive
swa, on the other hand, is invariably found in the initial position
(See Pp. 166—167). The *swa* in Beow. 1142 must therefore be either
a conjunctive adverb or a conjunction. The context calls for the
latter, a causal conjunction: "since". Malone cites the *swa* in
Beow. 2184 as evidence that causal *swa* is to be found in negative
clauses. Other cases he might have added are as follows:

2. ASHom. 13, 233:

> and wæron on heora modgeþance swiðlice afyrhte
> and gedrefde, *swa* hit nænig fyren wæs. (*"seeing that*
> there was no sin.")

3. ASHom. 13, 236:

> Wiste he drihten ana, hwa hi læwend and myrðra wæs,
> *swa swa* him nan þing bemiðen beon mæg. (*"since* nothing
> can be concealed, etc.")

4. Or. 86, 15:

> for þon ic ne mæg eal þa monigfealdan yfel
> emdenes areccan, *swa* ic eac ealles þises mid-
> dangeardes na maran dæles ne angite. (*"as* I am
> not acquainted, etc.")

5. Gen. 288 (See below, Pp. 168—169.)

6. Dan. 666 (See below, P. 167.)

Beow. 2184, cited by Malone, is as follows:

7.   Hean wæs lange,
> *swa* hyne Geata bearn godne ne tealdon, etc.
> (*"as* the children of the Geats did not, etc.")

VI. *Swa* in Conditional Clauses.

1. Rid. 88, 31:

> næfre uncer awþer his ellen cyðde,
> *swa* wit þære beadwe begen ne onþungan.
> (*"unless* [14] we were both, etc.")

2. Apollonius of Tyre, 93:

> Nim nu, lareow Apolloni, *swa* hit þe ne mislicie .. [15]
> (*"if* it is not displeasing to thee")

---

[13] For the use of "so that" (= "therefore") at the head of an independent
clause with back-reference to a preceding sentence of which it is semantically
a dependent clause, see Pp 167—168.

[14] Tupper (*Riddles of the Exeter Book* [glossary]) uses "where" here, but
I follow Grein, who makes an *ohne daß* clause out of it. Similar cases are to be
found in Old Saxon: Heliand 798. 813. 5777, et. al. See Sehrt's *Vollständiges
Wörterbuch zum Heliand*, P. 484, Col. 1, line 23 ff.

[15] In Moore and Knott: *Elements of Old English*, P. 93.

VII. *Swa* in Modal Clauses.

Here the *swa* is a conjunctive adverb of manner, and is always found in the initial position.

A. The simple *Swa*-clause.

1. Beow. 2331:

> breost innan weoll
> þeostrum geþoncum, *swa* him geþywe ne wæs.
> ("*as* his habit never was")

2. Gen. 1565:

> and him selfa sceaf
> reaf of lice, *swa* gerysne ne wæs. ("*as* was not seemly")

3. Rid. 3, 1:

> Hwilum ic gewite, *swa* ne wenaþ men . . ("*as* [16] men are not
> expecting, etc.")

Other cases: Beow. *2574. 2585.* Gen. *901.* Dan. *20.* CS. *412.* El. *838.* HP. *3, 43.* PB. *26, 92.* MM. *63.* PPs. *105, 22. 119, 5.* Or. *254, 9.* BR. *74, 19.* DG. *46, 6. 61, 6.* ASHom. *8, 59.* With *swa swa:* VPs. *38, 6.* DG. *13, 13.* BR. *18, 14.* PNT. *1269.* In an ellipsis: EH. *3, 49.*

B. *Swa* introducing the second member of a comparison of inequality.

1. Or. 180, 18:

> þa wearð Tiber seo ea *swa* fledu *swa* heo næfre ær wæs
> ("*so* swollen *as* it never had been.")

2. POT. 60—61:

> *swa* wlitiges cyndes, *swa* we secgan ne magon.
> ("*so* beautiful *as* we cannot express")

Other cases: Beow. *1046—1048* [17]. Jud. *67—68.* EH. *3, 189—90. 5, 859—62.* POT. *493—5.* DG. *69, 11.* AEx. *9, 24. 10, 6.* Swa . . . *efne swa* DG. *15, 31—33. 25, 29.* Swa eac. . . . . *swa:* EH. *1, 788—790* [17].

C. *Swa* in the sense of "as if".

1. WComp. 24:

> is nu *swa* hit no wære,
> freondscipe uncer. ("*as if* it had never been")

2. DG. 26, 29:

> and of þære tide he wearð *swa* fremde þære costunge, efne
> *swa* he næfre þone had on his lichaman næfde. ("*as if* [18] he
> had never had, etc.")

Other cases: Wand. *96.* DG. *15, 31—33* [18]. *66, 26.*

---

[16] Brooke (*EELit.* P. 142) has "how"; Warren (*Treas. Eng. Lit.* I: 45), "when".

[17] These might also be considered *swa . . . swa* clauses of result.

[18] For obvious reasons, these two cases are listed under Sub. B, as well.

D. *Swa* introducing the second member of as
"as" . . . "so" correlation.

1. BH. 57, 8 (See Pp. 169—170).
2. Chm. V—A, 13 (See Pp. 170—173).
3. Chm. V—B, 10 (See Pp. 170—173).

VIII. Non-conjunctive (Adverbial) Clauses.

1. Absence of such in the initial position.

Not counting 16 cases of adverbial *swah þeah*, there are 36
cases of non-conjunctive *swa* in the monuments examined. Of
these latter, 20 occur in the interior position of the clause and 16
at the end. There is not one indisputable case of adverbial *swa*
at the beginning of a clause. [19] Six cases have been put forward
as such, the twists and turns of which will be discussed in this
section.

1. Dan. 666:

heold hæleða gestreon and þa hean burh
frod, foremihtig folca ræswa,
Caldea cyning, oð þæt cwelm gesceod,
swa him ofer eorðan andsaca ne wæs
gumena ænig.

The *swa* in the above Grein translates as "wie", and Kennedy
obscures the matter with a transitional "and". Bouterwek and
Thorpe both begin a new sentence with "so". But no complete
stop is necessary, if we follow Grein's punctuation and consider
the *swa*-clause one of "cause" or "evidence". My translation is:

(He [Nebuchednezzar] guarded the heroes' treasure
and the lofty city, this wise and mighty leader of
the folk, Chaldea's king, until death overtook him,
for over all the earth there was no man to oppose
him.)

2. Gen. 733:

Forþon hie leng ne magon
healdan heofonrice, ac hie to helle sculon
on þone sweartan sið, *swa* þu his sorge ne þearft
beran on þinum breostum . .

Here Bouterwek and Grein both begin a new sentence with
swa, and translate "so." Even though this is done, the initial *so*

---

[19] I except, in this statement, the adverb of manner used in correlation with
the conjunctive (modal) adverb in the "as" . . . "so" combination. But in such
cases the *swa* is protected by the conjunctive *swa* in the preceding clause.

of the sentence leans on the preceding clause. In modern English, a "so that" clause is sometimes used to introduce a pseudo-independent clause. I say *pseudo* because the clause is semantically *dependent*, in spite of its standing alone. The "so that" has given up its more exact *result* notion for the related one of *inference* or *conclusion*, with back reference to the preceding clause. As an example consider:

John Macy: *World's Literature*, 165:

"The Pope at Rome was often the unifying personality at the head of the universal Church, who presided not only over the spiritual life but over the temporal affairs of the many countries and principalities of Europe; and at least one great and strong man, Hildebrand, Pope Gregory VII, was a supreme monarch with kings under his thumb. *So that* Europe did not quite cease to be Roman through these long centuries, etc."

Similar cases in Old English are: EH. 4, 3749 (See Latin original; also Sellars' translation) and AEx. 9, 10—11 (Cp. Latin).

What is one to call the *swa* (or *swa þæt*) in such cases? It is almost the toss of a coin. But since meanings are older than grammatical classifications, I prefer to put such cases on a semantic basis, and to class them as subordinating conjunctions ("so that"), even when they are at the head of an apparently independent clause.

On this basis, then, I render Gen. 733 ff. as follows:

(Hence they [Adam and Eve] may no longer
hold their heavenly kingdom, but they
must travel the dark road to hell, *so*
that thou [Satan] needst feel no sorrow, etc.)

3. Gen. 288 (Grein-Wülker punctuation): [20]

ic mæg hyra hearra wesan
rædan on þis rice. *Swa* me þæt riht ne þinceð,
þæt ic oleccan awiht þurfe
gode æfter gode ænegum: ne wille ic leng his geongra wurþan!

This Grein translates:

(. . ich mag ihr Herr wol sein
und dieses Reich beherrschen! *Drum* dünkt mir recht das nicht,
daß ich in irgend etwas brauche abzuschmeicheln
Gott der Güter eines: ich will länger nicht sein Jünger bleiben!)

---

[20] Professor Malone, in the article already cited, speaks of the possibility of such non-conjunctives at the head of a clause with "verbs of thinking." Misled by the punctuation of Grein-Wülker, I once took Case 3 to be of that type. But Case 3 is a causal clause, and no others are at hand. I remain, therefore, skeptical on this point.

Bouterwek places a comma after *ænegum* and translates:

> (. . ich kann ihr Herr sein, herrschen in diesem Reiche;
> *drum* dünkt es mich nicht recht, daß ich irgend wie,
> um eines Gutes willen, Gott schmeicheln sollte: nicht
> länger will ich ihm unterthänig sein.)

Kennedy reads:

> (I may be their lord, and rule this realm. It seemeth *no wise* right to me
> that I should cringe a whit to God for any good.)

With these I disagree. My judgment is that the colon used by Grein-Wülker after *ænegum* should be replaced by a comma, and that the "*swa . . . ænegum*" portion should be read as the antecedent clause, with the "*ne . . . wurþan*" as the subsequent, in a causal sequence. My translation follows:

> (*Since* it does not seem right to me that I should cringe a whit to God
> for any good, no longer will I remain his underling.)

4. BH. 57, 8:

> ne þæt to nahte nyt ne biþ þæt man godne mete
> ete oþþe þæt betste win on gebeorscipe drince,
> gif þæt he hit eft spiwende anforlæteþ þæt he
> ær to blisse nam and to lichoman nyttnesse; *swa*
> we þonne þa gastlican lare unwærlice ne sceolan
> anforlætan, þe ure saul big leofaþ and feded bið;
> *swa* se lichoma buton mete & drence leofian ne
> mæg, *swa* þonne seo saul, gif heo ne bið mid Godes
> worde feded gastlice hungre & þurste heo bið cwelmed.

Here Morris disregards his own punctuation somewhat, and translates:

> (It is all to no purpose for a man to eat good meat or at a feast to drink
> the best of wine, if it happeneth that he afterwards spews up and loses
> that which he previously received for enjoyment, and for the advantage
> of the body. *So*, then, we must not unwarily relinquish the spiritual
> teaching by which our soul liveth and is fed. *As* the body cannot live
> without meat and drink, *so* then the soul, if she be not spiritually fed
> with God's word, will perish through hunger and thirst.)

It is the first *swa* that that we are concerned with, but I have italicized those in the sentence following because I feel that this second clause is a restatement, in concentrated form, of the one immediately preceding it. I assume that the first *swa* is the adverb of manner in a defective correlative modal pair ("as" . . . "so"). A case of such omission of the conjunctive adverb is at hand[21]; viz.

---

[21] Cp. the following from OHG in E. Steinmeyer: *Die kleineren Ahd. Sprachdenkmäler*, P. 378, LXIX: Christ uuarth giuund] tho uuarth he hel gi ok gisund. that bluod forstuond: *so* duo thu bluod!

DG. 47, 12:

> Forþon þa oferhydigan blissiað for þam arum
> þe hi begytað, *swa* eac full oft þa eaðmodan
> for heora forsewennysse.

> (For *(as)* the proud are made glad because of their honor, *so* those that
> are humble very often rejoice over contempt and disgrace.)

Now the Latin original has both adverbs in this correlation:

> Nam *sicut* superbi honoribus, *sic* plerumque
> humiles sua despectione gratulantur.

With this case, then, as a parallel, I read BH. 57, 8 as follows:

> (*As* it is all to no purpose for a man to eat good meat, or at a feast to
> drink the best wine, if it happeneth that he afterwards spews up and
> loses that which he previously received for enjoyment and for the advantage
> of his body, *so*, then, we must not unwarily relinquish the spiritual teach-
> ing by which our soul liveth and is fed.)

5. Chm. V—A, 13:

> Judeas Crist ahengon, dydon dæda þa wyrrestan;
> hælon þæt hy forhelan ne mihtan: *swa* þeos dæd
> nænige þinga forholen ne wurþe þurh þa haligan
> Cristes rode. Amen.

Cockayne's [22] translation of this passage is:

> (The Jews hung up Christ, they did of deeds the worst, they hid that
> they could not hide; *so* may this deed be in no wise hidden through
> the holy rood of Christ. Amen.)

6. Chm. V—B, 10:

> Judeas Crist ahengon, gedidon him dæda þa wyrstan;
> hælon, þæt hi forhelan ne mihton; *swa* næfre ðeos dæd
> forholen ne wyrþe per crucem Christi

This Cockayne renders:

> (The Jews hanged Christ, they did to him the worst of deeds; they con-
> cealed what they were not able to conceal. *So* never may this deed become
> concealed. Per crucem Christi.)

Grendon [23] is in practical agreement with Cockayne in the
translation of these two cases.

Now these two examples seem at first glance to prove that an
adverbial *swa* may introduce a negative clause, but closer scrutiny
will show that the *swa* in each sentence is (as in Case 4, this
section) the adverb of manner of a defective correlative modal
pair, an independent clause standing in each case for what would
normally be the "as"-clause of an "as" . . . "so" correlation.

---

[22] O. Cockayne: *Leechdoms, Wortcunning and Starcraft of Early England.*
III: 60—61; I: 390—393.

[23] *Anglo-Saxon Charms*: American Journal of Folk-Lore, XXII: 105—237.

It is characteristic of most Teutonic charms that they are built on a simile frame, usually by way of reference to something in church or biblical tradition. Jacob Grimm long ago remarked this [24]:

> »Viele formeln beruhen auf bloßer *sympathie zwischen gleichnis und wirkung.* Das blut, das feuer soll so still stehn, wie Christus still am kreuz hieng (XLI sanguis, mane in venis, sicut Christus pro te in poenis; sanguis mane fixus sicut Christus crucifixus); wie der Jordan still stand bei der taufe (VIII); wie die menschen am jüngsten tag still stehn werden (XXXII). das feuer soll seine funken behalten, wie Maria ihre jungfrauschaft behielt (XXVI); dem wurm im fleisch soll so weh werden, als es Petro weh ward, da er seines herrn marter sah (XXXVI), etc.«

In the High German charms given by Grimm and others, the simile frame is regular, that is, a correlative clause of comparison, either complete or defective. Examples:

1 Steinmeyer: Ahd. Sprachdenk. 367, LXIII:

> *Soso* Krist gibuozta themo sancte Stephanes hrosse thaz entphangana, *so* gibuozi ihc it mid Kristes fullesti thessemo hrosse.

2 Steinmeyer: Ibid. 373, LXVI, 2:

> *also* sciero werde disemo . . . . . rosse des erreheten buoz *samo* demo got da selbo buozta.

3. Grimm III: 500, xxv, b:

> behalt dein funk und flammen, *wie* Marie ir jungfrauschaft und er behalten hat vor allen mannen

4. Grimm III: 502, xxxvi:

> ich gebut dir huf und horn, das du *als* lutzel zerbrechist *als* got der herr die wort zerbrach, do er himel und erd beschuof.

Professor Grendon [25], in his study of Old English charms, likewise calls attention to this "sympathie" . . . as he puts it, "the mention of something which often bears only a remote relation to the subject of the charm". He cites in particular the two Old English charms here under discussion (Cases 5 and 6, this section), giving as the formula, "The cross of Christ was hidden and has been found", and as the associated idea, "so may these cattle be found".

Now in expressing this "gleichnis" and "wirkung", apparently what is known to English as "upside-down subordination" was often resorted to, just as in the case of concessive clauses (See above P. 164. By that process, the subordinate clause assumes such importance in the mind of the speaker or writer that it becomes

---

[24] *Deutsche Mythologie* (Berlin, 1878), III: 508.
[25] Op. cit. P. 120.

an independent clause. What results is an asyndeton, in which each clause may stand alone. A case in kind is a Pomeranian charm cited by McBryde [26]:

> Das Kreuz ward verborgen ward wiedergefunden durch die Sankt Hellman — *Also* wahr muß der Dieb widerkehren und sich wiederfinden mit dem gestohlen Gut.

Except that the second clause here is affirmative, this charm is very much like the two we are considering, and one senses here, too, what would be normally an "as" ... "so" arrangement.

Another case is on record in which, although the same similitic idea is apparent, the construction does not show it in the slightest.

LWS. I, 392:

> Adiuro te infans si es masculus an femina per patrem et filium et spiritum sanctum ut exeas et recedas et ultra ei non noceas neque insipientam illi faceas. Amen. Videns dominus flentes sorores Lazari ad monumentum lacrimatus est coram Iudeis, et clamabat, "Lazare, veni foras!" et produit, ligatus manibus et pedibus, qui fuerat quatriduanus mortuus.

This I translate as follows:

> (I charge you, infant, be you man-child or woman-child, in the name of the Father, the Son, and the Holy Ghost, that you come out and withdraw, and further that you do not harm her, nor do any injury to her. Amen. The Lord, seeing the sisters of Lazarus weeping at the tomb, wept in the presence of the Jews and exclaimed, "Lazarus, come forth!" and he came forth, wrapped hand and foot, he who had been four days dead.)

Anyone can see that a conjurative simile is intended in the above:

> "As the Lord called forth Lazarus .... so I adjure you, infant, etc."

In a third charm, one for blood-stopping, the "gleichnis" alone is given, although the subsequent clause can be readily inferred from it. The case is from Cockayne (LWS):

> Wrið cristes mæl and sing ðriwe on ðir
> and pater noster. Longinus miles lancea ponxit
> dominum et restitit sanguis et recessit dolor;

> (Make a cross of Christ and sing this thrice over the place, together with a pater noster. The soldier Longinus pierced the Lord with his lance and the blood ceased to flow and his pain ended. — Cockayne)

Cockayne [27] gives us as a source for the above charm "a transcript forwarded by a friend". His ending it with a semi-colon indicates that he probably considered it incomplete. If that surmise is

---

[26] J. M. McBryde, Jr. *MLN* 21: 180—183. His source for this charm, as acknowledged by the author, is Ulrich Jahn: *Hexenwesen und Zauberei in Pommern.*

[27] Cockayne op. cit. I: 393.

correct, the complete charm very likely had some such sense as this:

> (*As* the Saviour's blood ceased flowing and His pain ended when the soldier Longinus pierced His side with a lance, *so* may this blood cease flowing and the pain end.)

Since, then, the simile was a frequent device in the charm, and since (as has been shown in Case 4, P. 169—170) the conjunctive adverb of the antecedent clause was sometimes omitted, these two cases (Chm. V—A, 13 and Chm. V—B, 10) may be considered defective correlative (modal) pairs, to be translated as follows[28]:

> (*As* the Jews hanged Christ, did to him the worst of deeds, tried to hide [29] what they could not hide, *so* may this deed never be concealed.)

VIII. Non-Conjunctive (Adverbial) *Swa* — (continued).

B. In the interior position.

1. Beow. 1709:

> Ne wearð Heremod *swa*
> eaforum Ecgwelan, Ar-Scyldingum;
> ("Heremod was not *thus* to the off-
> spring of Ecgwela, Honor-Scyldings.")

2. El. 477:

> Ne meahton hie *swa* disige deað oð-
> fæstan weras wonsælige.
> ("Yet might these vain and miscreant
> men *in no wise* work his death." — Kennedy)

3. EH. 5, 1989:

> Ne scealt ðu *swa* sprecan
> ("Thou shalt not speak *so*.")

Other cases: EH. *4. 189. 5, 2546.* VPs. *147, 20.* BH. *215, 12.* BR. *46, 18. 48,7. 9.* ASHom. *16, 316.* AGen. *17, 27* (note). *18, 21.* AEx. *8, 26. 10, 11. 21, 23.* DG. *50, 20.* LAS. *164, 21. 210, 8—1. 262, 4—1.*

C. In the final position.

1. Beow. 1471:

> Ne wæs þæm oðrum *swa*
> syðþan he hine to guðe gegyred hæfde.
> (".. not *so* with the other
> when he for battle himself had prepared." — Garnett)

2. Guth. 548:

> hit ne meahte *swa*
> ("It might not *so* befall.")

---

[28] The two versions differ only in minor particulars.

[29] I take the verb *hælon* to be a translation of a Latin conative form.

3. MM. 74:

> ne mæg don unlæde *swa*
> ("It shall not be *so* with the others.")
> Other cases: Beow. *2091*. And. *1393*. Gen. *718*. PPs. *107, 10*. VPs. *118, 85*.
> SS. *391*. ASHom. *10,614*. BH. *175, 36*. AGen. *4, 15. 18, 15. 23, 11. 42, 10.*
> *48, 18.*

I will now tabulate my findings:

I. *Swa þeah:* "nevertheless", "yet", "though"
    1. As a subordinating conjunction 2
    2. As a pseudo-conjunction 2
    3. As a simple adverb (interior, *13*; final, *3*) 16
II. *Swa þæt:* "so that" in Result Clauses 18
III. *Swa* (or *swa swa*) alone, as a true conjunction
    1. "Although" in Concessive Clauses 5
    2. "So that" in Result Clauses 17
    3. "As", "since" in Causal Clauses 7
    4. "If", "unless" in Conditional Clauses 2
IV. *Swa* (or *swa swa*) alone, as a conjunctive adverb
    1. "As" in Modal Clauses 24
    2. "As if" in telescoped Modal-Conditional Clauses 5
V. *Swa* as a pseudo-conjunction: "yet" 4
VI. *Swa* as a member of a correlative pair
    1. As a conjunctive adverb introducing the second member of a comparison 13
    2. As a non-conjunctive adverb (modal) introducing the subsequent clause of an "as" . . . "so" correlation 3
VII. *Swa* (non-conjunctive adverbial): "so", "thus"
    1. In the interior position 20
    2. In the final position 16

                  Total cases in the literature examined **154**

Let me make it plain before drawing my conclusions that the cases discussed above cover every negative clause in the whole body of Old English poetry, as well as those of a substantial and representative portion of the prose. Of my findings with regard to the poetry, therefore, there can be little doubt; and while an examination of prose monuments other than those I have studied may qualify my conclusions somewhat, that possibility is slight, seeing that the prose works I have examined are typical of the prose literature in general.

What conclusion, then, can be drawn from these **154** cases, as regards the position of *swa* in the clause? As would be expected in the **57** cases where the word is used as either a true or pseudo-conjunction, as well as in the **42** conjunctive adverb cases, the *swa* is found in the initial position. And of the **55** non-conjunctive cases, only **3** (those of the "as" . . . "so" clauses of comparison) are found at the beginning of the clause, and these are accompanied by an extenuating circumstance — the fact that the clauses in which they occur do not stand alone, but are accompanied by a preceding *swa*-clause. Since, then, in this collection of representative cases, there is not a single clear case of adverbial (non-conjunctive) *swa* in the initial position, one may with safety conclude that the appearance of *swa* at the head of a negative clause is *prima facie* evidence of its conjunctive character.

———

CHANGE OF MEANING BY ANALOGY

BY SAMUEL KROESCH
UNIVERSITY OF MINNESOTA

In spite of the great progress which has been made in the field of lexicography within the last few decades there is probably no phase of linguistic science which still leaves so much to be desired as the matter of the investigation into the causes and the development of semantic changes as well as the proper arrangement and recording of meanings.

Strangely enough the editors of some of the best High German dictionaries have been prone to regard these points less seriously than we should expect in view of the fact that the problems in the field of sematology are at the same time the most difficult and most important of all the problems of lexicography. The editors of the Grimm Dictionary, following an antiquated medieval tradition, carried out the plan of putting Latin synonyms in lieu of definitions in the German, a procedure justly criticised by Hermann Paul[1] and fortunately corrected in later serial issues. The defence of this plan by the editor, Jakob Grimm, is quoted in part below since it throws an interesting light on the views held on this matter at the time that great work was begun: "Auch wird man nicht die Verständlichkeit aller im Lateinischen gebrauchten Ausdrücke für alle Leser des Wörterbuches verlangen; die ihrer unkundig sind, hüpfen mit leichtem Fuße daran vorbei und finden sich dennoch zurecht, wie sie vorübergehen, wenn sie auf ein Wort gestoßen sind, dessen Gehalt sie gar nicht anzieht ... *Jeder Leser bringt eine Menge Verständnisse mit sich, die ihm den Zutritt zu den Wörtern leicht machen* ... Nicht zu verachten ist auch, daß der Gebrauch der

---

[1] *Ueber die Aufgaben der wissenschaftlichen Lexikographie.* Sitzungsber. d. philos.-philol. Klasse d. Bayer. Akad. d. Wiss. 1894, p. 63 ff.

fremden Sprache die Erklärung der unzüchtigen Wörter löblich verdeckt und dem allgemeinen Verständnis gewissermaßen entzogen wird" (DWB I XLI). If today these words make an impression almost of frivolousness in the face of so serious a task they may be excused, at least, on the ground that they were written many years ago before the study of semantics had received any serious attention. But the fact that the user of the dictionary is in one way or another to fill in the gaps in the semantic history of a word seems scarcely justified in a work like Weigand's *Deutsches Wörterbuch*, whose editor, Hirt, expresses himself as follows in the introduction to this work: "Mancher wird vielleicht eine eingehendere Darstellung der Bedeutungsentwicklung vermissen. Da aber die meisten heutigen Bedeutungen, die selbständigen durch ; getrennt, außerdem die mittel- und althochdeutschen genau angeführt sind, *so wird man sich bei einigem Nachdenken die Bedeutungsentwicklung leicht klarmachen können.*" [2] Certainly as long as this phase of lexicography is taken so lightly we need not expect a dictionary whose discussion of the development of meaning is on a par with other parts of the work. The users of the NED are much more fortunate in this respect in that the editors of that great undertaking, early recognizing the difficulties and importance of this problem, have given us a much more careful and informative discussion of the semantic history of a word than any that has appeared elsewhere.

It is undoubtedly much more difficult to trace the beginnings of semantic changes or the causes for these changes than it is to trace phonetic forms. For this reason there will always be gaps in the semantic history of a word, especially in the older dialects. But by no means all possible phases of semantic history have thus far been studied and it is hoped that many more avenues of approach to the field may be found. The present paper is an attempt to discuss one of these neglected avenues of approach, namely change of meaning by analogy with a closely associated language, in this case Latin.

For more than one thousand years High German was most closely associated with Latin. Old High German prose literature consisted almost without exception of translations from Latin originals. Our earliest records of the Old High German were the

---

[2] The italics in the two quotations are ours.

glosses, the principal means by which the German novice who knew only his mother tongue, the *lingua theodisca*, was introduced to the *lingua latina*, the language of the Church. These glosses, extending unbrokenly down almost to the end of the fifteenth century, form the beginning of our science of lexicography. The invention of printing and the consequent appearance of our first dictionaries made no great change in the method of recording the meanings of words. Down to the eighteenth century, in fact to Adelung's great work (1775), practically without exception German dictionaries recorded meanings in Latin. The most important of these are the well known works of Aler, Frisch, Frisius, Kirsch, Maaler, Schottelius, Steinbach, Stieler, etc., so often quoted by the DWB and others. The importance of this fact from a linguistic standpoint cannot be overestimated because it makes clear the condition of bi-lingualism which was universal among the writers of the Middle Ages, that is, among those who have left us the records of the older dialects. That this constant association of two languages with each other in the minds of thousands of individuals through centuries should have left few or no traces in the semantic content of the High German seems inconceivable, and yet there is little evidence of the recognition of any such influence in our High German dictionaries. A few most striking cases of analogical influence may occasionally be mentioned, but on the whole, meanings are universally regarded by the lexicographers as having developed spontaneously either from the fundamental or the secondary meanings within the word itself. This, for example, is consistently the attitude of Paul in his *Deutsches Wörterbuch*, in most other phases of its discussion of meanings a model of excellence, and for its size in this regard probably the best German dictionary published. Possible analogical influences receive no consideration at all. If OHG *zunga* shows the development of meaning "speech; a peninsula", these are regarded as natural semantic developments in the German, Lat. *lingua* and Gk. γλῶσσα being mentioned only to supply semantic parallels. The possibility of the borrowing of these meanings by the Latin from the Greek and in turn by the German from the Latin is not considered worth mentioning. That these three linguistic groups should have developed independently the same figurative expression for "language" is not an impossibility, but if two of them have been closely associated and if it can not be shown that these meanings had existed independently before this association, it is certainly not justifiable to disclaim possible analogical influence; for the transference of the semantic content of one language to another is no more remarkable than the commonly accepted transference of the phonetic peculiarities of one language to another.

The association of the highly developed Latin, the language expressing the advanced culture of the Roman civilization, with the crude and undeveloped Old and Middle High German was of the utmost importance for the latter. Naturally the introduction of the Roman-Christian culture and learning found the Old High German inadequate to express in the native form innumerable ideas familiar to the user of Latin. The result was a rapid development of the Old High German in two principal directions, the one, the enlargement of the vocabulary through the introduction of numerous loan-words from the Latin, the other, the enrichment of the semantic content of the native vocabulary. We are concerned here only with the latter development. The semantically highly developed Latin increased uses for native High German words principally in three ways. The first thru the formation of new German compounds, usually literal translations of Latin compounds, as, for example *circumdare: umbigeban, umbisellan* (cf. OE *ymbsellan*), which have sometimes been called translation loans. In the second type either a new or an old Germanic compound was used to express less exactly the meaning of a Latin word or compound, as, for example, *einlih* "einfach": *simplex;* "einzig": *unicus.* In these two types the native High German vocabulary was increased thru the formation, for the most part, of new native compounds needed to express ideas of the associated Latin. In the third type the High German word, unchanged in form, is given new meanings by its association with the Latin word and it is this type especially with which we are concerned here.

It is the nature of the human mind to associate linguistic phenomena in groups whether consciously or unconsciously. Not only single words may be thus associated but phrases, whole sentences, syntax, grammar, meanings, etc., all are grouped in the mind of the individual in an infinite variety of complications. In grammar, for example, there is the grouping of the different cases of the single noun, the different tenses, modes, persons, number of the verb, or the ramifications of the word stem into a great variety of forms related both phonetically and semantically. [3] For the bilinguist the strongest association is the synonym group, the word in one language recalling this or that synonym in the other. Even tho these are not exact equivalents, and this is usually the case, the one readily recalls the other and the uses of the one will be readily transferred to the other. This transference of usage often entirely unconscious in the bilinguist, results in the creation of new meanings for words and these usually in the less highly developed language. [4]

To illustrate, let us take the example used before. OHG. *zunga* and Lat. *lingua* both mean primarily that most useful part of our anatomy, the tongue. Let us suppose the OHG word was used only in the primary sense while the Latin word because of association with Gr. γλῶσσα had developed also such meanings as "speech, language; a peninsula, etc." The German bilinguist would be likely to use *zunga* also in these special uses because of the perseverative tendencies created by his use of *lingua*. Thus the semantically more highly developed language would enrich the less highly developed, because the former would have more uses for its words and these uses would be transferred to the other language in the mind of the user of both. This association would tend to the new use of the word *zunga* in the OHG even tho *sprāhha* might have been just as adequate to convey the thought. The writer has noted repeatedly, especially in Notker, that where the two languages were associated, as in translation, *zunga* always translated *lingua* in the sense "speech".

---

[3] Compare Paul, *Prinzipien der Sprachgeschichte* [6], p. 25 ff.: Borowitz, *Die Uebersetzungstechnik Heinrich Steinhöwels*, Hermaea XIII, p. 44 says: »Unsere ganze Sprechtätigkeit beruht ja auf assoziativen Vorgängen. Gleichartige Elemente verbinden sich im Bewußtsein zu Vorstellungsgruppen, und wird nun eins dieser Elemente in der Sprache reproduziert, so stellen sich die anderen auf assoziativem Wege, d. i. automatisch, ganz von selbst ein.«

[4] The majority of translations of the OHG and MHG period represented little more than literal, word for word transferences from one language into the other. Translation had not been developed as an art. Even as late as the fifteenth century this practice was common, as we may see from the words of Heinrich Steinhöwel (*Aesop*, Oesterley, p. 276), who, agitating for a reform in this matter, explains how he believes in translating "in ringem verstentlichem tüsch on beheltne ordnung der wort gegen wort, ouch nit gelyche sinn gegen sinnen, sonder offt mit zuogeletten worten."

In order to show in an especially striking manner the influence of the Latin on the development of meaning in the High German, let us take a case in which the Latin word represents a wide expansion of ideas new to the German, i. e. ideas introduced by the Roman-Christian culture. Such a word is Latin *ars*. This word meant primarily "skill in joining or making something" (cf. *artus*, Gk. ἀρτύω ἀρετή) and developed the following meanings, practically all of them used in the words to be discussed below; 1. any physical or mental activity, so far as it is practically exhibited; a profession, art. 2. Science, knowledge; (a) the theory of any art, science, etc., grammar, rhetoric, etc.; (b) the knowledge, art, skill, workmanship employed in effecting or working upon an object; (c) the object artistically formed; a work of art; (d) cunning, artifice, fraud; (e) a machine (Med. Lat. only). Being primarily a learned word, *ars* was acquired very early by the Old High German cleric learning Latin because it was the name for at least a part of his course of studies. The *trivium*, consisting of grammar, logic and rhetoric and the *quadrivium*, made up of arithmetic, geometry, music and astronomy were called the *septem artes liberales*. [5] Since the Old High German had no words to represent these ideas, either the Latin word itself (cf. Piper *Notker* I, 10, 11, 65, etc.), or a German word representing an idea synonymous with one of the meanings of *ars* might be used. In the OHG period this word was *list* "Kenntnis", i. e. "knowledge, science", which began to be used to translate *ars* at first, no doubt, only in this sense. But once associated with the Latin word in this meaning, it was easy to use it for the special branches of knowledge, the *artes liberales*, especially since there was no other word to express these meanings. In the *Regula Benedict.* we find *artis spiritalis* translated by *listi atumlihhun* (IV); *ipsas artes: dea selbun listi* (LVII); *artes diversos: listi missilihho* (LXVI); *in arte aliquo: in listi edeslihheru* (XLVI). Other correspondences are: *liberalium artium: buohliste* (Notker, Boeth. V); *theiwāri gougalares list* (Otfrid, *Evangel.* IV 16, 33) cf. *magicis artibus facta* (Hrab. Maurus in Matth. p. 147a); *magicae artes: zoubirliste* (Notker, Schilter, *Thesaur.* I 10a, 6); *ludicra arte: spilelisti (Can.*

---

[5] Cf. Specht, *Geschichte des Unterrichtswesens in Deutschland*, Stuttgart 1885; Hoffmann, *Der mittelalterliche Mensch*, Gotha 1922 and particularly Burdach, *Der Ackermann aus Böhmen. Vom Mittelalter zur Reformation* III, p. 334 ff.

cod. tegernsee); exclamat artem: seiccant list (Isidor, *Lib. de officinis eccles.*).

In order to express Latin derivaties of *ars* such as *artifex, artificium, artificiosus*, etc., new High German words were formed on the stem of *list*, e. g. *listarra: artifices (Reg. Benedict.* IV); *listwirker: artifex* (Dief. *nov. gloss.* 36 a); *listig: arteficiosus* (Greg., *Cura past.* IV); *listigemo; artificioso (Gl. monsee.*, Pez I 384); *listlihemo: artificiose* (Greg., *Cura. past* VI); *list: artificium* (St. u. Siev., *Ahd. Gl.* 474, 21). Once Notker (Piper I, 276) translates *artifex* by *zimberman*. For the MHG period we may add *listmachaere, listwerkaere, listwerke, listwürhte:* artifex (Lexer s. v.); *tusendlistelaere: milleartifex* (Berth. v. Reg., Pfeiffer 408). Other words found in the poetic literature of the period and therefore without their Latin counterpart, but clearly analogical in origin are: *listsache* "Zauberkunst" *(ars magica), listviur* "durch geheime Künste bereitetes Feuer" (Lexer *s. v.*), *der siben liste brunnen (Troj. Kg.* 1958), from *Tristan: arzetlist* (7780), *boslist* (2903), *houbetlist* (4780) *jagelist* (3420), *schuollist* (7971); *der list von nigromanze (Parz.* 617, 12), etc. The uses of *list* in the usual senses of *ars* extend thru the thirteenth and fourteenth centuries but with ever diminishing frequency: e. g. *astronomie den list von dem gestirne* (R. v. Ems, *Weltchr.* 1178), *zouberlist (ars magica)* Die A*pok.* H. v. Hesler 1291) *wen er can alle die liste* ("Zauberkünste") *die je wurdent (Lucid. D. Texte d. Mas.* 28, 66, 1); *Wan Jubal der fand schmides list (D. T. d. Mas.* 31, 1897). Gradually during the fourteenth and fifteenth centuries the varied meanings of *list* become restricted almost entirely to one sense of *ars*, viz. 2 (d) above, the prevalent meaning in the NHG today. The cause of this specialization of meaning is to be found partly in the increased use of the word with such MHG adjectives as *bose, arc, valsch, ubel*, etc. with the resultant compounds *arclistic, boeslistic, hinderlistic, überlist, trügelist*, etc., and partly to the gradual assumption of the other meanings by a synonym of *list*, namely *kunst*. By the sixteenth century the transference of the whole group of meanings of *list* with the exception of 2 (d) to *kunst* was accomplished and still other meanings of *ars* added which *list* seems never to have had.

OHG *kunst*, a verbal abstract of *kunnan*, NHG *können* was an exact synonym of *list* (cf. Goth. *lais* "ich weiß") meaning primarily "Kenntnis, Wissen". While *list* was associated with *ars* in the OHG period there is no indication that *kunst* was thought of in connection with our Latin word. The OHG translator, for the most part, associated *scientia* with *kunst* as seen by the following parallels from Graff, *Ahd. Sprachschatz s. v. chunsti: scientia; chunst kelirnis: scientiam doctrinae; kunstigo kelerto: scientes.* Once *chunste* renders *sapientiae* and *kunstiger: gnarus, potens in scripturis.* At that *kunst* does not seem to have been the word most usually associated with *scientia*, the translations of *wistuom* and *wissentheit* being even more numerous, at least with Notker. Now *scientia* was occasionally used in connection with the *artes liberales*, for instance by Notker (I, 65) *tiu scientia diu rhetorica heizet.* But *kunst* was not associated with *ars* in the OHG period as far as the writer was able to discover.

We come then to the MHG period. It is unfortunate that for the later OHG and the earlier MHG periods the lack of records of translations makes impossible the tracing of any semantic associations for our word. In the early MHG poetic works *kunst* seems to have been rarely used. A hasty glance through several thousand lines of the *Rolandslied, Kaiserchronik, König Rother* and the *Vorauer Alexander* fails to reveal a single instance of its use, whereas *list* is found numerous times. In the heroic epics it is used very seldom, in the *Nibelungenlied* only once (2222, 2), in the sense "Geschicklichkeit", against eight uses for *list*. That *kunst* had become popular by this time, however, is evidenced by the fact that derivatives such as *kunstec, kunstriche, kunstlich* are used by the author of the *Nibelungenlied*. An examination into the uses of *kunst* by the poets of the court epic shows an increasing use as a synonym of *list*, especially in the meaning "skill" (Geschicklichkeit, Fertigkeit, Kunstbegabung) which, as we have seen, is the fundamental meaning of *ars*. The most definite evidence of this is seen in those cases where *list* and *kunst* are used synonymously in the same passage, as in the following:

> In vernam von jägerie
> solher liste nie niht nie
> dar zuo liez er im sehen e
> wie man den hirz enbesten sol
> diu kunst gevallet mir so wol, etc. (*Tristan* 3302 f).

Hartman von Aue in discussing the education of the young Gregorius says:

> unt daz kint wart alsus
> in dem selben liste
> ein edel legiste
> diu kunst sprichet von der e. (1022 f).

In Wernher's *Marienleben* whose source was the *Vita beate virginis Marie et Salvatoris rhythmica,* the author, in referring to Mary and the art of dressmaking *(ars suendi),* says: . . . *kunde alle fröliche kunst* 5509). In 778 *list* is used for the arts of sewing, weaving, spinning, etc. When Wolfram von Eschenbach says of his hero Parzival (123, 13) *do lac diu gotes kunst an im* he is thinking of God as the *artifex,* the artist. As a variant of the *arzate list* above he has *dar zuo al der arzate kunst* (643, 21) (cf. however, *der list von nigromanzi* 617, 12). The same use of *kunst* as the *ars medicinae* is found in a passage of an old work of this period on medicine *daz den wech mit die rechten chunst geleret hat . . . die da geschriben habent die chriechischen arzet Ypocris,* etc. *Zwei deutsche Arznei-bücher aus dem 12. und 13. Jahrh.* Pfeiffer, *Wiener Sb.* 42, 127. Toward the middle of the thirteenth century *list* and *kunst* are still often used as synonyms. Compare the following from R. v. Ems *Weltchronik:*

> (532) und musycam den hohen list,
> mit der kunst man alle vrist.

> (679) mit kunstlichir liste kraft
> wuohs ouh ir liste meisterschaft
> an manegir kunst mit wisheit.

This author rather favors *list* in referring to the *artes liberales,* judging from the foregoing uses and from the following: (1178) astronomie den list von den gestirne; (15 766) der siben liste hohe kunst. For the manual arts, however, *kunst* seems now well established. Compare the following from the same author:

> (535) gelt, silbir, stahil, isin
> von dem selbin wisin
> wart dirre hohe list irdaht
> und zeiner kunst der welte braht.

> (686) ir kunst mit vlize worhte
> zwo siule der einiu ziegelin
> was und diu ander steinin
> . . . . . zwaz kunst von in do fundin was.

(539) des swester diu hiez Neoma ....
diu was von erst die mit begunst
irdahte wipliche kunst.
mit nadiln unt mit drihin
nejen, brettin, rihin
diz vant ir kunst do bi den tagen
nu kunde birsen, schiezen, jagen
Lamech durch chunst und durch bejac
dirre selbin chunst er pflac.

Thomasin von Zirclaria uses *kunst* and *list* interchangeably in reference to the *septem artes liberales*. Compare the following from his *Der welsche Gast:*

(8899) wir haben künste vil geschriben
der sint uz erwelt siben
liste heize wir die künst.

(9063) An die siben liste breit
von den ich iu han geseit
sint ander zwo künste groz
die enen sint übergenoz:
die heizent davon liste niht
wan in ze herschen geschicht
über die siben ......
die ein Divinitas ist genant
diu ander Physica.

Besides the two additional *artes* mentioned here Thomasin adds the *Decrete* and the *Leges* (9151). These with the original seven he calls the *einlef künstn* (9667). After the expansion of the educational curriculum beyond the original seven arts *kunst* seems to have been used regularly, *list* evidently remaining restricted to the original seven. From the fourteenth century on, therefore, *kunst* has taken on almost all the senses which *list* formerly had acquired from *ars* with the exception of the use prevalent today. This, for instance, is true of the uses of these words in Hugo von Trimberg's *Renner*. [6]

---

[6] An examination of Trimberg's *Renner* indicated that by this time *kunst* had already taken over the meanings of *list*. The latter was used only in the sense which it had in the NHG, whereas *kunst* while often used in rather indefinite senses, is a favorite word with the author. A rapid survey of the work showed *kunst* used eighty times to five times for *list*. A century earlier the proportion of usage for these words would have been the reverse.

We have thus far attempted to trace the expansion of the meanings of MHG *kunst* thru the literature of the period but without direct association with the Latin. This expansion may have been due to its close association with *list* rather than with *ars*, especially in the early period of its semantic development. From the fourteenth century on, however, we have again the Latin for comparison in the manuscript glosses and for the later centuries the Latin-German dictionaries, these sources showing an ever expanding use of *kunst* to parallel similar uses in the classical and medieval Latin.

In Diefenbach, *Glossarium, list* is mentioned once only in connection with *ars*. *Kunst*, on the other hand, appears as follows: *kunst, konst* (three times); *ars eterna: ewige kunst; artes liberales fry (vrighe) kunste, frige kunste, frihe konste, frie konst, frey chunst, kunst; artifex (artista): kunstiger, konstiger* (four times), *kunstner, kunstmeister, konstener* (twice), *kuoster, kuosta; artificium: ein werck der kunst; artificiose: künstlich; artificiosus: kunstig, kinstig, konstig, kunstick, kunstich, kunstlich;* Med. Lat. *artista: ein kunstiger, kinstiger, fri kunstiger, frey chunstiger.* The *Novum Glossarium* adds: *ars eterna: cunstekeit; artificium: kunstheit; artista: fry kinstig, süben künster; astrologia: kunst der sterne.* Once *ars* is glossed by *behendekeit* and once by *hantwerck*, probably with the connotation of the *artes manuales* cf. Dief. 352 c (mechanica).

The early German-Latin dictionaries are of importance in showing many special uses of High German compounds with *kunst* to correspond to or even translate certain long established Latin expressions. From Stieler, *Der deutschen Sprache Stammbaum im Fortwachs*, Nürnberg 1691, we take the following words with Latin equivalents, many doubtless formed by analogy or association with the latter: *Kunst über alle Künste: ars artium; kunstbeflissen: artis studiosus; kunstbegleiter: comes et socius artis; kunstbild: Opus artificis; kunstfeind: osor artium liberalium; kunsthasser: id.; kunstfeuer: ignis artificialis (cf. Fr. feu d'artifice); kunstgerät: instrumenta artium; kunstgeschmack: artis gustatus; kunstgesellschaft: collegium artificium; kunsthand: manus artificiosa, artifex; kunstlauf: stadium artium; kunstlehre: artificium; kunstprobe: specimen artis; kunstquell: seminarium artis; kunstrede: oratio artificiosa; kunstregel: regula artis, pl. principia artium; kunstschade: artium labes; kunstschlüssel: clavis artium; kunstschweiß:*

studium artis; kunstspiegel: speculum politissima arte perfectim; kunstspiel: ludus artificialis; kunststörer: abusus artis, kunststüm- pelung: id.; kunststück, kunstgriff: artificium; kunsttanz: saltatio artificiosa; kunstübung: artis agitatio; kunstverwandter: ejusdem artis studiosus; kunstwasser: aquae artificialis; kunstwerker: artifex; kunstzweck: finis artis. Other compounds of possible analogical origin found in the dictionaries of Aler, Kirsch, Schottel, Stein- bach and in the DWB are: *kunstfrei: immunis ob artem; kunst- freund, kunstliebend: artium amans; kunstgönner: fautor artium; kunstmaler: pictor artifex; kunstpfeifer: tibicen artifex; kunstsprache: sermo artificiosus; kunstverständig: artis peritus; kunstwerk: artis opus.* With *kunst* as the last element of the compound we have the following analogies, which could easily be increased: *apo- thekerkunst: ars pharmaceutica; baukunst: (ars) architectura; bild- hauerkunst: (ars) statuaria; dichtkunst: (ars) poetica; kriegskunst: (ars) duellica; kriegskünstler: bellandi artifex (Livy); redekunst: (ars) rhetorica; sprachkunst: (ars) grammatica,* etc. (the other *artes liberales); sittenkunst: (ars) ethica; sehkunst: (ars) optica; zergliederkunst: (ars) anatomia; scheidkunst: (ars) chymia; denk- kunst: (ars) logica* (Leibnitz.); *wapenkunst: (ars) heraldica; schau- spielkünste: artes theatrales.* An interesting analogical compound of this type is *notenkunst,* a direct translation of *ars notoria,* found in *Der Ackermann aus Böhmen* 26, 30. (Cf. the note in Burdach's edition p. 360 f.)

In later times these analogies extend even to French derivatives of *ars,* in *kunstgegenstand, kunstsache: objet d'art; kunstgenie: genie de l'art,* etc. In the eighteenth century the analogical expressions *die guten Künste: bonae artes* and *die schönen Künste: les beaux arts* were in common usage. Semantic analogies, in fact, becoming popular may attain a momentum which sometimes carries them to extremes. This was the case with the word *kunst* in its use by students of the seventeenth century who, facetiously identifying Latin *ars* with German *ars,* gave *kunst* the analogical meaning "podex". From this developed the compounds *kunsthummel* "Kotfliege" (Luther), *kunstkammer* id. and *kunstjucken.* (Cf. DWB, vol. 5 s. v.)

For the development of *kunst* "machine" by association with *ars* "machina" (Du Cange) we refer the reader to the author's article on the semantic development of the OE *cræft.* This parti- cular sense, found as early as the fourteenth century in Konrad von Megenberg's *Buch der Natur*, e. g. *künstendingel: mechanicum aliquid* 434, 20, was restricted mainly to mining machinery and produced such compounds as *feuerkunst, dampfkunst, wasserkunst*, etc. (Cf. DWB V Sp. 2683). Another analogical development of meaning found in K. v. Megenberg is *kunstig* in the sense "artificialis" contrasting with "naturalis". In his *Deutsche Sphaera* we find him using, or shall we say translating, *kunstig tag* in contrast to *natürleichen tag* (31, 14; 32, 8; 36, 26—28 D Texte d. Mas.), *kunstiger: artificialis* (7, 11, id.), and in his *Buch der Natur* (Pfeiffer, 478, 7) *künstleich: artificialis*, this, the usual sense of NHG *künstlich*.

The conclusions to be drawn from the foregoing discussion may be briefly expressed as follows. Semantic development contrary to the prevalent conception does not always represent a direct line of associative changes from the fundamental meaning of the word in the particular dialect. There are many cross-currents of semantic influence, due to the association of synonyms in the same or foreign dialects. These latter influences may be so strong as to blot out entirely the fundamental meaning of the word. This is illustrated in OE *cræft* (cf. *op. cit.*) where thru the influence of Lat. *virtus* and *ars* the fundamental meaning "power" was entirely supplanted by the meanings of these Latin words. It is true again of *list* and *kunst* whose fundamental sense "knowledge", becoming associated with the same sense in the Lat. *ars*, adopted most of the other meanings of the latter by analogy and discarded the original fundamental meaning altogether.

It is, therefore, erroneous to think of the meanings of a word as always derived the one from the other in a close concatenation from a fundamental meaning as source. True, that is the usual conception which the lexicographer has of his task today. This is not enough, however. Even tho such a chain of meanings is psychologically unimpeachable it may still be incorrect unless possible analogical influences are weighed in considering the semantic history of a word.

If, then, the development depicted here is correct, a very commonly accepted test for semantic relationship must of necessity lose much of its value. We refer to the use of the semantic parallel as a sign or proof of the correctness of a semantic association. For languages as closely associated as Latin and Greek or Latin and the Germanic dialects it would have almost no validity because such parallels would more naturally be explained as semantic analogies.

What has occurred with the words discussed here, has taken place in hundreds of similar cases, not always with the great abundance of deviations in meanings shown in the foregoing, but nevertheless, with associative transferences just as convincing as those seen in High German *kunst*.

DER WORTSCHATZ DES AHD. TATIAN UND DIE ÜBERSETZERFRAGE

VON TAYLOR STARCK
HARVARD UNIVERSITY

Es ist längst anerkannt, daß die ahd. Tatianübersetzung nicht die Arbeit éines Uebersetzers sein kann. Die Unbeholfenheit einiger Partien, die stellenweise, z. B. 77—82. 11 a und 99—103, fast interlinear sind, gegenüber anderen gut, wenn auch nicht vorzüglich übertragenen Kapiteln, muß jedem unbefangenen Leser auffallen.[1] In seiner ersten Ausgabe des T[2] hat Sievers es unternommen, die Abschnitte zu bestimmen, welche verschiedenen Uebersetzern zuzuweisen sind. Er hielt sich an die wechselnde Uebertragung verschiedener häufig auftretender Wörter, wo Zufall oder absichtliche Variation als bestimmende Faktoren leichter ausgeschieden werden können als bei gelegentlichen Ausdrücken. Er wählte also solche Wörter wie *quia = bithiu uuanta, uuanta, bithiu, thaz,* unübers.; *cum = mitthiu, thanne, thô, sôsô, sô;* usw. Er kam zum Entscheid, daß die Abschnitte 18, 45, 67, 104, 119, 135, 146, 175 als Anfangspunkte neuer Arbeiter zu betrachten seien. In seiner Rezension von Sievers Ausgabe[3] hat Steinmeyer

---

[1] Die Versuche von Arens, *ZfdPh* 29, 510 ff. und Walther, *Die deutsche Bibelübersetzung des Mittelalters,* Braunschweig, 1892, Sp. 446, wieder einheitliche Verfasserschaft für den ahd. T zu beweisen, sind verfehlt. Das von Arens herangezogene Material beweist noch nicht, daß gar kein Uebersetzerwechsel stattgefunden hat, nur daß die Grenzen der Uebersetzerabschnitte nicht alle richtig gezogen sind. Karl Förster, *Der Gebrauch der Modi im ahd. Tatian,* Kiel (Diss.), 1895, kam zum Schluß (S. 1): »Der Modusgebrauch erscheint im ganzen Werk einheitlich genug, so daß man sich auf diese Indizien hin für die Annahme der Uebersetzung von éiner Hand erklären müßte.«

[2] Paderborn, 1872, S. 48—53. Nachträge in der zweiten Auflage, 1892, S. LXX—LXXV.

[3] *ZfdPh* 4, 474 ff.

diese statistischen Aufstellungen weiter ausgebaut und korrigiert. Er legt überzeugend dar, daß ein häufigerer Uebersetzerwechsel angenommen werden müßte und ließ die Abschnitte anheben mit 4. 12; 13. 5; 17. 6; 45; 67; 77; 78. *1*; 79. 4; 82. 11 a; 86; 88. 13; 91. 5; 96. 5; 104. 1; 104. 6; 119; *125. 11*; *132*; *135*; 146; 175; *198*. Die kursiv gedruckten sah er als nur schwach bewiesen an. Sievers ließ nur 45; 67; 104; 119; 135; 146; 175 als sicher gelten und wies die übrigen als unbewiesen zurück.

Die ganze Frage blieb nun lange [4] ruhen, bis sie wieder von Friedrich Köhler in einer Leipziger Dissertation [5] aufgenommen wurde, der auf Grund syntaktischer Indizien und durch Anwendung des Rutzschen Verfahrens zur Unterscheidung der Stimmtypen, eine große Menge kleiner Abschnitte machte, gegen dreihundert an der Zahl, wobei er aber an nur wenige Arbeiter dachte, die sich im Laufe der Uebersetzung gegenseitig ablösten. Schließlich hat Leo Kramp die von Steinmeyer gewünschte stilistische Untersuchung angestellt [6], die es ihm ermöglichte, die folgenden Abschnitte festzustellen: 17. 2; 45; 67; 77. 1; 82. 11 a; 89; 96; 104; 119; 141 (Vers unsicher); 146; 175; 188; 197.

Bemerkenswert ist, daß zwei oder mehr Arbeiter an den folgenden Stellen übereinstimmen:

4. 12 Steinmeyer, Köhler; 17. 6 Sievers, Steinmeyer, Kramp, Köhler; 45. 1 Sievers, Steinmeyer, Kramp, Köhler; 67. 1 Sievers, Steinmeyer, Kramp, Köhler; 82. 11 a Steinmeyer, Kramp, Köhler; 104. 1 Sievers, Steinmeyer, Kramp, Köhler; 104. 6 Steinmeyer, Köhler; 119. 1 Sievers, Steinmeyer, Kramp, Köhler; 135. 1 Sievers, Steinmeyer, Köhler; 146, 1 Sievers, Steinmeyer, Kramp, Köhler; 175. 1 Sievers, Steinmeyer, Kramp, Köhler; 198. 1 Steinmeyer, Köhler, Kramp (ungefähr). Bei der großen Zahl der von Köhler gemachten Einschnitte ist es beinahe unvermeidlich, daß er immer mit einem der übrigen zusammentrifft. Doch darf jetzt als einigermaßen sicher gelten, daß an den obigen zehn Stellen oder in deren unmittelbarer Nähe wirklich ein Uebersetzerwechsel stattgefunden hat.

In einer umfassenden Arbeit über den Wortschatz des T [7]

---

[4] A. Hilscher, *Die Verfasserfrage im ahd. T.* I. Programm, Posen, 1901, war mir nicht zugänglich.

[5] *Zur Frage der Entstehungsweise der ahd. Tatianübersetzung*, Leipzig, 1911.

[6] "Die Verfasserfrage im ahd. Tatian", *ZfdPh* 47, 322—360.

[7] "Der Wortschatz des ahd. T. in seinem Verhältnis zum alts., angels., und altfries.", *PBB* 39, 1 ff., 229 ff.

hat Gutmacher reiches Material beigebracht, welches sich zur Lösung der Uebersetzerfrage verwerten läßt. Gutmacher hat gezeigt, daß ein großer Prozentsatz des Wortschatzes des T (461 Wörter, etwa 15 v. H. des gesamten Wortschatzes) Eigenheiten aufweist, die dem T gegenüber anderen ahd. Denkmälern ein recht eigentümliches Gepräge geben. Darunter sind 41 Wortstämme, die im ahd. nur im T belegt sind. Von diesen Wörtern, welche durch ihr Fehlen oder ihren beschränkten Gebrauch im übrigen ahd. Schrifttum ausgezeichnet sind, finden sich eine große Menge im alteng., alts., altfries. und altnfr. Nach Gutmachers Zählung sind von ca. 2030 Wörtern im T 280 den übrigen ahd. Quellen fremd und von diesen kehren 120 im alteng. bzw. alts., mnd., mnl. wieder. Die Tabelle am Schlusse seines Artikels macht diese Beziehungen deutlich. [8]

Es fragt sich nun, ob diese Eigentümlichkeiten des T gleichmäßig auf die ganze Uebersetzung verteilt sind, oder ob einige Partien im Wortgebrauch mehr mit dem übrigen Ahd. zusammengehen als andere. Haben die Uebersetzer im Kloster Fulda gemäß ihrer landschaftlichen Herkunft diese oder jene Eigentümlichkeit bewahrt? Sollten sich die von Gutmacher behandelten Wörter sehr ungleichmäßig verteilt finden, so liegt die Vermutung nahe, daß hier wirklich der Sprachgebrauch verschiedener Individuen wiedergespiegelt ist.

Eine statistische Prüfung des Wortschatzes in bezug auf die Verteilung der von Gutmacher besprochenen Wörter zeigt nun eine überraschende Gleichförmigkeit. Es fallen auf die Seite von Sievers Text durchschnittlich 2.5, auf die Seite der Hs. 2.3 Wörter. Mustert man die oben aufgezählten Abschnitte, wo mehrere Arbeiter übereinstimmen, so zeigen die folgenden eine größere Variation von der Norm: Prol. 4. 12 (3 Wörter auf die Seite); 104—118 (3. 42); 119—134 (1. 57); 146—174 (1. 96); 175—197 (2). Wenn aber diese Grenzen nicht ganz genau gezogen sind, könnte die Verschiebung von nur einem Vers schon einen nicht unbedeutenden Unterschied machen, da nicht selten drei bis vier dieser Wörter in ein paar Zeilen vorkommen, oder sie auf mehreren

[8] Die Schlüsse, die aus diesen Verhältnissen gezogen werden können, gab Braune in der umfassenden und methodisch wichtigen Abhandlung "Althochdeutsch und Angelsächsisch", *PBB* 43,361—445. Es handelt sich nach ihm beim T lediglich um einen altertümlichen Wortschatz und nur in einigen Fällen um angelsächsischen Einfluß.

Seiten ganz fehlen können. Es scheint daher geboten, Seite für Seite der Hs. den Wortschatz zu prüfen, und um so eher, da, wie schon Sievers bemerkte, der Uebersetzerwechsel fast immer mit dem Anfang einer neuen Seite der Hs. zusammentrifft. So gezählt finden sich größere Abweichungen von der Norm, als wenn man längere Abschnitte als eine Einheit betrachtet und der Text zerfällt in Abschnitte, die durch größere oder geringere Häufigkeit der tatianischen Wörter ausgezeichnet sind. Bezeichnen wir erstere als Typus A, letztere als Typus B. Es folgen hier diese Abschnitte, gezählt nach Seiten der Hs., und daneben in Klammern die entsprechenden Kapitel und Verse des Textes sowie auch die auf die Seite der Hs. fallende Durchschnittszahl der von Gutmacher besprochenen Wörter.

25 (Prol. 1—2. 1; 0); 26—27 (2. 1—11; 4); 28 (2. 11—3. 8; 2); 29—32 (3. 8—4. 17; 4); 33—36 (4. 18—6. 6; 1.25); 37—44 (6. 6 bis 13. 6; 3.37); 45 (13. 6—12; 0); 46 (13. 12—18; 4); 47 (13. 18—23; 1); 48—50 (13. 23—16. 1; 3.3); 51—54 (16. 1—19. 4; 0.75); 55—57 (19. 4—21. 8; 3); 58 (21. 9—22.2; 1); 59—61 (22. 2—25.4; 5); 62—64 (25. 4—31. 2; 1.3); 65—66 (31. 2—33.2; 3); 67—68 (33. 2—35. 2; 1.5); 69—70 (35. 2—38. 5; 4); 71—81 (38. 5—45. 5; 1.36); 82—85 (45. 6—51. 3; 3.25); 86—88 (51. 3—53. 14; 2); 89 (54. 1—8; 4); 90—92 (54. 8—57. 3; 2); 93 (57. 3—8; 6); 94—96 (58. 1—60. 16; 2); 97—103 (60. 17—67. 7; 3.71); 104—106 (67. 7—69. 7; 1); 107—112 (69. 7—76. 5; 4.5); 113—116 (76. 5 bis 79. 10; 1.5); 117 (79. 10—80. 3; 4); 118 (80. 3—7; 2); 119 (80. 7 bis 81. 3; 6); 120—121 (81. 3—82. 5; 2); 122—123 (82. 5—11; 3.5); 124—127 (82. 11—84. 5; 1); 128—129 (84. 5—85. 4; 5); 130—132 (86. 1—87. 7; 2); 133—134 (87. 7—88. 1; 4); 135—146 (88. 1 bis 91. 5; 1.58); 147—148 (91. 5—92. 5; 5.5); 149 (92. 5—8; 2); 150—152 (92. 8—95. 5; 3.66); 153—154 (96. 1—97. 1; 2); 155 bis 157 (97. 1—98. 3; 3.6); 158—162 (98. 3—102. 1; 1.2); 163—164 (102. 1—103. 5; 3.5); 165 (103. 5—104. 2; 2); 166—167 (104. 2—6; 4); 168 (104. 6—8; 1); 169—170 (104. 8—106. 1; 4); 171—172 (106. 1—6; 1); 173—174 (106. 6—107. 3; 2.5); 175—176 (107. 3 bis 108. 5; 0.5); 177 (108. 5—109. 1; 4); 178—179 (109. 1—110. 1; 1); 180—182 (110. 1—112. 2; 3); 183—185 (112. 2—113. 1; 1.5); 186—188 (113. 1—116. 1; 5); 189 (116. 1—3; 0); 190—191 (116. 3—6; 4); 192—194 (116. 6—118. 2; 1.66); 195 (118. 2—4; 5); 196—201 (119. 1—123. 2; 1.16); 202 (123. 2—7; 3); 203—204 (123. 7—125. 2; 1.5); 205—207 (125. 2—127. 1; 3); 208—209

(127. 1—4; 1.5); 210—212 (128. 4—129. 8; 4); 213—219
(129. 8—131. 24; 1.33); 220 (131. 24—132. 4; 3); 221—226
(132. 5—134. 3; 0. 66); 227 (134. 3—8; 4); 228 (134. 8—135. 1;
0); 229—231 (135. 1—19; 3.3); 232—237 (135. 19—138. 6; 0.66);
238 (138. 6—11; 4); 239 (138. 11—139. 1; 0); 240—243 (139. 1 bis
141. 11; 3.75); 244 (141. 11—16; 2); 245 (141. 16—20; 2); 246 bis
248 (141. 20—143. 3; 1.33); 249 (143. 4—8; 4); 250 (144. 1—145. 3;
0); 251—253 (145. 4—16; 4. 3); 254 (145. 16—19; 1); 255 (145. 19 bis
146. 2; 3); 256—266 (146. 3—152. 3; 1.09); 267 (152. 3—7; 3);
268 (152. 7—153. 4; 1); 269 (153. 4—155. 2; 4); 270—274 (155. 3 bis
159. 6; 1); 275—276 (159. 6—161. 2; 2.5); 277—280 (161. 2 bis
165. 4; 1.25); 281—282 (165. 4—167. 1; 3.5); 283—285 (167. 2 bis
170. 6; 1.66); 286—288 (170. 6—174. 6; 3.66); 289 (175. 1—176. 3;
2); 290 (176. 3—177. 4; 5); 291 (177. 4—178. 5; 2); 292 (178. 5 bis
179. 2; 5); 293—294 (179. 2—181. 4; 1); 295—296 (181. 4—184. 1;
2.5); 297—303 (184. 1—192. 1; 1); 304—305 (192. 2—194. 3;
4.5); 306 (194. 3—196. 1; 1); 307 (196. 1—7; 6); 308 (196. 7 bis
197. 6; 1); 309—310 (197. 6—199. 3; 3); 311 (199. 4—11; 2);
312—313 (199. 11—202. 2; 3.5); 314—318 (202. 3—209. 4; 1.6);
319 (210. 1—5; 4); 320 (211. 1—4; 1); 321—323 (212. 1—217. 1;
2.66); 324—327 (217. 1—221. 7; 1); 328 (222. 1—223. 3; 3);
329—331 (223. 3—228. 1; 1.66); 332 (228. 1—229. 3; 3); 333—335
(229. 3—233. 6; 0.66); 336 (233. 6—235. 3; 3); 337—339 (235. 3 bis
239. 3; 1); 340—342 (239. 3—244. 4; 3).

Wie erklärt sich nun diese Verteilung, wonach in kleineren
Abschnitten ein bedeutender Unterschied hervortritt, der in den
längeren wieder verwischt wird? Daß mehrere Uebersetzer be-
teiligt waren, darf als Tatsache gelten. Wenn diese sich so in die
Arbeit teilten, daß jeder nur einen kleinen Abschnitt übersetzte,
ehe er abgelöst wurde, dann darf man in den kleineren Abschnitten
Unterschiede erwarten, die in den längeren wieder verschwinden.
Das durchschnittliche Auftreten auffallender Wörter in längeren
Abschnitten muß sich notwendigerweise dem Durchschnitt in
der ganzen Uebersetzung nähern. Je größer der Abschnitt, desto
geringer der Abstand vom Durchschnitt des ganzen Werkes. Ist
nun aber ein bedeutender Unterschied bei den kleineren Abschnitten zu merken, muß gefolgert werden, daß der Sprachgebrauch
eines oder mehrerer der Uebersetzer sich weiter vom ahd. Sprachgebrauch entfernte als der von den übrigen.

Dabei muß aber mit verschiedenen Faktoren gerechnet werden,

die leicht ein verzerrtes Bild geben. Die Uebersetzung ist selbstverständlich durch die Wortwahl der lateinischen Vorlage bedingt. Daß *furistsizzento* nur an einer Stelle (45. 6, 7) vorkommt, erklärt sich durch das einmalige Auftreten von *architriclinus*. Ob ein anderer Uebersetzer einen andern Ausdruck (Gutmacher S. 11) gebraucht haben würde, entzieht sich unserer Kenntnis. Ein und derselbe Uebersetzer wird auch wohl freiwillig den Ausdruck variiert haben und ausnahmsweise ein veraltetes oder selten gebrauchtes Wort herangezogen haben. Ueber solche Variation in den ersten 16 Kapiteln handelt Kramp ausführlich. Ferner werden gewisse Wörter in der Klostersprache von Fulda Gemeingut geworden sein, so daß der heimische Ausdruck des Uebersetzers in Vergessenheit geriet. Das ist sicher der Fall bei *fluobar* und Sippe.[9] Immerhin ist die Häufigkeit der fremden Ausdrücke in einer Partie und die sparsame Anwendung derselben in einer anderen von Bedeutung, denn die Wahl gerade dieser Ausdrücke zur Uebertragung von selten oder nur einmal auftretenden lateinischen Wörtern könnte nicht durchweg auf reinem Zufall beruhen. Auch ist die Verteilung der Wörter, welche, was den Wortstamm anbetrifft, dem Ahd. sonst fremd sind, von großem Interesse. Sie finden sich beinahe ausnahmslos in Partien vom Typus A. Wo das nicht der Fall ist, läßt sich aus stilistischen Gründen leicht eine Erklärung geben oder der Anfangspunkt des neuen Uebersetzerabschnittes ist um ein weniges zu verschieben.

Die im Ahd. sonst unbelegten Wortstämme (Gutmacher 68 ff.) finden sich im T wie folgt:[10]

asni 133. 11 (Seite der Hs. 225). Typus B von S. 221—226 (132. 5 bis 134. 3). Köhler macht Einschnitte bei 132. 6 und 134. 3.

asneri 97. 3 (2) (S. 155). Partie Typus A reicht von S. 155—157 (97. 1—98. 3).

berd: 141. 28 (S. 247). S. 246—248 gehören Typus B an. Gerade davor sind die fremden Ausdrücke häufig und wieder danach auf S. 250. Köhler macht einen Abschnitt bei 141. 20 (S. 246), aber nicht 143. 3 (S. 248).

biril: 80. 6 (S. 118) Abschnitt Typus B.

---

[9] Es ist aber bemerkenswert, daß die Sippe von *fluobar* mit einer Ausnahme nur in Partien vorkommt, wo die fremden Ausdrücke sonst häufig sind (Typus A). Die Ausnahme ist 135. 19. Wenn man aber die Grenze vom Seitenanfang bis an den Schluß des Satzes verschiebt, dann fällt *fluobritun* in eine Partie Typus A.

[10] Ueber *fluobar* und Sippe siehe Anm. 9.

bruogo: 145. 5 (S. 251) Partie Typus A reicht von S. 251—253 (145. 4—16).

flah: 192. 2 (S. 304) Partie Typus A reicht von S. 304—305 (192. 2—194. 3).

gifehan: Die einzige Uebertragung von gaudere, und ist daher wenig beweiskräftig. Wie *fluobar* ist das Wort in die Sprache aller Insassen des Klosters übergegangen. Dasselbe gilt von *gifeho.*

girdinon: 74. 8 (S. 110); 97. 2 (S. 155). Beide Stellen in Partien vom Typus A, S. 107—112 und S. 155—157 (69. 7—76. 5 und 97. 1—98. 3). Köhler macht Einschnitte bei 70. 1; 77. 1; 97. 4; 99. 2.

hansa: 200. 1 (S. 312). Typus A von 312—313 (199. 11—202. 2).

gikeuuan: 141. 7 (S. 243). Typus A von S. 240—243 (139. 1 bis 141. 11). Köhlers Einschnitte: 139. 2 und 141. 12.

landeri: 199. 8 (S. 311). Typus B (199. 4—11).

liodar: 145. 15 (S. 253). Typus A von S. 251—253.

manduuari: 22. 9 (S. 60); 67. 9 (S. 104); 116. 3 (S. 190). Die zweite Stelle in einer Partie Typus B, doch ist der Grenzpunkt des Uebersetzerwechsels vielleicht zu verschieben. Steinmeyer, Sievers und Kramp machen Abschnitt bei 67. 1 (S. 103); Köhler bei 67. 3 und 67. 8. Die anderen beiden Stellen in Partien vom Typus A.

manzon: 58. 1 (S. 94). Typus B von 94—96 (58. 1—60. 16). Doch steht das Wort gegen Anfang der Seite und der vorgehende A-Abschnitt reicht vielleicht bis 59. 1.

melmi: 44. 9 (S. 77). Typus B. Beinahe sicher ist aber in der Mitte des langen Abschnittes S. 71—81 ein Uebersetzerwechsel. Köhler faßt 44. 7—14 zusammen, also ungefähr gerade diese Seite der Hs.

gimunt: 138. 6 (S. 238); 160. 3 (S. 276). Die erste Stelle in einer Partie Typus A, die diese Seite allein umfaßt. Bei Köhler wird 138. 7—10, ungefähr die S. 238, als ein Abschnitt zusammengefaßt. Die zweite Stelle auch in einer Partie Typus A.

gimuntigon: 4. 8 (S. 37). Typus A.

scuhenti: 13. 25 (S. 48). Typus A.

tuomo: Von den 6 Fällen kommen vier in Partien vom Typus A vor. Die Stelle 122. 3 (S. 201) fällt in eine Partie Typus B, doch fängt mit 123. 2 (S. 202) ein neuer Abschnitt Typus A an. Dieser beginnt aber wohl schon vor *tuomo*. Köhler macht einen Abschnitt von 122. 2—123. 6. Da der andere Fall von *tuomo* in 122. 1 zu finden ist, spricht dies dafür, daß der neue Uebersetzer mit dem Kapitel 122 anhob. Zu beachten ist aber, daß *tuomo* die einzige Uebertragung ist für »iudex«.

furuuergen: 92. 2 (S. 148). Partie Typus A reicht von S. 147—148. Der andere Fall, 129. 9 (S. 213) in einer Partie Typus B, aber gegen Anfang der Seite und Schluß des Kapitels. Köhler macht einen Abschnitt 129. 8—11. Der dritte Fall, 152. 6 (S. 267), in einer Partie Typus A.

aruuizan: Sechs Fälle, davon 22. 4 (S. 59), 92. 2 (S. 148), 113. 1 (S. 186), 244. 2 (S. 342) in Partien von Typus A. Bei 42. 3 (S. 74) steht das Wort am Schlusse eines Kapitels und am Anfang einer neuen Seite und es ist wohl mit einem neuen Einschnitt zu rechnen. Bei 152. 6 (S. 267) haben wir es wohl mit einer kurzen Partie Typus A zu tun, die nur diese Seite der Hs. umfaßt, 152. 3—152. 6. Köhler machte Einschnitte am Schlusse von 152. 3 und 152. 6.

uozarnen: Die fünf Fälle nur in Partien vom Typus A. Die Stelle 118. 2 ist sicher zum folgenden A-Abschnitt zu ziehen, der dann mit dem Anfang des Verses anheben würde.

uuabarsiuni: 210. 3 (S. 319) Partie vom Typus A.

Von den 120 Einschnitten, die hier gemacht werden, stimmen 98 genau oder ziemlich genau zu den von Köhler anerkannten. Und da die obige Einteilung vorerst mechanisch vorgenommen wurde, ohne Rücksicht auf Vers oder Satzschlüsse, ist diese Uebereinstimmung sehr überraschend. Eine schärfere Abgrenzung kann nur erzielt werden durch Heranziehung anderer Indizien, die häufiger auftreten als die speziell tatianischen Wörter. Eine solche Untersuchung aber würde weit über den Umfang eines Aufsatzes hinausführen. Ich gebe also im folgenden nur ein paar Proben von der näheren Bestimmung der Grenzen. Letzten Endes wird doch wohl die Schallanalyse angerufen werden müssen.

Grenze zwischen 3. 2 und 3. 4. Ob vor Schluß von S. 32 der Hs. (4. 17) eine Grenze zu ziehen ist? Im Prolog und dem ersten Kapitel kommen keine von Gutmachers Worten vor, in dem längeren zweiten aber acht, nämlich *rchtfesti, uuirouhbrunst, ungiloubfol, menigi, blidida, tougilta sih, lazzen, gifeho.* Vier von diesen und die lateinischen Worte, welche sie übersetzen, kommen nicht wieder vor, lassen sich also für unseren Zweck nicht verwerten. *Uuirouhbrunst*, 2. 4, übersetzt *incensum*, das aber 2. 3 durch *uuirouh* und *rouhennes* wiedergegeben ist. Dies scheint also eine freiwillige Variation eines einzigen Uebersetzers zu sein. Das sonst im Ahd. unbelegte Adjektiv *ungiloubfol* für *incredibilis* 2. 7, das nur an dieser Stelle der Vulgata vorkommt, findet sich auch 21. 8 und 233. 6 für *incredulus*. Die ebenfalls auf den T beschränkte Ableitung *ungiloubfulli* (*incredulitas*) steht 92. 5 und 241. 2; dagegen das geläufige *ungiloubo* 78. 6 und 92. 8. Köhler macht zwischen 92. 5 und 92. 8 einen Einschnitt, was auch zu dem verschiedenen Sprachgebrauch *ungiloubfulli* — *ungiloubo* paßt. Das Adjektiv *ungiloubfol* gehört also einem Uebersetzer vom Typus A an. *Gifeho*, 2. 6, die einzige Entsprechung von *gaudium*, scheinbar allen Uebersetzern gemeinsam bekannt, und *menigi*, 2. 3, das nicht auf den T beschränkt ist (Gutmacher 27 f.) sind für unseren Zweck nicht zu verwerten. *Huldi* 3. 4 = *gratia* ist zwar auch nicht speziell tatianisch, doch weicht der Gebrauch hier von anderen Stellen ab. *Gratia* heißt sonst *geba* 3. 2; 12. 1, 9; 13. 7, 9 oder *thanc* 32. 5, 6; 82. 3; 89. 2; 111. 2; 118. 2; 135. 25; 160. 2. Ob diesem Sprachgebrauch nach zwischen 3. 2 und 3. 4 ein Einschnitt anzunehmen ist? Ich glaube in der Tat, daß nach 3. 3 ein neuer Uebersetzer anfing. Weitere Stützen für diese Annahme finden sich in *uuis sin* 3. 6 für *cognoscere* gegenüber dem üblichen *furstantan* Prol. 4, obwohl die Bedeutung 3. 6 wie auch 5. 10 eine spezielle ist; *uxor* = *quena* 2. 1, 5, 8, 11 und später häufig, *gimahha* nur 5. 12 (Gutmacher S. 24); *benedicere* = *segenon* 3. 2 gegenüber *uuihen* 4. 12, 14; *salutatio* = *uuolaqueti* 3. 3, = *heilezunga* 4. 2. Bemerkenswert ist auch der Vergleich zwischen *ginemnis* 3. 4 und *nemnis* 2. 5; und der Orthographie *intfieng* 2. 11 und *inphahis* 3. 4.[11]

Grenze um 4. 12 bis 4. 15. Eine Grenze um 4. 12 scheint mir schon aus den von Steinmeyer und Köhler vorgebrachten Gründen sicher. Kramps Beweise für die Einheit von 1—17. 1 sind ungenügend. Auch die größere Kompetenz zugegeben, die in diesen ersten Kapiteln zutage tritt, bleibt doch nicht ausgeschlossen, daß wir es hier mit mehr als einem Arbeiter zu tun haben. Kramp betont selbst die Unbeholfenheit des Prologs und die Fehler 4. 7, 10. 1 und 10. 3, die schlecht zu seiner Annahme passen.

Zu einer Grenze um 4. 12 ist aber noch einiges hinzuzufügen. In 4. 8 wird *memorari* durch *gimuntigon*, aber 4. 15 durch *gihugen*

---

[11] Ueber die Verteilung von *int-*, *inph-*, *intph-* vgl. Sievers § 60. 6.

übersetzt. Letzterer ist der geläufige Ausdruck. *Aperire = gioffanon* 4. 12, = *intuon* 7. 2, später, 8. 7, wieder *gioffanon*. *Benedicere = uuihen* 4. 12, aber = *lobon* 7. 5; gleich darauf, 7. 7, wieder *uuihen*.

Grenze um 5. 1 bis 5. 6. Da die ersten fünf Verse dieses Abschnittes aus einer Namenliste bestehen, ist kaum festzustellen, ob sie dem Uebersetzer angehören, der bis Schluß von Kapitel 4 ging, dem von 5. 6 ff., oder noch einem dritten. Die tatianischen Worte sind S. 34—36 (5. 6—6. 6) selten: nur *girado, gimahha, gifeho* und *menigi*. Das erste übersetzt 5. 8 und 9. 1 *ecce*, was sonst durch *senu, nu, tho, thana* wiedergegeben wird. *Gimahha* für *coniunx* ist auf diesen Abschnitt (5. 8, 10, 12) beschränkt; das synonym *uxor* heißt 2. 5, 8. 11 und später häufig *quena*. Bemerkenswert ist auch das t in *tiurida* 6. 3, sonst, schon 6. 7, häufiger d. Dieser Wechsel braucht nicht vom Schreiber herzurühren. (Vgl. Sievers § 29.)

Grenze um 6. 6. Nun werden die tatianischen Worte häufiger; *gommanbarn* 7. 2 und *gotforht* 7. 4 kommen nur hier vor. Zu *gommanbarn* vgl. Gutmacher S. 4. Der Kontrast zu *thegankind* 9. 2 ist bemerkenswert. Unkombiniertes *barn* kommt öfters vor (2. 6; 3. 7; 13. 14; 22. 14; 62. 10; 127, 3; 131. 15; 139. 10), *thegan* unkombiniert gar nicht. *Progenies viperarum = cunni natrono* 13. 13 gegen *barn natrono* 62. 10 kommt gerade vor *barn* 13. 14, ist also vielleicht stilistischer Wechsel. Von den drei Uebertragungen von *filius* wird *sun* durchweg gebraucht, um das Vater-Sohn-Verhältnis auszudrücken, besonders häufig von Christus. *Kind* ist ohne Rücksicht auf das Geschlecht einfach »Nachkomme« und drückt entweder die geistliche Verwandtschaft (54. 4; 107. 3) oder die leibliche (alle übrigen Stellen) aus. Die einzige Ausnahme ist 67. 10, wo es im Kontrast zu *filia-dohter* gebraucht wird. *Barn* wird an keiner Stelle gebraucht, um das Vater-Sohn-Verhältnis auszudrücken, also nirgends = *sun*, sondern = *Kind*. Nur 3. 7 von Christus; 22. 14 und 127. 3 vom geistlichen Verhältnis zu Gott; 2. 6 von den Kindern Israel. Also am Wechsel von *barn* und *kind* ist wahrscheinlich auch ein Uebersetzerwechsel zu erkennen. Solcher Wechsel findet sich wie folgt: *barn* 2. 6 — *kind* 2. 7; *barn* 3. 7 — *kind* 4. 2 und 4. 11; *barn* 22. 14 — *kind* 22. 6; *barn* 127. 3 — *kind* 127. 2, 3; *barn* 131. 15 — *kind* 131. 16.

Zur Bestimmung dieser Grenze ist ferner anzuführen *uuuntaron*

200

mit *acc. rei* 6. 5, aber mit *ubar* 7. 7. Auch sonst ist der syntaktische Gebrauch dieses Verbums innerhalb ein und desselben Uebersetzer-Abschnittes konstant.

Grenze um 13. 23 (S. 48). Steinmeyer macht einen Einschnitt bei 13. 5 wegen des Auftretens der Präposition *fur-* statt *for-*; Köhler aus syntaktischen Gründen. Letzterer nimmt aber auch 13. 23 einen Einschnitt an, den ich ebenfalls anerkenne, weil hier die tatianischen Worte wieder häufig werden.

Grenze um 16. 1 (S. 51). Hier ist sicher ein Einschnitt, da die tatianischen Worte bis S. 55 (19. 4) beinahe ganz verschwinden, nur *mittilgart*, st., *sihuuaz*, *gotspellon*. Dazwischen liegt wenigstens noch ein Abschnitt bei 17. 6, wie Steinmeyer auf Grund des Auftretens von *antuuurtan* annahm.

Grenze um 19. 4 (S. 55). Eine Partie A reicht von 19. 4 bis 20. 9. Vielleicht kommt der Einschnitt zwischen 19. 2 und 19. 3. Vgl. die Orthographie *forlazanen nezzin* 19. 2 mit *forlazzanen nezin* 19. 3.

Grenze um 27. 1 (S. 63). Diese Partie reicht von 27. 1 bis 31. 1, doch sind wohl dazwischen weitere Abschnitte anzunehmen. Z. B. hebt mit 28. 1 wieder das Präfix *fur-* an. Das eine *for-* am Schlusse von 28. 1 ist wohl dem Schreiber aus Gewohnheit in die Feder geflossen.

Grenze um 31. 2 (S. 65). Der Schluß dieses Abschnittes fällt wohl um 33. 3, denn in diesem Verse wird *reddet* falsch mit *gelte* übersetzt, aber 34. 2 richtig mit *giltit*.

Grenze um 34. 1 (S. 67). Diese ist ohnehin auf Grund des Wortschatzes anzunehmen. Auf einen Wechsel deutet auch die Uebertragung von *merces* durch *mieta* 34. 1 und 35. 1 gegen *lon* 33. 2.

Aus Mangel an Raum müssen wir hier auf eine eingehende Analyse der hypothetischen Grenzen verzichten. Diese Grenzen, wie sie oben angedeutet wurden, sind aber nicht als endgültige Resultate anzusehen. Erstens ist die Statistik nach Seiten der Hs. aufgestellt worden und die Seitenanfänge der St. Galler Hs. stimmen nicht notwendigerweise genau mit denen der Urhandschrift überein [12]; noch ist anzunehmen, daß mechanisch bei jeder

[12] Ziemlich genau wird die Uebereinstimmung aber doch sein, wie aus dem Schlusse von S. 164 erhellt. Hier ist offenbar vom Kopisten ein Wort ausgelassen. Die lat. Vorlage lautet: *gaudebat in universis* (165) *quae . . .*, die Uebersetzung: *gifah in then* (165) *thiu.* Der neue Schreiber (δ) beginnt mit *quae — thiu* am Seitenanfang, denn γ war mit *then* mit seinem Pergament zu Ende gekommen.

neuen Seite ein anderer Uebersetzer anhob. Wie schon gesagt, würde die Statistik deshalb hier und da der Korrektur bedürfen. Solche Verschiebungen würden aber, wie die gegebenen Proben zeigen, eher die Hypothese stärken als untergraben. Sogar nach der provisorischen Einteilung ist die Uebereinstimmung mit Köhlers Resultaten überraschend genau. Er gibt in seiner Dissertation § 105 ein Beispiel für eine Gruppe von Abschnitten, die éinem Uebersetzer angehören könnten. Eine Prüfung derselben erweist, daß von den 53 darin vorkommenden tatianischen Wörtern 49 nur in A-Partien vorkommen oder A- und B-Partien gemeinsam sind. Von dem Rest, *gimahha, diacan, abafurhouuan, widarscouuan*, kommen *diacan* und *abafurhouuan* in unmittelbarer Nähe von Uebersetzereinschnitten vor, so daß bei einer geringen Verschiebung der Grenze sie einer A-Partie zufallen würden. Köhlers hypothetischer Uebersetzer wäre also einer vom Typus A.

Eine schärfere und definitive Abgrenzung könnte erst geschehen nach Aufstellung umfangreicher Tabellen, ähnlich der von Köhler gebotenen, aber mit Hinzufügung aller Eigentümlichkeiten des Wortschatzes, Stiles und der Orthographie, sofern letztere nicht vom Schreiber allein herrührt. Auf diese Weise könnte auch dann der Wortschatz der einzelnen Uebersetzer bestimmt werden.

Vorläufig scheinen folgende Schlüsse erlaubt:

1. Die an der Uebersetzung des T beteiligten Mönche lassen sich in zwei Hauptgruppen teilen. Die eine (A) bediente sich eines Wortschatzes, der erheblich vom Sprachgebrauch im Ahd. des frühen neunten Jahrhunderts abwich. Ob diese Abweichungen einfach als Altertümlichkeiten aufzufassen sind (Braune) oder auf Dialektverwandtschaft mit dem Niederdeutschen und Altenglischen hinweisen, ist für unseren Zweck einerlei. Die andere Gruppe (B) stand sprachlich dem Oberdeutschen näher. Eine Anzahl Ausdrücke aber, wie *millen, gifchon, fluobar* u. a. m., die dem Hochdeutschen sonst fremd sind, scheinen beiden Gruppen gemeinsam gewesen zu sein und sind als Bestandteile der in Fulda üblichen Klostersprache anzusehen.

2. Die Zahl dieser Uebersetzer genau zu bestimmen ist bei dem gegenwärtigen Stand der Untersuchung nicht möglich, doch wird

---

Das Versehen ist leicht zu erklären, wenn *universis* und seine ahd. Entsprechung *(allen?)* auch in der Vorlage am Seitenschlusse stand.

die Schätzung Köhlers, 10 bis 15, ungefähr das Richtige getroffen haben.

3. Die Uebersetzerabschnitte sind von ungleicher Größe, aber überschreiten selten oder nie die Länge von einer Seite der Hs. Die von Sievers, Steinmeyer und Kramp angenommenen langen Abschnitte sind alle weiter einzuteilen. Die Mehrzahl der Abschnitte heben annähernd oder genau mit dem Seitenanfang an, so daß die von Sievers (Einleitung LXXIV, § 125) und Köhler (S. 89—90) ausgesprochene Vermutung, die Uebersetzer hätten sich in der Arbeit beim Beginn einer neuen Seite abgelöst, wohl den Tatsachen entspricht[13].

---

[13] Oben S. 197, Z. 8 v. u. hätte auf Sievers Aufsatz in *PBB* 50, 416 ff verwiesen werden sollen. Er macht da den Versuch, eine Anzahl in Sagversen abgefaßte Abschnitte des T herauszuschälen, von denen einer (124.7 — 125.11) aus klanglichen Gründen Hrabanus Maurus zuzuschreiben sei. Merkwürdig ist, daß in diesen Abschnitten nur zwei der speziell tatianischen Wörter (*tuomo* und *uozarnen*) vorkommen.

Erst nach der Drucklegung des Aufsatzes fand ich Ernst Schröter, *Walahfrids deutsche Glossierung und der althochdeutsche Tatian*, Halle, 1926 und Baeseckes Artikel in *ZfdA* 58, 241 ff. Ich glaube, daß sich meine Schlüsse mit denen von Schröter und Baesecke gut vertragen werden.

RANDGLOSSEN ZUM MORIZ VON CRAON

VON JOHN L. CAMPION

UNIVERSITY OF PENNSYLVANIA

Das vortreffliche kleine Gedicht eines unbekannten Verfassers aus der Blütezeit des 13. Jahrhunderts, worüber man vergleiche neuerdings Ehrismann, Gesch. der deutschen Lit. 2, 2, 1, S. 127 f., bietet gerade durch den Umstand, daß es allein in dem bekannten Ambraser Codex aus dem Anfang des 16. Jahrhunderts überliefert ist, noch manches zu erwägen in bezug auf seine textliche Gestaltung. Durch seine ausgezeichnete Ausgabe in den »Zwei altdeutsche Rittermären« hat Edward Schröder 1894 das Gedicht dem Dunkel und der Vergessenheit entzogen und somit allgemein zugänglich gemacht. Von diesem Werkchen erschien 1913 eine zweite, 1920 bereits eine dritte Auflage. Wohl im Hinblick auf seine erste Bestimmung als Uebungsmaterial im Seminar hat Schröder einen möglichst konservativen Text geliefert und aus eben diesem Grunde ist es auch zu erklären, wenn die späteren Auflagen keine wesentlichen Unterschiede gegenüber der ersten aufzuweisen haben. Nur gelegentlich sind die Besserungsvorschläge andrer in den Text aufgenommen worden. Es sind also verschiedene Stellen stehen geblieben, die, wenn nicht gerade unverständlich, doch zum mindesten undeutlich oder dem Sprachgebrauch des Dichters zuwider sind. Im folgenden teile ich eine Reihe Vorschläge mit, die mir bei wiederholter Lektüre der Dichtung eingefallen sind, mache aber durchaus keinen Anspruch darauf, alle Schwierigkeiten gehoben, noch wo ich etwas gewagt, immer das Richtige getroffen zu haben. Es bleibt immer noch die dankbare Aufgabe, die Stellung der Dichtung innerhalb ihres Kreises und ihrer Periode genauer zu bestimmen. Daß wir es hier mit dem Werke eines begabten Dichters zu tun haben, leuchtet jedem ein, der die letzten hundert Verse durchliest.

98. 99. hat Schröder die Verderbnis so zu heilen versucht:
man zinste in, nû gernt sie hulde (daz ist doch ein ungelîchez leben).

Mit teilweise näherem Anschluß an die Hs. möchte ich lesen: *man zinste in, nû gebent sie hulde. (daz ist dechein ungelîchez leben)*: wodurch die Stelle erst verständlich wird, besonders die Aussage in Vers 100.

120. *ein lop erkôs sîn hant* ist mindestens eine auffällige Wendung und soweit ich sehe, sonst nicht belegt; vielleicht ist *er ze hant* statt *sîn hant* zu lesen.

233. *lîbes unde guotes* ist der formelhafte Ausdruck, wozu vgl. Wilmanns zu Walther 88, 2.

272. *hûs* in der Bedeutung »Familie, Geschlecht« scheint erst im 14. Jahrhundert vorzukommen. Um 1300 schreibt Heinrich v. Heßler, Apok. gegen den Schluß: *Heinrich ist mîn rechter nam, Hesler ist mîn hûs genant.* Unsere Stelle wäre somit der früheste Beleg für diesen Gebrauch.

273. Vorzuziehen wäre *der was ir dienstes bereit* mit Bezug auf die *grævinne* (268). Wegen des gewöhnlichen Dativs vgl. Wigalois 3149, 6226 usw.

277. *âne lôn* ist auffällig und drückt gerade das Gegenteil aus von dem, was man erwartet, denn der Held hat doch immer den Preis davongetragen, wie wir aus Vers 282 erfahren. *umbe lôn* würde dem Sinne nach besser passen.

301. Man setze einen Punkt nach *rât* gegen das Komma der drei Auflagen Schröders; ebenso Punkt statt Kolon nach *mâze* 354.

357. 358. Der Sinn dieser beiden Verse ist nicht klar. Der Ausdruck *als in daz mer ein slac* bedeutet ebensoviel wie »nichts, etwas, was nichts zu bedeuten hat« und paßt gar nicht zum Gedanken. Vielleicht ist der Stelle geholfen, wenn man *leider* statt *lieber* 358 liest. Danach wäre der Gedanke etwa folgender: »Es ist ihm ein harter Schlag, denn nichts könnte ihm unangenehmer sein«.

363. Ich möchte mit Haupt *an êre* lesen. Diese Wendung ist formelhaft; vgl. 1. Büchl. 1583 f. *der frume wirt niht mêre wan der schade an êre.*

373. Es ist wohl *den* statt *die* zu lesen. In der zweiten und dritten Auflage hat Schröder, einer Konjektur Wilmanns gemäß, eine Lücke von zwei oder vier Versen angesetzt. Es scheint uns aber dem Sinne nach nichts zu fehlen, besonders wenn man *baz gemeine* 374 in komparativer Bedeutung nimmt, eine Konstruktion, die dem 13. Jhrh. durchaus nicht fremd war; vgl. u. a. Gottfr. Tristan 3630 *baz lobebære*, 7744 *baz gemuot*, Iwein 3969 *baz ein sælic man* = *sæliger m. si* 374 bezieht sich natürlich auf *Üppic* und *Irre* (367).

429. Relatives *so* ist der Sprache Hans Rieds gemäß, nicht aber der des Dichters; es ist also mit *daz* zu ersetzen.

431. = M. F. 39, 13 (Dietmar von Eist) mit demselben rührenden Reim.

444. Die Form *mac* ist wohl durch Attraktion an *gemach* entstanden. Man lese dafür *muoz*, nach zahlreichen Stellen in den Wbchern.

477. In den beiden ersten Auflagen hat der Herausgeber das handschriftliche *aber* beibehalten und ich sehe nicht ein, inwiefern das *alter* der dritten den Vorzug verdient. Ungefähr denselben Gedanken hat Freidank 117, 10 *swem dicke leit geschiht den enwirret trûren niht.*

490 f. Schröders Text scheint der Hs. genau zu folgen, da er nichts in den Laa. bemerkt. Den Sinn kann man höchstens erraten. Ich möchte die Stelle etwa so verbessern: *miner sorgen, der ich tûsent hân, diu machent ûz ein iewederem dinc . . .*, d. h. »durch die vielen Sorgen, die ich bereits trage, wird jedes [weitere] Ding (Ungluck) verdreißigfacht«. Ich muß aber gestehen, daß ich mit diesem Versuche nicht ganz zufrieden bin.

496. Der Genetiv darf eigentlich nicht fehlen; vgl. Erec 6041 *got sî der mirs ein ende gebe.*

607. Den überladenen Vers kann man durch Streichung von ‚*der hant'* beseitigen. Vgl. Wig. 6331 *er zoch ir abe ein vingerlin*, was sich vielleicht auf Parz. 131, 16 f. bezieht.

661. In Anlehnung an die Hs. möchte ich mit Haupt zu *alle samt* zurückkehren; vgl. noch 699.

718. Lexer, Wbch. s. v. *strecken* zitiert: ‚*Ein segel hiez er ze iegelichem maste strecken'. daz* 717 darf aber nur auf *baniere* 714 bezogen werden. Danach heißt es vielmehr: »Eine Fahne ließ er an jeden Speer binden; die [Fahnen] waren [wie der Segel] alle weiß.«

727. Der Artikel ist entbehrlich, auch wird der Vers glätter, wenn man ihn streicht und dafür *unde* liest.

804. Lies *sis* statt *siz*.

875. Die hs.liche Lesart *gewieret*, ebenso wie Vers 953, verdient den Vorzug. Vgl. Lexer s. v. *wieren*, Haupt zu Erec 4636.

1062. Es ist nicht einzusehen, weshalb man die hs.liche Lesart *gegangen* mit Maßmann und Haupt nicht beibehalten sollte. Ein ‚*man gevangen'* hätte doch nicht wohl zum Helden gehen können. Vgl. noch Junker u. der treue Heinr. 1330 *da kam ein ritter gegangen.*

1160. Die schwache Flexion des Namens Veldeke ist die vorherrschende, wie bei Gottfr. v. Straßburg 4725 *von Veldeken Heinrîch*, wonach *meister* an unsrer Stelle zu streichen wäre. Auch Wolfram Parz. 292, 18 sagt einfach *hêr Heinrich v. V.*, wogegen aber Herbort im Troj. Krieg 17381 ihn *meister* nennt.

1311. Bech will lieber *niht* entbehren und zwar mit Recht. Vgl. die Laa. zum Iwein 588 sowie Erec 261, wo es ebenfalls überflüssig scheint.

1313. Wie der Konjunktiv *lebe* 1311 durch den Reim bewahrt blieb, so ist *gediene* hier zu lesen.

1513. *belangen* statt *verlangen* ist vorzuziehen; letzteres wird nur zweimal belegt, eins davon mit *nâch* Engelh. 15.

1523. Lies *zuo ir gân*, denn gemeint ist doch die Frau, nicht das Ehepaar.

1551. In den Laa. stellt Schröder die Frage ‚*erklancte er?*‘ Das Transitivum hätte aber ohne weiteres in den Text gesetzt werden sollen, doch vgl. Nibel. 2285, 4 *Nibelunges swert das guote vil lûte ûf Dietrîch erklanc.*

1645. Seit der zweiten Auflage hat Schröder *wert* für das überlieferte *wort* gesetzt. Dieses ist aber wohl beizubehalten, denn es hat hier die Bedeutung »Ruf, Leumund«. Vgl. Wbch. 3, 808, Erec 830, 2695. Lanz. 3414. Hartm. Lieder 211, 24 usw.

1673. Lies *swannez* wie Athis C 135 *swenniz dem manne missegât.*

1691. Lies *loup, blüemen unde gras*, wofür Belege wohl überflüssig sind.

1697 f. Zu der ganzen Situation vgl. Veldekes Eneide 11 368 f.

1780. Ist nicht *rede* aus 1777 geholt und *rîme* dafür zu lesen? *rîme rihten* Engelh. 213. Otte 751. Heinzlein 111, 9 usw. *rîme ungerihtet* Reinh. Fuchs 2249.

KLEINE BEITRÄGE ZUR TEXTKRITIK UND ERKLÄRUNG VON „DES MINNESANGS FRÜHLING"

VON JULIUS GOEBEL

UNIVERSITY OF ILLINOIS

Die nachstehenden Bemerkungen zum Text und zur Erklärung von »Des Minnesangs Frühling« waren ursprünglich als Teil einer Besprechung von Friedrich Vogts vorzüglicher Ausgabe (3. Auflage, 1920) bestimmt, kamen aber dann, als die feindliche Kriegsstimmung deutsche Studien in Amerika vernichtet zu haben schien, leider nicht zur Niederschrift. Ob sie es heute noch verdienen, bekannt gemacht zu werden, mag der Leser selbst entscheiden.

KÜRENBERG

In seinem ausgezeichneten Aufsatz: »Die Kürenberg-Literatur und die Anfänge des deutschen Minnesangs« (*Germanisch-Rom. Monatsschrift* Sept./Okt. 1927) hat Gustav Ehrismann kürzlich so ausführlich über den Kürenberger gehandelt, daß dem dort Gesagten nur wenig hinzuzufügen ist. Zu den beiden Strophen des ersten Tones möchte ich jedoch bemerken, daß die Weise in 7, 5, reimend mit 7, 14, beim Sammeln im 13. Jahrhundert wohl als Körner angesehen wurde, wodurch die beiden *liet* in diesem Tone für uns gerettet wurden.

7, 1. Bartschs Lesung »*fremden*« ist nach meiner Meinung wegen des Gegensatzes zu »*behalten*« 7, 3, Vogts »*scheiden*« vorzuziehen.

7, 2. Zu den Reimen »schedelîch: lobelîch« vgl. »gremelîch: heimelîch«, Rol. 23, 5.

7, 17, 18. Die Stelle im Rother 2931: *daz ist mir daz minnist —* ist mir einerlei, scheint mir die Ueberlieferung in C zu bestätigen und Vogts Aenderung unnötig zu machen. Der Sinn der beiden Zeilen wäre daher: *meine Freude wie alle anderen Männer sind mir dann einerlei.* Es ist das trostlose Elend nach verlorener Liebe,

das der Sänger ausdrücken will. Die Zeilen würden dann lauten:
daz mîn froide ist daz minnist und alle andere man.

7, 19, 20. Lachmanns geschraubte Erklärung dieser Zeilen, wie
Vogt sie umschreibt, ist nach diesem »freilich nicht ganz so plan
im Ausdruck, wie man es beim Kürenberger zunächst erwartet«.
Viel einfacher und einleuchtender ist es, in den Zeilen mit Ehrismann eine bekannte sprichwörtliche Wendung, den Gegensatz
von *leit* und *liep*, Liebesleid und Liebesfreud zu sehen.

8, 1. Zu dem *mir* wäre Anno 614: dô stuont *imi* ûf der vili
guote man, sowie Heliand 202 b (Heyne): ging *imu* heranzu-
ziehen.

8, 9 ff. Nach Ehrismanns Ausführungen darf auch diese Strophe
unserem Dichter zugesprochen werden.

8, 16. »so sprach daz wîp« scheint so nachgebracht, als könnte
es auch *fehlen*, ähnlich wie: 39, 7; 5, 6; 32, 3. 7.

8, 33. In betreff des viel behandelten Falkenliedes und seiner
vermeintlichen italienischen Quelle sei noch bemerkt: das *An-
deuten*, die Blüte des deutschen Liedes, fehlt im italienischen
Sonett, so daß Entlehnung von keiner Seite passen will, zumal
das deutsche Lied, knapp und rasch, ganz anderen Sachgang
hat als das italienische. Bei Kürenberg ist der Falke nur in die
Freiheit entflohen, *wieder wild geworden*, im italienischen Sonett
dient er nun bald *einer Anderen*. Da könnte also nur dieses jenem
nachgemacht sein, mit Weiterführung des Gedankens. Auch vergleiche man den reinen Schluß des deutschen Liedes mit der
verhüllten Zweideutigkeit des italienischen.

9, 19. 20. Nach *versuonde* sollte Komma stehen und nach *wol*
Ausrufungszeichen. *Wol* = euge!

10. 1. Könnte der *tunkel sterne* wohl auch Komet bedeuten?
Dafür scheinen mir die von Pfeiffer u. a. beigebrachten Stellen
weit eher zu sprechen als Vogts Deutung, »der schwach leuchtende,
der sich dem Blicke zeitweilig ganz entzieht«. Besonders die
Zitate aus Bertsch mitteld. Gedichte S. 16, 531 und S. 15, 511 ff.
(bei Pfeiffer, Germania 12, 224 ff.) würden schlecht zu dieser
Deutung stimmen, da hier der *tunkelsterne* gerade seines Lichtes
wegen gerühmt wird, dem an Leuchtkraft und Schönheit das
Licht aller sieben Planeten zusammengenommen nicht gleich-
kommt. Wozu auch die Mahnung Kürenbergs an die Geliebte,
sich zu verbergen wie ein ohnehin »schwach leuchtender« Stern?
Faßt man dagegen unser Liedchen als eine Art Morgenständchen

mit dem Hinweis auf den hell leuchtenden Kometen, der sich bei anbrechendem Tage zu verbergen scheint, dann wird die Mahnung des Dichters weit eher verständlich. Auch will mir der Vergleich der Dame mit einem glänzenden Kometen viel passender erscheinen als der mit einem »schwach leuchtenden« Sternchen.

DER BURCGRAVE VON REGENSBURG.

16, 15, 22. Vogt übersetzt die Strophe in seiner Mittelhochdeutschen Literaturgeschichte mit Beiseitelassung der Lesung in A C also: »Ich lag den Winter allein. / Schönen Trost gab mir ein Weib, / seit mir Freude kündeten / die Blumen und die Sommerzeit. / Das neiden mir Aufpasser. / Davon ist mein Herz wund. / Hilft mir nicht eine Frau mit ihrer Minne, / so wird es nimmermehr gesund.«

Ich glaube nicht, daß dies den Sinn des Dichters trifft, über den übrigens weder Lachmann-Haupt, noch Bartsch, der »vür sie mir vröide kunten« liest, ein Wort bemerken. Was sollte auch der Wunsch des Dichters, daß ihm eine Frau sein wundes Herz mit ihrer Minne heile, wenn eine andere ihn doch erfolgreich getröstet hat! Und würden ihm die Aufpasser nicht auch das zweite Liebesverhältnis verleiden?

Ganz anderen und, wie ich glaube, den richtigen Sinn erhält die Strophe aber, wenn wir mit A C lesen:

vüere sie mir mit, vröiden kunten
die bluomen und die sommerzît,

und *nîden*, ebenfalls mit A C, als Conjunctiv praet. fassen. Was ihm das »herze wunt« macht, ist die Erkenntnis, daß die Aufpasser ihm die Vertröstung auf die Sommerzeit mit ihrem Neid vereitelt haben würden. Darum hofft der Dichter am Ende der Strophe auf Heilung seines wunden Herzens durch die w i r k - l i c h e Liebe der Frau.

Für seine Annahme, daß 20, 17—21, 4 einen Wechsel bildeten, hat Vogt keinerlei Beweis vorgebracht.

SPERVOGEL.

20, 25—21, 4. Die schöne, wohl im Dienste eines edlen Geschlechts, dem er nach einem Unglück Trost zuspricht, gedichtete Strophe zeigt uns den Sänger als Berater, ganz wie auch 24, 25. In ähnlicher Weise beziehen sich ferner die Strophen 23, 5 und

24, 9 wahrscheinlich auf sein Verhältnis zu derselben Gruppe von Freunden oder Genossen.

21, 29. *Diu saelde dringet für die kunst:* mehr Glück als Verstand haben.

23, 4. *gerîten* = durchreiten (den Rhein).

23, 29. *disen halm.* Meint er das Stroh, auf dem er schlief?

23, 32. *strô*, gewöhnlich = Halm, auf dem Felde stehend mit der Aehre, vgl. Walther 66, 5, 7. Zugleich aber bezeugt die Waltherstelle 17, 35: *von grase wird ein halm ze strô,* daß *strô* auch die *gedroschenen Halme,* d. h. Stroh in unserem heutigen Sinne bedeuten kann, wobei an Stroh als Lager zu denken ist, wie auch Wilmanns in seiner von V. Michel besorgten 4. Ausgabe von Walthers Gedichten S. 104 betont. Die Stellen, die er hier für diese Bedeutung von strô heranzieht, und zu denen noch Winsbeckin 14, 2 zu fügen wäre, weisen sicher auf die Bedeutung Stroh, Strohlager. Ebenso hätte die bittere Bemerkung am Ende der Strophe, daß das *strô* wieder *ze miste* werde, wenig Sinn, wenn *halm* nicht auch ein Synonym von *strô* wäre.

66, 5, 7. Trifft meine Vermutung, daß der Sänger in dieser Strophe die Streu (den Haufen Stroh) besingt, auf dem er in seiner Armut schlafen muß, dann hätten wir in dem kleinen Kunstwerk ein Beispiel seines genialen Humors, der sich in sieghafter Geistesfreiheit über seine und seiner Genossen oft beklagte dürftige Lage hinwegsetzt.

26, 10. Hinter *erben* sollte Doppelpunkt stehen, um anzudeuten: d. h. einen solchen (erben).

26, 21. *Hergêr.* Daß wir in *Hergêr* den Namen des Dichters zu sehen haben, könnte von Vogt stärker betont werden als er es tut. Unter *Spervogel* wäre dann die Bezeichnung einer Geschmacksrichtung zu verstehen, der Fahrende verschiedenen Namens huldigten.

27, 20. *witzig*, d. h. nicht *alwaere* wie 27, 14.

29, 20. Dem Dichter schwebt augenscheinlich ein Herrenhof vor, in dem zweierlei Obst wächst, süßes und saures.

29, 23. *ein sîn nâhgebûr* = wohl der Sänger selber.

29, 24. *wir suln das obez teilen,* gemeint ist das *scheiden* der Guten von den Bösen, das auch Walther oft verlangt, z. B. 58, 35; 48, 29; 45, 28.

30, 4. Vgl. Walther 101, 22: *ich wil ze herberge varn.*

30, 21. *stuont sich*, vgl. 8, 1 ich stuont m i r nehtint spâte; ûf erstuont *sich* Gorijo dâr, M. S. D.[3] 37, 29 (Vom heiligen Georg); dô stuont imi ûf der vili guote man, Anno 614.

DIETMAR VON EIST.

33, 27. *bezzer* hier nicht, wie Scherer D. St. 2, 43, 66 will, im eigentlichen moralischen Sinn gemeint, sondern = *tiurer, werder*, wie bei Johansdorf 94, 14 und Meinloh 11, 7.

33, 34. In der Handschrift C sind diese beiden Verse ganz anders gemeint, ohne B wären sie, wie sie nun stehen, kaum herzustellen gewesen.

34, 2. der *mâze* nicht kennt.

34, 6, 7. wichtig für den Begriff *herze*.

34, 19. *Gedanke . . . frî*, vgl. dazu Hildebrand, DWb. IV. 1. 1. 1961 unter *Gedanke*. Erst von diesem Gedichte an finden sich überschlagende Reime und Waisen.

35, 32—36, 4. Die Strophe zeigt einen merkwürdigen Kampf des Frauenherzens um die *minne* und *mâze*.

36, 2. also auch das gewünschte *senen* 35, 35 nur mit w o h l - t u e n d e r *mâze*.

37, 22. *mîniu wol stênden ougen* — meine v o r h e r schönen Augen.

37, 30. Vgl. 6, 7 und Neidhart 11, 12.

38, 21. *nu reden wirz*, d. h. der Bote und die Frau!

38, 28. *ir keiner*, die Geliebte ist gemeint.

38, 31. *und ich* = da ich doch.

39, 1. *gelâzen* = loslassen.

39, 2. *sô hôh ôwî*, wohl soviel wie: hôhe klagen, hôhiu klage, wofür der Ausruf in der 3. Strophe spricht. Mit Schönbach u. a. in dem Refrain einen Schifferruf zu erblicken, kann ich mich nicht entschließen.

39, 33, 34 Kranz als Liebeszeichen.

40, 31 — ich liebe sie doch fort.

41, 1 *si* — die Leute, die Merker.

Auch über den Text und die Erklärung der übrigen Dichter des »Frühlings« wäre mancherlei nachzutragen, doch glaubte ich mich zunächst auf die am meisten umstrittenen Sänger der deutschen Frühzeit beschränken zu sollen.

THE PHONETIC AND MORPHOLOGICAL SETTINGS OF THE MIDDLE HIGH GERMAN CLIPT PRETERITS

BY ROBERT JAMES KELLOGG
OTTAWA UNIVERSITY

I. Origin of the Clipt Preterits : *gie, fie, lie.*

Professor Collitz in two clear and admirable articles [1] has discust the history and probable origin of the MHG clipt preterits *gie, fie, lie,* beside the full forms *gieng, fieng, liez.* The present inquiry is based primarily on Collitz's findings, but attempts to trace more fully (1) their basis in OHG preexistent clipt forms; (2) their phonetic background in MHG, and (3) to show how the shifting of this background conditioned both the original development and later disappearance of these forms. It thus constitutes a concrete study of the trend of linguistic development as shown in these forms. [2]

A brief summary of Collitz' articles may serve to refresh the memory of those who have already read them or to whet the appetite of those who have not yet done so. He points out the following facts:

The forms *gie, fie, lie* are the 1 and 3 sg. prets. which arose toward the end of the eleventh century in the transition period between OHG and MHG as doublets of the older historically correct preterit forms *gieng, fieng, liez* [3] from the reduplicating-preterit verbs *gân (gên), fâhen (fân), lâzen (lân).*

---

[1] Zu den kurzen Präterita gie, fie, lie, *MLN* XXXII 207—215, 449—458.

[2] This continuation of Professor Collitz' work along these special lines was begun several years ago with his kind permission and approval. The subject was first workt out under a Harrison Research Fellowship in Linguistic Psychology at the University of Pennsylvania in 1922—3, forming part of a larger study of the normal direction of structural development in language. Its only public presentation hitherto was in a lecture before the Germanic Society of the University of Pennsylvania. The present article is a revision and extension of certain portions of this lecture.

[3] For convenience the MHG forms are cited to represent both the OHG and MHG forms.

These clipt forms first appear clearly in the *Merigarto* and the *Vienna Genesis*. Collitz' investigation of the latter shows the clipt forms to be fully developt and used in alternation with the full forms according to more or less consistent rules.

As verse or sentence finals the clipt forms greatly predominate — for *gie* 17: 2, *fie* 9: 1, and *lie* 8: 5 — most of the exceptions being explainable by the exigencies of rime or poetic style.

As verse or sentence medials, the clipt forms are used before a following consonant, the full forms before a following vowel, as *gieng er; gie der, inpfieng in; impfie uon, liez uns; lie si.*

Collitz' figures show 42 regular to 8 irregular occurrences. If he should class *iu* in *giench Iudas* as a diphthong instead of a consonant + vowel, his figures would become 43: 7. Of these seven irregular uses, only one *(giench uon)* is a full form used before a consonant, the other 6 being encroachments of the clipt forms before vowels. There are in all 23 instances where Collitz' rule calls for full forms; they occur in 17 of these, while in 6 instances the clipt forms occur in their stead. This clearly proves Collitz' contention that these clippings were fully developt forms already intrencht in the speech consciousness of the folk. They also prove that the clipt forms were still extending their use at the expense of the original full forms.

Next, as to the possible origin of these forms: prior to their extant literary appearance, the verb *lâzen* develop a clipt 2 sg. impv. *lâ* from the present stem *lâz*. This appears in Notker, being used by him as the tiefton or reduced grade of impv. *lâz* [4]. Paul [5] and Braune [6] explain this form by analogy of the *-mi* verbs *gân* and *stân*. Collitz rejects this explanation as a starting point, believing the form *lâ* was due to the contaminative influence of the closely associated and partly synonymous 2 sg. impv. *tuo*. The development of *lâ*, however, necessarily brought *lâzen* into touch with *gân* and *stân*, so that from this point on Collitz' explanation agrees with and amplifies that of Paul and Braune.

Following the impv. *lâ* came the clipt pret. sg. *lie*, which occurs once in Notker and twice in the OHG Glosses; then the 3 sg. pres. ind. *lât* in the *Memento mori*, the *Prudentius Glosses* and the OHG Glosses. [4]

The clipt preterit *gie* makes its first extant appearance in *Merigarto*, [4] while *fie (entfie)* is first extant in the *Vienna Genesis*. [4] By the opening of the MHG period the whole present and preterit systems of the three verbs *gân, fân* and *lân* had been leveled, and in the present this parallelism extended to the verb *stân*. [7]

The rise of these clipt preterits was favored by the fact that the resultant distinction between singular and plural preterit stems brought them into line with the ablaut verbs generally, with which they had long been groupt in speech feeling. [8] Thus *gie: giengen, lie: liezen* are, in a general way, comparable to *sang: sungen, was: wâren*, etc.

With the NHG leveling of singular and plural pret. stems came also the disappearance of these clipt preterits *gie, fie, lie* and the revival and retriumph of the original forms *gieng, fieng, liez (ging, fing, ließ)*.

So much for a brief and therefore inadequate summary of Collitz' investigation, which the reader should by all means know at first hand.

---

[4] For references, see Collitz' article.

[5] *Mhd. Gramm.* 180.

[6] *Ahd. Gramm.* 351 A 2.

[7] The pret. *stuont* was not of the reduplicating type and so did not admit of a similar levelling.

[8] This grouping was in fact primitive, as the reduplicating verbs were ablaut verbs also in Gc. and IE.

II. Sandhi Principles Involved in the Rules of Vowel and
Consonant Sequence.

Owing to the tendency of verb forms to take a strong sentence stress, they are apt to be followed, especially in verse, by words of weaker stress. This is particularly true of monosyllabic verb forms such as the 1 and 3 sing. preterit forms. Furthermore the requirements of sentence connection most often favor the bringing of a subject or object pronoun or an article belonging to a noun subject or object, or an adverb or preposition next to the verb. For both these reasons the verb is most apt to occur before unstrest sequence, especially before enclitics or proclitics.

As a result, even in authors (such as Walther von der Vogelweide and Gottfried von Straßburg) who follow the rule of simple consonant and vowel sequence without regard to stress or sentence position, most of the actual combinations bring an unstrest word (most often a clitic) after the monosyllabic preterit form. Thus in *Tristan und Isolde*, the sentence medial occurrences of these clipt and full preterits and of *lâ/lâz* (including verse finals used as sentence medials) show 90% of unstrest consonant or vowel sequence [9]. Such unstrest sequence was therefore the main sandhi environment in which these forms developt.

Linking, or the tendency of words to run together in connected speech, is a familiar phenomenon in many languages, as in French liaison and Sanskrit rules of euphonic combination [10]. This tendency is strongest between adjacent strest and unstrest words, as Hitt. *ammu-ga* "mihi": Gr. ἐμοίγε: Go. *mi-k;* Lat. *hun-c, pot-est;* F. *donner-ai;* Eng. *for-give, home-ward;* Ger. *zu-m,* and especially such MHG combinations as *gruoztes* (= *gruozte si*) Nib. 1410 (Holzm. Ausg.), *zehant (ibid.), sine* 1409, *zir* (= *ze ir*) 161, *zen* (= *ze den*) 1417, *giengez* 432, *gienger* 653, *ranger* 641, *hieng in* (pronounced as *hiengin*) 642, etc. That is to say, a full word followed without any break by an enclitic or proclitic or other unaccented word tends to combine with it after the phonetic pattern of a dissyllabic word, this fusion taking place most easily with a consonantal final followed by a vocalic initial, or a vocalic final followed by a consonantal initial. This fusion may or may not be represented in writing, but in either event the phonetic

---

[9] These figures are based on a personal count of the forms.
[10] See Whitney *Skt. Gram.*, Ch. III.

pattern is the same. Thus *gienger, gieng er, gie der*, are all of the same general rhythmic and phonetic pattern as the dissyllabic 2 sing. pret. ind. *gienge*, the plural pret. ind. forms *giengen, gienget*, and the pret. subjunctive forms *gienge, giengest, giengen, gienget.*

In other words, the full preterit forms were regularly preserved only in sandhi combinations which were for speech feeling identical in rhythmic and general phonetic pattern with the dissyllabic preterit forms and whose sandhi combinations were practically internal. Where the full forms could not preserve this pattern, it was preserved by the development of the clipt forms. In case of encroachment in either direction, this rhythmic pattern is destroyed. The rise of the clipt forms was favored by these phonetic analogies, which could not however function independently to create them, but only as accessories to the inflectional groupings and levelings which C. notes in his article.

III. Preexistent Syncopating Verb Groups in Old High German.

A large number of clipt present and preterit forms were preexistent in the full OHG period. Such were: (1) the reduplicating clipt presents (the *gân*-group); (2) the sixth class clipt presents (the *stân*-group); (3) the "pure vowel" verbs (the *blân*-group); (4) verbs of the first weak conjugation with long stem-vowel followed by stem-final *-w-*; (5) the first ablaut class clipt presents and preterits (the *spî(w)an/spêo* group); (6) the second ablaut class clipt preterits (the *blou*-group); (7) the reduplicating clipt preterit *hio* "hieb"; (8) the clipt present and preterit forms of *hâben/hân*. Groupt with these in speech feeling, tho not involving syncopation, were (9) verbs showing consonant variation between sing. and plur. stems (the *zôh/zugum*-group). — With the exception of *hân* from *habên*, these forms were the result of normal phonetic shifting, so that syncopation was merely apparent — which was, however, the same thing for speech feeling as genuine syncopation.

1. The reduplicating verbs, because of their peculiar vocalization, formed in all periods of OHG (and earlier) a compact associative group. They were in IE straight ablauting verbs, and a considerable number were still so in primitive Germanic. All were inflectionally groupt with the ablaut verbs; and, after the leveling out of their initial reduplication, they agreed with the other strong verbs in their general consonantal pattern, and also came again to show

a difference of vowel between the present and preterit stems, which was certainly felt as ablaut. They were, therefore, for speech feeling simply a special class of strong verbs.

Within the reduplicating group, a smaller sub-group of three verbs, *gangan (gân), fâhan* and *hâhan*, showed still more intimate associations with each other. Their full stems and their inflections rimed thruout, and all showed in the present system phonetic variation based on the apparent weakening or syncopation [11] of the final stem consonants *(-ng)*. This parallelism was further increast (tho it never became absolutely perfect) by the fact that medial *-h-* was sporadically syncopated in all periods of OHG [12] so that completely syncopated forms of *fâhan* and *hâhan* occurred occasionally in writing and probably far more often in speaking.The resultant analogical proportion for speech feeling was therefore:

> *gangan|( )|gân|giang|giangun|gigangan*
> *( )|fâhan|(fân)|fiang|fiangun|gifangan*
> *( )|hâhan|(hân)|hiang|hiangun|gihangan.*

2. The closest external association of the reduplicating verbs was with the verbs of the sixth ablaut class, owing to the partial similarity of vowel gradation. In this class also there was a sub-group, consisting of *stantan|stân* and *slahan|(slân)*, [13] also showing apparent syncopation [13] in their present systems, and hence closely associated with the *gân-*group both by this syncopation and by the resemblance of the phonetic type of *stân* to *gân* and of *slahan* to *fâhan*, giving the approximate phonetic proportions *gangan: gân:: stantan: stân* and *fâhan: fân:: slahan: slân*. Their analogical proportion for the full and clipt forms was *stantan:* ( ): *stân: stuont: stuontun: gistantan::* ( ): *slahan: (slân): sluog (sluoc): sluogun: gislagan.*

---

[11] *Gân* of course was not a syncopation of *gangan* but an independent word going back to Prim. Gc. **gai-* and perhaps to IE **co-i-*. See Kluge *Et. Wtb.* s. v. *gehen.* (However, see Streitberg, *Urgerm. Gramm.*, p. 319.) — Similarly, *fâhan* and *hâhan* were differentiated from the participial stems *(gi)fang(an)* and *(gi)hang(an)* not by weakening but by grammatical change (Verner's Law). — See Braune, *Ahd. Gramm.* §§ 33 and 128 A 1 with further references there given, Wright *Gram. of the Go. Lang.* §§ 59 and 126 f.

[12] Braune, *Ahd. Gramm.* § 154 with A 1 and 7. — For the full development of these clipt present forms before the close of the OHG period, cf. the free use of such present syncopations as *fân, geslât, hân, hât,* etc. in *Memento mori.* — See Collitz *art. cit.*, p. 456 with n. 11.

[13] *Stân* < IE **stā-* was wholly independent of *stantan*, so that here also syncopation was apparent only, but none the less real for speech feeling; *slahan* < Gc. **slahan-* has *h* by grammatical change (Verner's Law) — see Braune § 346 A 2.

3. Closely associated with the *gân-stân* groups were the pure
-â- verbs, [14] which showed apparent syncopation in their present
formations, as *blâhen (blâjen)/blân* "blähen", *drâjen/drâen/drân*
"drehen", *knâhen/knâen/knâan* "kennen", *krâhen (krâjen)/krâen*
"krähen" (cf. noun *krâja (krâwa)/krâ* "Krähe"), *nâhen (nâwen,
nâjan)/nâen* "nähen", *sâjan (sâhen, sâwen)/sâen/sân* "säen", etc.
Originally they were reduplicating verbs with strong past participles showing apparent syncopation, as *giblâan (giblân)*, *gidrâan
(gidrân)*. Cf. also apparent syncopation in such weak formations
as *biknât* "bekannt". These syncopated forms continued into
MHG, as *blân/geblân, drân/gedrân (gedrât)*, beside such full forms
as *gedrœjet* and new syncopations as *gedrœt*.

The new analogical proportions offered *(blâhen:blân::sâhen:sân,*
etc.) were such as to associate themselves closely with *fâhan:*
fân::slahan:slân, etc., and added the important patterns of
syncopated past participles and new consonantal syncopations
and variations.

The possibility of speech feeling holding such forms as *blân/*
giblân for syncopated forms depends on the stem increments,
-h-, -j- and *-w-*, being not merely graphic, but actually pronounced.
For the proof of the actual pronunciation of the *-h-*, see Braune
§ 152 b). For the reality of the *-j-*, compare (1) the early shift
of these stems to the *-jan* conjugation, (2) their uniform umlaut
in MHG *sœjen, wœjen*, etc., (3) O. Sax. and Dutch forms in *-ian*,
(4) such Germanic *-i*-stem formations, as Go. *saian, waian* (: Lith.
vējas "wind": Skt. *vāyus* "wind", etc.), Go. *daddjan* "säugen"
(: OHG *tâen* < Gc. **daian-* < IE **dhēi-/dhǝi->* Skt. *dháyati:*
Armen. *diem:*OBulg. *doja:*OIr. *dínim*, etc.). — The genuineness
of the stem final *-w-* appears (1) in its dialect survival in MHG,
as in Upper Sax. and Thur. *mêwen, sêwen, wêwen* for MHG
mœjen, sœjen, wœjen [15], (2) in its OSax. survival in the old redupli-
cated forms *seu* (OEng. *sēow*) and *threu* (OEng. *þrēow*) beside the
newer weak forms *sāida, thrāida*, (3) in its uniform preservation
in OEng. *blāwan, þrāwan, sāwan*, etc.

Furthermore, many of these verbs show ablaut and stem-final
variations in IE relatively identical with those appearing in Germanic and OHG and MHG. Variation in phonetic form by ablaut
and suffixal extension was, as is well known, characteristic of IE

---

[14] Braune §§ 359 A 3, 351 A 3, 152 b.
[15] Kluge *Et. Wtb.* s. v. *2 weben.*

verbal roots generally, as in the Sanskrit and Greek present stem formations. Their occurrence in the pure vowel verbs in Germanic is therefore not an anomaly from the IE standpoint, but an interesting survival of a normal IE type of verb formation. See, for instance, Walde-Pokorny *Vergl. Wtb. d. idg. Spr.* under the roots *2bhel-/bhlē-/bhlō-* "üppig sprießen", the obviously identical *4bhel-/bhlē-/bhlē-s-/bhlō-/bhlō-s-* "aufblasen, schwellen, strotzen", the related (extended) roots *2bhlei-/bhlei-s-* "aufblasen, schwellen, strotzen, überfließen", whose dehnstufe *bhlēi-* is not listed by VWIS but occurs in Lat. *flāre*, OHG *blâjan*, etc., *bhleu-/bhlēu-* (dehnstufe in Greek citations) "aufblasen, schnauben, brüllen, schwellen, strotzen, überwallen", *8bhel-(/bhel-n-* or *bhel-s-)* "brüllen, bellen". The *-k-* and *-q-* extensions — which would yield Germanic forms in *-h-* (or *-w-* by Sievers' Law) — are cited by VWIS only under *bhleig-* and *bhleu-(k)-*, extensions respectively of *1bhlei-* and *bhleu-*, which are in turn extensions of *1bhel-* "glänzen", and as such obviously related to the other *bhel-* roots cited above. (For connection of meanings cf. Eng. *burst*, Fr. *éclater*, Eng. *blaze* beside Ger. *blasen*, etc.).

These IE variants yielded Gc. forms as follows: IE *bhel-* > MDu. *belen;* IE *bhel-s-* > OHG *bellan;* IE *bhlē-* > OHG *blâan* (distinguish from *blâjan* > later *blâen*); IE *bhlēi-* > Gc. *blēi-* > OHG *blâjan* (later *blâen*); IE *bhlē-s-* > Gc. *blēs-* > OHG *blâsan;* IE *bhlē-u-* > Gc. *blēu-* > OHG **blâwan* (accidentally not extant, but cf. OSax. and OEng. forms, and the *-w-* grade in other verbs of this group in OHG); IE *bhleiq- (bhleik-)* > Gc. *blēh(w)-* > OHG *blâhen;* IE *bhlō-* > Gc. *blō-* > OHG *bluoan:* IE *bhlō-i-* > OHG *bluojen (pluogen);* IE *bhlō-u-* > OHG *blouwen;* IE *bhlō-k-* > OHG *bluohen;* IE *bhlō-s-* > MHG *bluost;* OE *blōstma;* etc.

In other words, the stem variations of *blâan/blâjan/*blâwan/blâhen, blâsan, bluoan/bluohen/bluowen*, and other phonetically and semantically resembling verbs, agreed with and presumably were derived from similar variant formations in Indo-European. Theoretically *blâan, blâjan, blâhen and *blâwan* might as well have given separate words in OHG and other Germanic languages as did *bluoan* and *blâsan* — or speech feeling might have included the IE *-ō-* and *-ēs-* grades *bluoan* and *blâsan* in the group as variant forms of *blâan/blâjan* — cf. the Gc. *-ēi-*, *-ō-* and *-ē-* grades in Go. *saian/saisō/-sēþs*, and the inceptive *-s-* suffix as a tense sign in the sigmatic aorist and future in Sanskrit, Greek, Latin, Tocharian, etc.

Similar stem variations occurred in other IE roots — see, for instance VWIS sub rad. *mai-* "hauen, schnitzen" with its extended form *maid-* beside *(s)mē(i)-/(s)mī-* "hauen, abhauen, etc.", with which compare OHG *mâen/mâjen, meizan,* etc. See also *(s)nē(i)-* "spinnen, nähen" > Skt. *snāyati* "umwindet": Gr. *νῇ (*σνήϳει)* "spinnt": Lat. *nēre* "spinnen": MIr. *snīid* (fr. **snēi̯-*) "spinnt": OHG *nâjan/nâen/nâwen;* etc.

The pure vowel verbs were, therefore, contaminative OHG groupings of resembling stem formations reduced in speech feeling to the level of phonetic variants. Naturally these variations ⸍ did not occur equally in all verbs of the group, some originally having several variations, others one or none (as *tâen:*Go. *daddjan*), but the group once formed, variations tended to spread and assimilate in all verbs of the group. The name "pure â" is a misnomer.

Only one verb beside *blâhen* could have conceivably furnisht a starting point for the *-h-* formations, namely *drâen* > NHG *drehen*. Intrinsically, the etymological equation *drehen/drechsel* < OHG *drâ(h)en/drâchsil* ("Drechsler") < Gc. **þrēhv-* < IE* *tereq-* > Gr. *τρέπω*: Lat. *torqueo,* is both phonetically and semantically flawless. But, because of the character of *drâen* as a "pure" *-â-* verb, this connection is usually given up [16] in favor of Lat. *tero:* Gr. *τείρω/*τίτρημι* "rub, abrade, wear out, wear holes thru"/ *τόρμος, τρῆμα* "aperture, hole" (: Ger. *Darm* "gut") and the supposedly connected *τόρνος* "carpenter's compass, lathe-chisel (for wearing or rounding off)". Both Kluge and Boisacq further connect the root with Skt. *tarati* "goes thru, crosses".

But the *-â-/-âh-* verbs offer no bar to the connection of *drehen* with *drechsel,* but only a confirmation. IE *q* > OHG *hw/h/w,* as IE **quis* > OHG *hwer/wer,* IE **liq-* > OHG *lihum/liwum,* IE **seq-* > OHG *gisehan/gisewan;* cf. also *aha/ouwa* "water, stream", and other variations of *h/w* in orthography or derivation. The sound which could thus tempt double spelling must have been a velar *h* or *ch* [*hv* or *hᵘ*] with a *-u̯-* offglide. With the above noted occasional syncopation of *h* [12], we should therefore expect a Gc. **þrēhvian* to appear in OHG with the spellings *drâhen (drâen, drân), drâwen, drâjan,* several of which actually occur. Such a verb would fall automatically into the *-â-/-âw-/-âj-* group, or rather help to create it, and would tend to spread both *h* and *w* spellings and pronunciations to other verbs of the group.

[16] Kluge *Et. Wtb.* s. v. *drehen,* and *Darm;* and Boisacq *Dict. étym.* s. v. *τείρω*.

3 b. The pure -ô- (OHG -uo-) verbs [17] *bluoen, druoen, gluoen, gruoen, tuoen, muoen, spuoen,* showed the same extensions as the pure -â- verbs, frequently inserting -h- (as *muohen, bluohen*) or -w- (as *bluowen*), and showing apparently syncopated forms (as *muon, gluota, spuon, spuot*) in the present and preterit.

3 c. The verb *tuon* (Braune § 380 f.) inflects in the present system as a clipt -uo- verb, in the preterit and perf. ptc. approximately as a clipt pure -â- verb.

3 d. The pure vowel verbs therefore made several important contributions to the development of syncopating verb types: (1) They establisht types of (apparent) syncopation in pret. and perf. participle forms as well as in the present, thus strengthening the tendency to clipt formations as such, and also making a beginning of a connection in speech feeling between present and preterit syncopations. But their syncopated preterits (*drâta, sâta, spuota, tĕta,* etc.) could not associate closely with strong preterits (*sluoc, giang,* etc.) because of the difference of phonetic and inflectional pattern. (2) But their present syncopations closely paralleled and therefore strengthened those of the *gân* and *slân* groups. Compare, for instance, the phonetic and functional proportions *fâhan:fân::slahan: slân::blâhen:blân (::muohen:muon),* etc. (3) They establisht in advance a type of past participle syncopation suitable both for the reduplicating clipt presents and for *habên* in such forms as *giblân, gitân,* etc.

4. Verbs of the first weak conjugation with long stem vowel followed by stem-final -w- showed the same connection between present and preterit syncopations as did the pure vowel verbs. In these verbs also apparent syncopation came as the result of normal phonetic shifting, [18] the stem-final -w- disappearing necessarily before a consonant, and optionally before a vowel. As a result the preterit regularly showed syncopation, while the present and the perf. participle varied between syncopated and full forms. The two following verbs occur:

a) The verb *hîwen (hîen)/hîta/gihîwit (gihît)* was analogous thruout to the -w- forms of the pure vowel verbs, but because of the difference of vowel and the absence of an -h- grade, it could

---

[17] Braune § 359 A 4.

[18] Braune §§ 108, 110 A 1. These rules do not affect verbs of this class with short stem vowel, which therefore remained unsyncopated, as *frewen/frewita, gifrewit.* Cf. also the unsyncopated pret. plur. and past ptc. in verbs of the *spian-* group.

not show the same close parallelism to the *gân* and *slân* groups. It necessarily contributed, however, to the feeling for syncopation in all tenses and to the connection between present and preterit syncopations.

b) The verb *lâwen (lâen) /lâta/gilâwit (gilât)* "verraten" occurs in the pret. subjunc. forms *firlâti* and *gilâti* in Otfrid. The remaining forms are positively inferable from these and from Go. *lēwjan:* OEng. *lǽwen* "verraten" [19]. Observe the close parallelism to the *-w-* and clipt grades of the *blân-group*, to which *lâwen* could be admitted unchanged.

c) The verb *bûwan (bûan) /bûta/gibûwan (gibûan)* [20] originally belonged to the reduplicating conjugation, from which it retained the strong perf. ptc. into the MHG period. The old reduplicating pret. plur. *biruun* (from earlier **bibu(w)un*) occurs in Otfrid. But the pres. and pret. forms *bûwan (bûan)/bûta* wholly parallel *hîwen (hîen)/hîta, blâwen (blâen)/blâta*, etc. — The *-w-* in *bûwan* may be excrescent — see Feist *op. cit.* s. v. *bauan*.

5. Verbs of the first ablaut class with stem-final *-w-* suffered optional syncopation in the present system and regular syncopation in the preterit singular, according to the rules for the dropping of *-w-* noted in the preceding section [18]. They retained the full unsyncopated forms in the pret. plur. and perf. ptc. because of the short stem vowel of these forms. The verbs originally in this group were *spîwan (spîan)/spêo/spiwum/gispiwan* and *snîwan (snîan)/snêo/sniwum/gisniwan*. By contamination of these verbs *scrîan* created forms in *-w-* giving the gradation *scrîwan (scrîan)/screi/scriwum (scrirun)/giscriran*.

Besides further strengthening the feeling for both present and preterit syncopation and for the connection between them, the *spîan*-group added the further contribution of connecting these syncopations with the vowel gradation of ablauting preterit singular and plural forms. The later preterit singular forms of these verbs were *spê, snê, scrê*, giving a combined vowel and consonant variation of *-ê* (zero)-: *-iw-*. Such consonantal variation might at any time come to be felt as functional, just as the vowel variation was, for distinguishing the pret. sing. and pret. plur. stems.

---

[19] Braune, *Ahd. Lesebuch*, vocab. s. v. *gilâwen/firlâwen*, and *Ahd. Gramm.* § 363 A 4 d; Feist, *Etym. Wtb. d. goth. Spr.* s. v. *lēwjan*.

[20] Braune §§ 353 A 3, 354 A 3 d. — The perf. ptc. forms are inferred from the MHG forms.

6. Verbs of the second ablaut class with stem-final -*w*- showed apparent syncopation in the preterit singular under the rule of dropping final -*w*. Long -*û*- appears as the stem vowel of the preterit plural and perfect participle by the rule that -*uww*- > -*ûw*- [21]. The verbs involved are *bliuwan/blou/blûwun/giblûwan*, *briuwan/brou/brûwun/gibrûwan*, *kiuwan / kou / kûwun / gikûwan*, *riuwan / rou / rûwun / girûwan*, *niuwan / nou / nûwun / ginûwan*. By rule there should be optional syncopation after the long stem vowel in the present, the pret. plur. and the perf. participle, and this actually occurs in some instances, as *bliuan, blûun, giblûan*, but this is rare because of the opposing tendency to develop an excrescent -*w*- between -*u*- and a following vowel. — Their chief contribution was, therefore, that they reinforced the verbs of the *spîan*-group in offering a combined vowel and consonant variation between the pret. sing. and plural, namely, -*ou* + zero: -*û* + *w*-.

7. The reduplicating clipt preterit *hio* (later *hie*) from *houwan* (with stem-final -*w*-) was the sole instance of preterit syncopation remaining among the reduplicating verbs after the above noted shifts of pure-vowel and stem-final-*w* verbs to the first weak conjugation. Tense stems *houwan/hio/hiowun/gihouwan* showed as yet no such variation between the clipt and full preterit singular forms as later develept in MHG *hie/hieb*, but only the distinction between sing. and plur. stems, which was consonantal only. Tho not as common in literary use as *gân, fâhan* and *lâzan*, the verb *houwan* must have been common in the spoken language; so that the preexistence of this clipt preterit form is important both in itself and as the only preexistent form of the later reduplicating clipt preterit group: *gie/fie/lie/hie* ("hing")/*hie* ("hieb").

8. In the later OHG period the third class weak verb *habên* develept the syncopated present forms *hân* [22], *hâst, hât, hânt*, and the syncopated preterit *hâte*. The development of these shorter forms was favored (1) by the general speech feeling revealed by the various clipt present, preterit and participle forms noted in the preceding sections; (2) by weakened sentence stress, as these clipt forms of *habên/hân* occurred especially in the auxiliary use of the verb; (3) by the specific analogy of other syncopated forms, as *habên, hân, hât, hâte*, etc. beside *blâwen, blân, blât, blâte*, etc., or *lâwen, lâ(e)n, lâta*, etc. This analogical influence must have

---

[21] Braune §§ 334 A 4 and 5, 108, 110 A 1, 113 A 2.
[22] First extant use in Williram. — See Braune § 368 A 4.

come into play still more easily owing to the close resemblance in phonetic type, the distinction between the voiced bilabial spirant -b- and the voiced bilabial semi-vowel -w- being very narrow.

The clipt present forms of *habên/hân* became closely associated in speech feeling with the corresponding forms of *gân, stân*, etc., and as in the case of *blân/blâta, hîen/hîta, spîan/spê*, etc., helpt to establish still more firmly the connection between present and preterit syncopations in speech feeling.

That the clipt forms of *habên/hân* may have been much older in actual speech than in their common literary usage is indicated by the emergence of the auxiliary *hât* in the *Petruslied (Unsar trohtîn hât farsalt* . . .) in the ninth century. This in no wise affects the close relation of the *hân* forms to those of the *gân, stân* and *blân* groups, since these latter (apparent) syncopations were primitive.

9. The clipt preterits came under the larger category of consonant variation between the sing. and plur. preterit stems, under which they constituted the special case in which the first variant is zero. They were therefore strongly reinforced by the strong verbs showing grammatical change in the pret. sing. and plural. The consonantal equations involved were *d/t, h/g, s/r* [23]. The following verbs occurred: (a) in the first ablaut class, *sneid/snitum, leid/litum, meid/mitum, zêh/zigum, dêh/digum, rêh/rigum, wêh/wigum, lêh/ligum, reis/rirum;* (b) in the second ablaut class, *sôd/sutum, zôh/zugum, kôs/kurum, frôs/frurum, firlôs/firlurum;* (c) in the fifth ablaut class, *las/lârum, gas/gârum, ginas/ginârum, was/wârum.*

These variations, going back to Prim. Gc., show an establisht feeling for consonantal variation as a normal means of distinguishing sing. and plur. pret. stems.

10. To sum up, both present and preterit syncopations occurred in a considerable number of common verbs and were well intrencht in OHG speech feeling. Present syncopations occurred in the *gân* and *stân* groups, and preterit syncopations occurred alone in the -w- verbs of the second weak conjugation and in *houwan/hio.* Both present and preterit syncopations occurred together in all the other groups. In the weak verbs (*blân*-group, weak -w- verbs, *habên/hân*) syncopation made no difference between singular and plural preterit forms; in the strong verbs (*spîan*-group, *blou*-group, *hio*) it brought a new means of distinguishing pret. sing.

---

[23] Braune §§ 100 ff., 330 ff., 343.

and pret. plur. stems by consonant variation, which was groupt in speech feeling with consonantal variation by grammatical change.

IV. Preexistent Materials which were still Isolated in Old High German.

Certain other components of the later reduplicating clipt present and preterit group were preexistent, but were still isolated in the main OHG period. Especially to be noted are (1) the isolation of *houwan/hio* from the *gân*-group; (2) the isolation of *lâzan* from ill syncopating groups, and especially from the *gân*-group; (3) the isolation of the *gân*-group from all preterit syncopations; (4) the phonetic isolation between the *gân*-presents and preterits; (5) the isolation of the *gân*-preterits from all other preterit groups; (6) the resultant inhibition of a comprehensive clipt present and preterit group.

1. *Houwan/hio* was for several reasons not closely associated with the *gân/fâhan/hâhan* group. They had (apparent) present stem syncopation or weakening, *houwan* had only the full stem; they had only full preterit sing. forms, *houwan* had only the clipt form; the present stems were not of the same phonetic pattern; their vowel gradations differed thruout *(a/ia/ia/a* and *ou/io/io/ou)* in the main OHG period. So that, tho the type of a reduplicating clipt preterit was preexistent in *houwan/hio*, it did not yet touch the verbs *gân, fâhan* and *hâhan*.

2. The verb *lâzan* did not in the full OHG period belong to any of these syncopating groups, and had no special associations with the verbs *gân, fâhan, hâhan* or *houwan*. It had, to be sure, several general points of contact with these verbs in that it was (1) a reduplicating verb (2) of the same vowel gradation *(a/ia/ia/a)* as *gân, fâhan* and *hâhan,* and (3) in its main meaning of "loslassen, freilassen" the exact antonym of *fâhan* "fassen, fangen", and therefore already semantically associated with this word and with the phonetically resembling *fazzôn* "ergreifen". But it lackt the prime essential of membership in the *gân-fâhan* group in that it had no clipt present forms and it equally lackt the clipt preterit forms which might have associated it with *hio/hiowun* and the other groups of preexistent clipt preterits noted above.

3. Of the preexistent syncopating verbs most closely associated

with the *gân*-group, none exerted any analogical pressure on the *gân* preterit formations. *Stân* and *slahan* did not form clipt preterits; the *blân*-group and *hân* formed the weak preterits *blâta*, *hâte*, etc., whose phonetic pattern was both in stem and inflection exactly the reverse of a strong preterit, and hence furnisht no model for clipt strong formations. But, if a specific pattern and actual startingpoint should be found elsewhere, these forms would exert a strong general pressure toward its acceptance and spread.

4. The phonetic discrepancy between *gân*, *fâhan*, *hâhan* and their preterits *giang*, *fiang*, *hiang* prevented their forming a proportional group. *Fâhan* and *hâhan* had no present stems in *-ng* to group with the preterits *fiang* and *hiang*. *Gân* was so thoroly dominant over *gangan* in ordinary use that the normal functional association was certainly, *gân/giang* and not *gangan/ giang*, just as English is *go/went* and not the historically correct *wend/went* (cf. *send/sent*). Had the apparently syncopated presents really arisen out of syncopation of stems ending in *-ng-* they might have carried the preterit stems with them. As it was with the present and preterit stems phonetically isolated from each other, there was no urge in any form to connect up the two systems. The situation was exactly parallel to that in NHG *gehen/ging*, *stehen/stand* or English *go/went*, *stand/stood*, Fr. *je vais/j'allai*, Gr. ἔϱχομαι/ἦλϑον, and many others. In these very common words, each heterothematic form is strong enough to maintain its separate and self-sufficient existence. No English speaker, for instance, feels any urge to say *I *goed*, nor German to say *ich *gehte*[24], nor French speaker *je *vayai*.

This isolation was strengthened by their completely riming stems and inflections. Their phonetic pattern in *-iang* was shared by no other OHG words. As a result their association with each

---

[24] This explains why thru hundreds of years *gân* refrained from forming the preterit *gie* except temporarily under the very special circumstances we are considering. It is so obvious a priori, however, that *gân* must have formed its natural preterit *gie* as the starting point of the whole development! Thus, one of the best and keenest of American philologists wrote me: — "The outward mechanism of the genesis of those forms is simple enough: starting with the forms *gân-gie*, and the analogical infinitives *fân*, *lân* — the shorter forms *fie*, *lie* were added as parallels to *gân-gie-gienc*. *Gie*, of course, is originally the preterit of *gân*, while *gienc* is the preterit of *gangan*." — At the time I fully shared this seemingly self-evident view. Actual investigation shows it to be so wholly erroneous that I now refrain from giving the name of the honored friend who wrote it.

other was very strong, which drew them still more completely away from phonetic influence of their present forms. Furthermore these words were all of such common everyday use that each of them (especially *giang*) would have been able to stand alone as an irregular form if necessary. As a result these three verbs formed a compact, self-contained and inter-reinforcing group, which still holds a thousand years later in NHG *ging/fing/hing*.

5. For these same reasons OHG *giang/fiang/hiang* stood aloof from all other strong preterit groups. They offered no hold for specific analogical pressure from the strong clipt preterits *spê*, *blou*, etc., such a proportion (?) as *gân: giang:: spîan: spê* being absurd. — Their similar immunity against specific pressure from the weak clipt preterits *blâta*, *hâte*, etc. was noted under § 3 above.

6. In spite therefore of the preexistence of these types of clipt presents and preterits and of several forms of connection between them, these isolations had prevented the development of a consistent group of syncopating verbs as such. A comprehensive group leveling all syncopating verbs was manifestly impossible because of the heterogeneity of the conjugations involved. As to the preterits of the *gân*-group, their above-noted phonetic segregation both from their own present systems and from all syncopating preterits, apparently precluded the possibility of leveling them to the clipt type or of creating variant clipt forms beside them.

Obviously these gaps between the *gân* presents and preterits, and between the preterits and those of other verb groups, could be bridged, if at all, only from within the group by a verb with a phonetically regular present and preterit stem.

V. The Formation of the Reduplicating Clipt Present and Preterit Group.

1. The bridge from the present forms *gangan/gân*, *fâhan/fân*, *hâhan/hân* to their preterit forms *giang*, *fiang*, *hiang*, and also the bridge connecting these clipt preterit forms with those of other syncopating groups, were furnisht by the accidental entrance of *lâzen* [25] into the group in the late OHG period (about the turn

---

[25] As this movement overlaps the transition to the MHG period, it will be better at this point to change to MHG spellings of cited forms.

of the tenth and eleventh centuries) [26]. Collitz shows conclusively that the clipt impv. 2 sg. *lâ* originated independently of the influence of *gân* and *stân*, at least as far as appearance in writing is concerned. That this holds also for spoken usage would seem to be shown by the original disconnection between *lâzen* and *gân* noted above (IV 2) [27]. Both these conclusions are further borne out by facts found by Starck and Sehrt in the index which they are making of Notker's works. Starck notes (in a personal letter) that in his part of the work (all except Boethius and the last fifty Psalms) 21 instances of *lâ* occur, but no other contract forms of *lâzen*, and none at all of *gân* and *fâhen*. Sehrt informs me that he finds in the Boethius 7 instances of *lâ*, none of *lâz* and the single instance of *lie* (126, 2) referred to by Collitz; in his share of the Psalms he finds 5 instances of *lâ*, 6 of *lâz* and none of *lie*.

It was noted above that *lâ* first appeared as the unaccented grade of the 2 sg. impv. *lâz*. It is a significant coincidence that the clipt forms *haben/hân*, whose increast use (noted in III 8 above) came in this same century, generally occurred under non-stress conditions in the auxiliary use of the verb [22]. Compare also such syncopations as the dropping of *-z-* of unstrest *daz* in *daz ist > deist*, etc.

2. As soon as the present tense forms were establisht in speech feeling, [28] the verb *lâzen/lân* thereby became an equal member of the reduplicating clipt present group, with its formations thruout exactly parallel to those of *gân*, less perfectly so to those of *fâhen* and *hâhen*. The proportions may be shown as *(gangen* [29]*): gân:gang:gâ:gieng::lâzen:lân:lâz:lâ:liez::hâhen:hân:hâh:hâ:hieng*, etc.

3. The connection which *lâzen* formed between the present and preterit tenses rested on the parallelism in the phonetic patterns of *lâz* and *liez*, a parallelism wholly lacking in *fâ(h)/fieng* and *hâ(h)/hieng* and seriously disturbed in *gâ(ng)/gieng* by the larger use of the short form. The analogical proportion of *lâzen* was *lâz:lâ::*

---

[26] Collitz *art. cit.* pp. 450—456.

[27] We must assume that in all cases spoken forms first developt and formed the basis of their literary appearance. Also we should expect OHG literary usage to agree generally with spoken usage, because it was based directly on the folk dialects and not on any accumulated or artificial literary tradition.

[28] Collitz *art. cit.* p. 451 n. 6.

[29] This form was dying out, but the stem continued in undiminisht use in the past ptc., and in the impv. *gang*, derivative noun *ganc*, etc.; so that the proportion was not destroyed, altho weakened.

liez:(x), in which the speech feeling value of x was necessarily *lie*. It is not strange therefore that *lie* was the next form to emerge [30].

4. With the creation of the form *lie* beside *lâ*, giving the proportion *lâz:lâ::liez:lie*, connection was completed between the present and preterit system of the *gân*-group. Therewith the old reduplicating clipt present group became in nascent form the new Reduplicating Clipt Present and Preterit Group. The preterit *lie* at once establisht connection with the old clipt pret. *hio*, now shifted to *hie*, from the verb *houwen*, which thereby became a member of the group, tho lacking present syncopation [31]. The group thus came to contain the verbs *gân, fâhen, hâhen, lâzen* and *houwen*.

5. With the linking together of present and preterit syncopations of this group, each of these types of syncopation was greatly strengthened by the other, since they now fell for the first time into proportional groups of present and preterit forms. And from this came the impulse to the analogical creation of new forms, since most of the new proportions were defective in either their present or preterit formations as judged by the new patterns, and stem analogies also exerted pressure for the extension of the new system of syncopations to the perfect participle. For illustrations, see the schema of the reduplicating clipt present and preterit group given below.

6. The changing of the *gân*-group to the clipt present and preterit status brought it into line with the general plan of the preexistent syncopating verbs, most of which had both present and preterit syncopations coordinated with each other. This again workt to the mutual strengthening of both the old and new groups. This general connection was made concrete and precise by the pret. *hie/hiewen* which was already associated in formation with the other *-w-* syncopating preterits, as *blou/blûwen, spê/spiwen*, etc. This also resulted in a tendency to analogical extensions and the creation of new forms which will be noted below.

7. The individual verbs of the reduplicating clipt group were further reinforced by other words of similar phonetic form and

---

[30] Bo. 126, 2. — See Collitz *art. cit.* 456.

[31] That it was actually felt as in this group is shown by the later leveling of *houwen* to *hawen* on the pattern of *lâzen*, etc. — The present syncopation of *houwen* was resisted by the diphthong *-ou-*, as explained for the verbs of the *blou*-group in III 6.

meaning which showed the same or similar syncopations and gradations. These were partly true cognates or derivatives, as *ganc* (gen. *ganges*), *fanc, hanc,* showing the missing full present stems of these words; *houwe (höuwe)/hou (höu),* showing the missing syncopation of the present system of the verb. Note also *laz/lâz/lazzen* beside *lâzen, hâhel (hâl)* "kesselhaken" beside *hâhen/hân,* etc. Others were contaminative or congeneric associates showing accidental resemblances, as *gâhe/gâ* "eile" (schnelles Gehen), etc. In some cases such cognate and contaminative associates offered a new bond of resemblance between different verbs, as *gazze* (cognate of *gân*) and *faz* "faß"/*fazzen* "fangen" (contaminates of *fâhen*) beside *laz/lazze/lazzen* (cognates of *lâzen*) [32].

8. The interaction of all these factors will be seen more clearly and quickly in the following.

Schema of the Reduplicating Clipt Present and Preterit Verbs

GANGEN	[*gâhen*]	(*gazze*)	GÂN	⟨*gie*⟩	GIENG	GIENGEN	GEGANGEN
(*ganc*)	[*gâhe*]		[*gâ*]				⟨*gegân*⟩
⟨*fangen*⟩	FÂHEN	[*fazzen*]	FÂN	⟨*fie*⟩	FIENG	FIENGEN	GEFANGEN
(*fanc*)	[*fâch*]	[*faz*]					⟨*gefân*⟩
⟨*hangen*⟩	HÂHEN	—	⟨*hân*⟩	⟨*hie*⟩	HIENG	HIENGEN	GEHANGEN
(*hanc*)	(*hâhel*)		(*hâl*)				(clipt . . . . . .)
—	—	LÂZEN	⟨*lân*⟩	LIE	LIEZ	LIEZEN	GELÂZEN
		(*laz*)	LÂ				⟨*gelân*⟩
		(*lazze*)					
		(*lazzen*)					
HOUWEN	( )	—	. . . . .	HIE	⟨*hi(e)w*⟩	HIEWEN	GEHOUWEN
⟨*hawen*⟩			(*hou*)				⟨*gehawen*⟩
(*houwe*)			(*höu*)				(clipt: . . . . . .)
(*höuwe*)							

Preexistent forms (that is forms which had originated independently in any way up to the nascent formation of the new group) are printed in capitals. The missing forms whose new creation was demanded and subsequently effected by the analogi-

---

[32] NHG *lassen* has inherited the phonetic form of *lazzen*, the inflection of *lâzen,* and combines in its derivatives the meanings of both — cf. *lassen, ablassen, lässig, unablässig,* etc.

cal proportions of the new group are put in pointed brackets. Cognates of *gân*, *fâhen*, *hâhen*, *lâzen* and *houwen* are put in parentheses. Contaminatively associated words are put in square brackets. Spaces in parentheses indicate that the verb was phonetically unfitted to create the corresponding form. A dotted line denotes an actual gap in the series of formations. A solid line indicates that there is no real gap and that the space is to be ignored.

9. The schema is in general self-explanatory, but certain observations may help:

(a) The forms *gâhen/gâhe/gâ*, *gazze/fazzen/lazzen*, etc., had of course nothing to do with developing the clipt forms of *gân*, *fâhen* and *lâzen*, but after the clipt forms were developt, such side-associations helpt to bind these words into still firmer association.

(b) The forms *fangen* and *hangen* were in no sense preexistent, but were later analogical recreations, since the present stems had from Prim. Gc. on terminated in *h*. The clipt inf. *hân* "hangen" was largely inhibited by the preexistent and far commoner *hân* "haben". Also *hie* "hing" and *hie* "hieb" must have hampered each other, tho both were used.

(c) The new formations *hawen/gehawen* for the original forms *houwen/gehouwen* were analogical extensions on the pattern of the other four verbs of the group, and not a premature NHG shifting of *-ouw-* to *-au-*. The leveling proportions which produced the new forms were *gangen: gie: giengen: gegangen: :fâhen: fie: fiengen: gefangen: :lâzen: lie: liezen: gelâzen*, etc., which analogically demanded *hawen: hie: hiewen: gehawen*. Similarly, the full sing. pret. form *hi(e)w* is a new formation on the pattern of *lie: liez*. Both *hawen* and *houwen* yielded NHG *hauen* by regular shifting. — The *-h-* grade of the present stem was impossible for *hawen*, because the *-w-* was original and not for a velar. — The clipt inf. **hân* for *hawen* was inhibited by *hân* "haben" and *hân* "hangen". Both **gehân* "gehangen" and **gehân* "gehauen" were completely inhibited by *gehân* "gehabt".

(d) The phonetic analogical proportions of the other new formations *gie*, *fie*, *hie* "hing" and (later) *gegân*, *gefân* and *gehân* are self-evident.

10. The distinctive feature of the new group was its development of this special variation in the preterit singular with clipt and full forms side by side, as against the full form only in the pret.

plural. Variant syncopation in the present was shared with the *stân, slân, blæn* (earlier *blân*), *hîen* and *spîen* groups and the verb *haben/hân*.

VI. The Extension of the Clipt Present and Preterit Conjugation.

1. The fact that the other classes of preexistent syncopating verbs continued and strengthened their association in speech consciousness with the verbs of the reduplicating clipt group is shown by their tendency to retain or create forms which agreed with those of the new group. Old forms were preserved which agreed with the pattern of the *gân/lân* group, tho no longer regular in phonology from their own standpoint, as *drâte/gedrât (gedrân)* beside the newer regular *dræte/gedræt*. New forms were created on the particular or general pattern of the *gân*-group, as *geslân* beside *geslagen*, *lê* beside *lêch* from *lîhen*. Especially to be noted is the retention or creation of strong past participles of the *gân*-type for weak verbs, as *geblân* beside *geblæt*, *gehân* beside *gehât*, etc., thus showing the continuance of the OHG association of the *gân, stân, slân, blân* and *hân (habên)* groups.

2. The aggressive vigor of the now reinforced syncopating type is further shown by the tendency to level other verbs to its pattern of total conjugation. Thus *lîhen (lîen)/lê (lêch)/lîhen/ gelihen (geligen/gelien)* was completely leveled to the new type, which is the more significant in view of its belonging to another ablaut series. Partial levelings also occurred in which consonant variation replaced syncopation (cf. III 9 above), as *ligen (lîhen, lîan, lîn)/lac/lâgen/gelegen* (*-c* due to devoicing of final), *sehen (sên)/sach/sâgen/gesehen (gesên)* [33], *geschehen (geschên)/geschach/ geschâgen/geschehen (geschên)*, *slahen (slân)/sluoc/sluogen/geslagen (geslân)*, *twahen (twân)/twuoc/twuogen/getwagen (getwân)*, *tragen (trân)/truoc/truogen/getragen (getrân)* (*-g-* due to grammatical

---

[33] By Verner's Law the pret. plur. of *sehen* should contain a voiced velar spirant as stemfinal (OHG *saȝuum*, MHG *saȝuen*). This sound would be essentially a velarized or "throaty" *-w-*, which (lacking exact representation in the Latin alphabet) would most naturally be spelled in the various Germanic languages with the closely resembling *-w-*. (Incidentally this suggests a possible explanation of Sievers' Law; see PBB 5, 149 and Kluge, *Urgerm.* § 47.) But a throaty *-w-* is intermediate in sound between *-w-* and spirant *-g-*. — Could the variant spellings OHG *sâwun*, MHG *sâgen* be therefore simply approximations of the same sound? — Compare Gc. initial *w-* from IE initial velar voiced aspirate, and the Romance borrowing of this *w-* as *gu-* in Fr. *guerre, guichet*, etc.

change). — Part of these levelings were due to ordinary phonetic changes, so that speech feeling had merely to accept accomplisht results. — It is to be noted that in most of these verbs the pret. sing. showed only the weaker stem, the plural the full form. This did not however separate them from the clipt preterits in speech feeling, because, as Collitz notes, already in the transition period, the clipt singular stem had become the regular popular form.

VII. The Phonetic Background of the Clipt Present and Preterit Conjugations.

1. The larger phonetic background both of the reduplicating clipt present and preterit verbs and of the other syncopating verb groups was formed by the general system of phonetic variation which characterized OHG and MHG phonology. The vowel and consonant syncopations and variations in these various groups were themselves an essential part of the larger scheme, and were dependent on and sustained by it. The system went back in its beginnings to IE, and received successive accretions in both the Germanic and OHG periods. Its extreme development fell in the later OHG and the MHG periods and formed the necessary basis for the rise and spread of those groups.

2. For the scientific and historical discrimination of these variant formations see Braune, *Ahd. Gramm.*, division on "Lautlehre" and Paul, *Mhd. Gramm.*, chapter on "Lautwechsel". Our present purpose is rather to consider how these variations presented themselves to speech feeling, which is neither scientific nor historical. For naive speech feeling all these variations stood on a par with each other and were not discriminated according to historic origins.

3. These variations were due to diverse causes, partly corresponding to the different periods of their origins. Among the causes of consonant variation we may note: (1) Phonetic shifting (all periods), as *decken/dahte, hie/hiewen*, etc.; (2) grammatical change or Verner's Law, *fâhen/gefangen, zôch/zugen* etc.; (3) devoicing of finals, as *tac/tage, lamp/lember*, etc.; (4) syncopation (all periods), as *fâhen/fân, gibist/gîst*, etc. — By the action and interaction of these factors many words had come to show phonetic variation either in the same inflected form (as *fâhen/fân*) or between different forms of the same word (as *zôch/zugen*).

4. Among consonantal equations or interchanges which had thus develOpt we may note: (1) the optional or necessary omission of various intervocalic and final consonants, such as *h, g, j, w;* (2) inflectional, derivational and sandhi interchange of consonants, especially of *h, ch, k, g, nk,* and *ng;* (3) combinations of these into more extended series. It will be well to quote sufficient illustrations to show how widely and firmly these variation series were intrencht in MHG phonetic feeling.

5. Omission of intervocalic or final *-h-* appears, for instance, in such verbs as *sehen/sên, geschehen/geschên, hâhen/hân, fâhen/fân, slahen/slân, twahen/twân, ziehen/zien, lîhen/lîn, jehen/jên,* etc.; in such nouns as *mahel/mâl, lêhen/lên, blahe/blâ, stahel/stâl,* etc.; in such adjectives and adverbs as *hôch/hôhe/hô, nâch/nâhe/nâ,* etc.

For omission of *-g-* compare *maget/meit, jaget/jeit, slage/slâ gegen/gein, ligen/lien,* etc.

For omission of *-j-* compare *blæjen/blæn,* etc.

For *-w-* compare *schatewe/schate, lê/gen. lêwes, krâwe/krâ(e), farwe/fâr, læwe/lâw/lâ* "lau", *hîwe/hîe* "gatte", *spîwen/spîen, iwer/iur,* etc.

Sporadically occurred other real or apparent syncopations and clippings, such as *-t-* in *sitzen/saz, netzen/naz,* etc., *-z-* in *fazzen/fân* (viewed as folk-cognates), *gazze* (deriv. of)*/gân; -nd-* in *standen/stân -ng-* in *gegangen/gân: -r-* in *dâ/dâr, wâ/wâr, mêr/mê, zer-/ze-; -d-* in *geschadet/gaschât; -b-* in *haben/hân, gibit/gît; -t-* in *leiten/*pret. *lei-te; -p-* in *scharf/scherpfe, sleife/sleipfe,* etc.

6. It is clear that the average MHG speech consciousness must have had a deep-rooted feeling that all non-initial consonants, especially between vowels and in final consonants matching these in inflection or derivation, were regularly or sporadically subject to syncopation or elision. Hence MHG [34] phonetic feeling was predisposed on the basis of a host of apparently slurred or clipt forms to accept and preserve new formations of the same kind wherever other causes tended to their formation, or to regroup originally independent but resembling forms (such as *standen/stân, gangen/gân*) as syncopation variants of the "same" word.

7. Completely interwoven with the phenomenon of consonantal omission was that of consonantal variation and equivalence. The two occur conjointly in many words, so that the syncopated form

---

[31] MHG in this developmental sense includes the same tendencies in OHG — especially in later OHG — leading into MHG.

comes to count as the zero grade in the consonantal variation series, and consonantal weakening (such as *-ng-/-h/* etc.) is felt as a partial or incipient syncopation. Such consonantal variation series thus combined in varying proportions the results of syncopation, grammatical change, devoicing of finals, normal sound shifting, and contaminative blending of originally separate words. The distinction between these various causes was, as already noted, largely blurred or obliterated for speech feeling, and their results were felt as belonging together, the more so as the phonetic equations resulting from them frequently overlapt or duplicated each other, and hence necessarily blended into one series when they occurred in different forms of the same word.

The simple phonetic equations due to devoicing of finals (*b/p, d/t, g/c*, as in *wîp/wîbes, fienc/fiengen*, etc.) are too common to need extended illustration. They tended automatically to blend with similar phonetic equations resulting from grammatical change and in many cases with those due to phonetic shifting. Thus, devoicing blends with grammatical change to produce such equations as *d/t* in *lîden/leit/liten, sieden/sôt/suten*, etc. It blends with phonetic shifting to produce such series as *k/g/h* in *mac/maht/magen* and *touc/tugen/tohte*. It blends with phonetic shifting and grammatical change in the forms of *hâhen, fâhen, denken, bringen*, etc., to produce the more extended series *0/h/nk/ng*. Simple shifting produces *h/ch/k* in such groups as *dach/decken/dahte (dacte)*. Compare such further equations (due to simple or mixt causes) as *h/k* in *wurken/worhte; g/h/0/k* in *ligen/lihen/lien (lîn)/lac; h/0/ch/ g/* in the forms of *sehen, gesche(c)hen, dîhen, zîhen*, etc. It is clear that these and very many other similar equations must have developt the fixt feeling that *0/h/ch/k/g/nk/ng* were freely equatable and interchangeable in any order, selection or combination. Other equations due to mixt causes were *s/r* in forms of *wesen, rîsen*, etc.; *z/0* in such contractions as *daz ist/deist, ez ist/eist; b/p/0* in *haben/hân/gehabet/gehapt/gehât, gibe/gît/gip*, etc.; *n/0* in *ein/eime, dîn/dîme*, etc. *d/t/0* in forms of *queden, reden, baden, schaden*, etc. and their derivatives; and many others.

8. Because of these mainfold blendings and overlappings, all of these series of consonantal variations cohered in a general system of consonantal variation in MHG speech feeling.

9. Like consonantal variation, MHG vowel variation went back to several different origins. The following historical forms of

vowel variation may be noted: (a) ablaut, going back to primitive Indo-European, as *bîten/beit/biten/gebiten:* Go. *beidan/baiþ/bidum/ bidans:* Gr. πείθω, πέποιθα, ἔπιθον, πιθανός; (b) interchange of *e/i* and of *o/u* before various vowels in the following syllable, with or without an intervening nasal + consonant, as *helfen/hilfe, herde/hirte, zugen/gezogen, hof/hübesch, lieht/liuhten* (OHG *lioht/ liuhtan*), etc.; (c) umlaut, beginning in late OHG and developing further in the MHG period, as *gast/geste, hôrte/hœren, hûs/hiuser, houwe/höuwe,* etc.; (d) contraction (all periods, often fused with and practically a part of syncopation), as *lien/lîn, krâe/krâ, fâhen/fân, gibist/gîst,* etc.; (e) results of leveling out primitive reduplication, with the following contraction and phonetic shifting, as *halten/hielt, ruofen/rief,* etc.; (f) phonetic shifting leading to vowel variation, as *gefangen/fâhen, mêre/meist,* etc.

10. These several types of vowel variation blended together in varying combinations. Thus, original ablaut and the primitive Germanic variation *e/i, o/u, ie/iu* blend into larger series of vowel gradation in the ablaut verbs generally, as *nemen/nime* (Germanic variation)/*nam/nâmen/genomen* (ablaut); *ziehen/ziuhe* (Gc. var.) / *zôch* (abl.) / *zugen* / *gezogen* (abl. + Gc. var.), and many others. In other words, Germanic vowel variation [35] was normally superposed on preexistent ablaut, and subsisted only as an inseparable aspect of the same, the two together forming for speech feeling an enlarged ablaut series.

Similarly, umlaut is inseparably superposed on both ablaut and Germanic vowel variation, blending with them into still larger composite series. Thus it combines with ablaut in *graben/grebet/gruop/ grüebe,* in *tuon/tete/tâten/tæte/getân,* and in many others. It combines with Germanic vowel variation and ablaut in *sol/süln/solte/sölte, wellen/wil/wolte/wölte, mac/megen/mugen/mahte/mohte/mähte/möhte, nam/næme/nâmen/genomen, ziehen/ziuhe/zôch/zugen/züge/gezogen,* etc. It occurs alone simulating ablaut in *setzen/satzte,* which was surely associated also with *sitzen/saz/sæze/gesezzen.*

The results of phonetic shifting combine with ablaut in numberless instances, as in the preterits of the reduplicating verbs, such as *halten/hielt* (*-ie-* < OHG *-ia-* < earlier *-ea-,* etc. [36]) beside *ruofen/rief* (*-ie-* < OHG *-io-* < earlier *-eo-*).

---

[35] I venture to base this name on Braune's "urgermanische wandlungen", *Ahd. Gramm.* § 30 c.

[36] Braune §§ 349 and 354, and § III 1 of this article,

11. Both consonant and vowel variation frequently alternate or concur in the same word or in the same functional form and systems.

Thus in nouns the stem-distinction between nom.-acc. singular and plural forms may, in addition to variation of inflectional endings, show: (1) consonantal variation only, as in *tac/tage*, etc.; (2) vowel variation only, as *bach/beche;* (3) both consonant and vowel variation, as *lamp/lember, burc/bürge*, etc. Similar illustrations could be given for adjective stems, as *blint/blinde, voll/völliu*, etc.

In the comparison of adjectives arise (1) such consonantal equations as *kreftic/kreftiger*, etc.; (2) such vowel equations as *alt/elter*, etc.; (3) such combined vowel and consonantal equations as *junc/jünger, lanc/lenger*, etc. In the formation of adverbs from adjectives, we may note (1) *lanc/lange*, and (2) *schœne/schone, veste/vaste*, etc. In verbs occur (1) such consonantal equations as *gruop/gruoben, truoc/truogen, slahen/geslagen*, etc.; (2) such vowel equations as *halten/hielt, giengen/gegangen*, etc.; (3) such combined vowel and consonant equations as *siude/gesoten, zôch/zugen, fâhen/gefangen*, etc.

12. In the case of noun and adjective and adverb forms, vowel equations (chiefly umlaut) constituted the dominant form of phonetic variation, with consonant variation loosely associated with it as a possible minor variant. Essentially the same situation holds for the present indicative and imperative of strong or ablaut verbs, as *wirde/wirt/werden, gibe/gip/gebet, grabe/grebet/grap/grabet*, etc. (The form of vowel variation here involved is of course only partly umlaut, including also the primitive Gc. vowel variation *e: i, o: u.*)

13. But in the preterit system of the ablaut verbs, vowel and consonant variation were more strongly intrencht and more closely associated together. Vowel variation in the strong preterit included, not only umlaut as in noun, adjective and adverb formations, but original ablaut, original reduplication, Germanic vowel variation and umlaut. Consonant variation included not only devoicing, but also the historically older and functionally more vital phenomenon of grammatical change (Verner's Law) and sometimes the results of phonetic shifting. Phonetic variation of either or both kinds was felt as fundamental as a means of distinguishing singular and plural stems. Vowel variation alone

distinguished the two stems in such verbs as *beit/biten, hauf/hulfen, nam/nâmen;* consonant variation alone in *truoc/truogen, stuont, stuonden, gruop/gruoben, fienc/fiengen;* neither variation in *vuor/ vuoren, hielt/hielten, lief/liefen,* etc.; combined vowel and consonant variation in *dêch/digen, zôch/zugen, wart/wurden,* etc.

14. To sum up, extreme phonetic variation, partly functionless, partly serving to express functional distinctions, was the most characteristic feature of MHG phonology. It found its fullest manifestation in the preterit of strong verbs, whose phonetic equations may however be abundantly duplicated from other parts of speech. — This sweeping system of phonetic variation was the necessary background and milieu of the development and continuance of the various clipt present and preterit systems.

VIII. Decline and Fall of the Syncopating Conjugations.

1. All of these phonetic and functional variations, including those of the clipt preterits, subsisted in a still larger milieu of "regular" forms which showed no variation of stem, but used suffixes to indicate grammatical distinctions, as *nagel/nagele, zal/ zaln, bote/boten, machen/machte, keren/kerte, wonen/wonete.* As a result the clipt preterit verbs were exposed to two opposing tendencies, a narrower and at first intenser tendency to preserve the phonetic variation of singular and plural stems and to create new analogical forms on the same or resembling patterns, and a broader tendency to level out all useless stem variations. The basic strength of this levelling tendency obviously lay in its conformity to the fundamental analogical principles of language, and in its conducing to clearness and mental economy in individual instances. Its initial weakness lay in the fact that in all the declensions and conjugations in which the "regular" forms occurred, other forms with manifold phonetic variations occurred beside them, as *gast/geste, lê/lêwes, geschadet/geschât,* etc., etc.

2. The strength of this narrower tendency as applied to the reduplicating clipt present and preterit group rested on both internal and external factors: (1) Its forms were of frequent and familiar occurrence and able to hold their own individually; (2) they formed a compact group strengthened by (3) association with other syncopating present and preterit verbs and (4) association with verbs making phonetic distinction between the

preterit singluar and plural stems, and (5) fortified by the still larger background of phonetic variation noted above. As long as these interlinking factors continued unchanged, they maintained the clipt verbs as an impregnable group.

3. The intrinsic weakness of the group lay in (1) the impossibility of conforming some stems (as those ending in a vowel) to the formation, (2) the limited numbers of distinct clipt forms (thus *hân* must theoretically do duty for *haben, hawen (houwen), hâhen)*, and (3) the consequent frequent ambiguity in clipt forms leading to the partial or complete inhibition of some forms, (4) the impossibility of securing phonetic consistency and homogeneity in a group so constructed. By preexistent accident *gân, fâhen* and *hâhen* formed the compact group above noted. In spite of their strengthening effect in other ways, the addition of *lâzen* and *houwen* to the group (not to mention such later additions as *lê/lêch*) greatly decreast this compact homogeneity. — The possible growth of the group was therefore very limited, and the above noted tendency to exceed these limits, tended also to break down the group.

4. A more serious blow to the group was the general tendency to wipe out the distinction between preterit singular and plural stems which occurred in later MHG in the ordinary course of phonetic development and as a result of the leveling of vowel quantity according to position [37].

As a preexistent basis for the levelling of preterit singular and plural stems, these already had the same stem in the sixth and seventh class strong verbs (as *fuor/fuoren, hielt/hielten*) and in weak verbs generally (as *machte/machten, satzte/satzten, wolte-n,*) and in all preterit subjunctives [38] (as *næme/næmen. büge/bügen, lieze/liezen,* etc.). Likewise the 2 sing pret. ind. [38] in all classes had the stem of the plural indicative.

5. In the first class, as a result of the phonetic coalescence of $\hat{\imath}$ and *ei* [39] such verbs as *stîgen: steig,* etc. produced the confusing equation *steigen/steig/stiegen/gestiegen*. The necessity of being understood in speaking forced the elimination of the preterit singular stem *steig* and the consequent levelling of the preterit singular and plural to *stieg: stiegen*.

---

[37] See Behaghel, *Geschichte d. deutschen Sp.*[5], pp. 427—438; Curme, *Gram of the Ger. Lang.* 197—204 and p. 14.

[38] Subject to umlaut.

[39] Paul *Mhd. Gr.* §§ 20, 21.

In the 4th and 5th classes, as a result of the positional levelling of vowel quantity [40] the feeling that there was any distinctive difference between singular and plural stems was lost — the variation in *nam/nâmen*, *gab/gâben* became the necessary variation of the same stem in different syllabic positions. The later analogical leveling of vowel quantity in all forms of the same inflected stem completed the levelling to NHG *nāhm: nāhmen*, *gāb: gāben*, etc.

Thus five out of the 7 classes of strong verbs came independently of each other to have identical singular and plural preterit stems. These five classes (I, IV, V, VI, VII) contained about 60% of all strong verbs.

6. The 3d, 4th and 5th class preterits were strongly associated in speech feeling by the vowel of the present singular in gradation with that of the preterit singular in all three classes and also the perfect participle in the 3d and 4th classes. Compare *gelten: gilte: galt: gegolten, nemen: nime: nam: genomen*, and *geben: gibe: gap: (gegeben)*, etc. As soon as the singular and plural of the 4th and 5th classes were levelled, such 3d class plurals as *gulten, sungen*, etc., necessarily began to feel incorrect and were corrected (probably both unconsciously and consciously) to *galten, sangen*, etc., thus leveling the 3d class preterits.

In the 2d class, *bôt: buten:* ppc. *geboten* became partly leveled when mere phonetic shifting gave *bôt: buten: gebôten*, etc., whose seemingly irregular plural yielded to the combined pressure of these forms and of all other classes and levelled to *bōt: bōten*.

7. Thus, owing to phonetic shifting and consequent analogical readjustment, the distinction of singular and plural stems [41] disappeared from the strong preterits, where it had originally been intrencht most strongly of all. With it most of the analogical support for the clipt preterits *gie, fie, lie, hie* "hing" and *hie* "hieb" had disappeared from speech feeling.

8. These levelings of the singular and plural preterit stems were an integral part of a general movement in later MHG which leveled out most of the syncopations, vowel and consonant variations and phonetic doublet stems, and thus led to the NHG period of stabilized sounds and leveled stems. The leveling of quantity according to position, the falling together of *î* and *ei*,

---

[40] Paul *Mhd. Gr.* §§ 18, 19.

[41] Save for such vanishing remnants as *ward/wurden, sang/sungen*, and such pret. subjunctives as *gölte, stürbe*, etc.

and the analogical levelings of variant preterit stems in the second and third ablaut classes were noted above. By the regular shifting of both *ou* and *-au-*, the doublet pair *houwen/hawen* coalesced. By the normal mutescence of *-h-* between vowels, and the general leveling out of final *-ch/-h-*, such variations as *sehen/ sach/sâhen/gesehen* disappeared. By contaminative and analogical new formations, non-functional and antifunctional phonetic variations in noun, adjective and verb stems generally were leveled out, as *kraft/krefte, schate/schatewes, rêch/rêhes, nâch/nâhes, blâ/blâwes, fliegen/fliuge* [42], etc. As a part of this last tendency syncopated forms generally tended to yield to the corresponding full forms, as *geslân* to *geschlagen, treit* to *traget, deist* to *daz ist*, etc.

9. By the successive accumulation of such individual changes the phonetic character of High German speech became more fixt and gradually ceast to be prominently characterized by excessive phonetic variation. This change was partly precipitated, as noted above, by normal phonetic changes which either happened to level variant forms or made them so dissimilar that subsequent analogical leveling was necessary. The need for clearness also helpt in such ambiguous forms as *hân/hie*, etc. Other factors calculated to help were the impulse to purism and formalism connected with some forms of literary composition, and also with the development of an interdialectal and formal Kanzlei- sprache, and the tendency to precision and correctness which necessarily accompanied the more or less conscious and artificial spread of the Schriftsprache.

10. These cumulative changes constituted not only a normalizing and stabilizing of particular words and forms, but also a general shifting of MHG phonetic speech feeling and of the phonetic basis and background on which the syncopated verb formations had previously rested. The result was the collapse of syncopation as a system of stem formation and conjugation. — But here a caution is necessary. Just as the development of the reduplicating clipt preterits at the close of the OHG period involved regroupings but not the wholesale wiping out of older forms, so the downfall of this system at the opening of the NHG period did not mean the sweeping destruction of all clipt forms. Very many of these still survive in present-day German, but always at the price of

---

[42] But in separate stems the variation remained as *lieht/liuhten* > NHG *licht leuchten*.

various regroupings. Furthermore it does not mean that slurred or slovenly or abbreviated pronunciations of verbs and other words cannot take place in German as they do in other languages, but only that such slurring is no longer recognized as basic or standard by speech consciousness.

11. Among present-day survivals of clipt forms the following may be noted. The clipt presents *gehn* and *stehn*, with their full preterits *ging* and *stand*, have reverted to the OHG status, but they are no longer felt as clipt stems but as full stems with clipt endings and irregular preterits. *Schlan, empfahn* and *han* "haben" linger on as vanishing poetic echoes; *hast, hat, hatte* survive as accepted irregularities, but they are short-voweled and no longer felt as syncopations. The clipt preterits *spie* and *schrie* survive but they are no longer felt as clipt since all other forms of these verbs now have stems equally shortened. The same is true of the weak clipt preterits *blähte, drehte*, etc. — It is worth noting that all the survivals are long-time preexistent forms; the brand new clipt reduplicating forms *lâ, lân, lie, gie, fie, hie* "hing" are clean gone, and with them the preexistent *hie* "hieb", which was felt as one of them.

12. The revived vigor of the full or leveled stem type of conjugation is shown, as was formerly that of the syncopated forms, by analogical new formations, back-formations and restorations, and by undoing not only newer clipt formations but even some primitive OHG syncopations. We may note (1) the wiping out of the clipt forms *gie, fie, hie* "hing", *lie* and *hie* "hieb"; (2) the preservation of the full preterit *hiew* > NHG *hieb;* (3) the full restoration of the erstwhile languishing forms *gi(e)ng, fi(e)ng, hi(e)ng* and *lieβ;* (4) the displacement of the clipt forms of *haben*, except *hast, hat, hatte, hätte;* (5) the displacement of *lân* by *lassen;* [32] (6) the displacement of *slahen/slân, fâhen/fân, hâhen/hân* and all their clipt present forms by full forms of the type of *schlagen, fangen*, etc.; (7) the displacement of the clipt past participles *gegân, gefân, gelân, gehân* ("gehabt"), *geslân, geblân*, etc. by the full forms *gegangen, geschlagen*, etc.; (8) the creation of the dissyllables *gehen, stehen, sehen, gehe, stehe, sehe*, etc. beside the old clipt forms *gehn, stehn, sᵉhn*, etc., which are now felt merely as colloquial forms of the normal dissyllabic words, with a clipping of endings which can be applied colloquially to any verb if euphony allows. (9) By the conta·ninative inclusion of *tun* in this

clipt ending group, the restored full formations have wiped out
the last remnant of the -*mi* inflection as a primary formation
in German speech feeling [43].

VIII. The Bearing of the MHG Clipt Verb Formations on the
Problem of the Normal Direction of Linguistic Development.

1. This double reversal of the direction of linguistic development
— *gân* and its kindred clipt forms first refraining for centuries to
encroach on preterit formations, then thru a space of three or four
centuries forming an aggressive and conquering group, then again
rereversing the direction of their development and building again
the forms they had begun to destroy — is the most classic
illustration of the fact that not only the elements and special
groups of a language are subject to shifting and displacement,
but that along with them speech feeling itself is subject either
to a slow drift (often cumulative), or (with the breaking down of
old forms) to a more rapid displacement and re-formation. The
system of phonetic variation which reacht its overdevelopment
and culmination in the late OHG and early MHG period, had
developt slowly and cumulatively since Indo-European times.
At last its strength became great enough to inaugurate the new
formations and groupings of the clipt preterit type, at variance
with the older types of stem formation, but not disagreeing with
the accumulating total of phonetic variations. Then, at the close of
the MHG period, with the development of a new trend in phonetic
feeling, the new groupings based on former speech feeling col-
lapsed, and the direction of development was again reverst. But
every one of these diverse developments lay in the direction of
the then prevailing speech feeling.

2. This throws light on an important moot question, namely,
that of the normal order and direction of structural and morphological development. Do inflections and affixes normally form
by excretion and analysis, as -*er* in *kälber*, -*en* in *frauen* and -*z*- in
lie/*lie-z(en)*? Or do they normally form by accretion and composition, as in Fr. *donner-ai*, *triste-ment* and Ger. *ge-macht*, *faul-
heit*? Fortunately or unfortunately the adherents of both views
can bring an inexhaustible array of irrefragable illustrations and
proofs of their respective views.

---

[43] *Bin* is not an exception to this statement, as it is no longer felt as an analyz-
able inflected form.

3. The fact that all these divergent OHG, MHG and NHG developments agreed with the then drift of the language, and were in accord with the speech feeling and establisht norms which formed their basis and background, suggests a different principle which easily reconciles and includes both these opposing views: Speech feeling determines the form and direction of specific linguistic developments, and these are always in the direction of the establisht norms and patterns of the language in which they occur. The survival of new formations depends on their conformity to this rule.

4. It is for this reason that phonetic, structural, inflectional and syntactical types and shiftings usually occur, not detacht and in disorder, but in analogous and orderly groups, as in the case of the different groups of syncopating verbs considered above.

OLD PRETERITES OF THE FIRST ABLAUT CLASS IN THE 1671 WITTENBERG REVISION OF THE LUTHERAN BIBLE [1]

BY D. B. SHUMWAY

UNIVERSITY OF PENNSYLVANIA

One of the most interesting archaisms of the Lutheran Bible is the retention of the old preterite singular in *ei* of the first class of ablaut verbs. Rudolf von Raumer in his *Vorschläge zur Revision von der M. Luther-Bibelübersetzung*, Jena 1884, states that the Lüneburg Bible of 1677, the Nürnberg edition of 1692 and the Wittenberg edition of 1703 still preserve preterites like *bleib, treib*, etc. Virgil Moser in his interesting article: *Frühneuhochdeutsche Studien* [2] compared the 49 instances which he gives with the forms of all the editions at his disposal and points out that an Ulm edition of 1671 introduced the new forms with *ie* in two sevenths of the cases, e. g. always *erschien, biesz, schrieb* and predominantly *blieb*. He suggests that the disuse of the preterite in the Upper German dialects may have been the reason for the early disappearance of the form *ei*. It gave way, however, very slowly. Nearly thirty years later the Nürnberg edition of 1698 has only one new form to every four of the old. The Wittenberg edition of 1702 has the same proportion, whereas in the Nürnberg edition of the same year the new forms predominate in the proportion of three fifths to two fifths.

---

[1] This article is a rearrangement of one section of a longer paper: *The language of the 1671 Wittenberg Revision of the Lutheran Bible* which the author hopes will shortly appear in the *Germanic Review*. This revision was undertaken by the theological faculty of the University of Wittenberg and was published by Balthasar Christoph Wust. In the preface they state: »Zu dem Ende, dasz Lutheri Arbeit rein und wol erhalten werde, ist die H. Bibel noch unlängst widerum auffs neue von uns mit Fleiß durchgegangen und revidiert worden.« This *Vorrede* is dated Wittenberg March 10th, 1671 and is signed by the »Dechant, Senior, Doctores und Professores der theologischen Facultät daselbst«.

[2] *PBB.* 47 (1923), 357—407.

Just why Moser confined himself to examining only the 49 cases he gives I fail to see. They were certainly not the only occurrences of the sing. pret. of verbs of this class, for I noted no less than 160 instances, counting those given by Moser which I carefully compared. If he desired to make such an examination at all, it should have been based on all the instances occurring and not on just a few.

The edition of 1671 has made considerable progress in introducing the new forms. Moser's statement for 1622 is that *ei* is retained in all but two cases (Ex. 16, 10; Judith 4, 5) which already appear in the edition of 1545. In the Bible of 1671 66 new forms appear to 532 old forms, or about in the proportion of 1 to 8. Still this is much less than that in 1698 which has 1 to 4 and that of the Nürnberg edition of the same year which has 3 to 5, as we have seen. In the last quarter of the 17th century the old forms disappeared quite rapidly, still a goodly number continued over into the 18th century.

Taking the individual verbs in alphabetical order the statistics for the Bible of 1671 are as follows:

beissen: *beisz* twice: Num. 21, 9; Acts 20, 11.

bleiben: *bleib* 114 times: Num. 21, 9; 2 Sam. 13, 20, etc.; *blieb* 14 times: Gen. 28, 11; Tob. 2, 13, etc.

leiden: *leid* or *leyd* 4 times: Gen. 41, 55; 1 Pet. 223 etc.; none of *litt*.

(er)greiffen: *(er)greiff* 38 times: Gen. 44, 6; Matth. 8, 15, etc.; one of *griff:* 2 Mac. 14, 17.

reissen: *reiss* 70 times: Ps. 18, 20, etc.; once *zurisse*, ind.: Jdg. 14, 6.

reiten: *reit* 9 times: Deut. 22, 22; 1 Sam. 25, 20, etc.; once *du rittest:* Hab. 4, 8.

(er)scheinen: *(er)schein* 25 times: Gen. 12, 7; 18, 1, etc.; *(er)schien* 22 times: Ex. 16, 21; Matth. 1, 20, etc.; one of *erschiene* 2 Mac. 11, 8. One sees that the new forms are almost as numerous as the old.

schleichen: *schleich* once: Tob. 8, 15; *beschlich* twice: Gen. 41, 4; 42, 21.

schmeissen: only one case: *du schmissest:* Hab. 4, 13.

(be)schneid: *schneid* 11 times: 2 Sam. 10, 4 etc.;; *beschneid* 5 times: 1 Mac. 2, 46, etc.

schreiben: *schreib* 42 times: Ex. 24, 4, etc.; *schrieb* 8 times: Dan. 5, 5, etc.; *unterschrieb* once: Dan. 6, 10; *schriebe* once: Judith 4, 5.

schreien: *schrey* 33 times: Gen. 27, 34; Jonah 2, 2, etc.; none of *schrie.*

schweigen: *schweig* 10 times: Gen. 34, 5; Matth. 26, 63; Acts 15, 12, etc.; *schwieg* once: Gen. 24, 21. This instance is also found in the Bible of 1622, but not in that of 1545.

steigen: *steig* 31 times: Josh. 4, 19; 2 Sam. 7, 18, etc.; none of *stieg.*

streichen: *bestrich* once: Judith 16, 10; no other form.

streiten: *streit* 34 times: Ex. 17, 8; Josh. 10, 14, etc.; two false preterites: *streitet:* Jdg. 9, 45; *stritte:* Judith 5, 14.

treiben: *treib* 37 times: Gen. 3, 24; Jdg. 1, 20, etc.; *trieb* 15 times: Mk. 5, 40; Acts 7, 19; 18, 16, 18, etc.

weichen: *weich* 31 times: Gen. 12, 9; John 6, 15, etc.; no other form.
The preterite plural of verbs of this class conforms in every respect to the modern norm. Those with a long vowel are:

blieben: Num. 11, 5; 14, 38, etc.

schienen: 2 Mac. 10, 29, etc.

schryen: Ps. 22, 6, etc.

schwiegen: Acts 11, 18, etc.

stiegen: Josh. 4, 18, etc.

trieben: Ps. 107, 23, etc.

With short vowel:

bissen: Num. 21, 6, etc.

litten: Wis. 18, 1 or *lidten:* 1 Sam. 2, 5, etc.

wichen: Acts 1, 4, etc.
Weak verbs now belonging to the first ablaut class are:

gleichen: *ich gleichet:* Wis. 7, 9; *vergleichet,* ppl.: Prov. 27, 15. Strong forms of this originally weak verb do not appear before the 17th cent. Weak forms are found occasionally as late as Schiller.

leihen: *leiheten:* Ex. 12, 36, but the strong ppl. *geliehen* occurs: Jer. 15, 10, both instances being in Luther.

meiden: *meidete:* Tob. 1, 10; *meidet* (pret.): Tob. 1, 5; Job 1, 1. Weak forms are not found before the 16th century.

preisen: *preiseten:* Gen. 12, 15; *gepreiset:* Luke 4, 15. This verb from French *priser* was originally weak. Weak forms continue in part to the 19. century, tho strong forms appear as early as the 15th cent.

scheinen has the weak pret. *scheinete:* 1 Mac. 6, 39, as in L., otherwise the verb is strong, as above. The weak forms, which do not occur before the 16th cent., may be under the influence of the MLG.

schmeissen: in the meaning of "befoul", is conjugated weak: *schmeyste:* Tob. 2, 11. This verb which appears already in OHG. continues down to the 18th century.

speien: *speyete:* Jonah 2, 11; Matth. 15, 9; Wis. 11, 19; *ausgespeyet:* Lev. 18, 28; Num. 12, 13; 2 Peter 2, 22. Weak forms appear as early as the 12. cent. and are very common in the 16th and 17th centuries.

weisen: *anweisete:* Gen. 46, 28; *beweiseten:* 2 Mac. 14, 22; ppl. *beweiset:* Ps. 31, 22; *überweiset:* 2 Mac. 4, 45; *unterweiseten:* Acts 14, 21; *geweiset:* Matth. 3, 7. Strong forms of this originally weak verb begin in the 15th cent. and predominate since the 16th century.

A few instances of the old strong forms of *versiegen* were noted, which in older NHG. was *verseigen* and *verseihen,* e. g. inf. *verseihen*: Jer. 51, 36. The imperative is *verseige:* Is. 44, 27; the past ppl. *versiegen:* Ps. 107, 33; Hos. 9, 14; this latter form is used as late as Herder. The present tense of the new weak verb is also found inf. *versiegen:* Is. 19, 5; 3rd plu. *versiegen:* Sir. 40, 13.

"DER RIHTER UND DER TEUFEL"

BY ARCHER TAYLOR
UNIVERSITY OF CHICAGO

The tale which Chaucer's Friar tells on the road to Canterbury has recently been used to illustrate the proper editorial handling of traditional materials, — a subject involving the general reliability of Asbjörnsen and Moe's collection, — and the differences between literary and popular narrative style [1]. Since the tale has thus acquired an importance perhaps beyond its deserts, it is worth while to list and discuss briefly the dozen or so versions which have lately come to my attention [2]. These new texts show the longevity of the story versified by the Stricker

---

[1] R. Th. Christiansen *Festskrift til Hjalmar Pettersen* (1926); Jan de Vries *Het sprookje* Antwerp [1929] pp. 91 ff.

[2] About 30 versions are listed and 20 of them are discussed in my article "The Devil and the Advocate" *PMLA* XXXVI (1921) 35 ff. In that article certain matters call for comment either by way of correction or addition: (Note 3): The MHG text was first printed in Lassberg *Liedersaal* II (1846) 341 ff. There exists a modernization by K. Simrock which I have not seen; see F. W. Wander *Deutsches Sprichwörterlexikon*, s. v. "Anderes 7." (Note 11): Weber's text may be found in Reclam's *Universalbibliothek*. (Note 13): The story is reprinted in Tewaag *Erzählungen aus Hessen* (1888) p. 87. (Note 15): Usteri's text contains an incident involving goats which I failed to mention. (Note 22): The story is found in P. Kennedy *Legendary Fictions of the Irish Celts* (London 1866), pp. 147—8 = W. B. Yeats *Fairy and Folk Tales of the Irish Peasantry* (London 1888). (Note 25): The story is found in Zaunert *Deutsche Märchen seit Grimm* I 368. (Note 27): Correct the reference to read: p. 104 § 48 ¶ 149. (Note 33): Insert at the end of the first paragraph: Chauvin III 69 no. 39.

To the list in note 2 of my article I add several which I have not seen: (1) E. von Wolzogen *Schwankbuch* (1922) p. 75; (2) Th. van Rijswijck *Poetische Luimen* 44: (3) *Niedersachsen* I 110; (4) *Bienenkorb* 6, c. 69; (5) J. D. Ernst *Bilderhaus* (1675) I 769.

References are conveniently assembled in Feilberg *Bidrag til en ordbog over jyske almuesmål* (1886—1912) s. v. "ladefoged", "ridefoged" and Pauli's *Schimpf und Ernst* (ed. Bolte, 1924) n. 81. The texts in the *Dansk Folkemindesamling* (cited under no. 81 in Lunding *FF Commun.* 2) are printed in Kristensen *Danske Skjæmtesagn* (notes 17 and 28 in my article). Feilberg's reference to "Vang Reglo" deals with a different story, as does Kristensen *Fra Bindestue og Kolle* I no. 17.

and by Chaucer. It will be remembered that the story tells how the Devil, who is accompanying an avaricious advocate, refuses everything that is offered him until someone curses the advocate. The Devil seizes and bears off the advocate because the curse is sincere. In the Stricker's story we learn why the advocate is cursed, viz., because he has unjustly possessed himself of an old woman's cow. This explanation is not found in Chaucer and the exemplum tradition. Accordingly we may say with confidence that the three Finnish tales taken down in the last few years [3] are descendants of the oral tradition on which the Stricker drew [4]. This form of the story appears, therefore, to be very old and to have maintained itself only on the extreme border of the area in which the story was current.

Within that area another form became widely known, a form first reported by Caesarius of Heisterbach, later employed by Chaucer, and firmly established in exemplum tradition. This form, which is recognizable by the absence of the cow, has persisted in tradition on the shores of the Baltic. In addition to those previously known, I note three Danish versions [5] and one from Pomerania [6]. It is, furthermore, reported from what was formerly Austrian Silesia in a form which appears to have undergone literary embellishment [7]. Altered in still a different way, this traditional version is found in the homiletic writings of Peter Bornemisza (Abstemius), which appeared between 1573 and 1579. As Kirjály points out, this version is derived from the Hungarian Esopic tradition, for only there does the Devil hire himself out as a laborer and demand as pay whatever is seriously given to him [8]. Jan de Vries makes it clear that the Limburg version is a derivative of the exemplum tradition, as is also the Norwegian

---

[3] See the references in Aarne *FF Communications* 33 no. 821 C*. Copies of these three versions, which were taken down between 1908 and 1918, are in the University of Chicago library.

[4] E. g., "Ni vaimol ei ollu raha maksa ja ku henel ol yks lehm, ni see tultti ja myytti ja henee lehmäs men." (The old woman had no money to pay and since she had a cow, so they came and sold it and her cow was lost). The passage is quoted from Kallio no. 77. Similar passages occur in the other texts.

[5] *Skattegraveren* II (1884) 105 no. 470; E. T. Kristensen *Jyske Folkeminder* IV (1880) 341; E. T. Kristensen *Danske Sagn* VI (1900) 755 no. 761.

[6] Haas and Knoop *Bl. f. pomm. Volksk.* VIII (1900) 100.

[7] Czech v. Czechenherz *Zs. f. öst. Volksk.* X (1904) 144—45.

[8] "Deutsche Sagen und Schwänke in einem ungarischen Teufelsbuche" *Ungar. Jahrb.* I (1921) 245.

story taken down by Hans Ross [9]. Beyond pointing out that the oral Norwegian tradition, which forms the basis of the story printed by Asbjörnsen and Moe, follows the exemplum tradition, we need not enter into the discussion of the evidence so clearly and carefully presented by Christiansen. In this classification we cannot distinguish sharply between tales derived from the exemplum and tales derived from the oral tradition in which the exemplum finds its origin. I have little doubt that those versions which have bookish antecedents, e. g., Bornemisza, go back ultimately to manuscripts of the exemplum. On the other hand, it is altogether likely that many of these north German, Baltic, and Scandinavian versions derive directly from the oral tradition which gave rise to the exemplum.

An abbreviated form, which is first met with in the writings of Hans Sachs, is found again in recent Danish tradition [10]. In this form we have merely the weeping child which is offered to the Devil and the carrying off of the lawyer. This variation is rather frequent in the region where the story is most frequently told: it occurs three times in Danish and once in German tradition. A connection with Hans Sachs is unlikely, inasmuch as the omission of a single incident, and particularly of an incident forming part of a series, is an ordinary mishap in a tale's life.

A very corrupt version is found in a Danish manuscript play of the first quarter of the eighteenth century, but it offers no points of interest and appears to have suffered mutilation for the purpose of adapting the story to use as a sub-plot [11].

The distribution of these texts agrees well enough with the origin of the story in northwestern Germany. There it was early recorded and there it has remained in popular tradition, in Limburg, Westphalia, Hesse, Oldenburg, Bremen, Pomerania and Denmark. Elsewhere the story seems not to have become

---

[9] J. de Vries *Het sprookje* pp. 91 ff. (A text reformed from P. Kemp *Limburgs sagenboek*, which I have not seen) and pp. 95—96 (for the Norwegian tale). See also the references in R. Th. Christiansen *Norske folkeminne* II (Kristiania 1921) no. 1183. The story has received the number 1186 in Aarne-Thompson *FF Commun.* 74, where the reference to Christiansen's article should be corrected to read *Festskrift til Hjalmar Pettersen* and the number 1183 should be inserted after "Norw".

[10] See *PMLA* XXXVI 51 ff.; Jens Kamp *Danske Folkeminder, Aeventyr, Folkesagn, Gaader, Rim og Folketro* (Odense 1877) pp. 286—7 no. 898.

[11] See S. B. Smith *Studier på det gamle danske Skuespils Område* (Copenhagen 1883) pp. 117—23.

thoroughly acclimated: the oldest version, the Stricker's, leaves
no trace in the popular literature of southern and eastern Germany [12]. Versions reported from elsewhere than northwestern
Germany are either definitely literary in origin and association
or extremely corrupt.

Apart from the connection of the story with Chaucer, — a
point on which these new versions throw no light, — the most
interesting detail in the story's life is the preservation by Finnish
narrators of the form found in the thirteenth century verse
of the Stricker. Since his narrative was entirely inaccessible
until almost the middle of the nineteenth century and then
became known only to a small group of scholars, — Lassberg's
Liedersaal is a rare book and von der Hagen's Gesamtabenteuer
cannot have enjoyed a wide circulation, — we have one more
example of the tenacity of folk-memory. The nice question
remains whether the folk-versions of northwestern Germany and
Denmark likewise represent the independent preservation of a
story disseminated throughout European lettered circles by
Caesarius' exemplum.

---

[12] The text printed by Schmeller is, as I have pointed out (PMLA XXXVI 49
n. 20), a translation of Pauli's jest into the dialect of Aschaffenburg. Under no
circumstances is it evidence for the persistence of the tradition in Bavaria. This
disposes of the notion mentioned by de Vries (Het sprookje p. 90) that the story
is Bavarian.

A VIEW OF LESSING

BY WILLIAM GUILD HOWARD
HARVARD UNIVERSITY

On Lessing's birthday two centuries ago George Berkeley, then Dean, later Bishop, was aboard ship off the coast of North America. Three years earlier he had written of this region:

> There shall be sung another golden age,
> The rise of empire and of arts,
> The good and great inspiring epic rage,
> The wisest heads and noblest hearts.
>
> .   .   .
> Westward the course of empire takes its way — —

For the better part of the ensuing three years Berkeley dwelt on the shores of Narragansett Bay, reconciling himself as best he might to the necessary abandonment of his charitable plan for a college at Bermuda, but finding life in New England congenial, and leaving behind him a fragrant memory.

So far as I am aware, Lessing displayed no interest in our New England. The course of empire never engaged his attention, nor was he by nature endowed with missionary zeal. In spite of his passion for doing things and getting things done in his time and place, he was primarily a literary, philosophical, and theological scholar who rather kept within range of the Mediterranean beacons of civilization than turned his gaze towards these plantations as yet not very productive in contributions to learning. Nevertheless, it is pleasant to recall that in Lessing's time, even as Berkeley had found, there were institutions here respectable for age, as for other attributes, and a population of which an acute observer[1] could say that it had "retained to an incalculable degree qualities which had faded from ancestral England with the days of Queen Elizabeth"; namely, "spontaneity, enthusiasm, and

---

[1] Barrett Wendell: *A Literary History of America*, New York, 1900; cf. pp. 19, 77.

versatility." To a people so enduringly Elizabethan the venerator of Shakespeare would not have been indifferent. But he might have discovered additional characteristics: first, a sturdy individualism which, as to the spiritual realm, made every man, disdaining a mediator, bent upon proving himself one of God's elect, and as to the material, made him watchful over his interests in trade and at the town meeting; and secondly, so persistent a particularism that the smallest of the states became the last to ratify the Federal Constitution. Could any German fail to perceive herein a certain affinity between this people and his own? The Germans are a nation of individualists, and their proneness to particularism, keeping them for generations internationally impotent and to this day so inconveniently multiplying their political parties in the *Reich*, has more than any other single cause brought to pass, on the one hand, an infinite variety of separate existences — so picturesque and romantic when reflected in art — and has contributed, on the other hand, to create for them that fecundity of the inner life which qualifies them to be a people of poets and thinkers.

It is no accident that the Protestant Reformation originated in Germany. The Protestant Reformation was an assertion of confident, self-sufficient individualism; and Martin Luther, the Reformer, was a German to the marrow. So was Gotthold Ephraim Lessing. On many accounts the two names belong together. Such parallel as we draw may begin with the purely historical observation that without Luther there could have been no Lessing. It has been prettily said that of the many consequences of the Reformation — not all, certainly, salutary — one was the creation of a new institution of inestimable advantage to the community, the Protestant parsonage [2]. Nothing, surely, prevented the parish house of the Roman Catholic Church from being a source of social as well as spiritual light and warmth; it often was and still is; but the parish priest being celibate, the house was sterile. We of New England, at least, do not need a demonstration of what the difference means. We have only to remember how many of the makers of our history have been scions of clerical stock. Lessing too was the son of a Protestant parson.

To be sure, Johann Gottfried Lessing early became alarmed at his boy's free-thinking and no doubt remained, as Lowell

---

[2] Cf. W. Brecht: *»Einführung in das 16. Jahrhundert«*, GRM, III, pp. 340 ff.

shrewdly surmises, "like many other fathers, permanently astonished at the fruit of his loins". Other ministers among the orthodox were more than astonished as time went on; they waxed indignant and grew not a little apprehensive, lest the citadel in which they felt secure against open assault might come tumbling about their ears because a sapper and miner was dislodging its foundations. I should exceed the sphere of my competence if I undertook to define Lessing's theology, perhaps so if I even expressed an opinion of his religion, though the evidence for this is spread before us in sundry writings, whereas his theology is largely a matter of inference from imperfect testimony. In any case, I assume, we are more concerned with the spirit than the letter of his doctrine and should be most solicitous to discern his attitude towards the faith and the speculation of his time. It was a time when Protestant orthodoxy was far more rigid than Roman Catholic dogma, for all its positiveness, had ever been — a time, accordingly, when a generation of rationalists either abandoned Revelation altogether, as incapable of accommodation to reason, or firmly upheld it as susceptible of confirmation by logic and of proof on the basis of evidence furnished by the senses. With the former class Lessing was not impatient. At the age of twenty he composed his comedy *Der Freigeist*, describing the titular hero as "without religion, but of an abundantly virtuous disposition". In the course of the action this hero is made to acknowledge that a clergyman is not necessarily a hypocrite, and he is none too gently converted from his hasty intolerance, though not exactly converted to religion. With the latter class, on the contrary, Lessing contends as with those who abuse the greatest of our natural gifts, who subject to slavery that faculty through which alone man is capable of being free. He is of a mind to save Revelation from its friends. In other words, Revelation, he holds, is not to be preserved by any attempt to demonstrate that in reason it is a final formulation of truth; rather the truths of Revelation invite translation into truths of reason; and they can be so translated, if we perceive that Revelation is not a product but a process, is as yet only a partial, progressive communication of such truths as mankind has been successively ready to grasp, conformably with a Providential plan for the education of the human race. Shall we ever arrive at the entire comprehension of truth? We have all eternity in which to try. And what, though we do not? It is the endeavor and not the attainment that shall make us also perfect.

I would not mar by a single superfluous word the noble passage in which Lessing declares his choice [3]. But I may be permitted to adduce a private communication recently made to me by an eminent theological colleague [4], who thus confesses to an obligation both professional and personal:

> Some forty years ago, when I began to lecture on the Philosophy of Religion, I found in *The Education of the Human Race* and in *Nathan the Wise* the roots of the modern liberal theology, and had the happiness of impressing this view on successive classes. Lessing took an epoch-making step in the interpretation of religion, and this it was which so long ago arrested my attention and has remained my reassurance.

Lessing, then, who paid homage to Luther not the less sincere because occasioned by polemics with the Lutherans of his day, is a continuator of Luther in Luther's most important line of activity, that is, in the cause of religious emancipation. But if we take a large view of the two hundred years separating them, and properly appraise what each effectuated in his day and generation, we shall see Lessing as a second Luther in respect to a still more comprehensive achievement. It will not have escaped notice that I used just now an expression of Matthew Arnold's defining the relation in which he conceived Heinrich Heine stood to Goethe, that of a continuator. I should be the last to proclaim Heine a safe guide in either criticism or history. But he nevertheless often reveals no common penetration in his *aperçus*, and, journalistic though his language is apt to be, he has a knack at neat formulation. Heine [5] brings Luther and Lessing together as I have done, albeit for reasons that are not altogether mine. He calls Lessing the continuator of Luther; he says, "Germany has produced since Luther no greater and better man that Gotthold Ephraim Lessing. These two are our pride and our delight". He avers "that Luther is not only the greatest, but also the most German man of our history; that in his character are magnificently united all the virtues and the faults of the Germans, so that even in his personality he is a representative of wonderful Germany". Heine particularly refers to those mundane constitu-

---

[3] »Vater, gib! die reine Wahrheit ist ja doch nur für dich allein!« *Eine Duplik* (1778).

[4] Rev. Dr. Francis Greenwood Peabody.

[5] *Der Salon*, II, *Werke*, ed. Elster, IV, pp. 190, 191, 240.

ents which made Luther a rough and ready controversialist as well as a tender husband and father, a boon companion, and a poet. He speaks of these elements as "that earthly admixture, without which Luther could not have been a man of action. Pure spirits cannot act." We should say much the same of Lessing. He also was a man of action, the tenderest husband, a good companion, by no means a pure spirit, but a being of quick sympathies and sanguine temperament. Condemned by circumstances to a life prevailingly solitary, he greatly preferred the market-place; and the deeds to which he aspired, which in fact he performed, were no more than prepared in the closet. Lessing's historical mission was to be a Siegfried and to revive the Sleeping Beauty of German nationality.

The first half of the sixteenth century in Germany fell, admittedly, far short of the spacious times of great Elizabeth at the end of the century in England. But it was none the less a buoyant time of national vigor, of youthful promise, and of intrepid leadership towards better things for all mankind. Two forward movements got under way and for a while were fortunately united: one, the religious reformation, originating within the country and early assuming the form of a national crusade; the other, humanism, coming from without, but almost from the first appearing — by contrast to many of its aspects in Italy — as serious, moral, pedagogical, altruistic, democratic, national, intent upon raising German life to the plane of newly discovered humanity, not at all conspiring to set up an antique idol for indiscriminate worship. Erasmus and Reuchlin are the *oculi Germaniae*, Hutten is *Germaniae Libertatis Propugnator*, Melanchthon, the *Praeceptor Germaniae*. Nobody could regard Luther as a humanist otherwise than in principle. But in principle he is one: criticism, founded upon the independent interpretation of an authoritative text, is his instrument in theology, as it is that of Erasmus or Reuchlin in philology. Nobody, on the other hand, could be blind to the disintegrating tendency of classical scholarship in and of itself. It encourages the learned to smug satisfaction over against the unlearned; and if it lives in the world of Greek or Latin literature, it is *eo ipso* alienated from home. The gap between the learned and the unlearned which began to yawn wide almost immediately after the death of Luther was not invisible during his life-time, but it was not yet portentous. On the contrary, if Germany did not then produce a Shakespeare, she did give birth to a Hans Sachs — like the Englishman armed with small Latin and less Greek, but like him also in command of multifarious literature through translations. There is in the six thousand poems of the Nürnberg shoemaker an incontestable epic amplitude — more than that, there is a picture of contemporary Germany, such a conspectus of a civilization as Grillparzer declared to be the distinguishing mark of an epic poem [6]. Nor did Hans Sachs stand alone. Herder [7] was mayhap over-enthusiastic, but he found the *Reinke de Vos* of 1498 the greatest epic since Homer. And Hutten discovered an epic hero in Arminius.

It will be perceived that I now have in mind several of the suggestive pronouncements with which Goethe enriched the seventh book of *Dichtung und Wahrheit*. He speaks of the lapse of Germany into barbarism during the interval between Luther and Lessing, declaring that there had never been any lack of literary talent, but that there had been want of a national content for the forms of poetry, and adding that every nation which lays claim to greatness must have its epopoeia, "for which indeed the form of the epic poem is nowise necessary". We should identify the Elizabethan epopoeia, in this sense, with what is unfolded in Shakespeare's plays. Similarly, there is an epic energy stirring in the days of Luther; we see it in Hans Sachs; it is the same spirit when it prompts the leaders to utterance in the more immediate, more characteristically German, and less objective form of the lyric. The national content might be phrased as the ideal of a free church in a free state [8]. Goethe divined an epic hero in Götz von Berlichingen; and that Faust — also of the sixteenth century — in whom he symbolized striving, erring, and finally triumphant humanity is, for indomitable individualism, spiritually akin to the author of the war-song of faith, »Ein feste Burg ist unser Gott«, and likewise akin to that other patriotic warrior, "watch-dog" of the commonweal, as he modestly described himself, who undismayed reiterated to the end his slogan, »Ich hab's gewagt!«

The point which I am trying to make is, I trust, now apparent.

---

[6] »Lyrik, Epos, Drama, Aussicht, Umsicht, Ansicht«; cf. *Werke*, ed. Sauer, Wien, 1909 ff., Tgb. IV, Nr. 3186.

[7] Letter to Gleim, Apr. 12, 1793.

[8] Cf. Hutten, *Opera, passim*, and the "Wolfaria" in the *Fünfzehn Bundesgenossen* of Joh. Eberlin von Günzburg (1521).

I submit: the spirit animating Luther and Hutten is national, the tasks with which they grapple are present, and the vigor with which they express themselves gives earnest of illimitable achievement. Humanism has meant for them a broadening of view indeed, but chiefly a vivifying of what lies closest at hand.

I would not be understood to allege that when the German spirit, as above defined, fell into a torpor, it was in all respects a Sleeping Beauty which then awaited the coming of the appointed Prince. Confining myself to literature, I am aware of the crudeness of most of the prose and verse of the period which Wilhelm Schlegel characterized as »bürgerlich« and of which Wilhelm Scherer said that while it lasted aesthetic cultivation was at a low ebb. Certainly. But the crudeness was not a sign of degeneration; it was due partly to inexperience, partly to youthful indifference; the gravity of the issues at stake called for force and did not suffer luxurious elegance. Although beauty had not fully developed, character and capacity were there, when Germania was driven to hibernation through many winters of discontent.

It would be fantastic also to entertain the notion that Lessing was in all respects a representative German. He was not. As a very individualist he exercised his right to variation from the type. He was no lover of nature, of music, or of the formative arts; he was no sentimentalist or visionary of any sort; figuratively and also literally he was not a dreamer; he had no fondness for lyrical poetry — poetry was to him a means for the treatment of action: epic, therefore, or still better dramatic. In likening him to Siegfried I have regard to one feat only. Lessing read the *Nibelungenlied;* there is no indication that he was especially edified by it; certainly he had no share in Romantic enthusiasm for the Middle Ages, or in Rousseau's and Herder's enthusiasm for the primitive.

When Lessing came to the fore there were baroque extravagances to curtail and pseudo-classical errors to redeem — a thicket of thorns and brambles impeding progress to the Sleeping Beauty. But there was also a still more formidable obstacle. After a year's experience had shown the futility of trying to maintain a national theatre at Hamburg Lessing exclaimed [9], not without bitterness:

What a naïve idea, to provide a national theatre for the Germans, when we Germans are not yet a nation! I am not talking of a political constitution, but

[9] *Hamburgische Dramaturgie,* 101. St.

solely of moral character. One would almost have to say, the moral character of the Germans is the determination not to have any of their own. We are still the sworn imitators of everything foreign, especially the humble admirers of the never sufficiently to be admired French.

And yet a twelvemonth before this lament, in the very spring when the national theatre was started (1767), Lessing had himself given his fellow-countrymen, whether a nation or not, an example of national literature in *Minna von Barnhelm*.

Remarkable on many accounts, *Minna von Barnhelm* is in nothing more remarkable than for not being what we should expect a play to be which bears the sub-title »das Soldatenglück« and is advertised on its title page as »verfertigt im Jahre 1763«. Should we not at the very least expect the hero, Tellheim, to be every inch a soldier? Since none but the brave deserves the fair, we surely anticipate that the hand of Minna shall be the reward — perhaps delayed by some mischance, but still ultimately the reward — of conspicuous gallantry; and since we are at the height of an epoch glorious in Prussian history — glorious for all Germany, inasmuch as Prussia, by beating off a whole Continent of enemies, gave a new dignity to the German name, we instinctively raise our hands to applaud military glory effulgent in a worthy member of the victorious army. We are confronted, in fact, by nothing of the kind. Tellheim is as far from being a typical Prussian officer as a wearer of the king's coat could very well be. He is not even a Prussian subject — he is a volunteer in this service, he hardly knows why; he campaigns like a *grand seigneur* with a retinue of unreliable servants; the discipline in his battalion would scarcely pass muster in a provincial militia; he has been more than once under fire, he has been wounded, but we do not hear of his presence at Rossbach or Leuthen, and the great day for his command saw a brush with the enemy concerning which the chronicles are silent. This soldier, in short, deserves his fortune by exhibitions of magnanimity for which the war and its sequel give him opportunity, but which are altogether personal, in no sense military acts.

Nevertheless, the Seven Years' War is the epic stream which has caught up our magnanimous hero and which bears him, his comrades, their dependents and superiors along in its irresistible course. Somewhat after the manner of Diderot we have in *Minna von Barnhelm* a particular class of society isolated and its characteristic virtues displayed: personal honor, hardihood, mutual dependability, loyalty, *bonne camaraderie* — likewise some of the defects of these virtues exhibited. But Lessing avoids all commendation of the war in respect to either cause, conduct, or result. Instead, he gives us a vivid picture of its effects upon personal lives, such a picture as we have recently been able ourselves to contemplate in sordid reality. The principal figure in the foreground is distressed and distressing. Tellheim, dishonored and resentful, appears to be as little heroic as Achilles in his wrath; but both are heroes just the same; from the obscure retreat of the one as from the tent of the other we look out upon the theatre of mighty actions; and as Homer peoples the background of his picture with gods, so Lessing fails not to indicate, in the background to his, the potent personality of that Frederick whom the world has agreed to call the Great.

Goethe [10] describes *Minna von Barnhelm* as "the first theatrical production with a content, specifically of the time, taken from life of serious import", "the veriest offspring of the Seven Years' War, of perfect North-German national substance", "the revelation of a higher world than that of civic actuality or literary tradition". It is the earliest modern German drama and the prelude to the epopoeia of German classical literature. Furthermore, it is the masterpiece of a rationalist, a humanist whose acquaintance with Aristotle and Plautus made him but the more capable of being a German and the more eager to do for Germans what Plautus, in the light of Greek example, had done for Romans. But by "Germans" Lessing understood a community of individuals, not the constituent members of a state. Even love of country he confessed he could not comprehend; he felt no attachment to the soil — his nature was as little political as Goethe's was warlike. True, he never said patriotism was "the last refuge of a scoundrel" — he was too liberal for that — but he did think it "at most an heroic weakness" [11]. What he wished, therefore, to do with *Minna von Barnhelm* bore no semblance to adulation, had no part in propaganda; it was something more intimate, higher in aspiration and at the same time more vital; for he was a humanitarian — and now we recall that "earthly admixture" which Heine attributed to Luther. Lessing was a warm lover of his kind, who wished to move his fellows to quickly reactive

---

[10] D. u. W., VII.
[11] Cf. Letters to Gleim, Dec. 16, 1758, Feb. 14, 1759.

sympathy, and who knew — in the words of Gottfried Keller — that "you can bring round the bone and sinew of the people only with the full momentum of truth". In the ripeness of age Goethe admonished his disciples, "Let every man be in his own way a Greek, but see that he be one!" Lessing, before Goethe, was a Greek in *his* way, and this was the way of an enlightened spirit fructifying with formative life the responsive reality of experience. Reality so informed arose as a new art for the Germans of 1767. Criticism had penetrated the secrets of creation.

The distinctive excellence of *Minna von Barnhelm* resides in its authentic personalities, individuals, particularized, conceived in their integrity and produced before us in unaffected self-evidence. "What an admirable piece!" exclaims Grillparzer [12]. "Evidently the best German comedy. Comedy? Well, yes; why not? So genuinely German in all its characters, and precisely in that regard unique in German literature." Such praise from the censorious Austrian who, on the whole, looked askance at our North-German author, is doubly noteworthy, for its greater weight as coming from Grillparzer and for the technical question that it raises. What kind of comedy is *Minna von Barnhelm*?

Although Lessing in his youth was ambitious to become a German Molière, it does not appear that he assiduously sought instruction in the plays of that master. Everything in the German's theory and practice points to a more democratic ideal than can be found even in the splendid naturalness of him who studied the court and knew the city of Louis XIV. But in *Minna von Barnhelm* Lessing had a happy thought, comparable for fruitfulness with the fundamental idea of *l'Avare* or *le Misanthrope*, though not unaffected by the exaggerated virtuosity of *le Fils naturel* or *le Père de famille* — I mean that for the springs of action in his drama he envisaged not simply an interminable series of those incongruities, maladjustments, mishaps, and misunderstandings — including amazing credulity under the stress of passion — which prompt us to the reflection "What fools these mortals be!" — but also a fundamental incongruity upon which to erect a world quite out of joint. Something of the kind is suggested by the baffling sub-title to which I have already alluded. The initial impulse, however, which turns this whole world topsy-turvy is this: during a time of public warfare

---

[12] Tgb. II, Nr. 1142.

private virtue flourishes and lovers' joy reigns; when public warfare ceases righteousness and peace do not kiss each other, but peace brings in her train public wrong, private sorrow, and personal estrangement. Everything is now awry. Of the Prussian major, by nature generous to the point of lavishness, we might say — paraphrasing a gruesome verdict of Hebbel's passed upon another man [13] — that pertinacity has usurped the place of his soul; and of his Saxon betrothed, by nature bountiful as a May morning, that she becomes as capricious as April. Wishing to convert her lover to her own conception of realities, she institutes a stratagem in which she herself all too soon becomes inextricably ensnared. The lovers' quarrel eventuates indeed in a reintegration of love, but more because the Gordion knot is cut for them than because by themselves they could possibly have disentangled the snarl.

Criticizing Kleist's *Prinz Friedrich von Homburg*, Hebbel lays down a maxim that may be found generally useful in the interpretation of plays. The drama, he says, represents a thought which seeks to become a deed either through action or through patience. The protagonist, that is, is impelled by an idea, and antagonism to its realization gives rise to the action. If we should ask what Tellheim's idea is, the immediate answer would shape itself into some such formula as this: honor is the supreme good; without it, nothing is possible, and when it is impugned, no means are too costly, no sacrifice is too great, to restore it. Similarly, Minna cherishes the idea that love is the supreme good; without it, nothing is worth much; and everything inconsistent with it is negligible. It is obvious that both positions are tenable; that they are mainly characteristic of the two sexes; that in this absolute form they are irreconcilable; that, therefore, they might, as well as not, be factors in a tragedy; and that they are fit to yield a comedy when taken with uncompromising, not to say exaggerated, exclusiveness by persons who in reality are not only lovers, but also respectively a man and a woman of honor. Love is the fulfillment of the law; but Minna's means are totally inadequate to prove that love may defy the law. Doubtless, a good name is rather to be chosen than great riches; but there

---

[13] His own father : »ein herzensguter, treuer, wohlmeinender Mann; aber die Armut hatte die Stelle seiner Seele eingenommen«; *Werke*, ed. Werner, Berlin, 1913 ff., Tgb. I, Nr. 1323.

is something more substantial than the bubble reputation, as Tellheim, in his right mind, well knows: self-respect is a higher good than the respect of others. Thus the contestants are both in the right, and both in the wrong — wherefore, we may parenthetically remark, we have a comedy instead of a tragedy. Easier, however, though it be to sympathize with the untroubled gaiety of the good-hearted maiden than with the purblind stubbornness of the sorely troubled man, we are left with a sense that after all Tellheim is justified and has reinforced the truth of an assertion which, as we attribute it to him, has a far deeper meaning than on the lips of Lovelace:

> I could not love thee, dear, so much,
> Loved I not honor more.

Furthermore, it is plain that the foregoing generalities, that any such rationalistic formulations, not only disconcert aesthetic reaction to this drama, but also obscure what is most meritorious in the artistry employed. We have before us nothing so simple as protagonist, antagonist, victory or defeat, nothing so mechanical as thesis, antithesis, and synthesis. Neither Tellheim nor Minna is the mere embodiment of an idea, though Minna is unmistakably much the less complex and significant personality — as such, perhaps, the less entitled to prevail. And the significance of Tellheim's more ample endowment of human qualities is not made manifest by what he does in pursuit of an abstract ideal. The play is, indeed, not devoid of action, nor — especially in the conduct and the successive situations of the sharply individualized minor characters — of those appeals to indulgent humor which are the prerogative of comedy. But the plot, with its juggling of rings, in which Minna involves Tellheim, is neither very clever nor very useful, except as it furnishes occasion for exposition and argument: Tellheim seems to be in singularly unstable equilibrium and Minna to be singularly lacking in both perspicacity and foresight. These are, however, but the symptoms and the signs of passion. The real action is in the breast of the hero; the conflict between love and honor [14] he alone has fought out to a victory

---

[14] By "honor" I here mean a subjective standard of right conduct. Tellheim's self-respect will neither permit Minna to share his disgrace, nor permit him to live on her bounty. For the most part, however, — and notably in Act IV, Scene vi — Tellheim and Minna mean by "honor" something that can be taken away and restored, i. e. social recognition, objective approbation. Tellheim shares the extreme sensitiveness of the aristocratic and military caste on this score: "Caesar's

which he thinks secure, until the sudden apparition of Minna renews the struggle in an aggravated form.

That Tellheim, then, with all his imperfections on his head, is a man and a brother makes the deepest impression and, confirmed by the impressive verisimilitude of such another character as Werner, constitutes the revolutionary excellence of this composition. Such was, moreover, precisely the effect aimed at. Why, queries Lessing, all the toil and trouble of writing and enacting a drama, unless we desire to attain in the fullest measure what is fully attainable only on the stage? [15] Like any depiction of life, the drama will convey, at least by implication, a moral lesson — it may legitimately be produced for that explicit purpose.

> Ich hab' es öfters rühmen hören,
> Ein Komödiant könnt' einen Pfarrer lehren.

Hebbel, and sometimes Schiller, will construct a plot that almost literally conforms to the following definition:

> If we refer a general moral precept to a particular case, attribute reality to this particular case, and out of it compose a story in which the moral precept s intuitively perceptible, such a composition is called a fable.

These are the well-known words of Lessing [16], the maker of definitions. If we remember that *Fabel* means either "fable" or "plot", and if — as without unseemly violence we might do — we render the phrase »daraus eine Geschichte dichten« by "invent an action involving it", we may at the end substitute "drama" for "fable" and arrive at the definition, "such a composition is called a drama". But not in Lessing's sense; and he is a maker of distinctions before he makes definitions. To the dramatist, he declares, it is immaterial whether or not a general truth can be inferred from the action of his persons [17]. Again [18]:

> The drama lays no claim to a single, definite doctrine emerging from its plot; it aims either at the passions which the course and the peripeteia of its

---

wife must be above suspicion"; so long as his mind is befogged by egotism or hardened by opposition he makes no distinction between rectitude and repute. But when he clearly hears the call to altruistic duty, he casts to the winds the talisman to which he has been clinging: »Nein, das ist dringender« (IV, viii), »Lieber hier alles im Stiche gelassen« (V, i). This instinctive turning to the really preferable proves that his allegiance is after all neither to a phantom nor to a fetish. G. Kettner, in his admirable *Lessings Dramen* (Berlin, 1904), is too little discriminating on this point (pp. 96 ff.).

[15] *Hamburgische Dramaturgie*, 80. St.
[16] *Abhandlungen über die Fabel*, I (conclusion).
[17] *Hamburgische Dramaturgie*, 33. St.
[18] *Ibid.*, 35. St.

plot are capable of inflaming and sustaining, or at the pleasure which a true and vivid depiction of morals and characters affords; and both aims require a certain rounding out of the action, a certain satisfying ending — something that we can dispense with in the moral narrative, because in it, all our attention is concentrated upon the general proposition of which the particular case gives so illuminating an example.

Moreover [19]:

Since the illusion is far more potent in a drama than in a mere narrative, the persons in the former interest us far more than in the latter, and we are not satisfied with seeing their fate settled just for the present moment, but wish to rest forever content with the settlement.

And now we are prepared to answer the question, what kind of comedy *Minna von Barnhelm* is. It is a true comedy: it incites to laughter at manifold human frailty — in no wise to ridicule thereof — and it also moves to pity for well accredited people in affectingly real tribulations. Secondly, it is a serious comedy — Lessing himself authorizes the apparent oxymoron [20]; he who, for reasons that need no further exposition, welcomed the *tragédie bourgeoise* and was not inhospitable even to the *comédie larmoyante*. *Minna von Barnhelm* is but one degree removed from tragedy. As serious, it produces the effects peculiar to drama, and these are, in brief, the poignant impression of significant human experience. The more nearly this play approaches the gravity of tragedy, the more insistently it challenges consideration of the question whether it might not properly be classified with that species of drama extensively cultivated in the nineteenth century and found particularly adapted to the debate of problems, the species which the French call *drames* and the Germans *Schauspiele*. Such a piece is Sudermann's »Schauspiel«, *Die Ehre* — immeasurably inferior to *Minna von Barnhelm*, but not altogether dissimilar in subject [21]. Another such is Kleist's *Prinz Friedrich von Homburg*, which Hebbel denominates a tragedy notwithstanding its happy outcome, but with which I am in the habit of associating *Minna von Barnhelm*. As to frankly laughable scenes, these, in full accord with Lessing's theories — and with Shakespeare's practice — may have their place in any drama. But, after all, classification is a question only of convenience. It is pedantry

---

[19] *Ibid.*, 35. St.

[20] »Die ganz ernsthafte Komödie« (*Hamb. Dram.*, 21. St.).

[21] Sudermann would have us believe not only that "honor" has at best no more than a social sanction, but also that each social class has its own conventions in the matter. Cf. note 14 above.

and routine, *teste* Grillparzer [22], that judges by categories; true artistic sense knows only individuals. As a true and serious comedy, then, *Minna von Barnhelm* is one of not more than four in all German literature, the first in time and in quality — such perhaps as could possibly be achieved even by an unusually competent author only when an unusually fortunate conjunction of circumstances made ready to his hand a matter so actual, so national, so capable of transcendent purposes.

If one undertakes to speak of an excellent work of art, it is almost necessary to speak of the whole of art; for it comprizes the whole; and each of us can, to the extent of his ability, develop the general from such particular example.

Thus Goethe [23]; and the principle so enunciated must be my excuse for dwelling so long upon a single work of Lessing's. If the whole of art is comprized in it, so also may the whole artist be therein discoverable. Other points of view than those taken would be obvious and would be requisite to an exhaustive discussion; other works doubtless exhibit some of the author's qualities more conspicuously; and qualities to which we have not adverted might in all probability also be illustrated from the drama so characteristically his and so unmistakably indicative of a turn for the better in the course of German literature. But my purpose has been limited in respect both to the play and to the playwright. If our examination has correctly determined the significant aspects of the one, and thereby put in evidence the salient features of the other, we may at last dismiss our witnesses and concurrently take leave of Lessing himself — of that author who professed not to be a poet, who wrote most abundantly as a critic, but who showed in *Minna von Barnhelm* for the first, though not for the only time, that superior intelligence ennobled by benevolent intent can accomplish something indistinguishable from creation. Grillparzer — for all the difference between himself and Lessing — also a humanist, and, by his own confession, both a fantastic poet and a rationalist of the toughest fibre, handily supplies us with the following diagnosis [24]:

What constitutes the worth of Lessing is the union of artistic sense with logic. To be sure, neither the artistic sense is so pure, nor the logic always so

---

[22] Tgb. I, Nr. 798.
[23] *Ueber Laokoon.*
[24] Tgb. V, Nr. 4030.

sound; but in this combination they are perhaps unprecedented; — in fact, they are ordinarily even mutually exclusive.

For my part, I find no flaws in Lessing's logic; on the contrary, I find him frequently conducted by logic to revelations usually made only to intuitive perception. That his artistic sense should be inferior to Grillparzer's would seem not unnatural in one deficient in imagination. In him we discover no tumultuous flights of fancy; his eye never rolled in a fine frenzy. But neither was he prosily sober. Far from it; his very prose is alive in every turn, and alert reason is what made it so. There is the flavor of an ancient rhetorician's rule in this downright declaration of his [25]:

> He who correctly reasons also invents, and he who wishes to invent must be able to reason. Only those believe that one can be separated from the other who are not qualified for either.

We should, however, be doing Lessing an injustice in the very act of glorifying the clarity of his intellect. He could reason; but he was also the happy man that getteth understanding, and the still happier man that findeth wisdom; for wisdom is a moral acquisition — it is knowledge tempered by good will.

Berkeley abounded in good will and was wise, but his grandiose scheme for "planting arts and learning in America" does little credit to his practical understanding, or common sense. For one thing, arts and learning had been "planted" here by the first colonists — it would have been more expedient to foster the gardens already under cultivation than to clear the ground for a new one six hundred miles off-shore. The experience of six generations demonstrates this for the white settlers; "the course of empire" dealt in its own way with the red men. As to the multitudinous academic establishments of the present day, they have more to learn from the critical scholarship of Lessing than from the idealistic philosophy of Berkeley. Both men, be it said at once, were shining examples of devotion to unselfish, reasonable service. Berkeley, however, is an historical figure, whereas Lessing speaks to us almost as a contemporary. This is largely because of the eminently personal tone of all his utterances — the man everywhere stands forth greater than the sum of his achievements. But Lessing's humane learning is especially fit to provide for us, as it provided for him, a corrective of the individualistic and

---

[25] *Hamburgische Dramaturgie*, 96. St.

particularistic vagaries to which the idealist is exposed and from which, we may add, the materialist seldom escapes. Whichever we are, we need an anchorage in information; in order to master the present, we need to make the past live again, as he knew so well how to make it; and if peradventure we also invent, we still shall find, as he found, in the old the most reliable guide to the new.

REPETITIONS
AS AN ELEMENT IN LESSING'S WORKS

BY ALLEN W. PORTERFIELD
WEST VIRGINIA UNIVERSITY

The creative writer, endowed as he must be with an imagination that is at once plastic and agile, broadens his outlook, if he does not basically modify his point of view, with increasing experience. He evolves in that he abandons the immature and champions the mature. Despite the surface difference, for example, between the mood or matter of Kleist's *Hermannsschlacht* and that of *Prinz von Homburg*, it becomes obvious, even to the undergraduate mind, that the same genius wrote both plays. In this there is nothing unique; for it is always possible to trace a direct connection between the various and successive works of a great author.

It is only rarely possible, however, to locate so many complete repetitions as occur in the works of Lessing. In Shakespeare there is a similarity in tone and technic between any two of his comedies, or tragedies, or historical plays; the search for actual verbal or conceptual repetitions will lead nowhere. Goethe repeated [1] himself in the letter to Kestner regarding the liberal young lover in *Werther* and in the Gretchen catechization scene in *Faust*; search for repetitions elsewhere in Goethe will be idle. Such men as Thomas Hardy [2] and Jakob Wassermann [3] repeat but with them it is an affair of general atmosphere. The same applies to Knut Hamsun. With negligible exceptions his major works are very much alike. Lessing, on the other hand, overworked certain cardinal words, repeated pivotal expressions, exploited favorite

---

[1] Cf. *Wolfgang Goethe*, by Georg Brandes, New York, 1924, vol. 1, pp. 199—201.

[2] Cf. Percy Hutchinson in *The New York Times Book Review*, January 29, 1928.

[3] Cf. The present writer, *ibid*, June 22, 1924.

settings in his dramas, and drew again and again on set pictures for illustrations in his critical writings. With the possible exceptions of Hebbel and Schnitzler, who are also given to repeating themselves. Lessing's hardened and persistent habit in this regard is unique, while the silence on the subject that has thus far obtained on the part of those who have admired Lessing greatly and studied him diligently is without easy or immediate explanation.

In his *Lessing*, Erich Schmidt points to the connection between *Die Juden* and *Nathan*, speaks of the Tempelherr as »ein jüngerer Bruder Tellheims«, refers to *Nathan* as »der zwölfte Anti-Goeze«, and maintains that only Lessing could have written *Ernst und Falk, Beweis des Geistes und der Kraft*, and *Erziehung des Menschengeschlechts*. There is nothing in Erich Schmidt's chapter on style and language that would reveal the fact that he was in any way impressed by what remains a really striking feature [4] of Lessing's works. The case of Heinrich Bulthaupt [5] is wellnigh bewildering. There can be no doubt of his thorough knowledge of Lessing's dramas. He finds it »auffallend« that there is a similarity between *Miss Sara Sampson* (II, 8) and *Emilia Galotti* (IV, 5), and between the close of Acts I and III of *Minna von Barnhelm*, I and II of *Miss Sara*, and III and IV of *Emilia Galotti*. The similarities to which Bulthaupt refers exist; but they are not as noticeable as many others which have hitherto been ignored. Indeed some German writers seem to have dreaded the thought of emphasizing Lessing's repetitions, whether of words, dramatic settings, ideas, or critical illustrations. Hans Altmann [6] writes: »Man käme also in Versuchung, was unser Problem betrifft, eine Parallele zwischen der *Sara Sampson* und *Emilia Galotti* zu ziehen«. The "temptation" in this case is an idle one; Lessing repeated himself much more frequently than any other great, or classical, German writer.

Lessing himself was aware, to a degree at least, that he indulged in repetitions. In his *Beweis des Geistes und der Kraft* he wrote [7]:

---

[4] Under this caption cannot come such a writer as Paul Albrecht who, in his *Leszing's Plagiate*, 5 Bde., Hamburg u. Leipzig, 1888—1901, was not even generous enough to allow Lessing the established spelling of his own name. It is in a way fortunate that the author never turned to Lessing's "plagiarisms" from himself, otherwise his voluminous study would have been greatly increased.

[5] Cf. *Dramaturgie des Schauspiels*, Bd. 1, 10. Aufl., Leipzig, 1905, pp. 3—88.

[6] Cf. *Verdeckte Handlung in Lessings Dramen*, Königsberg, 1926, p. 46.

[7] Vol. XVIII, p. 29, of the *Cotta* edition, the edition which, for convenience sake, is referred to consistently. No attempt is made throughout the paper to

»Und so wiederhole ich, was ich oben gesagt, mit den nämlichen Worten«. In one of his *Gegensätze* he wrote (XVII, 276): »Ich muß bekennen, daß ich von einigen Gedanken dieses Aufsatzes bereits wörtlich Gebrauch gemacht habe ... Die Indiskretion ... weiß ich zu verantworten«. In his *Gedanken über die Herrenhuter* [8] he wrote (XVII, 16): »Man schreibt, wie man denkt; was man an dem gehörigen Ort ausgelassen hat, holet man bei Gelegenheit nach; was man aus Versehen zweimal sagt, das bittet man den Leser das andre Mal zu übergehen«. He had too the idea of repetition in mind when, in his *Theatralische Bibliothek*, he wrote (VII, 12): »Die Regel, daß man das, was bereits getan ist, nicht noch einmal tun sollte, wenn man nicht gewiß wüßte, daß man es besser tun werde, scheint mir so billig als bequem.«

Before attempting to enumerate and explain a representative list of Lessing's repetitions, a few words of warning are indispensable: the greatest of German scholars contradict each other as to the way in which Lessing's mind grew; and he himself made a number of statements about his own method of working and his own style, that ill accord with the established facts. Moreover, Lessing was given to obvious banter, so that it is not always easy to know precisely where he stood.

At the anniversary of his death in 1881, Wilhelm Scherer [9] came out with his studied survey and initiated the custom of dividing Lessing's active or creative life into sharply staked-off periods; but if we study his creative works along with his critical ones it becomes obvious at once that there were no such "periods", for they connote, and make imperative, breaks in his life. Lessing evolved with smoothness and a continuity as but few writers. Heinrich von Treitschke [10] contended that Lessing was quite indifferent to his works once he had written them. It is a misleading assertion. Lessing would write a work and then seemingly abandon it but only because he somehow knew that he would eventually return to the same theme, do it over, and make something immortal out of it. His *Juden* (1749) and *Nathan*

---

list the places in which Lessing quoted himself literally and insisted that his publisher reprint his quotation.

[8] Lessing said the same thing in his first *Anti-Goeze* (XVIII, 136).

[9] Cf. *Kleine Schriften*, Berlin, 1893.

[10] Cf. *Historische und politische Aufsätze*, 6. Aufl., Leipzig, 1885, vol. 1, pp. 56—74.

(1779) constitute a case in point. Gustav Kettner [11] contended that he hurt himself by beginning to publish when he had very little to say, and that he did not have much to say before he had passed the age at which Goethe and Schiller first acquired lasting fame. The truth is, Lessing developed very young; the ideas which were to make him famous were virtually all in his mind, in immature form, when he was thirty-one years of age, in 1760.

Then there was his lifelong habit of saying things apparently in order to throw people off their guard. In his personal letters he derided without ceasing the bookish person; yet his private library contained 6,000 volumes in 1760. He himself lived with books; yet he lampooned in his dramas the individual who sought the company of books rather than of men. In his twelfth *Literaturbrief* he wrote: »Man prahlt oft mit dem, was man gar nicht hat, damit er es wenigstens zu haben scheine«. Precisely the same idea is expressed in *Minna*.

An amusing illustration of his unwillingness, or his unconscious inability, to see himself as others saw him, is in his *Rettung des Cardanus*. He has become excited; he writes: »Wenn ich ein Mann von Ausrufungen wäre, so würde ich mich ganz und gar darinne erschöpfen. Ich würde mit manchem O! und Ach! zu verstehen geben, daß . . .« But this is exactly what he did throughout his life. His use of exclamations, interrogations, and dashes makes one of his pages look like that of a contemporary Expressionist.

Although an explanation of his indulgence in repetitions falls quite beyond the scope and purpose of this paper, it may be that it was his very vigor, his belief in himself, his wish to drive a few thoughts [12] home rather than break a lance for a great number of thoughts, that led him into the habit of repeating himself. In his *Philosophischer Nachlaß* he stated (XIX, 224) that it was much better to know one thing than several, provided one were certain that the thing in question was really known. Despite his seemingly wide range of interests, Lessing was not a man of marked versatility. In ethics, his one best and greatest thought was that character existed long before the laws that are supposed to control character were formulated. In art, he spent his life trying to show that a man cannot use the tactics in writing that

---

[11] Cf. *Lessings Dramen*, pp. 1—6.

[12] Cf. *Lessings Pädagogik, dargestellt auf Grund seiner Philosophie*, by Georg Mann, Langensalza, 1894.

are essential to success in the others arts. He worked these two ideas over and over, and in so doing repeated himself with a frequency that militates against pronounced claims to originality [13].

Lessing's theories [14] of art are not germane to the present subject. As to his idea that the thing comes before the classification – it was a part of his noble plea for tolerance – one illustration out of many must suffice. He wrote (XV, 107): »Es hat unzählige Dichter vor dem Martial bei den Griechen sowohl als bei den Römern gegeben, welche Epigramme gemacht, aber einen Epigrammatisten hat es vor ihm nicht gegeben. Ich will sagen, daß er der erste ist, welcher das Epigramm als eine eigene Gattung bearbeitet . . .«

The works on Lessing's language [15], with the exception of Lehmann to be noted later, confine themselves to themes that concern in no way the present investigation, which has to do, particularly at this point, with Lessing's vocabulary [16]. This was not large. He himself wrote in *Eine Duplik* (XVIII, 58): »Mir graulet, eine Menge unnötiger Worte machen zu müssen«. By »Worte« he really means »Wörter«; the distinction was rarely observed by him. In his *Rettung des Horaz* he wrote: »*Parcus* selten? Und *infrequens* auch selten? So verschwenderisch mit den Worten ist Horaz schwerlich gewesen«. Both statements are apposite although, as has been stated above, caution is always in place when Lessing comments on what someone has or does.

But taking him at his word, his vocabulary is limited, and the limitation is revealed first of all in his verbal repetitions. Any vigorous and voluminous writer has his favorite expressions; we think of Goethe's fondness for »gelassen«. But here is the point:

[13] Cf. *Studien zu Lessings Stil in der Hamburgischen Dramaturgie,* by Max R von Waldberg, Berlin, 1882. This study deals only with repetitions for emphasis, as when Lessing wrote: "Der Bediente hat ihn gerettet; dem Bedienten gehört das erste Wort". Martin Schütze published a somewhat similar treatise in 1907.

[14] His theory of art in *Laokoon* might be discussed to this extent: The one theory he laid down in *Laokoon* could be expressed in a single paragraph; what he did in this work of approximately 50,000 words was to repeat illustrations which, in his judgment, confirmed his theory.

[15] Cf. *Sprachliche Kleinigkeiten zu Lessings Jugendwerken,* by W. Creizenach in *Zeitschrift f. d. Wortf.,* Straßburg, 1901, pp. 31—32. The article deals largely with Lessing's attitude toward the use of Latin as opposed to German words.

[16] A vocabulary for *Nathan* would with negligible exceptions serve also as a vocabulary for *Minna;* but a vocabulary for *Herm. u. Dor.* would not be of great service to the student of *Clavigo.*

Goethe uses »gelassen« in *Hermann und Dorothea* and also in *Clavigo*, two works that bear not a shred of similarity to each other. Lessing on the other hand never wrote works that seem to contradict each other in tone and theme.

The observing reader cannot go far in Lessing without being struck by his exploitation of certain pivotal words, as opposed to mere particles that have no particular signification. We think of »erraten«, »schlechterdings«, »rechtschaffen«, and »retten« [17]. The word »schlechterdings« [18] occurs thirteen times in *Wie die Alten den Tod gebildet* (1769), a pamphlet of forty (Cotta) pages at least seven of which are taken up with illustrations and direct quotations from the Latin and Greek. There is no question but that Lessing used the word effectively, as when he wrote (the passage is relevant): »Zwar muß ich gestehen, daß ich damals, als ich den Ort im Laokoon schrieb, schlechterdings keine Auslegung kannte . . . »But there are least a dozen German words that would have served as adequate synonyms.

His attachment to the word »retten« is even more striking. He was under no obligation to use the word »Rettung« in connection with all those vindications which he wrote of men who, in his judgment, had been wronged, from Simon Lemnius on. He could have varied his captions [19] and produced the same, if not even greater effect. But he loved the idea embodied in »retten«. His greatest »Rettung« is *Nathan*. In it he endeavored to write a »Rettung« of a great idea. And impelled to frame an adequate reply to the embarrassing question Saladin had raised regarding the comparative worth of the three great religions, Nathan, recalling the story of the rings, exclaims: »Das wars! Das kann mich retten!« The drama might have been called »eine dramatische Rettung«. But even Lessing seems to have grown tired

---

[17] Lessing never used, seems indeed never to have known, the words *static* and *dynamic*, as Fichte, and other Romanticists, made them popular. He believed, however, that everything is dynamic, that is, capable of being changed, except death. In *Die Matrone von Ephesus* (V, 110) Antiphila says: "Aus den eisernen Armen des Todes ist keine Rettung".

[18] Cf. *Forschungen über Lessings Sprache*, by August Lehmann, Braunschweig, 1875. Lehman writes of "schlechterdings": "Gehört zu den auserkorensten aller Lieblinge Lessings". He points to "gegen 150" examples. There are more. He says nothing of "rechtschaffen".

[19] In his *Untersuchungen über Ramlers und Lessings Bearbeitung von den Sinngedichten Logaus*, Leipzig, 1903, W. Heuschkel takes the stand that Lessing wrote a "Rettung" of Logau just as truly as of anyone else.

of certain of his own repetitions. In the 77th *Literaturbrief* he wrote: »Und wie oft werde ich dieses abermals, abermals brauchen müssen!«

Lessing revealed however the trait under discussion most strikingly in his use of »rechtschaffen« [20]. There is no case on record among writers of the first class like it. It occurs in all of his works, creative, critical, and personal or private. He used it five times in *Der Schatz* (1749). Sometimes he used it merely in the sense of »ehrlich«, more frequently in the sense of »gediegen« or »tüchtig«, »gründlich« or »großmütig«, and occasionaly in the sense of »gehörig« or »recht«. On December 3, 1772, He wrote to Eva König: ». . . so müssen Sie ein Ende damit zu machen suchen. Auf die rechtschaffenste Art; das versteht sich: aber nicht auf die skrupulöseste.« In the 49th *Literaturbrief* he discussed the question: »Kann man ohne Religion rechtschaffen sein?« The word occurs there nineteen times in three pages.

Lessing's most informative use of »rechtschaffen« however is in his translation of Plautus' *Captivi* [21]. He regarded Plautus as the model writer of comedies and *Captivi* as his best work. He even rose to such heights of admiration as the following (VI, 143): »Ich bleibe also dabei, daß ,Die Gefangenen' das schönste Stück sind, das jemals auf die Bühne gekommen ist, . . . weil es der Absicht der Lustspiele am nächsten kommt und mit den übrigen zufälligen Schönheiten reichlich versehen ist«. He was to be sure very young when he wrote this. In the translator's [22] note he tells how carefully he followed the original, reproducing, where possible, even the stubborn puns of Plautus. Then we read his translation, in prose. The word »rechtschaffen« occurs ten times. What Latin terms did he render by it?

In his first use of it, there is no direct Latin equivalent: *talem adulescentem* is rendered by »so einen rechtschaffenen Jüngling«. There can be no objection to this: *talis* is a colorless word. We may translate *talis homo* by "such a good man" or "such a bad

---

[20] The *Deutsches Wörterbuch*, which devotes three columns to "rechtschaffen" says it was common ("häufig") in the 16th Century. Since words of this sort, as contrasted with slang or technical expressions, rarely come into use suddenly, it may be inferred that it was known in the fifteenth Century. Luther used it, though Grimm does not cite cases in which it was used by Lessing's more important contemporaries.

[21] The text of the *Captivi* used is that of E. P. Morris, Ginn & Co., Boston, 1898.

[22] Cf. *Lessings Ansichten von der deutschen Sprache*, by K. Behschnitt, Breslau, 1915. Behschnitt discusses Lessing as a translator.

man", depending on the context; and Lessing is accurate: the youth referred to in this case was "good".

In the second case »rechtschaffen« is used adverbially: *sed utrum strictimne adtonsurum* becomes »so wird er ihn rechtschaffen zerkratzen«. In the third instance, *hominem* unmodified is translated »rechtschaffener Mensch«. The fourth case is literal enough: *optumusque hominum es homo* becomes »du bist der rechtschaffenste Mann«. The fifth and sixth cases are both appropriate contextual forms of *bonus*. The seventh likewise: *huic homini optumo* is done into »diesem rechtschaffenen Manne«. In the eighth case it is again used adverbially: *irrogabo multam* becomes »ich will sie rechtschaffen strafen«. Likewise in the ninth: *satin*, containing the root of "genug", becomes »rechtschaffen«. The tenth and last case shows Lessing's accurate freedom: *quando ego te exemplis pessumis cruciauero* is translated »wenn ich dich rechtschaffen habe martern lassen«. There is no thought of accusing Lessing here, in any of these cases, of inaccuracy; but there are numerous synonyms for »rechtschaffen«, and a careful writer avoids so far as possible the betrayal of either verbal prejudice or mental inertia.

In the matter of rhetorical figures and dramatic settings, the present writer is not minded to accuse Lessing of either of these weaknesses; but he did take it easy. Having worked out a scene or situation in one drama he exploited his antecedent labors in the following drama. Of this there can be no doubt, as a selected list of illustrations will prove.

The least important of Lessing's finished dramas, *Damon* (1747) not excepted, is *Die alte Jungfer* (1749). In this comedy »das leidige Geld« plays a large rôle. We think of *Minna* and *Nathan*. The old maid's friend is referred to as a »Verschwender«, and the noun is used here in much the same sense as later in connection with Tellheim. The word »rechtschaffen« also occurs three times. And J. C. Edelmann, the theologian who had the intrepidity, at the very beginning of the eighteenth century, to doubt whether the entire Bible was inspired and whether every word of it should be accepted literally, is given a place of honor within the play. These might be mere coincidences; but the following cannot be.

The question has arisen as to who will make the best husband for the old maid. A certain Kapitän von Schlag is in the offing. After years of military experience he has been given an honorable discharge because of a wound; he can no longer engage in foreign service. He stands in high repute with the King, however. He is Tellheim.

But the old maid has her doubts. Herr Oront thereupon replies: »Verlangen Sie denn einen Mann, der stets zu Felde liegt?... Die abgedankten Offiziere sind die besten Ehemänner; wenn sie ihren Mut nicht mehr an den Feinden beweisen können, so sind sie desto mannhafter gegen ihre...« The word to be supplied is »Frauen«. Compare this with *Minna*. Tellheim has made out quite a case for his unfitness as a husband; he is a cripple. Minna says: »Ein Schuß hat Ihnen den rechten Arm ein wenig gelähmt. Doch alles wohl überlegt, so ist auch das so schlimm nicht. Um so viel sichrer bin ich vor Ihren Schlägen.« Two speeches preceding this Minna rejoices in the fact that Tellheim has been discharged; she can have him entirely to herself. Herr Oront advises the old maid, in case she is determined to marry an officer, to marry a discharged one, otherwise she will see but little of her husband.

Take the case of *Philotas* (1759). It is not like the Lessing we know; Heinrich von Kleist might have written it: it is patriotic. And it is a »Rettung«. Can Philotas, a prisoner of the enemy, accept the liberty that has been offered him without jeopardizing the cause of his father's forces? He cannot; so he takes his own life. There are three themes in the play that Lessing expanded, with striking literalness, in *Minna* and *Nathan*; the natural inability of those in high power to reward all men according to their merits, the significance of family resemblances, and the approach of Parmenio, the soldier, to Philotas in his cell. Philotas takes the same attitude, at first, toward his visitor that the Tempelherr and Saladin take toward Nathan in their initial interviews.

Let us look rather closely at *Minna* and *Nathan*. Fifteen years lay between the writing of these two plays. In both a war is just over. In *Minna* the two outstanding kingdoms of Germany are reconciled; in *Nathan* the three outstanding faiths are reconciled. In *Minna* there are two rings, and it makes but little difference which one either of the leading characters wears so long as it is worn in the belief that it is genuine. In *Nathan* there are three rings [23], and all the world knows the story that is written about

---

[23] The description of the stones in the ring is based on, or parallel to, Lessing's discussion of this subject in *Briefe antiquarischen Inhalts.*

them. Money is now a much needed and now a despised thing in both plays. Paul Werner will go to the Orient and take part in whatever war Prince Heraklius is waging. In *Nathan* the characters are already in the Orient, and Heraklius was Patriarch there at the time. The Uncle in *Minna* arrives before it is too late. The Uncle in *Nathan* was the cause of the clearing up. In *Minna* Riccaut gambles. In *Nathan* Saladin and Sittah play chess. Both recreations were indulged in, harmlessly, by Lessing. In *Minna* the titular heroine says to Tellheim: »Der König war eine unglückliche Karte für Sie: die Dame wird Ihnen desto günstiger sein.« This figure from the card table awas taken over into *Nathan* and adapted to the chess board.

A quite typical similarity of a broader nature, and one that does not become apparent without a measure of thought, is the rescue of the poodle by Just in *Minna* and the rescue of Recha by the Tempelherr in *Nathan*. Just is walking along the canal one winter day when he hears a voice (the *Stimme* motif is common to both plays). He goes down in the direction of the voice and saves a dog from drowning: »Es ist ein häßlicher Pudel, aber ein gar zu guter Hund.« Mistreat that dog as he may, it refuses to leave him. It is precisely so that the Tempelherr rescues Recha from the fire. He is not proud of his deed, for she is only a »Judenmädchen«, but she is a »Mensch« and should therefore be saved. He scorns her, but the more intense his hatred the less she is minded to leave him. In the end he comes to love her. Contrast this with the idea regarding the acceptance and recognition of gratitude expressed in the foreword to Lessing's *Sophokles*: »Ich kann nicht bewundert werden, aber ich werde Dank verdienen. Und die Vorstellung, Dank zu verdienen, muß eben so angenehm sein als die Vorstellung, bewundert zu werden.«

Just in *Minna* proposes to Werner that they waylay the Wirt as he comes from the "Tabagie" some evening and assassinate him, set fire to his house, or ruin his daughter. Werner will listen to no such schemes. The Klosterbruder in *Nathan*, following instructions from his hated chief (Lessing could never work with ease for or under someone else), proposes to the Tempelherr that they waylay Saladin some evening and dispose of him for good and all. The Tempelherr is incensed at the thought of such a crime.

The Wirt wants Franziska's credentials in *Minna*, and the

manner in which she gives them to him, with saucy impudence and more in detail than he had cared for, finds its parallel in the Tempelherr's detailed reply to the Klosterbruder in *Nathan.* The curt replies given Daja by the Tempelherr are a reproduction of the replies that Just gives in *Minna.*

In each drama a friend's friend is also a friend; the wish to pray is a prayer in itself; there is someone who cannot read or who claims this inability; someone »hat Galle«; the significance of friendship on short acquaintance is commented on; the principle of *Interessen* or *Zinsen* is set forth; the related rôles played by the head and the heart are discussed; in each play there is an eavesdropper who is badly repaid for listening-in; the »Reitknecht« is present in each play and in each Persia is in the background; the Tempelherr stands outside and refuses to enter Nathan's house precisely as in *Minna* Just disrelishes the thought of re-entering the hotel; Minna is dressed »völlig und reich, aber mit Geschmack« while Nathan describes the things he has brought back with him from Babylon as »so reich, und mit Geschmack so reich«; in *Minna* the »kostbarer Ring« had been received »von lieben Händen« while in *Nathan* the original ring was »aus lieber Hand«; the way the heroine tries to put herself in the right mood to receive someone who was loved long since and lost a while is identical in both plays, as is the manner in which someone is sent for by a certain character who may be in a position to influence the speedy arrival of the desired person.

Then there is *Emilia Galotti.* It is admittedly a new type of play: there is in it an element of fatalistic chance [24]. Of it Erich Schmidt says: »Als Komposition ist es die äußerste Leistung eines peinlich rechnenden Kunstverstandes, mit eisernen Klammern festgebunden, Szene auf Szene festgemauert, . . . kein Wort entbehrlich, weil nur das unentbehrliche gesagt wird.« If this be true, we should expect to find *Emilia* wholly different, in wording and setting, from Lessing's other plays. This is not the case, as some illustrations will show.

The widow Marloff in *Minna* says: »Sie würden sein letzter Gedanke, Ihr Name der letzte Ton seiner sterbenden Lippen gewesen sein.« Claudia says in *Emilia*: »Marinelli war das letzte

[24] Cf. *Lessings Dramen*, by Gustav Kettner, Berlin, 1904, pp. 230—237. Kestner's contention cannot be refuted, but after all chance, mere "Zufall", plays a heavy rôle also in *Minna* and *Nathan.*

Wort des sterbenden Grafen.« At the opening of the play, the Prinz »will ausfahren«, accompanied by Marinelli; in *Minna* Minna »will ausfahren« accompanied by Tellheim. The Gräfin Orsina comes to town very much as Minna did and for a somewhat similiar purpose. The »Schatzmeister« plays a rôle in *Emilia* not wholly dissimilar to the one he plays in *Nathan*. The Prinz is impressed by the smile on Emilia's lips; the Tempelherr discusses the same theme in *Nathan*. And in *Emilia*, as in virtually all of Lessing's dramas, the characters quote each other, somewhat after the fashion of the cut-back in the motion picture.

In *Emilia*, Claudia bemoans the »rauhe Tugend« of her husband much as Franziska and Minna bemoan the same trait in the men in *Minna* [25]. When Emilia refers to the Prinz as »ihn selbst«, she does precisely what Nathan and Daja do: »Bei ihm? Bei welchem Ihm?« Emilia tells Appiani how to dress exactly as Minna coaches Tellheim on this point. There are dreams in all of Lessing's leading dramas, though Lessing himself is alleged to have passed dreamless nights. Marinelli's attempt to have Appiani sent away on an important mission reminds of the services the Patriarch wished to have rendered by the Tempelherr. The taking off of Appiani is the actual carrying out of the plan, proposed but rejected, in *Minna* with the Wirt and in Nathan with Saladin. Marinelli insists that the Prinz has not read Orsina's letter; Minna and Franziska stage a similar scene. Orsina's reference to a happy, laughing »Geschöpf« finds its counterpart in *Minna*, where Minna contends that a happy creature is the most pleasing object that can be thought of. Orsina catches Marinelli in a lie just as Tellheim catches Werner in a lie and in both cases the word »ertappen« is used. This however was a common verb with Lessing.

At the beginning of the last act, Marinelli tells the Prinz that Odoardo can be seen from the window, going up and down the arcade, turning now to the right and now to the left. It is a scene that is repeated literally in *Nathan* in which Daja and Recha watch the Tempelherr. And throughout the entire *Emilia* the

---

[25] The present writer regards it as quite remarkable that Otto Spiess could write such a book as his *Die dramatische Handlung in Lessings "Emilia Galotti" und "Minna von Barnhelm"*, Halle, 1911, and never say a word about repetitions, for this phase of Lessing's work has a direct bearing on Spiess's theme.

same expressions occur: »mein rechtschaffener [26] Galotti«, »ein unbekannter Freund ist auch ein Freund«.

As to *Miss Sara Sampson*, it is obvious that Mellefont is the prototype of the Prinz and Marwood of Orsina. The Wirt of *Miss Sara* is the prototype of the Wirt in *Minna*; both use the same expressions. Sir William comes to the hotel »aus den rechtschaffensten Absichten«. Sara, like the Prinz in *Emilia*, has nothing but »Klagen« to report to Mellefont who asks her, precisely as it is done in *Emilia* by Marinelli in his interview with Appiani, why she should be so disturbed over the »Verschiebung einer Zeremonie«, the ceremony being the wedding. And throughout the entire play it is the setting familiar to the student of the older plays: »Vernunft« and »Verstand«, the »Bilder« created by the »Phantasie«, »Tugend« and »Laster«, the bad rôle played by »Schwärmerei«, the place in gallantry of »Schmeichelei«, and the distress caused a father by the fact that nothing separates him from his endangered daughter but »eine Wand«, a situation that re-occurs in *Nathan*.

Then there are Lessing's critical works. An analysis of them, by way of showing how his mind evolved with regard to the working out of the few truths that interested him, is quite out of the question: space makes such an analysis impossible while the aim of this essay makes it unnecessary. Let us again merely enumerate a typical list of obvious repetitions.

As has already been indicated, Lessing was interested in the truth that the species precedes the class. In 1776 he exclaimed (XIX, 136): »Baum ist doch sicherlich älteren Ursprungs als E i c h e , T a n n e , L i n d e.« He proved in *Nathan* that Mensch came first and was then followed by such classifications as Jude, Christ, Mohammedaner. When twenty years of age, May 31, 1749, he wrote to his father: »Die christliche Religion ist kein Werk, das man von seinen Eltern auf Treue und Glauben annehmen soll.« The Mohammedan says precisely the same to the Jew in *Nathan*.

With Lessing the truth was all that mattered. When Saladin

---

[26] Lessing's most interesting use of "rechtschaffen" in connection with a given individual is in *Laokoon* (X, 134): "Der weise und rechtschaffene Aesop wird dadurch, daß man ihm die Häßlichkeit des Thersites gegeben, nicht lächerlich." Moreover, there can be no doubt but that his general interest in the word moved him to write as follows in connection with Logau's *Sinngedichte* (VIII, 204): "Weil Recht ein Knecht itzt ist, dem Frevel hat zu schaffen."

asked Nathan for a definition of truth, Nathan said (lines 1868 to 1876):

> ... Wahrheit. Wahrheit!
> Und will sie so — so bar, so blank — als ob
> Die Wahrheit Münze wäre! — Ja, wenn noch
> Uralte Münze, die gewogen ward! —
> Das ginge noch! Allein so neue Münze
> Die nur der Stempel macht, die man aufs Brett
> Nur zählen darf, das ist sie doch nun nicht!
> Wie Geld in Sack, so striche man in Kopf
> Auch Wahrheit ein? ...

It is a world-famous passage, quoted time out of mind, and as though it were an original figure. The truth expressed is, or was at the time, largely original. The figure used to express the truth was based without the slightest modification on Lessing's experience while secretary to Tauentzien in Breslau (November, 1760 — April, 1765). And in 1769 Lessing wrote (XIII, 192): »Es wäre doch sonderbar, wenn nur d e r reich heißen sollte, der das meiste frisch gemünzte Geld besitzet.«

It was also in 1749 that Lessing wrote the preface to his elaborately planned work, *Beiträge zur Historie und Aufnahme des Theaters*, in which he worked out the very idea that constitutes the core of his last major work, *Die Erziehung des Menschengeschlechts*: the people as a whole can stand only so much truth at a time; it is not safe to go from milk to wine with a child. In the same year, 1749, Lessing wrote in *Der Freygeist*: »Ihm [d. h., dem Pöbel] die Religion nehmen, heißt ein wildes Pferd auf der fetten Weide losbinden, das, sobald es sich frei fühlt, lieber in unfruchtbaren Wäldern herumschweifen und Mangel leiden, als durch einen gemächlichen Dienst alles, was es braucht, erwerben will.« The two ideas [27] are so identical that comment is uncessary; and yet there lay no fewer than thirty-one years between the writing of them.

There is room for but one more illustration of Lessing's repetitions bearing on his search after moral truth. In *Eine Duplik* (1778) he wrote (XIII, 42) [28]: »Wenn Gott in seinerRechten alle

---

[27] In a letter to his brother Karl, Lessing also wrote: "Das zahme Pferd wird im Stalle gefüttert und muß dienen, das wilde in seiner Wüste ist frei, verkommt aber vor Hunger und Elend." Goethe uses the same figure in *Faust*, lines 1830—1833.

[28] The figure the Tempelherr uses (lines 3243—3249) about the block of marble washed on to the shore and the form chiseled from it is a direct echo from the 29th *Stück* of the *Hamb. Dram.* (XI, 218). A slight variant of the same figure occurs in the 40th *Brief antiquarischen Inhalts*.

Wahrheit und in seiner Linken den einzigen immer regen Trieb nach Wahrheit, obschon mit dem Zusatze, mich immer und ewig zu irren, verschlossen hielte und spräche zu mir: ‚Wähle!' ich fiele ihm mit Demut in seine Linke und sagte: ‚Vater, gib! die reine Wahrheit ist ja doch nur für dich allein!«

Few statements of this sort have been more frequently quoted; but Lessing made the same point, and made it effectively, on a number of other occassions and in other connections. In his *Hypothesen über die vier Evangelisten*, likewise 1778, he wrote: »Den wahren Weg einschlagen, ist oft bloßes Glück; um den rechten Weg bekümmert zu sein, gibt allein Verdienst.«

If we attempt to explain this repetition by saying that the figure merely chanced to be on his mind at the time we encounter grave difficulty, for in his *Rettung des Cardanus*, written twenty-four years earlier, he said: »Man bediene sich des Gleichnisses nicht, daß, wenn man einmal den rechten Weg wisse, man sich nicht um die Irrwege zu bekümmern brauche.« The case is typical: with each repetition the expression generally became clearer and more striking. Throughout his entire life, Lessing regarded himself as perpetually in quest of the Holy Grail of Truth; for the man who contended that he had already found the Grail he had but little use. Consequently he wrote in *Nathan* (lines 2150—2151):

Ich will mit Männern lieber fallen, als
Mit Kindern stehn.

Just as Lessing wrote a long line of plays in which he depicted a pert maid before this type of character found its culmination in Franziska, so did he write four separate works [29] on literature, with especial reference to the drama, before he had the matter culminate in the *Hamburgische Dramaturgie;* and before he wrote *Laokoon* he became the author of various shorter studies that culminated in *Laokoon*. Had he written only the *Hamb. Dram.* his stature, except for the motive of diligence, would hardly be diminished. His idea in all five of these works was: the Greeks are to be studied; the English imitated; the French avoided. As

---

[29] *Beiträge zur Historie und Aufnahme des Theaters* (1749), *Das Neueste aus dem Reiche des Witzes* (1751), *Theatralische Bibliothek* (1755), and *Briefe, die neueste Literatur betreffend* (1760). In the *Brief* of May 22, 1760, the word "recht-schaffen" occurs fourteen times in four pages and "unrechtschaffen" occurs once. Throughout all of these works "retten" and "schlechterdings" occur with established frequency, while "frischerdings" and "platterdings" occur once each.

to *Laokoon* and its predecessors, it was a lifelong contention with Lessing that the genres must not be mixed. There is only one place in his entire output where he seemed to favor the mixing of types (XI, 301): »Weil der Maulesel weder Pferd noch Esel ist, ist er darum weniger eines von den nutzbarsten lasttragenden Tieren?« Lessing had a superb sense of humor; and in this one case he was defending Euripides: »Was geht mich es an, ob so ein Stück des Euripides weder ganz Erzählung, noch ganz Drama ist.« In the Greeks Lessing could see nothing but perfection. But the distinctly unusual feature of all these five works is the fact that Lessing drew on the same men (Greek, English, French, and German) for his illustrations, or he discussed the works of the same men. The case is paralleled only by his lifelong references to and interest in James Thompson.

There is space for the discussion of only a few important repetitions in *Laokoon* and the *Dramaturgie,* such as Milton's blindness and »Nachahmung der Natur«. As to the latter, it was rather carefully treated in *Laokoon;* but that did not prevent Lessing from covering the same ground in the *Dramaturgie* [30]. As to Milton's blindness, Lessing admitted that the pictures of light in *Paradise Lost* were different from what they would have been had Milton been able to see; but he greatly admired Milton's ability in this connection. Such cases always interested him. In *Emilia,* Conti exclaims: »Oder meinen Sie, Prinz, daß Raffael nicht das größte malerische Genie gewesen wäre, wenn er unglücklicherweise ohne Hände geboren worden?« Under the caption of Johannes Vermaasen, in the *Kollektaneen* (XX), he wrote of the blind man who reached the point where he could differentiate colors by the sense of touch. He discussed the possibility of learning to speak if born without a tongue. He took a persistent interest in deaf-mutes. Such cases are so many »Rettungen«.

---

[30] Charles Harris calls attention to this in his edition (Holt), 1906, p. 329. In a note on the 70th *Stück* of the *H. D.,* Harris writes: "The first paragraphs of this number, in fact, sound like an echo of that work *[Laokoon]*." The note is well founded, although it is strange that Harris was moved to comment on this repetition and remain silent about the others. It is strange, for "echoes" of *Laokoon* and the *Hamb. Dram.* can be found in the most out-of-way places in Lessing's works. In *Die Matrone von Ephesus* (V, 124) Philokrates says: "Allen ziemt nicht alles. Dem Mann, dem Krieger ist eine Thräne vergönnt, aber kein Strom von Thränen." That idea runs through all of Lessing's major critical works.

But there is a much more important phase of the matter than this. It will be recalled that the late William James of Harvard created almost a sensation, at the beginning of the present century, by his theory of emotions, according to which we do not cry because we are hurt, rather we are hurt because we cry. Lessing, whom William James never mentioned, antedated James on this point by nearly one hundred and fifty years. In the 3rd *Stück* of the *Dramaturgie*, he made it plain that an actor, if he acts as though he were angry, will come to feel and actually be angry. In his *Auszug aus dem Schauspieler* (1757), he made precisely the same point; and in his *Rettung des Horaz* (1754), he made the identical point, apparently for the first time. It is improbable that there is another case on record like this. Moreover, the idea is exploited in the very heart of *Nathan*, when Recha says that »Ergebenheit in Gott von unserm Wähnen über Gott so ganz und gar nicht abhängt«. That is to say, a really pious disposition comes from good acting and not at all from theological speculation.

In *Eine Duplik*, one of the most valuable theological works Lessing ever wrote, he said (XVIII, 91): »Wer gewisse Dinge nicht sogleich fühlt, dem sind sie auf keine Weise fühlbar zu machen.« Six years prior to the writing of this, he had Orsina in *Emilia* say: »Ich fühle so was! — Und glauben Sie, glauben Sie mir: wer über gewisse Dinge den Verstand nicht verliert, der hat keinen zu verlieren«.

In a letter to Moses Mendelssohn (April 17, 1763) Lessing tells the story of the two barbarians who, seeing themselves for the first time in a mirror, are impressed by the fact that as they move the reflections in the mirror move. They conclude that the movements in the mirror and those of their own bodies derive from the same cause. Lessing carried this idea in his mind for nearly thirty years, and made most excellent use of it in the 73rd paragraph of the *Erziehung des Menschengeschlechts*. Probably he never fancied that his letters would become literature; it may be that he never intended [31] to create the situation that has resulted from the publication of his complete works. There is not the slighest reason to believe however that had Lessing lived to

---

[31] Lessing himself, however, seems minded to refute this argument in the foreword to *Sogenannte Briefe an verschiedene Gottesgelehrten* (XVIII, 252).

be a really old man he would have brought out an edition of his works in which the writings of his younger years would have been eliminated on the ground that the ideas contained in them are found in the later volumes.

In the 49th paragraph of the *Erziehung des Menschengeschlechts*, Lessing gives his idea of an appropriate style for an »Elementarbuch« that is to be read by »Kinder« and a »kindisches Volk«. He says: »Bald plan und einfältig, bald poetisch, durchaus voll Tautologien, aber solchen, die den Scharfsinn üben, indem sie bald etwas anders zu sagen scheinen und doch das nämliche sagen, bald das nämliche zu sagen scheinen und im Grunde etwas anders bedeuten oder bedeuten können.«

With the reading public that Lessing here visualizes, he himself had, directly, very little to do: he wrote neither for "children" nor for a "childish race". He gives, nevertheless, a fair description of his own style. It may after all be that he had his own age, his own contemporaries in mind when he insisted that in order to be understood it was necessary to be plain, picturesque, and repetitive.

On December 16, 1771, he wrote to Eva König: »Lassen Sie uns ruhig sein, und das Beste hoffen, und jeden Augenblick nur immer das tun, was Rechtschaffenheit und Klugheit für das Gegenwärtige von uns fordern. Rechtschaffenheit und Klugheit — beide zugleich, meine Liebe!« Lessing was as honest a man as Germany knew in his day; and he strove without ceasing not merely for personal intelligence but for intelligence on the part of his contemporaries.

Conclusion: In 1766, Lessing published *Laokoon*, the germinal ideas of which can all be found in the various works he had previously written on the general subject of the plastic arts. In 1769, he published the *Hamburgische Dramaturgie*, which is a rounding-up and a practical application of what he had already written on dramatic criticism and related themes. In 1779, he brought out *Nathan der Weise*, which is a condensation of his dramatic practices to that date. In 1780, he finished *Die Erziehung des Menschengeschlechts*, which is a résumé of his old ideas on the broad subject of human and civic evolution. His contention that the Old Testament was good enough for a primitive people but that the New Testament became necessary as mankind grew in mental and spiritual ability, and that a third Testament would in time become indispensable is nothing more than an expansion of the idea set forth in *Nathan* about the Judge who is to come in thousands of years and hand down a decision in the light of such wisdom as will by then have accumulated. And his strange excursion, in the *Erziehung*, into the domain of metempsychosis? That too is a matter of repetition.

WIELANDS BRIEFWECHSEL
MIT JOHANNES GOTTFRIED GURLITT

VON W. KURRELMEYER
JOHNS HOPKINS UNIVERSITY

Johannes Gottfried Gurlitt, geboren den 11. März 1754 in Halle, gestorben den 14. Juni 1827 als Direktor des Johanneums in Hamburg, war von 1779 bis 1801 Rektor der Schule des Klosters Bergen bei Magdeburg, wo auch Wieland die Jahre 1747—1749 verlebt hatte. Gurlitt widmete sich besonders dem Studium der klassischen und orientalischen Sprachen, und war während seiner ersten Jahre in Kloster Bergen besonders mit der Uebersetzung Pindarischer Oden beschäftigt. Neun derselben sind in Wielands T e u t s c h e m M e r k u r abgedruckt: die Hefte 5—8, 12 des Jahres 1785 bringen je eine Ode, das 9. und 10. Heft je zwei; abgesehen vom 9. Hefte (September), welches mit Wielands eigenem Aufsatze: U e b e r d i e R e c h t e u n d P f l i c h - t e n d e r S c h r i f t s t e l l e r eröffnet wird, steht jede Ode am Anfang des betreffenden Heftes.

Vor etwas mehr als Jahresfrist erwarb ich zwei Briefe Wielands an Gurlitt, die über die Pindarischen Oden handeln; Bernhard Seuffert stellte mir dann seine Auszüge aus zwei Briefen Gurlitts an Wieland zur Verfügung, die im Germanischen Museum zu Nürnberg aufbewahrt sind. Später verglich ich selbst die Originale im Germanischen Museum, um Seufferts Exzerpte, die zu anderen Zwecken gemacht worden waren, zu vervollständigen.

Die Wielandschen Briefe liegen nicht im Original, sondern in alter Abschrift vor. Der Schreiber scheint des Griechischen und Französischen unk dig gewesen zu sein: die Briefe sind daher nachträglich von a..derer Hand korrigiert und wie es scheint, zum Druck vorbereitet worden. Sie scheinen jedoch unveröffentlicht zu sein, wie auch Gurlitts Name bei Goedeke IV, 1, 539—544 nicht vorkommt.

Das Format der Briefe ist Quart: das Papier des ersten trägt als Wasserzeichen den Namen J Kool & Comp, darüber einen gekrönten Löwen; der zweite Brief weist denselben Namen auf, aber ohne Löwen.

Der Text folgt hier in der vom Korrektor hergestellten Fassung; kleinere Versehen des Schreibers sind nur ausnahmsweise notiert worden:

Hochgeehrtester Herr,

Die Einrückung ihrer Uebersetzung der zweyten Isthmischen Ode [1] Pindars in No. 5 des Merkurs d. J. [2] wird Ihnen bereits bewiesen haben, daß mir Ihre Zuschrift mit den drey Pindarischen Oden richtig zugekommen ist. So nachtheilig es auch diesem *principi novem Lyricorum* bey uns Teutschen, so wie bey den übrigen heutigen Erdbewohnern ist, daß d e r I n h a l t seiner Gesänge auf die Siege in den öffentlichen Kampf-Spielen, aus bekannten und ganz natürlichen Ursachen, beynahe gar nichts interessantes für uns hat, und so viel er auch in einer Uebersetzung (von dem Unterschiede der Sprache nichts zu gedenken) blos durch den Umstand verliehrt, daß er in der Uebersetzung bloß gelesen, und nicht gesungen wird, da es doch zum Wesen der lyrischen Poesie der Griechen, und ganz besonders der Pindarischen Oden, gehört, nicht nur g e s u n g e n und mit I n - s t r u m e n t e n b e g l e i t e t, sondern sogar g e t a n z t zu werden: so bin ich doch, in Ansicht des Nutzens, den eine gute Uebersetzung des kostbaren Restes, der von den mannichfaltigen Werken dieses Dichters auf uns gekommen ist, unserer Litteratur verschaffen könnte, gänzlich der Meinung des Herrn v. *Chabanon* in dessen, im 58ten Bande der *Memoires de l'academie des B. L. et I.* eingerückten, *Discours sur Pindare et la poesie lyrique* ich das Gründlichste und scharfsinnigste gefunden habe, was meines Wissens über den Werth dieses Dichters, über die Dichtart, worin er gesungen und über den Gebrauch, der von seinen Werken

---

[1] 'Isthmischen' vom Korrektor in freigelassenem Raum nachgetragen, 'Pindars' am Rande.
[2] Pindars zweyte Isthmische Hymne auf des Xenokrates, des Akragantiners, Wagensieg steht im Mai-Heft S. 97—103. Bis einschließlich August werden Gurlitts Beiträge als »Hymne« betitelt, von September an steht »Ode«.

(ungeachtet des wenigen Verhältnisses, so sie zu uns zu haben scheinen) wenigstens von denjenigen gemacht werden kann, welche sich zur musicalischen Dichtkunst gebohren fühlen.

So wenig Gewicht ich auch meinem Urtheil über die mir anvertrauten Proben Ihrer Uebersetzung beylege, so kann ich doch nicht umhin, Sie, meines Ortes, zur Fortsetzung einer Arbeit aufzumuntern, wobey Sie zwar, wie nahe Sie darin der Vollkommenheit immer kommen mögen, weder auf den Dank der Nation, noch auf Belohnung von unseren Fürsten und Großen, noch auf ein zahlreiches Publicum von Lesern rechnen können, wo durch Sie Sich aber [3] gewiß um unsere Litteratur, um die kleine Anzahl der Liebhaber der Alten, welche in ihrem Studio derselben fremden Beystand nöthig haben, und besonders um die edlere Klasse unserer studierenden Jünglinge, die in die Mysterien der griechischen Musen eingeführt zu werden wünschen, ein wahres und großes Verdienst machen werden.

Der Merkur taugt allerdings wegen seiner Verbreitung durch den ganzen Umkreis unserer Sprache, zu einer Bühne, wo ein Gelehrter, der sich mit Untersuchungen dieser Art zu befassen Lust hat, Proben seiner Arbeit auf stellen kann, um das Urtheil der Kenner darüber zu hören. Da Ihnen aber dieses letztere nicht anders, als in einem hohen Grade günstig seyn kann, so kann es wohl schwerlich Ihre [4] Meynung seyn, sich blos auf die Isthmischen [5] Oden einzuschränken: Sie werden uns den ganzen Pindar geben, und da dieses ein höchst mühsames Werk *de longue haleine* ist, vielleicht für gut finden, von Zeit zu Zeit das Publicum durch Einrückung eines Stückes in den Merkur, oder ein andres Journal daran erinnern, daß Sie Sich mit dieser Arbeit beschäftigen, ohne darum den ganzen Pindar nach und nach so stückweise geben zu wollen, wodurch Sie einer künftigen Ausgabe mehr schaden, als nützen würden. Vielleicht würde auch eine vorläufige Abhandlung über Pindar, den Geist und Character seiner O d e n (warum H y m n e n? [6]) und in wiefern er, ungeachtet der W a h r h e i t des Horazischen *Pindarum quisquis studet imitari* auch noch izt von Lyrischen Dichtern mit Nutzen studiert werden können (zu welchem allen der oben berührte

---

[3] 'aber' nachgetragen vom Korrektor.
[4] 'Ihre' ursprünglich 'Ihrer'.
[5] 'Isthmischen' vom Korrektor in freigelassenem Raum nachgetragen.
[6] Hymnen vgl. oben, Anm. 2.

Discours, des *Mons. de Chabanon* Ihnen vielleicht einige Dienste thun könnte) nicht überflüssig seyn, das Publicum auf Ihre Arbeiten aufmerksam zu machen und dazu vorzubereiten. Sollte Ihnen dieser Vorschlag der Ausführung werth scheinen, so biete ich Ihnen den Merkur dazu mit Vergnügen an, wenn Sie anders nicht durch das *honorar* von 5 rthl per 1 Bogen abgeschreckt werden, welches bey dem dermaligen zerrütteten Zustand des teutschen Buchhandels, alles ist, was der Herrausgeber eines schon 12 Jahre daurenden Journals thun kann.

Ich bin mit sehr vorzüglicher Hochachtung, Mein Herr,

Dero

ergebenster Diener

Wieland

Weimar d 1 Jun 1785.

Gurlitts Antwort umfaßt fünf Quartseiten:

Kloster Berge, 20. Jul. 1785.

Wolgeborner Herr,

Hochgeschäzter Herr,

Das gütige Schreiben, womit mich Eu. Wolgeboren beehrt haben, hat mich sowol durch seinen lehrreichen Inhalt, als durch die nachsichtige u.[7] für mich vorteilhafte Beurteilung meiner Arbeit u. durch die wolwollende Bereitwilligkeit meine Arbeit zu fördern, ganz außerordentlich erfreut: ich sage Ihnen daher den verbindlichsten Dank dafür. — Den ganzen Pindar zu geben [8], bin ich nicht Willens, weil ich es nicht besser tun zu können glaube, als Gedike; und wenn ich auch manches wenigstens anders darstellen u. erklären dürfte, so mag ich [9], da ich ihn u. er mich kennt, doch wenigstens nicht den Schein eines Wetteifers mit ihm annehmen. Ich habe daher blos die Nemeischen u. Isthms. Oden übersetzt, welche ich schon seit Jahr u. Tag fertig liegen habe. Vor ungefär einem Jahre ließ ich die e r s t e und zehnte Nems. in die Dessauischen Berichte [10] etc. (ich glaube, im Aug.

---

[7] u., darnach 'vor-', gestrichen.

[8] geben, darnach 'will' gestrichen.

[9] ich, darnach 'mich' gestrichen.

[10] Gemeint sind: B e r i c h t e d e r a l l g e m e i n e n B u c h h a n d l u n g d e r G e l e h r t e n , Dessau und Leipzig, die vom April 1781 bis Dezember 1784 erschienen. Gurlitts Beiträge stehen im 8. und 9. Stück, 1784.

u. Sept.) einrüken, welche zweie der besten sind; u. vor etwa
3 Monat sendete ich 3 Isthms. an einen Freund, um sie ins
Museum [11] einrüken zu lassen, habe sie aber noch nicht darinne
gefunden; welches jedoch an der Saumseeligkeit meines Freundes
liegen mag. Noch liegen mir also 10 Oden ungedrukt da, dann
habe ich alle noch nicht von Gedike [12] und von niemand, als dem
steifen ganz unpoets. Dam̄, übersetzten Oden geliefert. Eu. Wolgeboren [13] würden sich nun um meine geringe Arbeit sehr verdient machen u. mir die größte Gefälligkeit erzeigen, wenn
Sie diesen 10 Oden Raum in ihrem Journale vergönnten. Denn
ich weis, daß meine Arbeit alsdann allgemeiner bekan̄t wird,
als wenn ich sie besonders herausgebe: auch haße ich das wider-
holte Umherschreiben u. Pazisziren mit den Buchhändlern. In
dem Vertrauen auf Ihre Güte u. in Rücksicht auf Ihr Anerbieten,
wenigstens noch einige aufzunehmen, lege ich hier die Hälfte
derselben bei, u. ersuche Sie ergebenst, mir, wo möglich, baldigst,
mir in zwoon Zeilen zu [14] melden, ob ich den Rest übersenden
solle. Denn ihn sogleich beizuschließen achte ich für unbeschei-
denen Mißbrauch Ihres Anerbietens. Willigen Sie ein, so bin ich
gesonnen, es in der Jenaischen Litteraturzeitung [15] bekan̄t zu
machen, daß ich nun alle von Gedike noch nicht übersezten Oden
des Pindar übersezt habe, u. wo sie befindlich sind. — Ziemlich
deutlich, dünkt mich, habe ich sie abgeschrieben, damit dem
Sezer u. Korrektor hinfüro nicht wieder dergleichen Fehler
entwischen, als in No. 6, welche den Sinn verunstalten könten
z. B. g l e i c h w o n n i g [16] statt g l e i c h n a h m i g; e r g r e i f t
statt e r g r i f f [17]; E r z b ä n d i g e n d e n W e z s t e i n statt

---

[11] Gemeint ist Boies D e u t s c h e s M u s e u m: Gurlitts Beiträge finde ich
dort nicht. Dagegen enthält der Jahrgang 1786 drei seiner Nemeischen Oden.

[12] Friedrich Gedike, seit 1779 Direktor des Friedrichswerderischen Gymna-
siums zu Berlin, hatte Pindars Olympische Siegshymnen (Berlin, 1777) und
Pindars pythische Siegshymnen, mit erklärenden und kritischen Anmerkungen
(Berlin, 1779) herausgegeben. Chr. Tob. Damms V e r s u c h e i n e r p r o -
s a i s c h e n U e b e r s e t z u n g d e r g r i e c h i s c h e n L i e d e r d e s
P i n d a r war 1770, 1771 in Berlin erschienen.

[13] Wolgeboren darnach 'Da' gestrichen.

[14] zu, darnach 'verl' gestrichen.

[15] Eine Bekanntmachung Gurlitts habe ich ın ᴅer Jenaischen Literaturzeitung
1785 nicht gefunden.

[16] Die gerügten Druckfehler finden sich im Merkur wie folgt: 'gleichwonnig'
S. 200, 8; 'ergreifft' S. 198, 1. 2; 'Erzbändigen den' S. 202, 15; 'Olympios'
S. 195, 6.

[17] vor Erzbändigen 'Erb' gestrichen; darnach 'den' gestrichen.

Erzbändigenden; Kampfeserretter Olympios
statt Olympias. Jezt kann ich [18] den von Eu. Wolgeboren
mir angegebenen Stoff zu einer Abhandlung über die Brauchbar-
keit Pindars für den heutigen Lyriker nicht sogleich benuzen, weil
es mir an Zeit gebricht. Denn teils kosten mich meine Schul-
arbeiten den grösten Teil der Zeit, u. diese verrichte ich doch
gern mit Treue u. Fleiß, weil schriftstellerische Arbeiten dem
Beamten vielleicht mehr Glanz u. Ruhm, aber nur die gewissen-
hafte Abwartung des Berufs an jedem Abend von neuem Ruhe
u. Zufriedenheit giebt. Teils habe ich auch jezt schon meinen
Abriß der Geschichte der Philosophie [19] zu
meinen Vorträgen unter die Presse gegeben, und habe also bis
Michaëlis nicht die mindeste Zeit etwas anders zu unternehmen.
Aber auf die Michaëlisferien gedenke ich nicht nur die benannte
Abhandl. gröstenteils auszuarbeiten, sondern nebenher auch noch
eine andre, in welcher ich mich bemühen will, die großen unnach-
amlichen Schönheiten der 4ten Pythischen Ode, wo die herrliche
Episode vom Argonautenzug ist, auseinander zu setzen, wen ich
anders nicht über der Arbeit finde, daß leztre Abhandlung in die
erste sehr bequem verwebt werden kann. Den Band der *Memoires*
wo Chabanons Abhandlung steht, werde ich aus der Wolfenbüttl.
Bibl. erhalten.

Ich nehme mir die Freiheit, Eu. Wolgeb. hierbei auch mit ein
Paar kleinen Schriften [20] aufzuwarten. Ich wünschte Ihr Urteil
von denselben in einer Rezension im Merkur, oder im Anzeiger
zu vernehmen, wenn Sie es der Mühe wert achten. — Ziehen
Sie aber aus dem allen ja nicht den Schluß, daß ich Lust zum
Vielschreiben u., welches sehr häufig damit verbunden ist, Hang
zum Nachläßigschreiben hätte. Ich mag vielleicht schlecht schreiben; aber, ist dieß, so ist es nicht die Folge der Nachläßigkeit,
sondern des Mangels an Talenten, die ungeachtet alles Bemühens,
ungeachtet der behutsamsten u. überlegtesten Fortschritte im
Arbeiten, doch nichts mittelmäßiges hervorzubringen vermögen.
Als ich den Pindar ausarbeitete habe ich ein Vierteljar des Abends

---

[18] ich, darnach 'die' gestrichen.

[19] Das im Jahr 1786 bei Müller in Leipzig erschienene Buch ist im A n z e i g e r
d e s T e u t s c h e n M e r k u r, November 1786, S. CLXXXIII ff. angezeigt.

[20] Eine Anzeige der Schriften habe ich im Merkur nicht gefunden: es handelt
sich wohl um Gurlitts E i n l e i t u n g u n d A n m e r k u n g e n z u R o s e n-
f e l d s U e b e r s e t z u n g d e r z w e y B r a u t g e s ä n g e d e s C a t u l l s
u n d z w e y e r O d e n d e s H o r a z, Leipzig, 1785.

nicht gegeßen, um nur einmal wieder neben den gehäuften Amts-
arbeiten mit etwas hervortreten zu können. Denn ich hatte in
6 Jahren gar nichts schreiben können, und auch vorher warens
nur kleinere Piecen u. zwar in der morgenländischen Litteratur,
die ich nachher gegen die griechische u. römische Litteratur u.
Philosophie ganz vertauscht habe, wie es mein Amt samt meiner
Neigung von mir heischte. Denn wer wird nicht lieber die großen
Griechen u. Römer, als die Araber lesen? Eu. Wolgeboren ver-
zeihen mir diesen Egoismus. Ich hatte dabei zur Absicht, mich
Ihnen einigermaßen darzulegen, wie ich bin; u. einem Manne,
wie Sie sind, etwas näher bekant zu werden, muß mir höchst
schäzbar seyn. — Unter Versicherung meiner unbegränzten Hochachtung u. Ergebenheit verharre ich

Eu. Wolgeboren

gehorsamster Diener

Gurlitt

N. S. Mit dem mir von Eu. etc. bestimten Honorarium bin
ich völlig zufrieden; nur ersuche ich Sie mir dasselbe, erst nach-
dem alles eingerükt ist, im Ganzen zu übermachen, weil ich es zu
einer Reise nach Göttingen bestimt habe. — Noch wage ich es,
Ew. etc. um eine Gefälligkeit im Namen meines Kollegen, des
Oberlehrer L o r e n z , zu ersuchen. Dieser wünscht das M i n e -
r a l k a b i n e t c h e n n e b s t d e n d r e i (b e s o n d e r s g e -
d r u k t e n) B r i e f e n ü b e r d i e G e b i r g e v o n H n.
B e r g s e k r e t a i r V o i g t zu besizen. Dürfte ich bitten dasselbe durch Ihren Bedienten an mich einschließen zu lassen u. mir
die Auslage am Honorar. abzuziehen?

Wäre es möglich, zuweilen zwei Oden auf einmal [21] einzurüken,
so wäre mir dieß noch angenehmer; und dann würde auch früher
Plaz für die 2 Abhandlungen gewonnen. Besonders sähe ich es
gern, daß [22] noch eine neben der zweiten Nems. Ode eingerükt
würde, weil diese sehr kurz. — Ich wünschte übrigens, daß auch
diese Uebersezungen einigermaßen Ihren mir schäzbaren Beifall
erhalten. Mühe habe mir deßhalb gegeben, u. selbst zu denken
gesucht; welches Eu. Wolgeboren auch den Anmerkungen hin
u. wieder ansehen werden. (Schluß des ersten Briefes.)

---

[21] einmal, darnach 'anz' gestrichen.
[22] daß, darnach 'zu' gestrichen.

Wolgeborner Herr,

Hochgeehrtester Herr Hofrath,

Da ich aus fortdaurenden Einrüken meiner Pindarischen Oden
ersehe, daß Eu. Wolgeb. nicht unzufrieden mit denselben sind;
so laße ich mir das eine desto größere Aufmunterung zu den ver-
sprochenen Abhandlungen seyn, an welchen keinen Fleiß sparen
will. Ungeachtet ich nun zwar in den ersten zwei Monaten noch
nicht möchte ganz daran gehen können, so habe ich doch schon
vorläufig wegen der Abhandlung von Chabanon nach Wolfenbüttel
geschrieben, aber daher die Antwort erhalten, daß diese Abh.
weder in dem von Eu. Wolgb. angegebenen 58 Bande der *Memoir
de l'Acad. des B.L. & I.* noch in irgend einem andern Bande stehe.
Nun muß ich freilich sagen, daß ich in meinem Apparat, wo ich
ziemlich alles gesam̄elt habe, was über Pindar geschrieben ist,
nichts von einer Abh. im 58 Bande der genan̄ten *Mem.* fand,
wol aber eine Bemerkung antraf, daß Chabanon im 32 u. 35 Bande
etwas über Pindar, ich glaube aber blos Uebersezungen der
Pythisch. Gesänge eingerükt habe, welche er a. 72 zu Paris unter
dem Titel: *les Odes Pythiques de Pindar, traduites avec des
remarques* nebst einer Abh. über das lyr. u. Pindarische Gedicht,
herausgegeben. Ob nun diese Abh. schon im 32 oder 35 Bande
der *Mem.* gestanden habe, weis ich nicht. Besizen Eu. Wolgb.
die *Mem.* selbst, so ersuche ich Sie ergebenst mir gelegentlich nur
mit ein Paar Worten Auskunft zu geben, damit ich den Band
einem Bibliothekar mit Gewisheit bestimmen kan̄. Wenn alles,
auch die Abhandlungen, eingerükt sind, werde ich dem Hofr.
Heyne [23] alles zusam̄en überschicken, und zur Beurteilung vor-
legen, wovon ich ihm bereits schon vorläufig Nachricht gegeben
habe, als ich neulich an ihn schrieb.

Mit diesem Schreiben nehme ich mir die Freiheit, dem Herrn
Hofrath die Musikalien, deren ich neulich schon gedachte, zu
übersenden, mit dem ergebensten Ersuchen, sie, wenn es anderer
Umstände halber wol angeht, dem T. Merkur stükweise, wenn u.
wie viel Ihnen auf einmal gefällig ist [24], anzufügen. Da Ihre
Demoisells Töchter, wie ich aus dem [25] im Okt. des T. Merk.
befindlichen Tonkünst [26], und auch aus Hn. v. Alxingers Gedichte

---

[23] Gemeint ist Christian Gottlob Heyne in Göttingen.
[24] ist, darnach 'einzu' gestrichen.
[25] dem, darnach 'die' gestrichen.
[26] Tonkünst ist wohl Schreibfehler für Tonstük, welches weiter unten vor-

im T. Museum [27] ersehe, selbst Kunstverständige sind, so werden
Sie dieselben bald können entscheiden lassen, ob diese Stüke der
Publikazion werth sind. Ich hoffe aber, so wol derselben, als des
Herrn Hofraths eignes Urteil wird für dieselben ausfallen. Auch
das längste Stük, Gerstenbergs vortrefl. Mohrenlied, wird kompreß
gedrukt sehr gut können eingerükt werden. — Das Honorar für
diese Tonstüke überlaße ich ganz Ihrer Bestimmung; denn ich
bin ganz überzeugt, daß Eu. Wolgeb. dafür so viel bestimmen
werden, was Sie nach den ganzen Unständen bestim̄en können.
— Wenn ich über die Folge der Stüke in der Einrükung mein
Urteil sagen darf, so glaube ich würde es gut seyn mit [28] zween
der besten Stüke den Anfang zu machen; etwa mit No. 7 u. 8
mit Klaudius u. Goethens zwei herrlichen Liedern. Ich habe der
N a c h r i c h t , welche ich den erstern Stüken beizufügen bitte,
darnach eingerichtet, überlasse es aber im̄er noch des Hn.
Hofraths Gutbefinden, obs so seyn soll. Mit dem s c h l a f e n -
d e n M ä d c h e n u. d e m M o h r e n l i e d No. 10 u. 12 würde
etwa kön̄en der Beschluß gemacht werden, so daß die Liebhaber
von dem jungen Tonkünstler mit ihrer Zufriedenheit an seiner
musikal. Tafel empfangen u. demittirt würden. So rathete ungefär, wen̄ ich dem Ernste etwas Scherzhaftes beifügen darf,
die Rhetorik des vorigen Jahrhunderts u. auch wol noch die
jezige hin u. wieder [29], mit starken Argumenten zu beginnen u.
zu enden u. die schwachen Kinder derselben in der Mitte von
vorne u. hinten zu deken.

Eu. Wolgebor. würden mir eine große Gefälligkeit erzeigen,
wen̄ Sie mir von jedem beifolgenden Tonstüke ein E x e m -
p l a r [30] besonders abziehen ließen, weil ich sie nicht mehr besize,
weshalb ich auch ergebenst ersuche, sie so aufbewaren zu lassen,
daß nichts davon verloren geht.

In einem meiner vorigen Briefe war ich so frei, den Herrn Hofr.
zu ersuchen, das Voigtische Werkgen nur durch Ihren Bedienten
einsiegeln u. mit einer Aufschrift an mich begleiten zu lassen.

---

kommt. Das Oktober-Heft des M e r k u r s enthält eine Musik-Beilage: Lied, mit
Melodie von Caroline W. Der Text: Glänzender sinket die Sonne dort in das
wallende Meer, ist Caroline R. unterzeichnet.

[27] In meinem Exemplar des D e u t s c h e n M u s e u m s 1785 finde ich
keine Komposition eines Alxingerschen Liedes.

[28] mit, darnach 'dre' gestrichen; zween könnte auch als zwoon gelesen werden,
während die Form zweien zu erwarten wäre.

[29] wieder, darnach 'die' gestrichen.

[30] E x e m p l a r : über der Zeile ist 'Blatt' nachgetragen.

Ich hätte noch vorschlagen können, daß Sie blos die Güte haben möchten, Hn. Voigt den Zettel nebst der Aufschrift an mich zuzuschiken u. ihn bitten zu lassen es abzuschiken. Es ist hier in solchen Dingen mit unserm Buchhändler Scheidhauer nichts anzufangen, u. Hrr. K. Lorenz braucht es notwendig zu seinem Fache.

Außer den Musikalien sende ich Eu. Wolgeb. noch [31] einige kleine Uebersetzungen von einem hiesigen Lehrer, welcher mich ersucht hat sie beizuschließen, u. es dañ Eu. etc. Urteil zu überlassen, ob Sie die Bekañtmachung in Ihrem T. M. verdienen oder nicht, so wie er auch das Honorar dafür Ihrer gütigen Bestiñung überläßt. Ich habe die Uebersetzungen nicht mit dem Original verglichen, aber aus seiner mir bekañten Stärke in der Engl. Sprache u. aus seiner Uebung im deutschen Styl vermute ich gewiß, daß sie gut sind.

Ich empfele mich Eu. Wolgb. Gewogenheit u. Zuneigung u. verharre unter Bezeugung meiner unbegrenzten u. unveränderlichen Hochachtung und Ergebenheit

Eu. Wolgebor.

ergebenster Diener

Gurlitt

Kloster Berge
16 Nov. 1785.

Wahrscheinlich kamen Wieland die verschiedenen Zumutungen Gurlitts etwas zudringlich vor: in dem folgenden Antwortschreiben werden weder die »Paar kleinen Schriften« Gurlitts, noch die kleinen »Uebersetzungen von einem hiesigen Lehrer«, noch Voigts Mineralkabinetchen erwähnt, um dessen Zusendung Gurlitt zweimal gebeten hatte.

Hochgeschätztester Herr,

Was werden Sie von mir denken, daß ich Ihnen den Rest Ihrer Pindarischen [32] Oden, nehmlich soviel davon, als in dem nun zu Ende gehenden Jahrgang 1785 des T. Merkurs nicht Platz gefunden, wieder zurük schicke, ungeachtet ich in Ihrer Arbeit

---

[31] Am Rande ist mer nachgetragen: 'noch erlauben Sie mir vierbitte um akkuraten Druk der Musikalien. Ich oder mein verstorbener Freund möchten sonst die Fehler auf unsre Rechnung kriegen'.

[32] ursprünglich 'Phindarischen'.

die Hand eines Meisters erkenne, und Ihre Uebersetzung für die
einzige halte, die einen der griechischen Sprache wenig kundigen
und überhaupt einen jeden, der (aus welcher Ursache es sey) den
Pindar nicht im Original s t u d i e r t hat, mit dem Geiste und
der Manier dieses Dichters völlig bekannt machen, und ihm Ver-
ständniß und Genuß seiner oft so schwer zu verstehenden Gesänge
beybringen kann. Ich mußte aber den Gründen, die mir meine
associés [33] vorlegten, diesen Artikel im Merkur, der nun bereits
7 Monatsstücke durcl. *continuirt* worden, mit dem heurigen [34]
Jahrgange zu beschließen, um so mehr nach geben, da wir (wie
alle Herrausgeber solcher Journale, die mehr von Ungelehrten,
als Gelehrten gekauft werden) nicht blos auf die innere Güte
eines Artikels, oder auf das, was *ad palatum* der kleinen Zahl der
Leser [35] ist, sehen können, sondern noch dem Geschmack und
den Wünsche der des großen Haufens uns *accomodiren* müssen, für
welche (wie uns von mehreren Orten gemeldet wurde) diese
Pindarische *deliciae* [36] würklich schon zu oft aufgetischt worden
sind. Wie sehr ein Gelehrter, der für Pindars lyrisches Genie [37]
und die Schönheiten seiner Oden Sinn und Empfänglichkeit hat,
auch immer Freude daran haben kann, ihm in seinen Adlers-
flügeln zu folgen, so können wir uns doch nicht verbergen, daß
diese Siegesgesänge, im Ganzen genommen, für teutsche Leser
aus dem 18ten Jahrhundert, beynahe gar kein Interesse mehr
haben, noch haben können; und daß also ein Journal, das für
eigenliche gelehrte und Philologische Artikel sich noch weit
weniger *qualificirt*, als das D e u t s c h e M u s e u m, eigentlich
kein schicklicher Platz ist, eine lange *Suite* von Pindarischen
Stücken dem Publico aus zu stellen. Ich bin überzeugt, daß Sie,
mein hochgeschätztester Herr, dieses selbst einsehen, und sich
also durch die Zurücksendung der hiebey [38] gelegten Stücke, auf
keine Weise [39] beleidigt finden werden.

Meine unmaßgebliche Meynung wäre, daß Sie nun wohl am
besten thäten, Ihre Bemühung auf eine eigne Ausgabe Ihrer
Uebersetzung Pindars mit allen dazu nöthigen Commentarien

---

[33] *'associés'* in freigelassenem Raum vom Korrektor nachgetragen.
[34] 'heurigen' in freigelassenem Raum vom Korrektor nachgetragen.
[35] 'Leser' vom Korrektor über ein jetzt unleserliches Wort geschrieben.
[36] *'deliciae'* aus *'delicie'* korrigiert.
[37] 'Genie' aus 'Chenie' korrigiert.
[38] 'hiebey' aus 'hierbey' korrigiert.
[39] 'Weise' korrigiert aus?

und Abhandlungen zu wenden; wo vielleicht wohl gethan wäre, wenn Sie den Text neben Ihrer Uebersetzung mit abdrucken ließen. An einem Verleger dazu wird es Ihnen schwerlich fehlen können. Die Ausgabe der *Memoires de l'academie des Belles-Lettres*, die ich besitze, ist in Groß 12 oder vielmehr [40] *median* 12⁰, *à Paris chez Pancouke* 1772, nach und nach *continuirt* bis zum 80sten *volume*, welches das letzte ist, so ich von meinem Buchhändler in Strasburg bis dato erhalten habe. In dieser Ausgabe finden sich

1) eine *Dissertation* vom *Abbé Fraguier* über Pindar, im *vol.* 2.

2) eine Uebersetzung der 1. 2. 4. 5. 12. und 14 Olympischen und der 1 und 2 Isthmischen Ode, vom [41] *Abbé Massieu* (im 6. 8. und 14. *volume* zerstreut.

3) *Recherches* [42] *sur la vie et les ouvrages de Pindare* im 23ᵗ *volume*.

4) Ein *discours sur Pindar et sa poesie lyrique* im 58ˢᵗ *volume*

5) Uebersetzungen [43] nebst Einleitung und Anmerkungen [44] der 7. Olympischen und der 1. 2. und 3. Pythischen Ode von *Mons. de Chabanon* in besagten 58sten *volume*, sehr interessant und schön gedacht und geschrieben [45].

Für [46] die in den T. M. in diesem Jahre eingerückten Stücke lege hier eine kleine Erkenntlichkeit bey, womit für lieb u. willen zu nehmen bitte. Arbeiten dieser Art müssen durch das Vergnügen, das man selbst darin findet, belohnen, oder sie würden die undankbarste unter allen seyn. Ich muß auf das Hesiodische und Sokratische καθδύναμιν ἔρδειν [47] provociren: wäre ich ein König oder *Nabob* [48] von Bengalen, so sollte [49] weder ein Pindar, noch ein Uebersetzer desselben, wie Sie, über meine Munificenz gegen seltne [50] Talente zu klagen haben.

---

[40] 'vielmehr' über 'viertel' (?) geschrieben.

[41] 'Ode, vom' korrigiert aus 'oder, des' (?).

[42] '*Recherches*' in freigelassenem Raum vom Korrektor nachgetragen.

[43] 'Uebersetzungen' korrigiert aus 'Uebersetzung'.

[44] 'Anmerkungen' korrigiert aus 'Anmerkung'.

[45] Der Satz 'sehr . . . geschrieben' wurde vom Schreiber am Rande nachgetragen; der Korrektor strich diesen nicht sehr deutlichen Nachtrag, um ihn auf dem unteren Rande zu wiederholen, wobei er zuerst die Worte 'beides (nur 4 und)' schrieb und dann strich, während 'u. schön' vergessen und später nachgetragen wurde.

[46] 'Für' kein Absatz; der Korrektor bemerkt: 'NB abgesezt und eingerückt'.

[47] Vgl. Hesiod, Werke und Tage V. 336: κὰδ δύναμιν δ' ἔρδειν.

[48] 'Nabob' aus 'Nabot' korrigiert.

[49] 'sollte' aus 'sollten' korrigiert.

[50] 'seltne' aus 'seltene' korrigiert.

Die mir neulich [51] ebenfalls zum Gebrauch des Merkurs zugeschickten [52] Lieder-Compositionen [53] muß ich auch wieder zurück
gehen lassen, weil beschlossen ist, künftig (zumal seit dem Tode
des Herrn von Seckendorf) gar keine Musik mehr [54] im Merkur
zu liefern. Ich versichre Sie aber bey meiner Ehre, daß diese mir
anvertrauten Compositionen [53] beständig im meinem [55] Schreib-
tische eingeschlossen gewesen sind, und daß von keinem derselben
Abschrift genommen worden ist.

Bin ich auf irgend eine Weise im Stande Ihnen einige Gefällig-
keiten zu erweisen, so soll es wenigstens an meinem Willen nie
fehlen. Denn ich schätze und ehre die leider so selten unter uns
werdenden Gelehrten Ihrer Art, und werde daher nur mit dem
Leben aufhören, wiewohl ich des Vortheils Ihrer persönlichen
Bekanntschaft entbehre, einer Ihrer aufrichtisten und wärmsten
Freunde zu seyn.

Weimar d 18 Dec 1785.
   raptim! [56]   *Wieland*

Die von Wieland zurückgeschickten Oden hat Gurlitt dann im
Deutschen Museum und in Wiedeburgs humanistischem Magazin
untergebracht. Nach seiner Uebersiedelung nach Hamburg be-
nutzte er sie dann noch einmal zu Schulprogrammen; im Jahre
1816 wurden diese Programme unter einem Sammeltitel vereinigt:
P i n d a r s   P y t h i s c h e   S i e g s g e s ä n g e   ü b e r s e t z t
m i t   A n m e r k u n g e n   v o n   J.   G u r l i t t,   D r.   d e r
T h e o l.,   P r o f e s s o r   u n d   D i r e c t o r   d e r   L e h r -
a n s t a l t e n   d e s   ʾo h a n n e u m s   z u   H a m b u r g,   w i e
a u c h   P r o f e s s o r   a m   a c a d.   G y m n.   u n d   M i t g l i e d
d e r   S c h u l d e p u t a t i o n   e i n e s   h o c h a n s e h n -
l i c h e n   S c h o l a r c h a t s   d a s e l b s t.   i n   II   P r o g r a m m -
m e n. Angehängt ist Pindars erster und zehnter Siegsgesang.
Hamburg, 1816 (München, Staatsbibliothek A. gr. a. 783. 4).
Das auf diesen Titel folgende Vorwort ist vom 28. April 1816
datiert. Der folgende Text besteht aus elf besonders paginierten

---

[51] 'neulich' aus 'nemlich' (?) korrigiert.
[52] 'zugeschickten' aus 'zugeschiktenen' (?) korrigiert.
[53] 'Compositionen aus' 'Compositions' korrigiert.
[54] 'mehr' vom Korrektor nachgetragen.
[55] 'meinem' aus 'meinen' korrigiert.
[56] 'raptim' vom Korrektor nachgetragen.

Programmen aus den Jahren 1810—1816, die jedoch nicht in numerischer Reihenfolge stehen. Eine Anmerkung zeigt die ursprünglichen Erscheinungsjahre an; von den nicht im Merkur veröffentlichten waren erschienen: Nem. 1. in den *Ber. d. Buchh. d. Gel. 1784, St. 8;* Nem. 8 im *d. Museum 1786 St. 3;* Nem. 9 das. *St. 4;* Nem. 10 in den *Ber. der Gelehrtenbuchh. 1784 St. 9;* Nem. 11 im *d. Museum 1786, St. 9;* Isthm. 1 in *Wiedeb. hum. Mag. Neuiahr 1788*, S. 39; Isthm. 3 in *Wiedeb. hum. Mag. Johannis 1787* S. 280; Isthm. 4 das. Ostern 1788, S. 165; Isthm. 7 in *Wiedeb. h. Mag. Ostern 1787*, S. 345; Isthm. 8 das. Johannisstück 1788 S. 199.

—————

A LETTER OF GOETHE

BY BERT J. VOS
INDIANA UNIVERSITY

This letter, hitherto unpublished, reads as follows:

Ew Hochwohlgeb

übergebe, auf Sereniss. Befehl, beyliegendes Pro Memoria mit der Bitte davon Gebrauch zu machen. Noch füge ich bey daß Hr. Lips wünscht, wenn es thulich wäre, vorerst ohne Charackter hier zu existiren. Es würde ihm nach seiner Denkungs art angenehm und in seiner gesellschaftlichen Lage vortheilhaft seyn. Im Adreßkalender könnte er bey der Zeichen-Academie aufgeführt werden. Es ist ein gar wackerer Mann und tüchtiger fleißiger Künstler, der viel Nutzen stiften wird.

Ew Hochwohlgeb

W. d. 18. Decemb.   gehorsamster Freund

1789   und Diener

JWvGoethe

Our letter was acquired by purchase during the latter part of 1923 from the firm of Geering in Basel. As a supplement to the letters of the Weimar Edition it would bear the number 2793a. It is written, entirely in Goethe's hand, on a single sheet measuring $18^1/_2$ by $23^1/_4$ cent. The water-mark shows a dancing bear with trainer, both in profile. Along three of the edges of the sheet there is a scroll in water-mark. The top, where there is no such scroll, shows signs of having been trimmed, perhaps to the extent of $3^1/_2$ cent. The Weimar edition of the letters, at least in the volume (9) that would come in for consideration here, volunteers practically no information concerning the paper used in Goethe's letters, such chance remarks as that the paper of one letter is the same as that of another being of little real help.

Johann Heinrich Lips, the subject of the communication, is, of course, well-known as an engraver and painter of the period. It was especially for his ability as copper engraver that Goethe was intent upon drawing him to Weimar. The conditions of this engagement will be found described in Goethe's letter to Lips of March 23, 1789. For the eight volumes of the Schriften published by Göschen Lips furnished six engravings, the frontispiece of the Iphigenie volume, the frontispiece of the Egmont volume, the frontispiece and vignette of the Tasso volume, and the frontispiece and vignette of the Faust volume. Of these his engraving after Rembrandt for the frontispiece of the Faust volume is best known.

Lips was apparently not to have regular classes in the Zeichenschule; see No. 2738 of the Briefe: »Vorerst also soll ich Ihnen 150 rh. jährlich anbieten, welche Durchl. der Herzog zahlen, wogegen nichts von Ihnen gefordert wird, als daß Sie einigen jungen Leuten, welche bißher sich im Kupferstechen ein wenig geübt haben ... Anleitung gäben ...« Compare also letter No. 2796: »Von den Stunden Mittwochs und Sonnabends wird er wohl zu dispensiren seyn.« This will serve to explain the sentence in our letter »Im Adreßkalender könnte er bey der Zeichen-Academie aufgeführt werden«, which might seem rather singular in the case of a man called to Weimar specifically as Professor in the Zeichenschule. The Pro Memoria that was enclosed, and which appears to have been lost, I take to have been a statement of the conditions under which Lips took up his residence in Weimar, a statement that had the signature, or at least the approval, of the Duke. Lips had arrived in Weimar on November 13, as we know from Knebel's Tagebuch (WE., *Briefe* 9, 358). Goethe's letter to the Duke of November 20 has the passage: »Lips ist angekommen, seine Gegenwart wird viel gutes und erwünschtes stiften«, with which the phrase from our letter »ein ... Künstler, der viel Nutzen stiften wird« may be compared.

The addressee of the letter is, I take it, Christian Friedrich Schnauß. For the facts of the life of Schnauß we have the brief article of Ruland in the *Allgemeine Deutsche Biographie*, the vivid sketch [1] by Max Hecker in Volume V (1925) of the *Jahrbuch der Sammlung Kippenberg*, and an autobiography [2] published by Beaulieu-Marconnay.

The autobiography is deeply disappointing. It would seem

[1] Ein neuaufgefundener Brief Goethes von der zweiten Schweizerreise, *Jahrbuch* V, 5—12.

[2] Ein Weimarischer Beamter des achtzehnten Jahrhunderts, von Carl Frei herrn von Beaulieu-Marconnay, *Zeitschrift für deutsche Kulturgeschichte*, Neue Folge, IV. Jahrgang (Hannover *1875*), pp. 649—702. I have used the copy in the library of the University of Illinois.

almost impossible that a man of the learning and culture of
Schnauß, living in so stirring a period and in such close proximity
to genius, should not feel the need of self-expression in connection
with the literary life of the day. And yet the account is absolutely
barren of anything of this nature. The student of the economic
life of a Saxon duchy during the second half of the eighteenth
century will find copious information on the state of the weather,
on the prices current of grains and victuals, on usages at weddings,
christenings, and funerals (or, at least, on the expenditures
incident thereto), but the student of literature will in no way
find reflected the cultural relations of the most important period
of German literary history. When Goethe is mentioned, it is,
as likely as not, to chronicle his presence at a Schnauß family
wedding or christening.

Schnauß had since 1772 had a seat and vote in the Weimar
Privy Council and became a little later the director of the Ducal
Library and the Coin Cabinet. Although Ruland does not tell us,
it also appears that he and Goethe were jointly in charge of the
Zeicheninstitut. This is shown, among other things, by letter
No. 3232a in Volume 30 of the Weimar Edition, which contains
the Nachträge to the earlier volumes. Here Schnauß and Goethe
have together signed an »Unterthänigste Anfrage« to the Duke
requesting that Heinrich Meyer be given the »Character« of
Professor in the »hiesiges Fürstliches Zeichen-Institut«.

Including the present one, we have altogether thirteen letters
of Goethe to Schnauß. So far as the Weimar Edition affords a
clue, all of these letters from Goethe to his colleague are in his
own handwriting, as was perhaps to be expected. Six of them
deal directly with some phase of the activities of the Zeichenschule.

The formulae of salutation and subscription agree with this
theory. »Gehorsamster Freund und Diener« of the close could,
in fact, have been used toward only very few persons of Goethe's
circle. Striking correspondences with other letters to Schnauß
serve to enforce this argument. It will not be necessary to take
more than three of these.

On January 2, 1790, about a fortnight after the date of our
own letter, Goethe writes to Schnauß as follows:

Mit herzlichem Wunsche zum Eintritt in das neue Jahr, sende
ich den mir kommunicirten Extracktum Protocolli zurück.

Es wird einen guten Effeckt haben, wenn Ew. Hochwohlgeboren Herrn Lips auf der Akademie einführen und vorstellen
wollen. Von den Stunden Mittwochs und Sonnabends wird er
wohl zu dispensiren seyn, da er nur zum Unterrichte der jungen
Künstler da ist, und solche ihn zu Hause sprechen und seinen
Rath und Lehre einhohlen können.

. . . .

Ew. Hochwohlgeb.

gehorsamster Freund und Diener

Goethe.

Again, under date of December 14, 1796:

Ew. Hochwohlgeb.

erhalten hierbey den von Serenissimo gnädigst genehmigten Vortrag
und werden die Güte haben das weitere gefällig expediren zu lassen.

. . . .

Die Ackten folgen hierbey mit dem Wunsche, daß Sie solche
noch lange ins neue Jahrhundert führen mögen.

Unter Anwünschung eines glücklichen Eintritts ins nächste
Jahr verharre mit wahrer, lebhafter Hochachtung

Ew. Hochwohlgeb.

gehorsamster

Diener und treuer Freund

Goethe.

Here the »Vortrag« corresponds to the "Pro Memoria" in our
letter.

Finally, a letter of November 20, 1795:

Vielleicht fänden Ew. Hochwohlgeboren es in diesem Augen-
blicke nicht ungünstig, wenn wir bei Serenissimo unsers Ab-
wesenden, guten Meyers gedächten, demselben den Charackter
als Professor erbäten und ihn in dem neuen Adreßkalender unter
die Lehrer an der Zeichenschule, nach Professor Kestner setzten.
Sie sind mit mir einig, daß er in mehr als Einem Betracht diesen
öffentlichen Aveu verdient. Ich wünsche zu hören, daß Sie sich
recht wohl befinden.

Ew. Hochwohlgeboren

gehorsamster

Goethe.

The Adreßkalender of the above and of our letter is, it may
be added, the Hof- und Adreß-Kalender of Weimar.

RHYTHM AND MELODY AS PARODISTIC MEANS IN HEINE'S UNTERWELT

BY ERNST FEISE

THE JOHNS HOPKINS UNIVERSITY

In Heine's *Neuen Gedichten* we find a cycle of five poems, entitled *Unterwelt*, four of which present, transferred into a bourgeois atmosphere, the melancholy myth of Pluto, Proserpina, and Ceres, while the fifth, a stirring lyric complaint, suggests the underlying motif of the poet's own experience. In poem no. 1 Pluto, envying the fate of Sisyphus and the Danaides yearns for his bachelor days when the strident voice of his termagant wife did not drown out the barking of Cerberus. But Proserpina, in poem no. 2, is in no happier mood; in the cursed rat hole, as she calls her consort's royal residence, Charon, baldheaded and spindle-legged, and the judges of the dead with their bored faces are her only table guests. The summer vacation which Ceres proposes for her daughter is therefore gladly accepted by Pluto (no. 3), who, drinking punch with Lethe, will be happy to forget his wife, while she is sporting with village clowns at the harvest dance on earth. The cruel prosaic directness of the diction combined with the burlesque irony of a consummate stanzaic art, the structural importance of highly accented rhymes linked in a complex system but of a vulgar connotation [1], the monotonous staccato rhythm, the commonplace vocabulary and syntax — every means of artful unpoetic expression is combined to create the impression of bleak and hopeless distress. And in the middle of this cycle, as a climax, we find, prefixed by some verses of

---

[1] Geselle — Hölle — Gebelle; Proserpine — Miene; Ehejoche — Rattenloche; Ceres — gewähr' es; Himmel — Bauernlümmel; verschnaufen — saufen; traurig — vertraur' ich — schaurig — versaur' ich usw.

Heine's own make, three stanzas of Schiller's *Die Klage der Ceres*, anonymously quoted as "those plaints known by all of you".

The effect of this interpolation is most startling: "What a platitudinous declamation, what hollow, high-sounding phrases in Schiller's poem!" is our first reaction. But our puzzled astonishment gives way to a second and growing impression, a resentment against the parodist and his frivolous play with a fellow poet's artistic creation, which he has somehow succeeded in depreciating. But if, at last, we are able to overcome our offended sense of aesthetic propriety and analyze the rhythmic jugglery performed before our ears we cannot but marvel at the keenness of acoustic instinct, of parodistic roguery involved.

Even then we have not sounded the deepest meaning of this apparent desecration of another creator's *geprägte Form*, as we shall see later. For the present, we must stop to consider what rhythmic means Heine has used to produce the desired effect in the third poem of this cycle [2].

His own introductory stanza consists of eight lines with four crossed, alternating feminine and masculine rhymes (a˘b a˘b c˘d c˘d), which, however, have no tectonic function since the strongest stop, marked by a period, occurs after line 3 (Erde) instead of, as we should expect, after line 4; all other verse-end stops are more or less veiled by the syntactic unity of the resulting two sentences and the concurrent rise of the voice in at least every last syllable of each verse (this end rise, by the way, being characteristic of the whole cycle). The beginning of the line, in contrast, is marked by a distinct melodic fall, which starts in the arsis and continues throughout the first trochee; this downward tendency is repeated in every foot and creates the monotonous trot peculiar to the whole stanza, a movement which is not relieved but rather reinforced by the arrangement of the four arses in two degrees of intensity and on two contrasting tone levels. They follow, to use the technical term employed by Eduard Sievers [3], Type B (light heavy light heavy or low high low high)

---

[2] The text is printed below on p. 313.

[3] See Eduard Sievers: Rhythmisch-melodische Studien, Heidelberg 1912 p. 46 and Metrische Studien (*Abhandlungen der Kgl. Sächsischen Gesellsch. d. Wiss., Phil.-hist. Klasse B.* 21, p. 58 ff.).

with the exception of line 6 which accents heavy light light heavy.
The diagram of the curve would accordingly look like this:

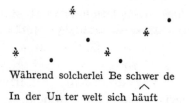

Während solcherlei Be schwer de
In der Un ter welt sich häuft

The tempo is fast. The ratio of the duration of arsis and thesis
is about even, for the accented syllables are cut short and level,
without a pronounced crescendo and decrescendo, not counting,
of course, the slight circumflection of the word before the pause
(häuft, läuft usw.). The voice quality which the stanza demands
for an adequate rendering is high and hard, the character con-
versational.

The meter of Schiller's poem is identical, but in rhytm and
melody it differs completely from Heine's introduction. To be
sure, the stanza, although containing four additional lines, shows
the same system of crossed, alternating maculine and feminine
rhymes; but while Heine's quatrains could be strung along
indefinitely like beads on a thread, the three component parts
in Schiller's poem, again subdivided by two and two, really
form a structural unity to which nothing could be added, from
which nothing subtracted without destroying the melodic harmony. The experiment, for instance, of skipping in an organic
reading from line 4 (Und des Eises Rinde springt) to line 9 (In
dem Hain erwachen Lieder) will reveal that the voice drops far
too low and arrives with the end of line 12 at an impossible
guttural level (»Die Stimme rutscht nach hinten« [4]). The reason
for this fact must be sought in the melodic composition of the
whole stanza, which seems to move in a preestablished balance
between the rather high start and the low end cadence.

A detailed analysis shows that the last (third) quatrain of the
stanza repeats the melodic movement of the first, only with a
decidedly stronger cadence and on a lower level. Each quatrain

---

[4] Concerning "freie und gehemmte Reproduktion" see Sievers, Ziele und
Wege der Schallanalyse (in Festschrift für Streitberg, Heidelberg 1924, p. 69—70
and Gunther Ipsen und Fritz Karg, Schallanalytische Versuche, Heidelberg
1928).

again is split into two chains, the two lines of which form a melodic unit. The first chain prefers a longer rise and short fall or a double rise and fall (see stanza I line 1 and 2), while in the second chain the long fall predominates (I, 3 and 4); in both cases the second line serves as a cadence to the first, i. e. 1 to 2 and 3 to 4.

Ist der holde Lenz erschie nen Hat die Er de sich ver jüngt

Die besonn ten Hü gel grü nen Und des Ei ses Rin de springt.

This melodic subordination is still more striking in the middle quatrain, where the flattened curve of the first two lines permits a long unbroken fall, while the second chain keeps up a rather high level of sustained interest and thus affords the last quatrain a sufficiently high start for the range of its cadence.

Aus der Ströme blauem Spiegel Lacht der un be wölk te Zeus

Milder we hen Zephyrs Flü gel Au gen treibt das junge Reis

Needless to say, then, that in contrast to Heine's dipodic types we have an up and down in scales with at least three virtually equal dynamic accents to the verse, that in contrast to Heine's end rise we have a fall at the end of every line and vice versa a rise at the beginning and were it only in a semivocalic m or l or in the circumflection of a long vowel (Reis!).

The diversity of tone direction is increased through the fact that the unaccented syllables do not invariably drop to a monotonous plane of indifference but have a strong part in shaping the described profile of the curve. The tempo is slow, the voice warmer and lower and of a singing quality, due to the swelling and ebbing of the tone cut of the arses, which have double the quantity of

$$<> \qquad <> \qquad <>$$

the theses (erschienen, verjüngt, Zeus, especially noticeable at line ends). If we read the poem in Schiller's Suabian dialect this latter peculiarity will stand out more strikingly; in that case the melody curves, although not changing in shape, would present their symmetrical mirrored reflection, so to say, of high and low.[5]

Our observations may then be tabled in the following abbreviated form:

	Heine	Schiller
Stanzaic structure:	open	closed
Tempo:	fast	slow
Accent:	predominantly dynamic (types)	predominantly melodic (scales)
Rhythm:	dipodic	monopodic
Rhythmic phrasing:	staccato	legato
Accented syllables:	cut short and even	long, cescendo-decrescendo
Unaccented syllables:	falling	following general tone curve
Line start:	falling	rising
Line end:	rising	falling

To complete the picture of this radical difference between the work of two poets we must still mention the criterion of the Becking curves. It has been established [6] that there are three principal curves, one of which (and only one) may be beaten (with the index finger of the right hand) to any individual production of prose and poetry while it is being read. The first, in the shape of a reversed Arabic 6 ($\mathcal{J}$), would, for instance, be called for by the works of Goethe. The second, in the shape of an horizontal 8 (∞), would apply to Schiller's works and thus in our case to *Die Klage der Ceres*. The third, in the form of an

---

[5] Concerning this phenomenon of "reversion" see Sievers' Rhythm.-Mel. Stud. p. 63 ff.

[6] Eduard Sievers: Ziele und Wege der Schallanalyse, l. c. p. 74 ff.

horizontal crescent (◡), will prove to be applicable to Heine's verse.

A diagram may illustrate the execution of the two curves in question at least for one line of each writer:

Abbildung

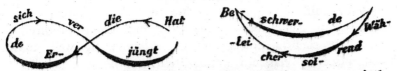

Thus far we have intentionally discussed the stanzas of the two authors as if they were two productions reproduced individually and in strict separation. Yet, we have experienced that the very effect Heine aimed to create was caused by the law of inertia, so to say, which forced us to carry over the insidious rhythm of the prefatory stanza in every characteristic feature and to superimpose it upon the organically different rhythm and melody of Schiller's poem. The most striking result is a change to dipodic movement, not, however, as we should expect, a continuation of type B but a breaking up of the monopodic lines into whatever types their gait, if accelerated, would most easily permit: Pegasus assuming the jagged trot of a jaded carthorse:

> Ist der hòlde Lénz erschienen?
> Hàt die Érde sìch verjùngt?
> Dje besónnten Hùgel grünen,
> Uñd des Eíses Rìnde springt.
> Aùs der Strôme blaùem Spiegel
> Làcht der únbewölkte Zeús,
> Mílder wèhen Zéphyrs Flügel,
> Aúgen treibt das jùnge Reís.
> In dem Háin erwàchen Lìeder,
> Ùnd die Òreáde spricht . . .

and so forth until, completely out of breath and aware of the ridiculousness of our rendering, we stop and consider into what trap we have fallen. It is significant, by the way, that Heine in his first draft (in 1840) of the cycle and in its first publication [7] quoted only two stanzas of Schiller's poem and that he added the third stanza later, probably in order to facilitate the transition to his own fourth poem (»Meine Schwiegermutter Ceres«) from

---

[7] *Zeitung für die elegante Welt* 1842 Nr. 11, 15 Januar. See Walzel's edition 2, 399.

the last lines of this stanza, which read as follows: »Ihre Träne bringt kein Zeuge Vor der bangen Mutter Blick«. His immediate auditory impression of the rhythmic jest was at that time, of course, worn away sufficiently so as to make him unaware of the observation that the psychological compulsion of his prefatory lines weakened with the length of the quotation.

What could have moved Heine to such an unprecedented parody of a truly poetic creation of one of his brethren in Apollo, to such a desecration of an avowedly well known masterpiece of classic German literature? Is it a parallel to his unsavory attack on Platen? Was it born of an innate aversion of one poet to another? An examination of all his utterances concerning Friedrich Schiller (facilitated by the index of Walzel's edition) must convince us that this is not the case, that Schiller is one of the German writers whose statue this iconoclast has left unturned. He calls him »den edelsten, wenn auch nicht den größten Dichter der Deutschen« (Reisebilder III, Kap. 33).

Let us remember the tone of bitter despair pervading the whole cycle, a cycle which culminates in the poet's realization of having robbed his wife of youth and happiness:

> Wiedergeben
> Kann ich dir nicht die Jugendzeit —
> Unheilbar ist dein Herzeleid;
> Verfehlte Liebe, verfehltes Leben [8].

He who so fervently wished for a life in Hellenic beauty and innocence after all never tasted the pagan love of Aphrodite but remained — his version of *Tannhäuser* (1836) demonstrates it — a Nazarene contenting himself with the love of »Frau Venus, die Teufelinne«. Thus his satire of the the Persephoneia legend is a veiled outcry at the realization of the gulf which separates his *petit ménage* with a little Parisian *grisette* from the world of Greek classic lore and love. Schiller's *Klage der Ceres*, dragged down to the level of platitudinous burlesque, is only the symbol in the symbol, the parody a heartrending masterpiece of selfirony.

---

[8] This poem was published later than the other four (*Zeitung für die elegante Welt* 1842, Nr. 104, 31. Mai), perhaps for discretion's (and Crescentia's) sake; even if it was not written with the others there can be little doubt that it presents the quintessence of the cycle.

UNTERWELT.
III.

Während solcherlei Beschwerde
In der Unterwelt sich häuft,
Jammert Ceres auf der Erde.
Die verrückte Göttin läuft
Ohne Haube, ohne Kragen
Schlotterbusig durch das Land,
Deklamierend jene Klagen,
Die euch allen wohlbekannt:

»Ist der holde Lenz erschienen?
Hat die Erde sich verjüngt?
Die besonnten Hügel grünen,
Und des Eises Rinde springt.
Aus der Ströme blauem Spiegel
Lacht der unbewölkte Zeus,
Milder wehen Zephyrs Flügel,
Augen treibt das junge Reis.
In dem Hain erwachen Lieder,
Und die Oreade spricht:
»Deine Blumen kehren wieder,
Deine Tochter kehret nicht.«

»Ach wie lang ist's, daß ich walle,
Suchend durch der Erde Flur!
Titan, deine Strahlen alle
Sandt' ich nach der teuren Spur!
Keiner hat mir noch verkündet
Von dem lieben Angesicht,
Und der Tag, der alles findet,
Die Verlorne fand er nicht.
Hast du, Zeus, sie mir entrissen?
Hat, von ihrem Reiz gerührt,
Zu des Orkus schwarzen Flüssen
Pluto sie hinabgeführt?

»Wer wird nach dem düstern Strande
Meines Grames Bote sein?
Ewig stößt der Kahn vom Lande,
Doch nur Schatten nimmt er ein.
Jedem sel'gen Aug' verschlossen
Bleibt das nächtliche Gefild',
Und solang' der Styx geflossen,
Trug er kein lebendig Bild.
Nieder führen tausend Steige,
Keiner führt zum Tag zurück;
Ihre Träne bringt kein Zeuge
Vor der bangen Mutter Blick.«

SWEDISH WITCHCRAFT AND THE MATHERS

BY ADOLPH B. BENSON
YALE UNIVERSITY

By September 22, 1692, nineteen persons had been hanged for witchcraft in Massachusetts, besides one who, "in accordance with the old criminal law practice, had been pressed to death for refusing to plead." The excitement ran indeed so high, we are told, that two dogs accused of witchcraft were put to death. — "A certain degree of reaction, however, appeared to be taking place," says an authoritative resumé of the history of the matter, "and the magistrates who had conducted the proceedings began to be alarmed, and to have some doubts of the wisdom of their proceedings. Cotton Mather was called upon by the governor to employ his pen in justifying what had been done; and the result was, the book ... "The Wonders of the Invisible World," in which the author gives an account of seven of the trials at Salem, compares the doings of the witches in New England with those in other parts of the world, and adds an elaborate dissertation on witchcraft in general. This book was published at Boston, Massachusetts, in the month of October, 1692."[1]

The governor had selected Cotton Mather, the eminent divine, teacher and writer, to defend or explain the execution of the witches (and that of Mr. George Burroughs, "a minister of the Gospel, whose principal crime appears to have been a disbelief in witchcraft itself"), because it was he who had been the most ardent believer in witchcraft and the most relentless spirit in the prosecution of the victims. He was readily and energetically assisted in his furious campaign by his equally credulous father, Increase Mather, the president of Harvard College, who after the famous accusation of Mrs. Hale, a clergyman's wife, published *A Further Account of the Tryals of the New England Witches* . . .

---

[1] Introduction to *The Wonders of the Invisible World*, London 1862, viii.

To Which is added Cases of Conscience[2] *Concerning Witchcraft and Evil Spirits personating Men*. The above-mentioned books by Cotton and Increase Mather, now very rare, were both reprinted in London in the year 1693. For this paper the writer has been using the London edition of 1862, which contains both works and an informative introduction [3].

But what has the Massachusetts witchcraft mania to do with Swedish witchcraft and the Mathers? Just this: In his cited book of defense, *The Wonders of the Invisible World*, Cotton Mather, for instance, makes bold to strengthen his own argument and position by quoting a story of the ravages and punishment of the witches in the province of Dalecarlia (Dalarne) in Sweden. A few references are made also in Mather's work to witchcraft visitations in England, Scotland, Denmark, Germany and France; but his argumentative *pièce de resistance*, so far as fortifying himself by foreign proof is concerned, appears to be the "Extracts from Dr. Horneck showing the Similarity in the Circumstances attending the Witchcraft in New England and that in Sweedland." [4]. In fact, the title-page of the original announces among four special matters to be treated the following item: "A Short Narrative of a late outrage committed by a knot of Witches in *Swede-Land*, very much resembling, and so far explaining, that under which *New-England* has laboured." In other words, because of a strong alleged resemblance between the cirsumstances and events of the witchcraft epidemic in Sweden and that of New England, the former became a main prop for the argument of Cotton Mather's

---

[2] A question of "conscience" was raised, whether or not the devil could assume "the shape of an innocent and pious person [like Mrs. Hale] for the purpose of afflicting his victims." *Ibid.*, ix.

[3] An examination of the witchcraft books by the two Mathers reveals a credulity which to-day is unbelievable of course. That two theologians, who have always been regarded as able scholars also, could ever descend to such abysmal ignorance and superstition as are evidenced in these writings seems indeed incredible. Yet the horrible truth is all too plain. True, many prominent clergymen, scholars, magistrates and physicians, all over the world were temporarily blinded by the witchcraft delusion; but a large percentage of these ultimately realized the error of their ways, and those who did not in despair commit suicide repented and used their influence to check the revolting madness. Not so the Mathers. Not only Increase and Cotton clung doggedly to their original beliefs and assurances, but the latter's son Samuel appears to have continued far into the eighteenth century to champion his father's claims. The "vanity of superior intelligence and knowledge was so great in the two Mathers [Increase and Cotton] that they resisted all conviction." Cf. *Ibid.*, xii.

[4] *Ibid.*, xiv.

The Wonders of the Invisible World. And it should be remembered
that the author claimed first of all to be "an *Historian*," and not
an "Advocate" of witchcrafts [5]. His father claimed the same
distinction. In view of its historical interest we shall here reproduce
in full Cotton Mather's account of Swedish witchcraft in Mora,
Dalarne [6].

"**But** is *New-England* the only Christian Countrey, that hath
undergone such Diabolical Molestations? [asks the author] No,
there are other Good people, that have in this way been harassed;
but none in circumstances more like to *Ours*, than the people of
God, in *Sweedland*. The story is a very Famous one; and it comes
to speak English by the Acute Pen of the Excellent and Renowned
Dr. *Horneck*. I shall only single out a few of the more Memorable
passages therein Occuring; and where it agrees with what happened
among ourselves, my Reader shall understand, by my inserting
a Word of every such thing in **Black Letter.**

I. It was in the Year 1669 and 1670, That at *Mohra* [Mora] in
Sweedland, the **Devils** by the help of **Witches**, committed a most
horrible outrage. Among other Instances of Hellish Tyrany there
exercised, One was, that hundreds of their Children, were usually
in the night fetched from their Lodgings, to a Diabolical Rendezvous, at a place they called, *Blockula*, where the Monsters that
so Spirited them, **Tempted** them all manner of Ways to **Associate**
with them. Yea, such was the perilous Growth of this *Witchcraft*,
that Persons of Quality began to send their Children into other
Countries to avoid it. [7]

II. The Inhabitants had earnestly sought God by **Prayer;**
and **Yet** their Affliction **Continued.** Whereupon **Judges** had a
Special **Commission** to find and root out the Hellish Crew; and
the rather, because another County in the Kingdom, which had
been so molested, was delivered, upon the Execution of the
Witches.

III. The **Examination,** was begun with a Day of **Humiliation;**
appointed by Authority. Whereupon the Commissioners **Consulting,** how they might resist such a Dangerous Flood, the **Suffering
Children,** were first Examined; and tho' they were Questioned

---

[5] *Ibid.*, 110.

[6] Professor George H. Ryden of the University of Delaware first called my
attention to the following account.

[7] "Blockula" in this paragraph is of course intended to be "Blåkulla"; "Elfdale", below, the modern "Elvedal"; and "Fahluna", "Falun."

One by One apart, yet their **Declarations All Agreed.** The **Witches** Accus'd in these Declarations, were then Examined; and tho' at first they obstinately **Denied,** yet at length many of them ingeniously **Confessed** the Truth of what the children had said; owning with Tears, that the **Devil,** whom they call'd *Locyta,* had **Stopt** their **Mouths;** but he being now **Gone** from them, they could **No Longer Conceal** the Business. The things by them **Acknowledged,** most wonderfully **Agreed** with what other **Witches,** in other places had confessed.,

IV. They confessed, that they did use to **Call Upon** the **Devil,** who thereupon would **Carry** them away, over the Tops of Houses, to a Green Meadow, where they gave themselves unto him. Only one of them said, That sometimes the *Devil* only took away her **Strength,** leaving her **Body** on the ground; but she went at other times in **Body** too.

V. Their manner was to come into the **Chambers** of people, and fetch away their children upon Beasts, of the Devils providing: promising **Fine Cloaths** and other **Fine** Things unto them, to inveagle them. They said, they never had power to do thus, till of late; but now the Devil did **Plague** and **Beat** them, if they did not gratifie him, in this piece of Mischief. They said, they made use of all sorts of **Instruments** in their Journeys: Of **Men,** of Beasts, of **Posts;** the *Men* they commonly laid asleep at the place, whereto they rode them; and if the children mentioned the **Names** of them that stole them away, they were miserably **Scurged** for it, until some of them were killed. The **Judges** found the marks of the Lashes on some of them; but the Witches said, **They Would Quickly Vanish.** Moreover the Children would be in **Strange Fits,** after they were brought Home from these Transportations.

VI. The **First Thing,** they said, they were to do at *Blockula,* was to give themselves unto the Devil, and **Vow** that they would serve him. Hereupon, they **Cut Their Fingers,** and with **Blood** writ their **Names** in his **Book.** And he also caused them to be **Baptised** by such **Priests,** as he had, in this Horrid company. In **Some** of them, the **Mark** of the **Cut Finger** was to be found; they said, that the Devil gave **Meat** and **Drink,** as to *Them,* so to the Children they brought with them: that afterwards their Custom was to *Dance* before him; and *swear* and *curse* most horribly; they said, that the Devil show'd them a great, Frightful, Cruel *Dragon,* telling them, **If They Confessed Any Thing,** he would let loose that Great Devil upon them; they added, that the Devil had a **Church,** and that when the **Judges** were coming, he told them, **He Would Kill Them All;** and that some of them had **Attempted To Murder The Judges, but Could Not.**

VII. Some of the **Children,** talked much of a **White Angel,** which did use to **Forbid** them, what the Devil had bid them to do, and **Assure** them that these doings would **Not Last Long;** but that what had been done was permitted for the wickedness of the People. This **White Angel,** would sometimes rescue the Children, from **Going In,** with the Witches.

VIII. The Witches confessed many mischiefs done by them, declaring with what kind of **Enchanted Tools,** they did their Mischiefs. They sought especially to **Kill The Minister** of *Elfdale,* but could not. But some of them said, that such as they wounded, would **Be Recovered,** upon or before their Execution.

IX. The Judges would fain have seen them show some of their **Tricks;** but they Unanimously declared, that, **Since They Had Confessed,** all, they found all their **Witchcraft** gone; and the Devil then **Appeared Very Terrible** unto them, threatning with an **Iron Fork,** to thrust them into a Burning Pit, if they persisted in their Confession.

X. There were discovered no less than *threescore and ten* Witches in One Village, **Three And Twenty** of which **Freely Confessing** their Crimes, were condemned to dy. The rest, (**One** pretending she was with Child) were sent to *Fahluna,* where most of them were afterwards executed. Fifteen Children, which confessed themselves engaged in this Witchery dyed as the rest. Six and Thirty of them between *nine* and *sixteen* years of Age, who had been less guilty, were forced to run the Gantlet, and be lashed on their hands once a Week, for a year together; twenty more who had less inclination to these Infernal enterprises were lashed with Rods upon their Hands for three Sundays together, at the Church door; the number of the seduced Children, was about three hundred. This course, together with **Prayers,** in all the Churches thro' the Kingdom, issued in the deliverance of the Country.

XI. The most Accomplished Dr. *Horneck* inserts a most wise caution, in his preface to this Narrative, says, he, *there is no Public Calamity, but some ill people, will serve themselves of the sad providence, and make use of it for their own ends; as* Thieves *when an house or town is on Fire, will steal what they can.* And he mentions a Remarkable Story of a young Woman, at *Stockholm,* in the year 1676, Who accused her own Mother of being a Witch; and swore positively, that she had carried her away in the Night; the poor Woman was burnt upon it: professing her innocency to the last. But tho' she had been an Ill Woman, yet it afterwards prov'd that she was not *such* an one; for her Daughter came to the Judges, with hideous Lamentations, Confessing, That she had wronged her Mother, out of a wicked spite against her; whereupon the Judges gave order for her Execution too.

But, so much of these things; And, now, *Lord, make these Labours of thy Servant, Profitable to thy People."*

While these quotations speak for themselves, for the most part, a few comments seem appropriate. In the references to what we may call the historical background we find certain statements and inferences that are essentially correct. That a particularly contagious form of witchcraft raged in a remote part of Dalarne, Sweden, in the seventh and eighth decades of the seventeenth century is well known. Every Swedish reader will have heard of the witches' flight to *Blåkulla* and may in Cotton Mather's account recognize some other features of demonic tactics so often proclaimed in Swedish legends of the devil and his servants. But the Boston Puritan and his father either accepted everything that they had read at its full face value, or they were the biggest scoundrels that Puritanism ever produced. Cotton either did not heed or wish to heed the wholesome caution set forth by his source in regard to making false accusations against innocent persons. To apply the moral of Dr. Horneck's counsel to his own actions either did not occur to him or, if it did, he slyly simulated innocence and approval of his own doings by calmly and hypocritically reproducing the story of the girl from Stockholm who had wrongly accused her mother of being a witch. It is obviously a case either of the most unthinkable blindness or the vilest pretense, and a dispassionate judgment forces us to admit that it must have been the former.

But why, in the first place, should an enlightened doctor of theology from Boston seek his heaviest polemic ammunition in the peasant district of distant Dalarne? Was it not sufficient to note that *"Now Hundreds* [of witches] *are discovered in one*

Shire [in England] ?" [8] Why carry devilish witchcraft coals to Newcastle? Cotton Mather evidently needed what he considered far more tangible and convincing evidence and so turned to a country beyond Great Britain, the land of his own ancestors. It is an extremely interesting Scandinavian influence with which we are dealing here. It is an unfortunate one perhaps, considering that this is probably the first Scandinavian influence we have on a New England book—and Swedes will not be particularly proud of it—but it is one possessing curious interest nevertheless. And we shall see later, that unless we consider Cotton Mather in all respects an idiot his method of procedure is in reality something of a tribute to Sweden.

Cotton Mather mentions a Dr. Horneck as his source. This was Anthony Horneck, a German who had settled in England and who had written "An Account of what happened in the Kingdom of *Sweden in the Years 1669, 1670 and upwards*. In relation to some Persons that were accused for *Witches;* and Tried and Executed by the King's Command . . . Done into the High-Dutch, by Anthony Horneck D. D." He had then translated it into English, as we have seen. [9] This English version had, furthermore, been incorporated in Joseph Glanvil's *Sadducismus Triumphatus or a full and plain Evidence concerning Witches and Apparatus*, of which a second edition appeared in 1681 and a third in 1689. It seems to have been a very popular work and a fourth edition, a copy of which the writer has examined, came out in 1726 [10].

Glanvil's book containing Horneck's account of witchcraft in Sweden proved a godsend—if I may use that term—to the Mathers when the governor of Massachusetts demanded a reckoning. "Executed by the King's Command" said the official Swedish report of the convicted criminals. Under the unbearable pressure of the Swedish state clergy, Dalecarlian witchcraft had finally, at least nominally, received an official recognition; it had nominally been attested by certain high but frightened personages;

---

[8] *Ibid.*, p. 88.

[9] In his article on "Witchcraft" (1868) James Russell Lowell included an account of witchcraft in Sweden. He speaks of the witches' flight to "Blockula" and of the executions at "Mohra". Lowell undoubtedly used the same source, though I once believed that he might have received an oral account of the persecutions from Longfellow, who had been in Sweden. Cf. my article on "The Essays of Fredrika Bremer in the *North American Review*", PMLA, XLI, 754, note 12.

[10] See pp. 474—499 for the account of Swedish witchcraft.

and so victims were thereafter dispatched "by the King's Command." This was just what the Mathers needed—more authority to execute "by the King's Command"; and if this had been done in old civilized Sweden, it should of course be done in the more recent settlements of Salem and Boston—according to the light and logic of the Mathers. Here was welcome proof not only of the prevalence of witchcraft in general but that the learned divines of Massachusetts had in their prosecution of witches acted justly in the past. As we have seen, they made the most of their data. It was not brought out, of course, that the most appalling cases of Swedish witchcraft, especially those among Dalecarlian children occurred in the backwoods, so to speak, and that their treatment could hardly be considered a model for an enlightened urban community in any land, not even for the Boston of 1692. But Sweden was in the seventeenth century everywhere held in high regard; the victories of the Protestant champion Gustavus Adolphus had not yet been forgotten; Swedish people had made a permanent settlement on the American shore not so many years after the Pilgrim Fathers; Scandinavian culture was closely akin to the Anglo-Saxon, and therefore any "evidence" from Sweden carried weight and was eagerly sought. So Cotton Mather's method may indirectly be considered a tribute to that country. It is at least doubtful, too, whether examples of witchcraft from southern Catholic Europe would have been considered valid in a Salem court of 1692.

Of course mere chance may have played a part in Cotton Mather's sources. In his zeal, hurry, and fanatic excitement he grasped the information nearest at hand and did the best he could with the matter at his immediate disposal. Among these was the popular work on witches by Glanvil, containing happily Horneck's work on witchcraft in Sweden, perhaps the best and most suitable foreign account extant on the subject. Tales of Swedish witchcraft had been very popular in England and Germany, and especially the more flagrant examples of intercourse with Satan, from remote districts, appealed to the morbid interest of high and low alike. The fact that devilish things happened in far-off Scandinavia added a gloomy, romantic and highly effective glamor to the stories. Then when Mather found what he could parade as a governmental stamp of approval of the method of punishment, he no longer hesitated to adopt the Swedish material for his chief defense.—We shudder to think that the Swedish witchcraft accounts may in the Massachusetts trials have influenced Cotton Mather's merciless attitude toward innocent defendands. But this possibility is very remote: no foreign evidence could have made the Mathers more adamantly bigoted in their inner convictions regarding witches than they already were. When some of their more rational neighbors later began to see the light, the Mathers stubbornly commenced to collect material and take such other measures as they deemed imperative to prove their bitterly contested ideas and statements, to enforce their opinion upon others, and to maintain their old position at all hazards.

We have noted that Increase Mather came to his son's assistance in defending the powers of witchcraft. His *Cases of Conscience Concerning Witchcrafts*, also, contains striking references to Swedish witches and Lapland magic. . . . "It is not usual for devils", says Increase, "to be permitted to come and violently carry away persons through the Air, several miles from their Habitations: Nevertheless, this was done in *Sweedland* about twenty years ago by means of a cursed Knot of Witches there" [11]. The case of the Swedish girl from Stockholm who in 1676 had falsely accused her mother of diabolical relations is told by Increase[12] as well as Cotton; and he also tells the story of "A Witch in *Sweedland* [who] confessed, that the Devil gave her a wooden Knife; and that if she did but touch any living thing with that Knife; it would die immediately". . . . [13] The fame of the Laplander's magic, so pronounced in many European travelogues of the time, had reached America also. Increase Mather had absolute faith in the Laplander's power of "second sight" which was quite independent of any guilty associations with ordinary witchcraft" . . . This is common amongst the *Laplanders*," asserts the learned president of Harvard College, "who are horribly addicted to Magical Incantations: They bequeath their *Daemons* to their Children as Legacy, by whom they are often assisted (like Bewitched Persons as they are) to see and do things beyond the Power of Nature. An Historian who deserves Credit, relates, that a certain *Laplander* gave him a true and particular Account of what had happened to him in his Journey to *Lapland;* and

---

[11] *Cases of Conscience* (bound in one volume with his son's *Wonders of the Invisible World*, London, 1862), 242.

[12] *Ibid.*, 280.

[13] *Ibid.*, 249.

further complained to him with Tears, that things at great distance were represented to him, and how much he desired to be delivered from that Diabolical Sight, but could not; this doubtless was caused by some Inchantment" [14].

No further comment is necessary. To-day the chief importance of what we have attempted to describe in this paper lies in the historical fact that the witchcraft polemics of the Mathers disclose definite Swedish influence on two New England writers as early as 1692.

---

[14] *Ibid.*, 246.

ANGLIST AND *ANGLICIST*

BY KEMP MALONE
THE JOHNS HOPKINS UNIVERSITY

The terms *Anglist* and *Anglicist* are not recorded in the *New English Dictionary* or the *Century*. In *Webster's* only *Anglist* is given; it is defined as "one versed in English linguistics". In the *Standard* both terms appear: *Anglist* is defined as "one skilled in English philology"; *Anglicist*, as "one who is in sympathy with or advocates anything promoting the interests of England or the English language or people". From the following quotation it appears that *Anglicist* has been in the language for nearly a hundred years:

Macaulay . . . at once became the leader of the Anglicists [in the controversy of 1835][1].

Anglist, on the other hand, seems to be a recent importation into English from the Continent. The term is based on a Latin noun, either *Anglia* "England" or *Anglus* "an Englishman". *Anglicist*, on the other hand, is based on a Latin adjective, *anglicus* "English". The difference in etymology corresponds closely to a difference in meaning, although this difference is obscured, or even distorted, by the definitions given in the dictionaries. *Anglist* is a learned or technical term which, so far as I am aware, has never had any vogue in popular speech. On the Continent it is applied to an authority on England and the English. Such an authority is a man who has devoted himself to the scientific study of the national culture of England, either as a whole (and he is the Anglist *par excellence*) or in some aspect or aspects. The term may therefore be applied to a historian of English politics, economics, literature, language, laws, customs, what not. This broad connotation did not desert the term when it was imported into English, and although *Anglist* can of course be applied to an authority on English linguistics the definition

---

[1] V. A. Smith, *Oxford History of India*, p. 670.

quoted above from *Webster's* must be condemned as too narrow. The definition given by the *Standard* is less objectionable, if we take *philology* in the broad sense, as "the scientific study of a national culture". But since this word is so often used in a much narrower sense, the definition of *Anglist* in the *Standard* is misleading and not to be recommended.

Anglicist as an English word has a very different history and background. It was no importation, but a native coinage, and was first used as a popular rather than as a learned term. In the controversy of 1835, an Anglicist was a man who advocated the use of the English language as the medium of instruction in schools for the natives of India. The term thus had, at first, a very limited scope, and was closely tied up with a particular aspect of English culture, viz., the English language and the literary monuments written in that language. With the settlement of the controversy the word seems to have gone out of popular use, but it has been seized upon as a technical term, in the sense "an authority on the English language and English literature". This usage fits in admirably with the etymology and the previous history of the word alike, and enables us to make a neat distinction between *Anglist* "authority on England", and *Anglicist* "authority on English". The definition of *Anglicist* given in the *Standard* is obviously too broad. The editors are to be commended, however, for recording the word, which seems to have eluded all other lexicographers.

But *Anglicist* is by no means an isolated term; on the contrary, it is only one of a group, and must be considered in its relations to the other members of the group. *Latinist* is another noun in *-ist* based on a Latin adjective. According to the *NED* it means "one who is versed in the Latin language; a Latin scholar". Here we have a definition far from good but highly characteristic of the dictionary makers when they come to deal with words of this type. As a matter of fact, *Latinist* has two meanings in English, and these meanings are different enough to deserve separate treatment. In the learned world, a Latinist is an authority on Latin. In popular use, however, anyone who can read Latin with tolerable ease and accuracy may be called a Latinist. Thus, Macaulay uses *Latinist* in the popular sense when he says of Samuel Johnson,

He read little Greek . . . but he had left school [at the age of 16]

a good Latinist, and he soon acquired . . . an extensive knowledge of Latin literature. [2]

Other words similarly formed are *classicist, medievalist, modernist, orientalist, Gothicist, Italianist, Romanist* and *Germanist*. These words are all recorded in the *NED*. The first is defined as (1) "an upholder or imitator of classic style or form;" (2) "one who advocates the school study of the Latin and Greek classics". The *Century* gives, besides, the meaning "one versed in the classics", and *Webster's* and the *Standard* likewise recognize this meaning. In present use, I think, four meanings of *classicist* ought to be distinguished: (1) an authority on Greek and Latin; (2) one who, without being an authority, is more or less versed in Greek and Latin; (3) a propagandist for Greek and Latin studies in our schools; (4) one who belongs to, follows or upholds any movement called classical, in literature, music or the arts generally. The first two of these meanings correspond to the two meanings of *Latinist* and are therefore of interest to us in this connection. Parallel to *classicist* is *medievalist*, which the *NED*. thus defines: "one who studies or is skilled in medieval history or affairs; one who practises medievalism in art, religion, etc." The other dictionaries hardly improve on this definition. In my opinion four separate meanings of the word ought to be given: (1) an authority on the Middle Ages, or on one or more aspects of medieval civilization; (2) a student of medieval culture; (3) a propagandist for medieval studies in our schools; (4) a defender or advocate of anything called medieval. It will be noted that *medievalist* in its first or learned sense differs from *classicist* in that it does not have primary reference to language and literature. The same must be said of *Gothicist*, which the *NED*. defines as "one who affects or is conversant with the Gothic style, especially in architecture". *Webster's* and the *Standard* give similar meanings; the word is not recorded in the *Century*. On the other hand, *Orientalist*, according to the *NED*, means "one versed in Oriental languages and literature". Here "versed" must be taken in a technical or learned, not in a popular sense; our word does not seem to have acquired a popular meaning distinct from its learned meaning. A better definition for it would be "an authority on Oriental languages and literatures". *Italianist* is defined in the *NED*. as "one who Italianizes";

---

[2] *Works*, ed. Lady Trevelyan, vol. VII, p. 325.

in the *Standard*, as "one who imitates Italian characteristics". These meanings are loose and obviously popular; in learned circles the word means "an authority on Italian". I have not found a corresponding popular meaning "one who has a knowledge of Italy and of the Italian language" but I suspect the word is sometimes used in such a sense. Certainly *Germanist* has a parallel use; in the *NED.* it is defined (1) as "one who has a knowledge of Germany and of the German language", and (2) as "one versed in Germanic or Teutonic philology". To these definitions *Webster's* and the *Standard* add a third: "one learned in the German language". The last two definitions evidently represent learned or technical terminology. They would be better put as (2) "an authority on Germanic", and (3) "an authority on German". The restriction to linguistics, implied in the definition of *Webster's* and the *Standard*, cannot be justified. The first definition reflects popular usage, of course; its learned or technical counterpart, "an authority on Germany", is ignored by all the dictionaries. One definition of *Romanist* in the *NED.* is "one who makes a special study of Romance languages or philology". This definition is not recorded in the *Century*, *Webster's* or the *Standard*.

From this survey, to which other terms might have been added (as *humanist*, *activist*, *naturalist*), we may conclude that nouns in *-ist* based on a Latin adjective are not infrequent in English, and that they are given very inadequate treatment by the dictionaries. Nouns in *-ist* based on a Latin substantive are also at home in the English language, but not at home in the dictionaries. I have already mentioned *Anglist*. Another word of this type is *linguist*. Here the *NED.* for once makes a distinction between the popular and technical meanings. It defines *linguist* (1) as "one who is skilled in the use of languages; one who is master of other tongues besides his own", and (2) as "a student of language". The first of these definitions is happy, but the second is unhappy, for "student" is not the right word. The second definition ought to read, "an authority on linguistics". And curiously enough the editor proceeds to mark this meaning as obsolete! No one who reads even cursorily our learned publications of today can fail to note that *linguist* in its technical sense is still very much alive. And this present use is by no means a revival of a meaning long dead. On the contrary, the meaning in question can be found in perfectly good nineteenth-century authors. Thus, Macaulay, in the same essay on Samuel Johnson from which I quoted above, uses *linguist* in the technical sense. He says,

There, too, were Gibbon, the greatest historian, and Jones, the greatest linguist, of the age [3].

The reference is to Sir William Jones, whose researches in the comparative grammar of Sanskrit, Latin and Greek led to the greatest single discovery, perhaps, in the history of linguistic science and justify the comparison with Gibbon. Here Macaulay's meaning is clear. He is speaking of eminent authorities, not schoolboys, and he has in mind their scholarly achievements, not their mere acquaintance with times and tongues other than their own. In other words, to Macaulay *linguist* meant "an authority on linguistics", and the editor of the *NED*. responsible for marking the term obsolete in this sense made a bad blunder. Other words that belong here are *Dantist, Celtist, Slavist, Romancist, Semitist* and the like. The *NED*. defines *Dantist* as "a Dante scholar", and "scholar" evidently means not a mere student but an authority on the subject. Less satisfactory is this dictionary's definition of *Celtist* as "one who studies the Celtic languages". The *Century* gives a much better definition: "one engaged or versed in the study of Celtic language, literature, antiquities, etc." I should distinguish between two meanings of this word: (1) an authority on the Celts, and (2) an authority on Celtic. Both meanings are learned, and the word apparently has not developed a distinct popular sense. For the second meaning the term *Celticist* is obviously more appropriate, but this term, though actually in use, is not recorded in the dictionaries. Similarly, *Slavist*, defined in the *NED*. as "one skilled in the Slav languages and literature; a Slavonic scholar", actually has two meanings: (1) an authority on the Slavs and (2) an authority on Slavic, and for the second meaning *Slavicist* would be a more appropriate term. *Romancist* is explained in the *NED*. as "a writer or composer of romances; a romantic novelist". So far as I know, this word is never used to mean an authority on Romance philology. We have already seen that *Romanist* may have this meaning. Neither *Romanist* nor *romancist* however strikes one as very suitable for the Romance philologist, and the term *Romanicist*, though unrecorded in the dictionaries, seems to be the only word that fits the case. Similarly,

---

[3] *Works*, ed. Lady Trevelyan, vol. VII, p. 345.

Germanicist is the obviously appropriate term for the authority on Germanic, while *Germanist* ought to be reserved to the authority on German. The authority on Germany must also be called a Germanist, since the resources of the English language do not permit of a distinction here. Finally, *Semitist* is defined by the *NED.* as "one versed in Semitic languages, literature, etc.; a Semitic scholar". Here again we must distinguish two meanings: (1) an authority on the Semites and (2) an authority on Semitic. For the latter meaning a term *Semiticist*, though in theory preferable, is rather heavy from a phonetic point of view, and so far as I know it does not occur.

The terms which we have been considering vary more or less in age and historical development, in spite of their similarity of form and meaning. Insofar as they are used in scientific nomenclature, a certain amount of system, and fixity of usage, is manifestly desirable. This end is best attained, I think, along the lines which I have indicated. As an example of the systematic working-out of the terminology, I present the following, on the theme "Iceland".

> *Icelander* "a native, an inhabitant, or a citizen of Iceland."
> *Icelandist* 1 (popular meaning) "one well acquainted with Iceland".
> 2 (technical meaning) "an authority on Iceland",
> *Icelandicist* 1 "one well acquainted with the Icelandic language or literature".
> 2 "an authority on Icelandic linguistics or philology".

In the case of Egypt, India and China a special terminology exists which has some interest in the present connection. The scientific study of China and Chinese civilization is called *Sinology*, and an authority in this field is known as a *Sinologist*. Similarly we speak of *Indology* and *Egyptology*, and of the *Indologist* and the *Egyptologist*. But this system of terms seems to have little or no tendency to spread, and it is defective in that it makes no provision for a distinct term to denote the linguistic and philological field. Moreover, such a term as *Icelandist* has in its comparative brevity a true advantage over *Icelandologist*. Most important of all, it has the great advantage of actual existence, and this advantage will probably prove decisive.

THE ETYMOLOGY OF *STIR* 'PRISON'

BY LOUISE POUND
UNIVERSITY OF NEBRASKA

The word *stir*, in the sense of prison, has considerable American currency. The "crook" jargon of the "talkies" makes frequent use of it, and it appears in newspaper accounts of crime and criminals and in fiction dealing with the underworld. Herbert Yenne in an article on "Prison Lingo" in *American Speech* (II, 280) mentions it as used by occupants of prisons in the sense of penitentiary. The word is not of American coinage, however, but is plainly an importation from the Old World. What is its history?

The Century Dictionary enters as a sixth meaning under the standard noun *stir*, from the verb *stir* (Old English *styrian*, rouse agitate, etc.), the following:

> A house of correction; a lockup; a prison. Thieves Slang. Mayhew, London Labour, 1851, I, 421. "I was in Brummagem and was seven days in the new 'stir'" (prison).

The New International Dictionary and *The Standard* also include *stir*, in the sense of prison, under the familiar noun *stir*. *The Oxford Dictionary* enters it as a separate substantive with the meaning of prison. The same citation from Mayhew follows and no etymology is suggested.

Apparently the history of the term has not been carefully traced. Perhaps, in the absence of links pointing toward the older forms, its ancestry cannot be certainly supplied. It seems to me far likelier, however, that the word, if coming from the Old English, is to be associated, not with the verb *styrian*, agitate, but with the noun *stēor(stier, stȳr)* defined in Old English dictionaries as meaning (1) steering, guidance (2) rule, regulation (3) restraint, discipline, check, correction. The phonetic development from either *stēor* or *stȳr* is normal, if we keep in mind the sixteenth-century coalescence of *-er, -ir, -ur, -or*. The shortened vowel of a Middle English *stēr* or *stīr* might have arisen out of compounds like *stēorness, stȳrness*, correction, discipline, or *stēorlēas*, without restraint, *stēorwirþe*, deserving reprobation, etc. Or compare *sir*, shortened from *sire*. On the semantic side the development of *stir* from Old English *stēor* seems even more probable than on the phonetic side.

If the etymology proposed here be sound, lexicographical entries should henceforth associate the underworld word with the verb *steer* rather than, as hitherto, with the verb *stir*.